INFANT DEVELOPMENT

Lawrence Erlbaum Associates Ltd., Publishers
27 Palmeira Mansions
Church Road
Hove
East Sussex, BN3 2FA
U.K.

British Library cataloguing in Publication Data

Infant development.
  1. Children. Development.
  I. Slater, Alan M. II. Bremner, J. Gavin, 1949–
155.4

ISBN 0–86377–126–2

Printed and bound by BPCC Wheatons, Exeter.

INFANT DEVELOPMENT

EDITED BY

Alan Slater
Department of Psychology
University of Exeter

Gavin Bremner
Department of Psychology
University of Lancaster

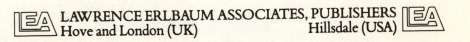
LAWRENCE ERLBAUM ASSOCIATES, PUBLISHERS
Hove and London (UK)   Hillsdale (USA)

Contents

List of Contributors   ix

Preface   xi

PART 1 PERCEPTUAL DEVELOPMENT

Introduction *Alan Slater*   3

1. Development of Basic Visual Functions   7
    Janette Atkinson and Oliver Braddick

    Introduction   7
    Pick-up of Basic Visual Information   8
    Development of Selectively Sensitive Visual Channels   12
    Indicators of Visual Cortical Function   18
    Development of Binocularity   20
    Oculomotor and Attentional Control   21
    Plasticity and Abnormal Visual Development   24
    Some Unanswered Questions   29
    Glossary   32
    References   36

2. Visual Memory and Perception in Early Infancy   43
    Alan Slater

    Introduction   43
    The New-born Baby's Window on the World   44

Preparedness for Visual Perception   45
Visual Activity and Memory at Birth   47
Neural Mechanisms Underlying Early Visual
    Capacities   50
Locus of Habituation in the New-born   50
Persistence of Visual Memory   51
Orientation Selectivity   52
Perception of Form   53
Static or Dynamic Stimuli?   57
Perception of Visual Space   58
Movement Perception   59
The Visual Constancies   60
Perception of Faces   64
Conclusions   67
References   69

3.   Events and Encounters in Infant Perception   73
     George Butterworth

Introduction   73
Dynamic Approaches to Perception   73
Events in Infant Perception   74
Biological Motion   76
Intersensory Events   78
Encounters in Infant Perception   79
Conclusions   81
References   82

4.   The Perceptual World of the New-born Child   85
     Tom Bower

Introduction   85
The Sonic Guide   86
New-born Reaching   89
New-born Imitation   90
Perception of "Pure" Human Movement   91
Conclusions   94
References   95

PART 2   COGNITIVE DEVELOPMENT

Introduction   *Gavin Bremner*   99

5.   Object Permanence in Infancy   103
     Paul Harris

Introduction   103
The Object Hidden by a Screen   106
Search under a Cloth   112

Conclusions   119
References   120

6.   Development of Spatial Awareness in Infancy   123
Gavin Bremner

Introduction: Piaget, Objects, and Space   123
Position Coding and Spatial Orientation   124
Active Movement, Postural Control, and Spatial
Orientation   132
Conclusion: A Model of Spatial Development   137
References   140

7.   Development of Problem-solving in Infancy   143
Peter Willatts

Problem-solving Behaviour   143
Problem-solving Strategies   145
Piaget's Theory   148
Problems with Piaget's Theory   153
Developmental Influences on Problem-Solving   168
Conclusions   175
References   177

PART 3   SOCIAL INTERACTION, EARLY LANGUAGE,
AND EMOTION
Introduction   *Gavin Bremner and Alan Slater*   185

8.   Early Social Development   189
Rudolph Schaffer

Introduction   189
Some Conceptual Guidelines   190
Social Pre-adaptation   192
The Changing Nature of Social Interaction   194
Attachment   200
The Respective Roles of Infant and Parent   206
References   208

9.   Early Language Development   211
Martyn Barrett

Introduction   211
The First Words of the Infant   212
Linguistic Developments during the Period of Single-word Speech   217
Lexical Development in the Single-word Period   218
Pragmatic Development in the Single-word Period   226
The Transition to Two-word Speech   230

    Conclusions   238
    References   238

10. The Social Structuring of Infant Cognition   243
     Andrew Lock, Valerie Service, Alfredo Brito, and Penelope
     Chandler

     Introduction   243
     A Social Constructivist Approach to Development   244
     A Little History   248
     Developing a Social Perspective on Language
         Development   251
     The Interactive Foundations of Imitation and
         Analysis   254
     Interaction and the Development of Language and
         Cognition   258
     Discussion   265
     References   271

11. Linking Emotion and Thinking in Infant Development: A
         Psychoanalytic Perspective   273
     Cathy Urwin

     Introduction   273
     Psychoanalysis and Thinking: Freud   275
     Melanie Kline and Infant Development   277
     Two Case Studies   284
     Discussion   293
     References   298

Author Index   301

Subject Index   309

Contributors

Janette Atkinson, Cambridge University
Martyn Barrett, Royal Holloway & Bedford New College
Tom Bower, University of Texas at Dallas
Oliver Braddick, Cambridge University
Gavin Bremner, Lancaster University
Alfredo Brito, Universidad de Murcia
George Butterworth, Stirling University
Penelope Chandler, University of Bristol
Paul Harris, Oxford University
Andrew Lock, Lancaster University
Rudolph Schaffer, Strathclyde University
Valerie Service, Lancashire Polytechnic
Alan Slater, Exeter University
Cathy Urwin, Cambridge University
Peter Willatts, Dundee University

Preface

Questions about, and interest in, the period of infancy have been with us for many thousands of years, but curiously it is only in the last 30 years or so that research has begun to construct a complete picture of early development. Two factors in particular contributed to this state of affairs. First, infancy by definition is the period "without speech", which means that one cannot question infants about their experiences. Second, infants display a limited repertoire of non-verbal behaviours, which makes it difficult to gain an understanding of their world from their spontaneous activities. Thus, an important enterprise has been the development of techniques, methodologies, and procedures that allow us to study the infant's world. Of course, as our knowledge of infancy has expanded, so too has our awareness of the complexity of early development and our awareness of the many aspects of this development about which we still know very little: Many of the exciting and controversial topics in current infancy research simply did not exist a few years ago.

The aim of this book is to provide authoritative accounts of important areas of development in infancy, to elucidate and clarify the processes of early development and growth, and to point to those many areas where there exist lively theoretical controversies. Our intention was always for the book to have a particularly British "flavour", since infancy is a flourishing area in this country. We approached our contributors with clear suggestions as to the chapters we hoped they would write. The end result, we hoped, would be a well-integrated book, providing coverage of the major areas of infant development, namely perceptual, cognitive, social, emotional, and early language development.

Our contributors have served us well, and we feel that all of our hopes for the book have been realised, but of course it is for the reader to judge this rather than us! We should note that in order to keep the book to a manageable length it has not been possible to include chapters on *all* the topics with which researchers are currently concerned, so that there are not, for example, separate chapters on temperament, types of parenting, and the origins of play. However, it seems to us that the quality and contents of the chapters included compensate for the unavoidable omissions.

The major issues and controversies in infancy research are identified in the introductory comments that are found before each of the three major sections of the book. These introductions are also intended to enhance integration of chapters and contents, and to provide linking comments across sections. In each of the chapters, the authors give careful attention to theoretical concerns, so that the major theories concerning infant development receive an airing in at least one, and sometimes several, of the chapters. Most chapters provide extensive reference sections so that the reader with specific interests will find reference to a great deal of additional relevant literature.

The book is intended for a wide readership. Read in conjunction with the introductory comments, the chapters will be understandable to those with little knowledge of infancy research. Since the authors present data and theory at the forefront of current knowledge, the book will also be useful for postgraduates, lecturers, researchers, and other professionals with an interest in the field.

The editors contributed equally to the preparation of the book and the order of their names was decided by the toss of a coin.

Alan Slater
Gavin Bremner
1989

1 PERCEPTUAL DEVELOPMENT

Perceptual Development: Introduction

Alan Slater

The four chapters in Part 1 concentrate particularly on visual perception, a bias that is justified on two counts. First, vision is the modality that has been most studied in infants, with very little work, for example, on taste and smell. Since the pioneering work of Robert Fantz in the 1960s, using particularly the visual preference method and habituation procedures, a wide variety of different methods of investigation have been developed to explore infants' ability to extract visual information from the environment. Second, vision is one of the most important means of extracting the environmental information that leads to normal cognitive and social development. Whereas other inputs, particularly those reaching the auditory system, will provide important information, it is clear that humans have evolved to rely heavily on vision at all ages.

As we might suspect, the new-born baby's visual world is quite different, and much impoverished, when compared with the adult's. Indeed, visual acuity at birth is so poor that an adult with the neonate's level of visual acuity would be legally registered as blind. While the new-born is far from the visually helpless creature that this might imply, it is clear that visual capacities develop rapidly in the first few months from birth. In Chapter 1, Atkinson and Braddick explore this development, describing in detail the information picked up and transmitted by the visual system, as the infant begins the business of understanding a world of objects. The basic visual functions they discuss include acuity and contrast sensitivity, colour vision, eye movements and oculomotor control, discrimination of spatial relationships, and the development of binocular vision. Throughout, they relate early developments to neural development and to the development of the visual cortex. An important section in their chapter considers the role of plasticity in visual development, and what happens when "vision goes wrong". Such instances of abnormal visual development help to increase our understanding of normal development, but are especially important in enabling us to detect and treat infants at risk of some degree of visual handicap. Atkinson and Braddick provide an invaluable glossary of terms that will help the reader who is not familiar with these areas of enquiry.

Some of the same topics are covered in Chapter 2 but from a rather different perspective. Atkinson and Braddick pose the question "what does the baby see, and how do the basic visual capacities develop?", whereas Slater has a greater emphasis on "what sense can the infant make of what he/she sees?". Topics covered in this chapter include preparedness for visual perception, the development of visual memory, changes in form perception in early infancy, perception of space, depth and movement, the visual constancies, and perception of the human face. Slater also discusses the extent to which infants can be considered "active" seekers of stimulation, the role of dynamic, changing stimuli on the detection of organisation in visual perception, and the extent to which infants can be thought of as making perceptual inferences from visual input.

Our knowledge of early perception has increased immeasurably in recent years, and the chapters both reflect this knowledge and also point to areas where many questions remain unresolved. One lively topic of investigation concerns the role of the visual cortex in early vision and Chapters 1 and 2 reach rather different conclusions on this issue, with orientation selectivity having a key role.

Butterworth's chapter continues the progression developed from Chapter 1 to Chapter 2. We have now moved away from questions to do with the development of the visual structures with which the infant analyses the world, to consider some of the ways in which infants are able to obtain information about the environment from the ever-changing, dynamic flux of stimulation that impinges on all the senses. Butterworth argues that young infants perceive "events" and "encounters" and superordinate aspects of perception (what J. J. Gibson called "higher-order" variables of stimulation) rather than perception being constructed from successive "snapshots" of the world. Butterworth illustrates his theme with reference to many interesting and ingenious experiments that have recently appeared in the literature: newborns' imitation of adults' facial gestures; detection of structure from biomechanical motion in the form of point light displays; perception of occluded objects; sensitivity to intersensory information; and response to "looming objects".

Bower continues the theme developed by Butterworth and often uses similar examples. He describes his own and Aitken's research using the sonic

guide in which blind infants are given the same information about the world
of objects in space that would normally be provided by vision, but through
the different modality of audition. Changes in sound intensity and quality
specify the movement, size, and texture of objects to the infant. He reports
that blind infants, if they are provided with the sonic guide young enough,
grow like sighted children without the delays in understanding the spatial
world that usually characterise the blind child. Like Butterworth, Bower
argues that infants respond to higher-order variables of stimulation, and he
argues that detection of these variables is not modality-specific, that is, the
infant responds to equivalence of sensory input independently of the sensory
modality which provides the input. This thesis touches on theoretical issues
about which we may expect some future research. In an earlier publication
Butterworth (1983) argued that when new-born infants turn their eyes in the
direction of a sound stimulus they *expect* the sound to have a visual
consequence—i.e. they expect to see the thing that produced the sound. This
is a clear statement that from birth, infants can differentiate the sensory
information given by the different modalities. Butterworth and Bower are in
agreement that infants detect and respond to higher-order variables of
stimulation, and that event perception is not a modality-specific process:
whether, and at what age, the infant can discriminate the information
provided by the different modalities is a topic of enquiry that will exercise
researchers in the years to come.

The terms "perception" and "cognition" are often distinguished in that
the former refers to the basic detection and processing of sensory information, whereas the latter refers to the ability to extract sense, meaning, and
understanding from this information. Although these distinctions, in practice, are often difficult to make, Chapter 1 and to a lesser extent Chapter 2 are
concerned with perception, while Chapters 3 and 4 begin to move beyond
perception to explore its relationship with cognition. Cognitive development
is the focus of Part 2 of the book, Chapters 5 to 7, as we develop the theme of
infants' understanding of the uniquely human world they experience.

REFERENCE

Butterworth, G. 1983. Structure of the mind in human infancy. In L. P. Lipsitt & C. K. Rovee-
Collier (eds), *Advances in infancy research*: Vol. 2, Norwood, N.J.: Ablex Publishing Corp.

1 Development of Basic Visual Functions

Janette Atkinson and Oliver Braddick

Visual Development Unit,
Department of Experimental Psychology,
University of Cambridge,
Cambridge CB2 3EB

INTRODUCTION

Visual capabilities develop rapidly over the period of infancy, and especially over the first few months. In this chapter we shall look at this development from an information-processing point of view, analysing the processes that act on the sensory input to extract the information needed to understand a world of objects. Often these processes can be related to mechanisms in the developing nervous system. The detail and precision with which we can analyse visual development in these terms is based on a large body of knowledge about adult visual perception, and about the neural machinery of vision in other mammals. The reader's understanding of the topics we discuss will be deeper if there is a familiarity with the material in an up-to-date textbook on vision, such as Frisby (1979), Goldstein (1984), Bruce and Green (1985) or Barlow and Mollon (1982); the glossary at the end of the chapter may also help with unfamiliar technical terms. Terms that are italicised in the chapter are explained in the glossary.

The infant's ability to use vision must be determined in part by the quality of the basic information picked up and transmitted by the visual system—detail, *contrast*, and colour. Quite thorough recent reviews are available on how these aspects of vision develop in infancy, so they are outlined only briefly below. We then look in more detail at the development of the selective processes that act on this information to begin its transformation into a description of pattern, shape, and depth, and discuss the problems of the infant's control of visual processing. Finally we shall outline some of the ways in which the development of vision may be abnormal.

PICK-UP OF BASIC VISUAL INFORMATION

Acuity and Contrast Sensitivity

The best-known measure of how effectively the visual system picks up information is visual *acuity*. *Preferential looking (FPL)* or the occurrence of a visual *evoked potential* (*VEP*) can be used to assess the finest *grating* for which an infant can detect a pattern as distinct from a uniformly blurred grey field. These methods show a rapid increase in acuity in the first 6 months of life (see reviews by Dobson & Teller, 1978; Atkinson & Braddick, 1981a; Banks & Salapatek, 1983). Generally accepted acuity estimates are: at birth, 1 *c/deg*; at 2–3 months, 2–5 c/deg; at 6 months, 6–20 c/deg. (The variation is both between individual infants and between studies.) Higher estimates come from some recent VEP studies (Norcia & Tyler, 1985). FPL measures are usually considered conservative, since the fact that a pattern was not preferred cannot prove that it was not detected. (However, in the case of flicker detection, 3-month-olds' performance in FPL is 90% of the adult performance (Regal, 1981) suggesting that it is possible for the method to come very close to the true limits of detection.)

Functionally, infant acuity values can be looked at from two perspectives. On the one hand, acuity in the first months is very low compared to adult values of 30–40 c/deg; in fact a new-born would meet legal criteria for blindness. On the other hand, the nearby objects with which young infants are primarily concerned (notably social stimuli) give large retinal images and much of the critical information about them is available even with an acuity of 1 c/deg—see for example the simulated face images in Atkinson & Braddick (1984). So the important uses of vision in the first few months are probably not constrained much by acuity limitations, although these limitations may well contribute to the infants' apparent inattention to distant objects, whose images are much smaller.

Acuity describes visual performance in the special case of resolving details that are very close together. However, a more general measure is contrast sensitivity—how well does the visual system convey small differences in light and dark which may be gradual in space as well as abrupt? Contrast sensitivity, like acuity, shows rapid increases to near-adult levels during the first year (Atkinson & Braddick, 1981a; Banks & Salapatek, 1981; Norcia & Tyler, 1985). However, the form of the *contrast sensitivity function* does not remain constant in this improvement. Older infants, like adults, are more sensitive to contrast over moderate spatial ranges (medium *spatial frequen-*

cies) than to very gradual variations in intensity (low spatial frequencies), but infants under 2 months do not show this low-spatial-frequency cut. The most likely explanation is that the neural process of *lateral inhibition*, which improves mid-frequency sensitivity relative to low frequencies, is not developed in the *receptive fields* of the young infant's retina.

Optical and Neural Development in Spatial Information Transmission

What underlying development brings about these improvements in transmission of spatial information by the infant's visual system? The first stage of this transmission is the formation of an optical image on the retina, where information is lost if the image is blurred. The basic optical structure of the eye is good from birth, but infants' *accommodation* responses are initially inaccurate and improve over the same period that acuity and contrast sensitivity are found to improve (Braddick, Atkinson, French, & Howland, 1979; Banks, 1980a; 1980b). Poor focus causes blur; but conversely accommodative responses can only correct errors of focus if the visual system transmits the information to distinguish blurred images from sharp ones. It appears that the latter is the important relationship in very young infants: limits on acuity lead to inaccurate accommodation, rather than accommodative blur limiting acuity. However, the refractive error of *astigmatism*, which is common in infants, may be a significant limit on acuity in many infants beyond 3 months (Howland, Atkinson, Braddick, & French, 1978; Atkinson & Braddick, 1981a).

These limits on acuity must then arise for neural rather than optical reasons. The neural signals of vision are initiated by light falling on retinal *photoreceptors*. In particular, adults' high acuity depends on the cone receptors, which are particularly densely packed in the central *fovea*. In the early months, these foveal cones have a very immature form that is presumed to be less sensitive, and are not yet concentrated in number in the central fovea (Youdelis & Hendrickson, 1986). This lesser density would place a limit on acuity below adult values, although it is doubtful whether changes in this factor alone can account for the early development of acuity. To achieve a mature fovea, the positions of *receptors* must change in development; this rearrangement also has consequences for eye movement control which are discussed later (see pp. 21–22).

The changes in the contrast sensitivity function, discussed earlier, imply that the changing form of *retinal ganglion cell* receptive fields is a significant factor in early development. The organisation of these receptive fields might be expected to affect response to high spatial frequencies (acuity) as well as to low. The axons of the retinal ganglion cells form the fibres of the optic nerve, which acquire their *myelin sheaths* progressively over the first few months. Neural transmission must be impaired by incomplete myelination, although it is not clear what this entails for functional vision. All these factors potentially set limits on visual information before it enters the brain. The importance of the early part of the pathway in acuity development is suggested by measurements on *lateral geniculate* cells in the monkey. The highest spatial frequency to which these cells respond increases with age, over a similar range to the animals' behavioural acuity (Blakemore & Vital-Durand, 1981). It would be perilous to assume a simple quantitative relationship between single cell responses and the sensitivity of a whole system as observed in behaviour. However, these data can at least be taken as opposing any idea that the signals entering the brain are mature from birth, and simply await the brain's development of the capacity to process fine detail.

Neither would it be true, however, to suppose that the new-born brain is ready to process high-acuity information but has to wait for the maturing peripheral visual system to deliver it. The processing power of the *visual cortex* depends on the interconnections between neurones, and these increase dramatically in number between 2 and 6 months of age (Garey & De Courten, 1983). It seems likely that rich cortical connectivity is necessary to define the fine structure of receptive fields that can deal with fine detail and subtle contrast. However, what is probably more important is that these connections also define the pattern-analysing capabilities of visual cortex, which are considered in the section on visual channels. (see pp. 12–18).

Colour

Our ability to separate and recognise objects depends heavily on picking up information about wavelength (colour) differences. The developing infant also seems to pick up this information from an early age. The technical issues involved in posing questions about colour vision, and answering them effectively in young infants, are lucidly discussed by Teller & Bornstein (1987) and Werner & Wooten (1979). Here we outline the various levels at which this issue can be approached, and current experimental conclusions on them.

First, the cone receptors, on which colour vision depends, give daylight vision a characteristic *spectral sensitivity*. The effectiveness of different wavelengths in infant vision is sufficiently close to that for adults (Dobson, 1976; Peeples & Teller, 1978) to indicate that infants 2 months and under are using cones. However, this cannot prove that all three cone types are functioning, or that infants can separate and compare their signals for colour discriminations.

For a visual system with only one functional class of cones, any two coloured lights could be made to look the same if their intensities were suitably adjusted to equalise the stimulation of that cone type. Teller, Peeples, and Sekel (1978) used FPL to show that 2-month-old infants could detect patches of most colours against white surrounds, no matter what the relative intensities. This implies that they have at least two types of cone. Certain colours were apparently not distinguished from white; this is characteristic of *dichromacy* (using two mechanisms rather than the three of full adult colour vision). However, the infant's dichromacy does not correspond to the common forms of colour blindness which are due to lack of a "red" or "green" cone mechanism (Hamer, Alexander, & Teller, 1982). It has been argued that young infants may lack information from the third "blue" cone mechanism, and adaptation experiments by Pulos, Teller, & Buck (1980), consistent with this, found evidence for blue cones in 3-month-old but not in 1-month-old infants. But other tests have shown, even in 1-month-olds, performance that would depend on using "blue" cone signals (Varner et al, 1985; Volbrecht & Werner, 1987).

The weight of evidence, then, is that infants are *trichromatic* at a very early age. An interesting possibility is that before about 3 months, even if they possess "blue" cones, infants may not use the signals from them very effectively. In primates, "blue" cone input apparently contributes to signals that go to the visual cortex but not to the signals that are routed subcortically (see Mollon, 1982). Any functional signs of dichromacy before 2–3 months may then reflect an immature cortical pathway, which is likely on other grounds (see pp. 18–19).

The evidence outlined for multiple cone types depends on infants detecting differences across a boundary between side-by-side colours. These differences will be present in the pattern of signals from at least one of the cone mechanisms. Although the infant has to be able to process the different cone signals separately to detect the boundary, the detection does not necessarily depend on comparing each cone signal with the others, which is the essential basis of real colour vision. *Habituation* testing, however, requires the infant to distinguish colours that are presented successively. Bornstein's (1976) positive results using this method, then, not only show that 3-month-olds are trichromats, but also that by this age they can use the balance among the three cone signals to define recognisable hues.

DEVELOPMENT OF SELECTIVELY SENSITIVE VISUAL CHANNELS

Selectivity vs. Unidimensional Processing

Studies of acuity and contrast sensitivity tells us what information is available via the infant's visual system about the distribution of light and dark, that is, pattern or spatial contrast in the image. However, this evidence has been obtained from very simple performances, such as preference for a stripe pattern over a blank screen. These only require the infant to differentiate between the presence and absence of spatial contrast. To be functionally useful, the visual system must encode this distribution in a way that brings out significant properties of the visual world. At least for the early stages of visual processing, this is believed to be done by the activation of selective channels (Braddick, Campbell, & Atkinson, 1978). That is, the visual system as a whole may respond to a broad range of orientations, spatial frequencies, or *binocular disparities*; but at some level the system is divided into parallel channels, each of which responds only to some narrower subrange of these stimulus dimensions. There is much psychophysical evidence in adults for this sort of selectivity, and it is characteristic of the neurones found in the *striate* and *extra-striate areas* of primate cortex.

Comparisons of patterned with blank fields in procedures such as preferential looking tap only a one-dimensional or "intensive" aspect of visual processing. Effectively, analyses of preference experiments treat each stimulus as having a "strength" or "intensity", and try to order stimuli in terms of which is "stronger" for the infant. For example, Karmel and Maisel (1975) proposed a measure based on the density of contour in the field, and this has been developed in Haith's (1978) proposals that the new-born's looking behaviour is directed to maximise activation of visual cortex, as predicted from "contour variability, amount and location" (Pipp & Haith, 1984). The most sophisticated version of this intensive approach uses *linear systems analysis*. In this analysis, contrast sensitivity data are used to predict how strongly the infant's visual system responds to the contrast in any given pattern (from knowledge of the spatial frequencies into which the pattern can be analysed). These calculations give effective predictions of infants' preference behaviour in many cases (Banks & Salapatek, 1981; Gayl, Roberts, & Werner, 1983; Banks & Ginsberg, 1983). However, the fact that, in these experiments, stimuli can be ordered along a single dimension does not tell us whether and at what age the infant's visual system is performing a richer analysis that can distinguish stimuli in more ways than just one. Several lines of evidence suggest that the multiple selective channels needed for this analysis are not functioning at birth, but that they come into play in the first months of life. Such selective sensitivity can allow the infant to respond not just to the "strength" of stimuli but to their pattern or configuration.

Orientation Selectivity

Stimuli which are equal in the amount and contrast of contour can differ in the orientation of the lines and edges that they contain. Selectivity for narrow ranges of orientation is a property which distinguishes neurones of the visual cortex from those in lower parts of the visual system, so infants' orientation selectivity is not only important for understanding their pattern perception, but is also an indicator of whether their cortex is functional.

A direct test of orientation selectivity can be made by evoked potential (VEP) testing of infants (Braddick, Wattam-Bell & Atkinson, 1986). If we simply switched the orientation of a stripe pattern that the infant was looking at, many points in the pattern would change from light to dark or vice versa, which could elicit an evoked potential response even from neural mechanisms which were completely indifferent to orientation. However, changes in orientation can be included among a series of jumps which produce, on average, equally great luminance and contrast changes without orientation change (see Fig. 1). In this case, any response which is specifically synchronised with the orientation changes must arise from mechanisms which are genuinely selective for orientation rather than simply responding to contrast change.

On this test, infants first show an orientation-specific response around 6 weeks of age on average, implying that the cortical mechanisms which respond selectively to particular orientations are not functionally effective before that age. If the perceptual discrimination of different orientations is based on the differential responses of these mechanisms, one would expect infants to be capable of such discriminations after 6 weeks but not before. In testing these discriminations, it is important to be sure that they cannot be done by an infant using only intensive variations. For instance, vertical and horizontal contours may have different effects because the former yield more frequent signals when crossed by (predominantly horizontal) eye movements; or the common astigmatism of infancy (Howland et al., 1978; Mohindra, Held, Gwiazda, & Brill 1978) may mean that one of these directions appears in sharper contrast than the other. For these reasons we unfortunately cannot be sure that the horizontal–vertical discrimination which Slater and Sykes (1977) found in new-borns was truly based on orientation. Contours at opposite oblique orientations are much less subject to these criticisms. Maurer and Martello (1980) and Cohen and Younger (1984) have both shown behaviourally (using habitutation methods) that 6-week-olds can discriminate obliques, but no one has yet tested the younger infants who from the VEP results would be expected to fail. Of course, since we do not know for sure the detailed neural mechanisms controlling either the VEP or the behavioural discrimination, we cannot assume that the two measures of infant visual performance will necessarily go together.

DYNAMIC ORIENTATION–REVERSAL STIMULUS

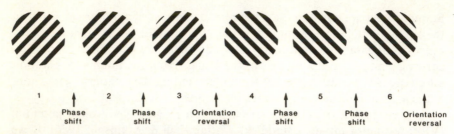

FIG. 1.   Stimulus sequence used to elicit orientation-specific visual evoked potentials (VEP). Patterns 1–6 are samples from a continuous sequence running at 25 frames/second. At the points marked "phase shift" there is a shift of the grating, causing local contrast changes, but no orientation change. Between patterns 3 and 4 there are also local contrast changes, but in addition a reversal of the grating's orientation. A VEP signal which is synchronised with the orientation reversals and *not* with the phase shifts is not simply a response to contrast changes, but must arise from mechanisms which respond differently to different orientations.

A curved line is one which contains different orientations along its length, so the finding that new-born infants prefer curved figures over their straight-line counterparts (Fantz, Fagan, & Miranda, 1975) could indicate that even these new-borns are using orientation information. However, it is possible to think of other ways that the curved and straight-line stimuli differ. For example, near sharp corners in the latter there would be a maximum in the activation of non-oriented spot-shaped contrast detectors. This illustrates how many alternative possibilities there are in the spatial analysis of pattern, and how much care has to go into designing experiments that can test whether infants (or adults) are performing a particular kind of analysis.

Spatial Frequency Selectivity

In the linear systems analysis discussed earlier (see p. 12), the visual system is considered as transmitting some of the spatial frequencies in the image strongly, but others weakly or not at all. However, we know that the adult's visual system is not unitary in its response to spatial frequencies, but contains a set of parallel channels, each of which responds to a restricted spatial frequency band (Braddick, Campbell, & Atkinson, 1978; Braddick, 1981a). That is, the visual system transmits separately information about the coarse, large-scale pattern of light and dark in the image (low spatial frequencies), information about fine detail (high frequencies), and the various levels of scale in between. Physiological experiments (De Valois, Albrecht, & Thorell, 1982) show that single cells in the visual cortex have this property of responding selectively to different, limited frequency bands. It is still controversial what part this division among selective channels plays in the overall process of perception, but it is clearly an important part of the pattern-analysing function of the visual cortex.

Psychophysical tests for the existence of spatial-frequency-selective channels are possible with infants as well as adults. For example, a one-dimensional visual *noise* background masks detection of a grating most effectively if the noise and the grating stimulate the same channel. Using this and other techniques in an FPL study of infants' grating detection, Banks, Stephens, and Hartmann (1985) showed that 6-week-olds behaved as if their detection depended on a single channel which responded to all spatial frequencies within their range, whereas 12-week-olds used at least two, and possibly more, independent spatial frequency channels. It seems, then, that selectivity for spatial frequency within the infant's visual system develops at a very similar time to that for orientation.

Discrimination of Spatial Relationships

Analysing visual patterns into separate spatial frequency bands does not by itself provide an adequate basis for pattern perception. This is because the same frequency components can make very different patterns depending on the spatial relationship, or relative *phase*, between them. For example, the two grating patterns illustrated in Fig. 2 have the same five components, but in one case these components are lined up at the point of steepest *luminance* change (*"zero-crossings"*), whereas in the other they are randomly positioned. They appear very different, so information defining the phase relationship must be represented in the visual system. Just how this is done is still controversial (see e.g. Stromeyer & Klein, 1974; Badcock, 1984; Field & Nachmias, 1984). One popular view is that there exist channels which are selective for particular phase relationships within a limited frequency band (Atkinson & Campbell, 1974; Field & Nachmias, 1984). For example, a channel which responded best when the zero-crossings of different components coincided would be an *odd-symmetric* detector that was strongly activated at edges, while one responding when peaks coincided would be *even-symmetric* and activated best at a bright band in the image. Thus an infant's ability to discriminate patterns such as those of Fig. 2 may reflect the maturation of a further class of selective channels. In any case, an infant who can discriminate these patterns must not only be sensitive to the intensive variable of activity in one or more spatial frequency channels, but must also somehow be able to process spatial relations between or within the outputs of these channels. Testing such discriminations, then, allows us to study the infant's sensitivity to spatial configuration with stimuli whose intensive aspects can be well controlled.

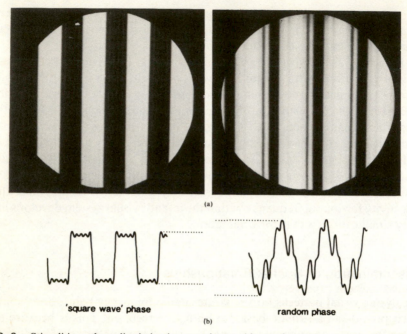

'square wave' phase   random phase

(b)

FIG. 2.   Stimuli in a phase discrimination experiment. Above: the gratings seen by the infant. Below: waveform showing the variation in luminance across each pattern. The two patterns are each made by combining the same components (with spatial frequencies in the ratios 1:3:5:7:9), but the relative phase of these components is different.

Habituation experiments (Braddick, Atkinson, & Wattam-Bell, 1986) show that 3-month-old infants can readily discriminate the stimuli of Fig. 2. This is a genuine recognition of the patterns, not just of the particular local contrast they contain, since they recognise each pattern as the same even when its overall contrast is changed. One-month-olds, however, show no recognition that the two patterns are different, although it is clear that they can detect the relevant components in both patterns. Kleiner and Banks (1987) have come to similar conclusions about the basis for infants' preference for face-like patterns. They found (Kleiner, 1987) that one-month-olds' apparent preference remained just as strong for a checker pattern which contained the same frequency components as their schematic face stimulus, but with relative phase altered to make it quite un-face-like to adults; for two-month-olds, however, the preference was determined by the phase relations characteristic of the spatial configuration of a face. Dannemiller and Stephens (1988) reached similar conclusions from a study of positive and negative face images.

For the younger infants, then, visual behaviour seems to be controlled by the variable of contrast; they are sensitive to the fact that a spatial pattern is present, but not to its configuration. By 2–3 months, mechanisms that can represent specific pattern relationships seem to have come into play. The one-month-old's detection of pattern contrast without positional relationships seems similar to some degraded forms of adult vision: For example, in peripheral vision it is possible to detect pattern components, but lose information about spatial phase relationships (Braddick, 1981b; Stephenson & Braddick, 1983; Rentschler & Treutwein, 1985), and something similar happens in the disorder of *amblyopia* where one eye's vision is degraded by disuse in childhood (Hess, 1982; Lawden, Hess, & Campbell, 1982).

In amblyopia and peripheral vision, interference or "crowding" effects are found between adjacent contours (Hilton & Stanley, 1972; Bouma, 1970; Lettvin, 1976), which may be due to a loss of the positional information that can effectively keep nearby parts of a pattern distinct. The "externality effect" (Milewski, 1976; Bushnell, 1979, 1982) shown by infants under about 2 months may be partly related to such a loss; in this effect an external contour interferes with infants' abilities to recognise internal pattern detail. (However, other factors are probably important also; the fact that a moving internal pattern can overcome the externality effect suggests that the relative attention-gaining power of interior and exterior is such a factor.)

Phase discrimination tasks tap an ability to process spatial relationships, which is important not only for grasping the configuration of features, but also for defining significant local features themselves. This idea is exemplified in Julesz's (1981) concept of "textons". Julesz explored what kinds of difference between visual textures could lead to the immediate perceptual segregation of one textured area from another. He found a statistical rule that, in most cases, produced pairs of textures which could not be segregated from each other. These pairs of textures contained the same spatial frequencies, but in different phase relationships (Julesz, 1980). However, textures containing certain special local feature types ("textons") formed exceptions to this rule that texture segregation is generally "phase blind". For instance, short oriented line segments are one type of texton, whose presence causes a texture to be distinctive.

Current theoretical approaches to vision (e.g. Marr, 1982) try to determine a set of spatial *primitives*—simple elements such as edges, line terminators, and "blobs", which are, as it were, the letters of the alphabet in which a representation of the visual image is expressed. Julesz proposed that textons are such primitives, and that they are encoded by specific detectors. Such detectors can be thought of as capturing significant local phase relationships in the image.

Patterns containing textons, then, can be useful tools for testing when the selectivity for specific spatial relationships develop in early infancy. This has been done using Julesz's (1981) "iso-third-order pair", illustrated in Fig. 3. The conspicuous difference in appearance between the "odd" and "even"

FIG. 3.   "Iso-third order" textures of Julesz. The textures are generated by statistical rules so that the same combinations of three dots occur in the "even" (left) and "odd" (right) textures, but the combinations of four dots are quite different, as shown by the outlined groups of dots. In discrimination experiments by Atkinson et al. (1986) infants were shown the two textures successively, not side by side as here (and no groups of dots were outlined).

corresponds to a difference in the distribution of edge and terminator textons (which can alternatively be described as a difference in spatial phase relationships). Habituation experiments (Atkinson, Wattam-Bell, & Braddick, 1986) have shown that three-month-old infants can discriminate these patterns but 1-month-olds cannot. This result fits in with the idea that the mechanisms needed to encode spatial configurations develop over the 1–3-month period, even though infants may have from birth adequate sensitivity to detect the spatial variations of light and dark in the patterns.

INDICATORS OF VISUAL CORTICAL FUNCTION

The striking developments of visual spatial selectivity that we have discussed occur within the rather brief period of 1–3 months, along with many other rapid and radical changes in visual behaviour (Atkinson, 1984). It has been proposed (Bronson, 1974) that the transition around 2 months represents the emergence of cortical visual function, with earlier visual behaviour having its neural basis in subcortical structures such as the *superior colliculus*. Orientation selectivity is a well-known property of cortical cells, and is not found in neurones of the superior colliculus in primates (Schiller, 1984). Spatial frequency selectivity is also a feature of cortical cells but not of the earlier stages of visual processing. Generally, the processing of spatial configuration is believed to be a cortical function. Whereas humans and monkeys with striate cortical damage show a surprising degree of visual function when appropriately tested (Humphrey, 1974; Weiskrantz, 1986), they still seem to have extreme deficits in visual tasks requiring configurational information. One interesting deficit shown by Humphrey's (1974) destriate monkey was the inability to locate pieces of food when they were surrounded by an outer contour, a similar failing to the externality effect found in 1-month-old infants.

The infant under 2 months shows a very marked immaturity of the functions which are later served by the visual cortex. However, it would be unwise to assume that the cortex is completely non-functional up to this age, and there are other related possibilities. First, cortical neurones may respond from birth, but show much less selective responses than in their mature function: Pettigrew (1974) describes this kind of finding in kittens. Second, the new-born cortex may contain only some subset of functional neurones, or may not be receiving some particular class of input needed for full function. Maurer and Lewis (1979) provide an example of such a theory, although one which has many problems in detail (Atkinson, 1984). Finally, it may be the neural outputs of cortex, as much as its inputs or processing, which are immature. Atkinson (1984) suggests that in development, cortical mechanisms have to establish their control over subcortical processing; we shall return to this issue in discussing oculomotor and attentional control.

Anatomically, there is no doubt that the visual cortex shows rapid development in the first months of infancy. Although all the cortical cells are formed before birth (Rakic, 1977), their pattern of interconnection is initially very sparse compared to what it later becomes (Conel, 1939; 1947). The number of synapses in samples of human visual cortex can be counted and shows a surge between 2 and 6 months (Garey & De Courten, 1983). A sparsely connected cortex must surely have less complete and sensitive function than a richly connected one; but we do not really have any idea how little or how much function we should expect from the structural immaturity of new-born visual cortex.

DEVELOPMENT OF BINOCULARITY

It would be a mistake to claim that visual cortical function emerges in development in a unitary way. The interaction of signals from the two eyes is a key feature of cortical organisation, which like orientation selectivity is not found lower in the visual pathway. However, there is clear evidence that this interaction begins later in development than does orientation selectivity.

The purpose of combining signals from the two eyes is not just to superimpose them, but to register the ways in which they correspond, and detect the disparities between them that are the basis of *stereoscopic depth* perception. The most revealing responses for studying binocular function, then, are those which occur specifically in the presence of binocular correspondence or *disparity*. For example, when non-corresponding random dot patterns seen by the two eyes suddenly come into exact correspondence, a visual evoked potential signal can be picked up. These signals are not detectable at birth but first appear around 13 weeks of age (Braddick et al., 1980; Petrig et al., 1981; Braddick, Wattam-Bell, Day, & Atkinson, 1983). Other studies have used behavioural responses to stereoscopic disparity (Fox, Aslin, Shea, & Dumais, 1980; Held, Birch, & Gwiazda, 1980; Fox 1981; Birch, Gwiazda & Held, 1983). A review of these varied experiments (Braddick & Atkinson, 1983) shows striking agreement that binocular function is generally first found between 12 and 17 weeks. (All studies find quite marked variation between individual infants; age-based "landmarks" should not be taken too rigidly in this rapid early development.)

These measures of cortical binocularity imply a form of selectivity: Neurones that require correlated inputs from the two eyes for optimal activation. This selectivity arises only some weeks after the infant's visual cortex has become active and pattern selective (see pp. 13–19). This implies that over those weeks the visual cortex is working in a binocularly unselective way. What could this "non-binocular" vision be like? One possibility is that in this stage, any cortical neurone receives signals from the right eye or from the left eye but not from both. The development of binocularity would then be the establishment of new connections that brought these signals together. Shimojo, Bauer, O'Connell, and Held (1986) make the opposite proposal; on their view the cortical neurones receive binocular inputs but these are initially broad and unselective, giving no special response when these inputs are correlated. These specific proposals for binocular development are examples of two quite general types of theoretical possibility. In the first, perceptual development is the formation of new connections, creating a kind of responsiveness that was not present before; while in the second, initially unselective connections become restricted, allowing a set of selective responses to be differentiated.

By "binocular selectivity" so far we have meant a selectivity for correlated vs. non-correlated inputs. Stereo vision depends on a more refined selectivity: the ability to respond differentially to different disparities. It is possible to envisage a system which initially responded uniformly to binocular correlation over a range of disparities, with disparity selectivity developing later (Braddick & Atkinson, 1983). Shimojo et al. (1986) and Birch, Shimojo, and Held (1985) provide some evidence against this, showing correlated/uncorrelated discriminations and stereoscopic discriminations to have a similar developmental course, although differences between the stimuli used in the two classes of test mean that the case is not quite conclusive. Birch et al. (1983) also show a very rapid increase in *stereoacuity* (the minimum disparity that can be discriminated) between about 14 and 20 weeks of age. Whether the ability to distinguish different disparities necessarily means that those disparities signify different depths to the infant is another question again, which cannot be answered by experiments which are restricted to investigations of disparity (see Yonas & Pick, 1975).

OCULOMOTOR AND ATTENTIONAL CONTROL

So far, we have treated vision as an essentially passive business of processing and transmitting the information that arrives at the eyes. However, these operations are under the perceiver's active control, overtly by means of eye movements that select what information is to be picked up, and covertly by internal orienting and attending processes.

From birth, eye movements are an indicator of the infant's visual processing. In some respects, they show a maturity that is quite unlike the infant's other motor responses. For instance, the *saccadic* movements that shift fixation appear to have basically similar dynamics to those of adults (Hainline et al., 1984). New-borns also show a similar pattern of *optokinetic nystagmus* (*OKN*) to adults; these repetitive eye movements induced by a large area of moving pattern consist of smooth movements following the pattern interspersed with saccade-like flicks returning the eyes in the reverse direction. However, there are important differences between neonates and adults in the way that eye movements are elicited.

Control of Saccadic Shifts of Fixation

A striking finding is that 1-month-olds frequently require a sequence of repeated small saccades to fixate a target, rather than the single accurate movement made by older infants and adults (Aslin & Salapatek, 1975). This may reflect the fact that in the new-born's developing retina, receptors have not yet reached their final positions (see p. 9). Consequently, a target which stimulates a particular set of receptors initiates a saccade towards the field location which those receptors will ultimately encode, rather than to their present location (Aslin, 1987). The resulting undershoot means that one or more further saccades are required to foveate the target.

Aslin's argument implies that the 1-month-old's saccadic control is based on an effective stimulus–response link that happens to be not yet appropriate. However, Aslin and Salapatek (1975) also showed that the average latency of a saccadic shift of fixation was considerably longer in infants than adults. A number of studies (Tronick, 1972; Harris & MacFarlane, 1974; MacFarlane, Harris, & Barnes, 1976; van Hof-van Duin & Mohn, 1986) also show that the region of the visual field to which a change of fixation can be elicited is very restricted in young infants. The ability to redirect fixation to a stimulus also seems to be much more limited by distance in 1-month-olds than in older infants (McKenzie & Day, 1976; De Schonen, McKenzie, & Bresson, 1978). It is doubtful whether these are purely sensory limitations of the visual field, as they are much more marked if a central target remains visible when the target for re-fixation appears (Harris & MacFarlane, 1974; MacFarlane et al., 1976). Rather, it seems that that the younger infant's difficulty is in the control of a shift of visual attention, especially when there are competing demands such as simultaneous central and peripheral targets.

This age difference is also apparent in the patterns of behaviour seen in preferential looking (FPL) testing. Infants of 3 months and older make brisk, decisive fixations, while 1-month-olds often show a longer latency to shift fixation away from the centre and then look from screen to screen, with the observer needing much longer to make a choice of which screen is holding the child's attention more effectively (see Atkinson, Braddick, & Moar, 1977; Braddick & Atkinson, 1987). When FPL is used to determine acuity, the younger infants also appear more sensitive to variables such as screen size; it has been suggested that they are unable to handle the competition for attention between the high-contrast edges of the screens and their internal patterns, when these are close together in the case of small screens (Atkinson, Pimm-Smith, Evans, & Braddick, 1983).

A "Gating" Function in Oculomotor Control

The eye movement to look at a new target is sometimes spoken of as a "fixation reflex". The neural basis for such a reflex would plausibly be in the superior colliculus, where in one layer neurones may be found with visual receptive fields in a particular field location, and in connected positions in another layer there are neurones involved in the initiation of saccades towards that same location (Wurtz & Albano, 1980). However, a purely reflex mechanism could not handle most normal situations, where the field of view contains many objects which cannot all trigger such a "reflex" simultaneously. Rather, if visual control of a saccade is mediated by connections in the superior colliculus, these connections must effectively be turned on and off ("gated") by mechanisms which can select a target for fixation on the grounds of its pattern, significance, and novelty. This selection would require processing of a complexity which is believed to occur in the cortex, not in the midbrain. The increasingly effective control of fixation seen over the first months of life, especially in competitive situations, may well reflect the establishment of functional control by cortical systems over subcortical visuomotor pathways.

A similar issue arises in the control of *smooth pursuit* movements. These are tracking movements in which the rate at which the eye turns is well matched to the speed of a moving target. Young infants can follow a moving object, but use a series of saccadic jumps; they generally do not follow a target with smooth pursuit until after 2 months of age (Aslin, 1981). However, if the same moving target is duplicated many times to fill a large region of the visual field, then smooth eye movements following the target occur as the "slow phase" of the resulting OKN (Atkinson & Braddick, 1981b).

OKN is an evolutionarily primitive oculomotor response controlled by subcortical pathways, which helps to stabilise the field of view during head and body movements. In smooth pursuit of a small target, any stationary background objects will be swept over the retina, forming a potential stimulus for OKN opposing the pursuit movement. Thus, successful pursuit requires some kind of inhibition of OKN. The new-born's inability to pursue may not be due to a lack of neural machinery that can generate a smooth eye movement, but to the higher parts of their visual system lacking the power to turn off subcortical pathways whose OKN response opposes the pursuit.

Binocular and Monocular OKN

Perhaps the clearest evidence on the developing integration of cortical and subcortical oculomotor mechanisms comes from monocular OKN. The OKN response of infants under 2–3 months only appears complete when both eyes are open. The response controlled by vision of either eye alone is asymmetrical: It can be elicited only by left-to-right field motion for the left eye or by right-to-left motion for the right eye (i.e. from *temporal* towards *nasal* field in each case) (Atkinson & Braddick, 1981b). It is known from animal work (see Hoffman, 1979) that the temporal-to-nasal direction of OKN depends on an entirely subcortical sensory-motor pathway, while the opposite direction requires neural signals transmitted from the visual cortex down to the subcortical centres which control the OKN response, as indicated in Fig. 4. The appearance of the nasal-to-temporal response around 3 months, then, is consistent with the idea that at this age, cortical mechanisms first become functionally connected to subcortical visual processing. We have suggested earlier that such connections allow a selective cortical processing to assert control over more reflex subcortical visuomotor mechanisms.

PLASTICITY AND ABNORMAL VISUAL DEVELOPMENT

It is obviously of human importance to understand how the course of visual development in infancy can be distorted by abnormal conditions. It is also scientifically important, because it is only by studying alternative paths of development that we can analyse how the course of development is controlled, and in human beings it is only through pathology that variations on the normal conditions of visual development can be observed.

Strabismus and Amblyopia

The most common, and intensively studied variations are in terms of the relationship between the two eyes. Between 2 and 8% of children develop *strabismus* (squint), in which the two eyes become permanently misaligned, and/or *amblyopia* (a functional loss of visual performance, usually in one eye, which is not due to visible eye disease and which is not improved by spectacle correction). Physiological studies in cats and monkeys (see reviews by Blakemore, 1978; Movshon & Van Sluyters, 1981; Mitchell, 1981) have shown that neural development can be modified in ways that may be related to these disorders. If an animal has one eye covered in early life, or its image grossly blurred, that eye loses almost all connections to the visual cortex. It is believed that nerve fibres carrying signals from the two eyes effectively compete for access to cortical neurones, and that more actively stimulated inputs have an advantage in this competition. This may be a general process in development, to ensure that the brain becomes responsive to significant inputs at the expense of inactive ones.

The animal model of having one eye covered is similar to the conditions, such as a dense cataract clouding one eye, which produce the strongest form of human amblyopia. It is reasonable to suppose that in this *deprivation amblyopia*, the affected eye has become functionally disconnected from the brain. *Anisometropic amblyopia*, resulting when one eye is blurred more than the other due to a greater refractive error, appears to be a less extreme form of the same thing.

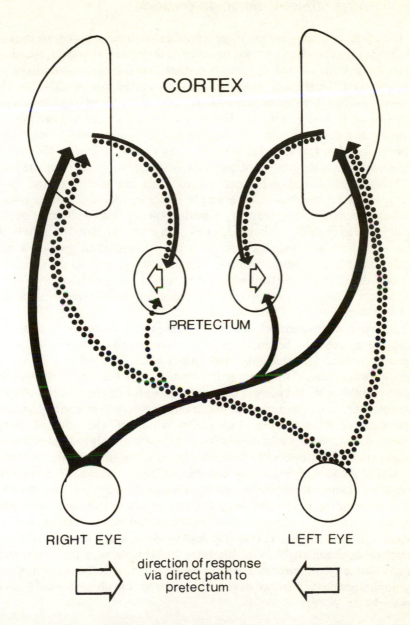

CORTEX

PRETECTUM

RIGHT EYE

LEFT EYE

direction of response
via direct path to
pretectum

FIG. 4. Pathways controlling OKN eye movements, as found in the cat. OKN is controlled by a subcortical nucleus in the pretectum on each side of the brain that receives direct input only from the eye on the other side, and responds to one direction of movement only. Thus, for the right eye to follow leftwards stimulus motion (or vice versa), signals must follow an uncrossed pathway via the right cortex descending to the right pretectum. This route via cortex appears to be inoperative in young infants.

The effects of strabismus are more complicated. In animals whose eyes are made misaligned, each eye retains its input to the cortex. However, the visual cortex is far from normal: It lacks neurones that combine inputs from the two eyes (the binocularly selective units discussed on pp. 20–21). This suggests that to establish and maintain cortical connections requires not just activity, but the kind of correlated activity that occurs when the two eyes are receiving the same stimulus. A developmental process which establishes connections when two stimulus events regularly co-occur could obviously be important beyond the context of binocular vision; it could act to create brain mechanisms which respond selectively to other regularities in the visual world. However, the binocular example indicates that the system cannot build up selectivity to any arbitrary stimulus pairing. With a constant squint, the object seen centrally with one eye will always appear, say, 10° right in the other eye's field, and yet no connections are established to give these field regions input to a common neurone. The nervous system has the capability to establish and dismantle connections according to the pattern of inputs, but only within a range that is apparently prespecified as an intrinsic constraint on the system.

If strabismic children lack cortical neurones with binocular inputs, they would be expected to be impaired in functions such as stereopsis, which depend on binocular selectivity, and this is what is found in clinical and experimental studies. However, it is common that the deviating eye also becomes amblyopic, and there is no obvious basis for this in the physiological findings; there must be some other mechanisms, besides the control of input to the visual cortex, which can functionally "switch off" the vision of one eye in whole or part. We must be careful, then, in how we apply animal models of neural plasticity to human development. Most of the animal data have been in terms of the *number of cells* receiving input from each eye; this would not necessarily connect closely to the acuity of vision through that eye, which is the usual clinical measure. In any case, loss of acuity is a very incomplete description of the amblyope's visual problem. Subjective reports and discrimination tests suggest that amblyopic vision is also "scrambled"(Hess, Campbell, & Greenhalgh, 1978; Braddick, 1981b). Perhaps the inputs from the amblyopic eye to the cortex are not simply attenuated, but somehow lose positional specificity; if so, we have no idea of what the physiological basis of this might be.

Critical Periods

Neural modifications of binocular relationships cannot be induced at all stages throughout life. They are only possible in a "critical period" in which the system is plastic (in kittens, for instance, this plasticity is maximal only between 3 weeks and 3 months of age). This is also the only period in which the effects of visual deprivation on binocular relationships can be reversed (Blakemore, 1978). However, it should not be assumed that all aspects of visual function are modifiable in the same period; in fact, it is likely that there are many critical periods for the plasticity of different functions, some of which we discuss later.

Can any critical period be identified for human vision? Tests for binocular function, in individuals who suffered strabismus at different ages (Banks, Aslin, & Letson, 1975), suggest that plasticity of the human binocular system declines quite rapidly from about 2 years, and this is in line with clinical experience. (Critical periods do not end abruptly, and the latest stage at which it is possible to induce any change is likely to be much later than the period of highest plasticity.)

What about the onset of plasticity? An indirect argument is that a time when connections are being rapidly established is likely to be a time when those connections are highly modifiable (Hickey, 1981). Such a period would also be expected to see corresponding improvements in visual performance, and in fact in kittens the critical period agrees well with the period over which behavioural acuity rises to adult values (Mitchell et al., 1976). The evidence earlier in this chapter would then suggest high sensitivity in the first year, and especially the early part. As discussed in "The development of binocularity" (see p. 20), the onset of binocularity occurs rather later than that of pattern-vision functions, but the period of rapid binocular development is still within the first 6 months. Monitoring of changes in infant acuity during therapeutic occlusion of one eye (Jacobson, Mohindra, & Held, 1983) supports the idea that the visual system is highly modifiable in the first year, but gives no clear evidence for any initially non-plastic period.

The plasticity we have discussed so far has been in the balance and combination of binocular inputs. Indeed, it has been argued that the visual system has to be modifiable specifically because binocular connections require a precision of detailed organisation which cannot be achieved by a predetermined pattern of development (see Mitchell, 1981). However, plasticity is not restricted to binocular relationships. The distribution of selective orientation-tuning in cortical cells can be modified by exposing the young animal exclusively, say, to near-horizontal orientations (Blakemore & Cooper, 1970; Rauschecker & Singer, 1981). The human analogy is believed to be *meridional amblyopia*; severe astigmatism in childhood can mean that the retina has never received any well-focused contours in a particular orientation, and acuity for lines in that orientation is found to be poor in later life, even if the astigmatism is then corrected to give sharp optical images (Mitchell, Freeman, Millodot, & Haegerstrom, 1973; Gwiazda, Bauer, Thorn, & Held, 1987). As another example, the normal development of motion-sensitive neurones depends on exposure to visual motion

(Cynader, Berman, & Hein, 1973). Thus other aspects of vision besides binocularity can be disrupted by anomalous input, and different functions may show a sequence of distinct critical periods (Daw, Berman, & Ariel, 1978). Presumably the modifiability which allows disruption must also serve some constructive role in the normal development of these functions.

Development of Strabismus, Binocularity, and Refraction

The commonness of strabismus and linked disorders suggests that binocular relationships must be a peculiarly vulnerable aspect of visual development. If the visual system is to detect small binocular disparities, the images must be kept aligned with high precision by the *vergence* movements of the eyes. Conversely, to control these movements, the binocular disparities arising from convergence errors must be detected. In principle, this delicately interdependent system could be disrupted by problems in either the disparity-detection or the vergence-control part of the loop.

An infant who intrinsically lacked cortical neurones with binocular input would have no means to register disparity and hence to prevent the eyes wandering into misalignment. Albinos (both humans and other species such as Siamese cats) have a congenital misrouteing of the visual pathways such that binocular inputs cannot come together: Presumably the strabismus they show is a consequence of the inability to register disparity. It is possible that similar defects in detection can arise for reasons other than albinism. However, this does not appear to be the general cause of strabismus. Longitudinal study (Wattam-Bell, Braddick, Atkinson, & Day, 1987) has shown that at least some infants who subsequently develop strabismus develop effective cortical binocularity first. Thus the lack of stereopsis and other binocular function usually found in strabismics can be secondary to the strabismus, rather than necessarily being its cause.

In strabismics who initially develop binocular function, some force must override the control of eye alignment by disparity. In many cases this force appears to be associated with accommodation. Accommodation and vergence normally form a closely coupled system, so that accommodating on a near target causes the eyes to converge even without disparity information (accommodative vergence). A child with marked *hyperopia* (long-sightedness) needs to accommodate more vigorously than normal even for distant objects. Such children have a high risk of developing strabismus, and it is believed that this occurs because the extra accommodative vergence is so strong, that it overcomes the child's ability to maintain convergence on a target by disparity control.

This implies a surprising limit on the developmental flexibility of the visuomotor system. The vergence required to match a particular degree of accommodation must change with growth, so one might expect the response to be modifiable, and to become suitably adjusted to the pairing of accommodation and vergence that produced sharp images when disparity was nulled. However, to cope with a growing separation of the eyes, the ratio of vergence to accommodation would have to increase, while to avoid accommodative strabismus the opposite change would be needed. Experiments in adult adaptation (Miles & Judge, 1982) suggest that the former change occurs much more readily than the latter. Once again, the system appears to be plastic, but only within fairly specific constraints.

Hyperopia, or other *refractive error*, is not of course fixed through life but is itself plastic. Most infants are somewhat hyperopic, but generally this refractive error tends to reduce over the first 5 years of life, as does the astigmatism which is very common in infancy. It has been hypothesised that this *emmetropisation* is an active adaptation (Banks, 1980a). That is, the blurred vision due to early refractive error might somehow be able to control the growth of the eye so as to reduce the error. Certainly, eyes which are deprived of patterned input can become grossly myopic, as if this process was no longer under adaptive control (Raviola & Wiesel, 1978). In more normal development, however, some types of refractive error become emmetropised more readily than others, in ways which are not easy to explain by the action of an adaptive process (Atkinson & Braddick, 1987).

SOME UNANSWERED QUESTIONS

We may have a wealth of detailed information about early visual development, but many central questions remain unanswered. Sometimes this is because of the specific difficulties of acquiring unambiguous information from infants, but often also because we may not know how to formulate the questions properly even for adult perception.

To go beyond a stage of local primitive features, perceptual processes must group similar features that occur within a region or along a boundary, and segment the visual field into separate regions or objects. Some early observations by Salapatek (1975) with stimuli of the kind illustrated in Fig. 5 suggest that this kind of segmentation may be remarkably ineffective for 3-month-old infants, but we know almost nothing about its development.

Perceptual processing also needs to bind together the different features that occur at the same location; without such a process, the perceiver would detect redness and squareness without identifying them as attributes of a unitary red square. Again, we do not know whether infants who can process the separate features can necessarily also link them in this way. Triesman (1985; 1986) argues that the linkage can occur only when focal attention is directed to the location that contains the features. We have suggested (see

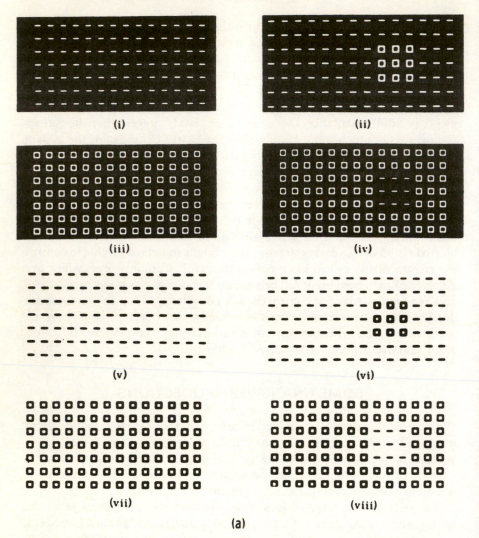

(i)   (ii)

(iii)   (iv)

(v)   (vi)

(vii)   (viii)

(a)

pp. 21–23) that between 1 and 3 months the infant gains greater control in selecting a field location as the target of an eye movement. Does this developing ability also allow a location to be selected for the purpose of binding different features at that location? Generally, can infants orient attention internally, as well as by overt eye movements?

Focal attention, and perhaps also spatial visual processes that do not require attention, must act on a region of a particular size. The precision with which spatial properties and relationships can be represented in perception

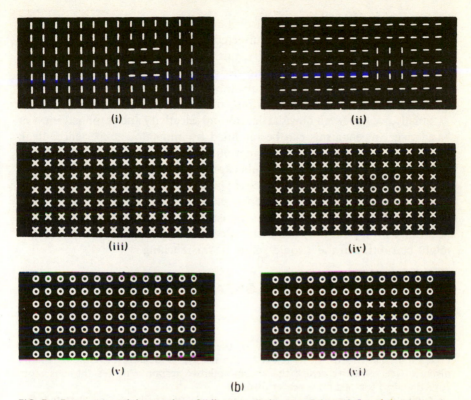

FIG. 5. Patterns containing patches of "discrepant" elements. Salapatek found that 3-month-old infants did orient to the discrepant patch in the cases shown in (a), but this can be explained as a response to differences in average luminance or contrast. Three-month-olds showed no evidence of orienting to the discrepancies in (b), where luminance and contrast are uniform. From Salapatek, (1975). *Infant perception from sensation to cognition, vol 1.* Academic Press.

will depend in part on how small this "patch size" can be (Braddick & Atkinson, 1987). Possibly some of the young infants' insensitivity to spatial relations (see pp. 15–18) may be due to an inability to organise processing in sufficiently fine patches, but we still lack a sufficiently clear-cut test of this ability. Further, only some of the properties of objects are defined over very local regions; Others require larger-scale processing, so for effective perception it is necessary to work with a hierarchy of patch sizes. We do not know whether visual perception develops from a "shallow" single-level process to a deeper hierarchy, or whether it is intrinsically hierarchical and multi-scale from the beginning.

In this chapter we have treated the flow of visual information as being from a "raw" visual input to higher-level, more abstracted representations.

However, there are good reasons to believe that in adults, lower-level visual processing can be modulated and directed by knowledge incorporated in the system at a higher level. Classically, this "top–down" processing has often been held to depend on learned knowledge; but in fact we know little about what high-level representations are available to the infant at what stage, and less about what top–down flow of information they may control.

Finally, we have seen how the developing selectivity and responsiveness of basic visual mechanisms can be modified by anomalous experience. If an operation such as combining information from the two eyes is susceptible to redirection in development, we would expect that the richer and more flexible processes controlling object and scene perception must also follow developmental routes that depend on experience. Developmental anomalies in these processes may not be as obvious as a misalignment of the eyes, but it would be strange if they did not occur. The effects of such anomalies in perception might be subtle but they would surely be far-reaching.

GLOSSARY

Bold type within an entry indicates a term which is explained under its own heading in the glossary.

Accommodation: The adjustment of the eye to bring objects at different distances into sharp focus. In its relaxed state the eye is focused for some maximum distance (see **refractive error**); the accommodative response makes the lens more curved and so focused for a nearer distance.

Acuity: A measure of the finest spatial detail which can be detected and signalled by the visual system. In infants (and often in adults) this is measured as the highest **spatial frequency** grating (of high contrast) which can be distinguished from a uniform field of the same average **luminance;** in adults an alternative approach is to determine the smallest letters which can be recognised.

Amblyopia: Poor vision, usually in one eye, which is not due to visible pathology and cannot be improved by correcting any **refractive error.** Rather, it is a developmental consequence of "disuse" of that eye. Sometimes known as "lazy eye".

Anisometropic amblyopia: In early life one eye may have a sharp optical image while the other is blurred due to uncorrected **refractive error.** The latter eye may then suffer permanently poorer vision or **amblyopia,** even when any remaining refractive error is corrected.

Astigmatism: A **refractive error** in which different orientations (e.g. horizontal and vertical lines) are not in focus at the same distance. It is due to the optical surfaces of the eye being partly cylindrical rather than perfectly spherical curves.

Binocular disparity: Objects nearer or further than the fixation point appear in different positions in the fields of the two eyes. Binocular disparity is a measure of this difference in position. The detection of disparity is used in **stereopsis,** and to control **vergence** eye movements that align the two eyes for a single target.

C/deg. (abbreviation for cycles per degree):   One cycle of a **grating** comprises one light stripe plus one dark stripe. The number of cycles that cover one degree of visual angle is a measure of the grating's **spatial frequency.** Thus if each light or dark stripe is

1 minute ($\frac{1}{60}$ of a degree) wide, one cycle covers $\frac{1}{30}$ of a degree, and the spatial frequency is 30 c/deg.

Contrast: The difference in **luminance** between the light and dark parts of an image, usually expressed as a percentage or fraction defined by: contrast = (Lmax − Lmin)/(Lmax + Lmin) where Lmax is the luminance of the lightest points and Lmin is the luminance of the darkest points.

Contrast sensitivity function: The relationship between ability to detect contrast in a sinusoidal **grating**, and the grating's **spatial frequency**. The highest spatial frequency for which the contrast sensitivity function can be measured corresponds to the limit of visual **acuity**.

Deprivation amblyopia: In early life, the image in one eye may be severely degraded or completely obstructed (e.g. by cloudiness of the lens in cases of cataract, or by severe droop of one eyelid). This eye is likely to suffer a permanently poor vision or **amblyopia** even after the obstruction is removed.

Dichromacy: See **trichromacy**.

Disparity: This is short for **binocular disparity**.

Emmetropia: See **refractive error**.

Emmetropisation: The process by which **refractive errors** (principally **hypermetropia** and **astigmatism**) tend to reduce in the early years of childhood.

Even-symmetric: Describes a **receptive field** which is organised so that any region on one side of the centre line has an identical region in the corresponding position on the other side. Its optimal stimulus is something like a dark or bright bar. Cf. **odd-symmetric**.

Evoked potential: An electrical signal, detected from the surface of the scalp, that reflects some brain response to a sensory event. The signal is known to be related to the sensory event because it occurs with a consistent delay following the event.

Extra-striate areas: Areas of the primate cerebral cortex that lie outside the **striate cortex**, but whose cells transmit and process visual information. They are believed mostly to gain their visual input (directly or indirectly) from the striate area, but to process it in specialised ways (e.g. motion processing in area MT; colour processing in area V4).

Fovea: The central area of the retina that has the highest density of cone **receptors** and **retinal ganglion cells,** and hence the highest **acuity**. Foveation is the act of moving the eyes in order to bring some object into this part of the field of view.

FPL: Forced-choice **preferential looking** (q.v.)

Grating: A pattern of repeated parallel stripes. In a sinusoidal grating the rise and fall of luminance across the stripes follows a sine curve, so the grating contains only a single **spatial frequency** component.

Habituation: A method of testing visual discrimination. The decline in looking time is measured as the infant habituates to repeated presentations of the same stimulus, and compared with the looking time to a novel stimulus which is then presented. A reliable increase in looking time is evidence that the infant can discriminate between the original stimulus and the novel stimulus.

Hyperopia (= **hypermetropia**):   A form of **refractive error** in which the eye when relaxed is focused beyond infinity, so objects at all distances will be blurred unless greater than normal effort of **accommodation** is made.

Lateral geniculate nucleus (l.g.n.):   A body of cells in the thalamus which receive visual input from the **retinal ganglion cells** and transmit it on to the **striate cortex.** These cells do not show the orientation-specific responses or binocular interaction that are characteristic of striate cortex.

Lateral inhibition: Property of the **receptive fields** of **retinal ganglion cells.** Light in the receptive field centre and in a surround region generates opposite responses (excitation and inhibition) which can cancel out if both regions are illuminated. Thus the cell responds strongly to local contrast but not to near-uniform illumination of its receptive field.

Linear systems analysis: An analysis of how effectively spatial **contrast** information is signalled by the visual system. Any pattern can be mathematically analysed into its **spatial frequency** components and the transmission of each component by the visual system is calculated from the **contrast sensitivity function.** The analysis assumes that the overall signal transmitted is the sum of these calculated components. (The same analysis can be applied to temporal as well as spatial signals, and to systems other than the visual system.)

Luminance: Light intensity—a measure of physical energy, but adjusted to take into account the **spectral sensitivity** of the eye to different wavelengths. Not quite the same as brightness, which strictly is a subjective measure of apparent intensity.

Meridional amblyopia: A difference of acuity for different orientations (e.g. poorer acuity for horizontal than for vertical lines) that cannot be improved by spectacles. It is the result of long-term exposure to greater blur in one orientation, as a result of uncorrected *astigmatism* in early life.

Myelin: A fatty sheath around nerve fibres that greatly increases the speed at which nerve impulses are transmitted.

Nasal: The part of the visual field of either eye that is on the side towards the nose. (Opposite = **temporal.**)

Noise: Generally, a signal which varies randomly. In visual experiments with gratings, "one-dimensional noise" is a stripe pattern whose intensity varies randomly from stripe to stripe; mathematically it contains a continuous and wide range of spatial frequencies.

Odd-symmetric: Describes a **receptive field** that is organised so that, for any region which has a positive response, there is a corresponding region the other side of the centre line which has a negative response. Hence the most effective stimulus will be something like a light–dark edge. Cf. **even-symmetric.**

OKN (optokinetic nystagmus):   Repetitive eye movements which occur when a large part of the visual field is filled with uniformly moving pattern: The eyes follow the motion (slow phase), then flick back (fast phase), and this cycle is repeated.

Phase: To describe a pattern in terms of its **spatial frequency** components, it is necessary to state for each component not only its amplitude (contrast) but also the relative positions at which the peaks of the sine-wave components fall. The phase of a sine wave is a measure of the position of its peaks (or of its **zero-crossings**).

Photoreceptor: See **receptor.**

Preferential looking (PL):   A method in which an infant's preference for looking at a pattern over a blank screen of matched luminance is used to indicate the infant's ability to detect the pattern. Most modern studies use forced-choice PL **(FPL)**, in which an observer has to decide, solely from watching the infant's looking behaviour, which screen contains the pattern. Above-chance performance by the observer is then evidence of the infant's detection.

Primitive: One of the elements or symbols out of which a representation is composed. Thus, an oriented line segment might be a primitive at some level of spatial vision; the more detailed information which was used to define a line segment as present would be lost in this representation.

Receptive field: For a cell at some level in the visual pathway, the region of the visual field in which stimulation can elicit some response. In many cases, distinct regions of the field can be mapped in which light produces excitation and inhibition respectively.

Receptor: The rod and cone cells of the eye that generate neural signals when light falls on them. Cones serve for high-acuity colour vision in bright light; the rod system is sensitive to dim light but has poor acuity and no colour vision.

Refractive error: The "normal" (or emmetropic) eye, when relaxed, is focused at infinite distance. Refractive errors are deviations from this ideal: If the eye is focused at too close a distance, the error is myopic, whereas if its optical power is too weak it will require some effort of **accommodation** even to focus at infinity, and the error is hyperopic.

Retinal ganglion cells: Neurones in the retina which collect information (indirectly) from the **photoreceptors** and transmit it down the optic nerve (whose fibres are the axons of these cells). Retinal ganglion cells have roughly circular **receptive fields** with **lateral inhibition** between centre and surround regions.

Saccade: The type of eye movement made to **foveate** a new target object. Saccades are rapid flicks that follow a preset pattern of velocity and cannot be altered "in flight".

Smooth pursuit: Eye movements that maintain the image of a moving object on the fovea, and so are matched to the rate at which the object moves across the field of view. They cannot normally be generated except as a response to a moving object.

Spatial frequency: For a repetitive pattern such as a grating, the number of complete cycles which occur in a unit distance (see **c/deg**). Thus a high-spatial-frequency grating has narrow stripes, while a low-frequency grating has broad stripes. Mathematically, any pattern can be considered as the sum of a range of spatial frequency components—sinusoidal gratings each of which has its own spatial frequency, orientation, amplitude or **contrast,** and **phase.** Low-spatial-frequency components determine the coarse distribution of light vs. dark areas, whereas high frequencies determine the fine details.

Spectral sensitivity: The response of the visual system, or of some element within it such as a particular class of cone receptors, as a function of the different wavelengths in the spectrum. The three types of cone have different but overlapping spectral sensitivity curves. The balance of their different responses to a single light depends on the wavelengths present in the light and so gives information about colour.

Stereopsis or **stereoscopic vision:**   The ability to use **binocular disparity** to distinguish the relative depth or distance of points in the visual field.

Stereoacuity: A measure of the finest **disparity** that leads to a visually detectable difference in depth.

Strabismus (often called "squint" in Britain):   A condition in which the axes of the two eyes cannot be brought parallel, so one eye is used to fixate an object while the other deviates. The deviating eye may be directed inwards (convergent strabismus or "crossed eyes") or outwards (divergent strabismus).

Striate cortex: The region at the back of the cerebral hemispheres which receives visual input from the **lateral geniculate nucleus** and connects to other, **extra-striate,** visual areas. It is believed to carry out the initial operations in the analysis of visual pattern and binocular disparity.

Superior colliculus: Structure in the midbrain which receives input from the retina, by a separate branch from that going to the **lateral geniculate nucleus** and **striate cortex.** It is involved in the control of eye movements and perhaps other spatial orienting behaviour.

Temporal: The part of the visual field of either eye that is on the side away from the nose. (Opposite = **nasal.**)

Trichromacy: The property of human colour vision that means a mixture of three primary colours is necessary and sufficient to match any arbitrary colour. It is a result of the existence of three types of cone **receptor** with different **spectral sensitivities.** Some "colour-blind" individuals have only two cone types, require only two primaries to make colour matches, and are called dichromats. An individual with normal colour vision is called a trichromat.

VEP: Visual **evoked potential.**

Vergence: Eye movement in which the axes of the two eyes swivel relative to each other (unlike **saccades** and **smooth pursuit** in which the two eyes move together). Vergence includes convergent movements, when the eyes turn inwards, and divergent movements, when they turn outwards.

Visual cortex: **Striate cortex.**

Zero-crossing: A waveform such as the plot of luminance variation with position (e.g. in Fig. 2) passes through the zero line (average luminance level) at certain locations, called zero-crossings. A zero-crossing will generally be present where there is a light/dark edge in the image.

REFERENCES

Aslin, R. N. (1981). The development of smooth pursuit in human infants. In D. F. Fisher, R. A. Monty, & J. W. Senders (eds), *Eye movements: Cognition and visual perception.* Hillsdale, N.J: Lawrence Erlbaum Associates Inc.

Aslin, R. N. (1987). Anatomical constraints on oculomotor development: Implications for infant perception. In A. Yonas (ed.), *20th Minnesota symposium on child psychology.* Hillsdale, N.J: Lawrence Erlbaum Associates Inc.

Aslin, R. N. & Salapatek, P. (1975). Saccadic localization of targets by the very young infant. *Perception and Psychophysics, 17,* 293–302.

Atkinson, J. (1984). Human visual development over the first 6 months of life: A review and a hypothesis. *Human Neurobiology, 3,* 61–74.

Atkinson, J. & Braddick, O. J. (1981a). Acuity, contrast sensitivity and accommodation in infancy. In R. N. Aslin, J. R. Alberts, & M. R. Petersen (eds), *The development of perception: Psychobiological perspectives:* Vol. 2. *The visual system.* New York: Academic Press. (Pp. 245–277).

Atkinson, J. & Braddick, O. J. (1981b). Development of optokinetic nystagmus in infants: An indicator of cortical binocularity? In D. F. Fisher, R. A. Monty & J. W. Senders (eds), *Eye movements: Cognition and visual perception.* Hillsdale, N.J: Lawrence Erlbaum Associates Inc.

Atkinson, J. & Braddick, O. J. (1984). Human visual development. In J. Nicholson & B. Foss (eds), *Psychology survey IV.* Leicester: British Psychological Society. (Pp. 1–37).

Atkinson, J. & Braddick, O. J. (1987). Infant precursors of later visual disorders: Correlation or causality? In A. Yonas (ed.), *20th Minnesota Symposium on Child Psychology.* Hillsdale, N.J: Lawrence Erlbaum Associates Inc.

Atkinson, J., Braddick, O. J., & Moar, K. (1977). Development of contrast sensitivity over the first three months of life in the human infant. *Vision Research, 17,* 1037–1044.

Atkinson J. & Campbell, F. W. (1974). The effect of phase on the perception of compound gratings. *Vision Research, 14,* 159–162.

Atkinson J., Pimm-Smith E., Evans C., & Braddick O. J. (1983). The effects of screen size and eccentricity on acuity estimates in infants using preferential looking. *Vision Research, 23*, 1479–1483.

Atkinson, J., Wattam-Bell, J., & Braddick, O. J. (1986). Infants' development of sensitivity to pattern 'textons'. *Investigative Ophthalmology and Visual Science (supplement), 27*, 265.

Badcock, D. R. (1984). Spatial phase or luminance profile discrimination? *Vision Research, 24*, 613–623.

Banks, M. S. (1980a). Infant refraction and accommodation. *International Ophthalmolology Clinics, 20*, 205–232.

Banks, M. S. (1980b). The development of visual accommodation during early infancy. *Child Development, 51*, 646–666.

Banks, M. S., Aslin, R. N., & Letson, R. D. (1975). Sensitive period for the development of human binocular vision. *Science, 190*, 675–677.

Banks, M. S. & Ginsburg, A. P. (1983). Early visual preferences: A review and new theoretical treatment. In H. W. Reese (ed.), *Advances in child development and behavior*. New York: Academic Press.

Banks, M. S. & Salapatek, P. (1981). Infant pattern vision: A new approach based on the contrast sensitivity function. *Journal of Experimental Child Psychology, 31*, 1–35.

Banks, M. S. & Salapatek, P. (1983). Infant visual perception. In M. M. Haith & J. Campos (eds), *Handbook of child psychology*: Vol 2. *Biology and infancy*. New York: Wiley. (Pp. 435–571).

Banks, M. S., Stephens, B. R., & Hartmann, E. E. (1985). The development of basic mechanisms of pattern vision: Spatial frequency channels. *Journal of Experimental Child Psychology, 40*, 501–527.

Barlow, H. B. & Mollon, J. D. (eds) (1982). *The senses*. Cambridge: Cambridge University Press.

Birch, E. E., Gwiazda, J., & Held, R. (1983). The development of vergence does not account for the development of stereopsis. *Perception, 12*, 331–336.

Birch, E. E., Shimojo, S., & Held, R. (1985). Preferential-looking assessment of fusion and stereopsis in infants aged 1–6 months. *Investigative Ophthalmology and Visual Science, 26*, 366–370.

Blakemore, C. B. (1978). Maturation and modification in the developing visual system. In R. Held, H. Leibowitz, & H. L. Teuber (eds), *Handbook of sensory physiology*: Vol. VIII. *Perception*. Heidelberg: Springer-Verlag.

Blakemore, C. B. & Cooper, G. F. (1970). Development of the brain depends on the visual environment. *Nature, 228*, 477–478.

Blakemore, C. B. & Vital-Durand, F. (1981). Postnatal development of the monkey's visual system. In *The fetus and independent life: Ciba Foundation symposium 86*. London, Pitman. (Pp. 152–171).

Bornstein, M. H. (1976). Infants are trichromats. *Journal of Experimental Child Psychology, 21*, 425–445.

Bouma, H. (1970). Interaction effects in parafoveal letter recognition, *Nature, 226*, 177–178.

Braddick, O. J. (1981a). Spatial frequency analysis in vision. *Nature, 291*, 9–11.

Braddick, O. J. (1981b). Is spatial phase degraded in peripheral vision and visual pathology? *Documenta Ophthalmologica Proceedings Series, 30*, 255–262.

Braddick, O. J. & Atkinson, J (1983). Some recent findings on the development of human binocularity: A review. *Behavioural Brain Research, 10*, 71–80.

Braddick, O. J. & Atkinson, J. (1987). Sensory selectivity, attentional control, and cross-channel integration in early visual development. In A. Yonas (ed.), *20th Minnesota symposium on child psychology*. Hillsdale, N.J: Lawrence Erlbaum Associates Inc.

Braddick, O. J., Atkinson, J., French, J., & Howland, H. C. (1979). A photorefractive study of infant accommodation. *Vision Research, 19*, 319–330.

Braddick, O. J., Atkinson, J., Julesz B., Kropfl W., Bodis-Wollner I., & Raab E. (1980). Cortical binocularity in infants. *Nature, 288*, 363–365.

Braddick, O. J., Atkinson, J., & Wattam-Bell, J. R. (1986). Development of the discrimination of spatial phase in infancy. *Vision Research*, *26*, 1223–1239.

Braddick, O. J., Campbell, F. W., & Atkinson, J. (1978). Channels in vision: Basic aspects. In R. Held, H. Leibowitz, & H. L. Teuber (eds), *Handbook of sensory physiology*: Vol. VIII. *Perception*. Heidelberg: Springer-Verlag.

Braddick, O. J., Wattam-Bell, J., & Atkinson, J. (1986). Orientation-specific cortical responses develop in early infancy. *Nature*, *320*, 617–619.

Braddick, O., Wattam-Bell, J., Day, J., & Atkinson, J. (1983). The onset of binocular function in human infants. *Human Neurobiology*, *2*, 65–69.

Bronson, G. W. (1974). The postnatal growth of visual capacity. *Child Development*, *45*, 873–890.

Bruce, V. & Green, P. (1985). *Visual perception: Physiology, psychology, and ecology*. London: Lawrence Erlbaum Associates Ltd.

Bushnell, I. W. R. (1979). Modification of the externality effect in young infants. *Journal of Experimental Child Psychology*, *28*, 211–229.

Bushnell, I. W. R. (1982). Discrimination of faces by young infants. *Journal of Experimental Child Psychology*, *33*, 298–308.

Cohen, L. B. & Younger, B. A. (1984). Infant perception of angular relations. *Infant Behavior and Development*, *7*, 37–47.

Conel, J. L. (1939, 1947). *The postnatal development of the human cerebral cortex:* Vols. 1 & 3. Cambridge, Mass.: Harvard University Press.

Cynader, M., Berman, N., & Hein, A. (1973). Cats reared in stroboscopic illumination: Effects on receptive fields in visual cortex. *Proceedings of the National Academy of Sciences of the USA*, *70*, 1353–1354.

Dannemiller, J. L. & Stephens, B. R. (1988). A critical test of infant preference models. *Child Development*, *59*, 210–216.

Daw, N., Berman, N. E. J., & Ariel, M. (1978). Interaction of critical periods in the visual cortex of kittens. *Science*, *199*, 565–567.

De Schonen, S., McKenzie, B., & Bresson, F. (1978). Central and peripheral object distances as determinants of the effective visual field in early infancy. *Perception*, *7*, 499–506.

De Valois, R. L., Albrecht, D. G., & Thorell, L. G. (1982). Spatial frequency selectivity of cells in macaque visual cortex. *Vision Research*, *22*, 545–559.

Dobson, V. (1976). Spectral sensitivity of the 2-month infant as measured by the visually evoked cortical potential. *Vision Research*, *16*, 367–374.

Dobson, V. & Teller, D. Y. (1978). Visual acuity in human infants: A review and comparison of behavioral and electrophysiological studies. *Vision Research*, *18*, 1469–1483.

Fantz, R. L., Fagan, J. F., & Miranda, S. B. (1975). Early visual selectivity. In L. B. Cohen & P. Salapatek (eds), *Infant perception: From sensation to cognition*: Vol. I. New York: Academic Press. (Pp. 249–346).

Field, D. J. & Nachmias, J. (1984). Phase reversal discrimination. *Vision Research*, *24*, 333–340.

Fox, R. (1981). Stereopsis in animals and human infants. In R. N. Aslin, J. R. Alberts, & M. R. Petersen (eds), *The development of perception: Psychobiological perspectives*: Vol. 2. *The visual system*. New York: Academic Press. (Pp. 335–381).

Fox, R., Aslin, R. N., Shea, S. L., & Dumais, S. T. (1980). Stereopsis in human infants. *Science*, *207*, 323–324.

Frisby, J. P. (1979). *Seeing*. Oxford: Oxford University Press.

Garey, L. & De Courten, C. (1983). Structural development of the lateral geniculate nucleus and visual cortex in monkey and man. *Behavioural Brain Research*, *10*, 3–15.

Gayl, I. E., Roberts, J. O., & Werner, J. S. (1983). Linear systems analysis of infant visual preferences. *Journal of Experimental Child Psychology*, *35*, 30–45.

Goldstein, E. B. (1984). *Sensation and perception* (2nd ed.). Belmont, Calif.: Wadsworth.

Gwiazda, J., Bauer, J., Thorn, F., & Held, R. (1987). Meridional amblyopia *does* result from astigmatism in early childhood. *Clinical Vision Sciences, 1,* 145–152.

Hainline, L., Turkel, J., Abramov, I., Lemerise, E., & Harris, C. M. (1984). Characteristics of saccades in human infants. *Vision Research, 24,* 1771–1780.

Haith, M. M. (1978). Visual competence in early infancy. In R. Held, H. Leibowitz, & H. L. Teuber, *Handbook of sensory physiology*: Vol. VIII. *Perception*. Berlin: Springer Verlag. (Pp. 319–356).

Hamer, R. D., Alexander, K. R., & Teller, D. Y. (1982). Rayleigh discriminations in young infants. *Vision Research, 22,* 575–587.

Harris, P. & MacFarlane, A. (1974). The growth of the effective visual field from birth to seven weeks. *Journal of Experimental Child Psychology, 18,* 340–348.

Held, R., Birch, E. E., & Gwiazda, J. (1980). Stereoacuity of human infants. *Proceedings of the National Academy of Sciences of the USA, 77,* 5572–5574.

Hess, R. F. (1982). Developmental sensory impairment: Amblyopia or tarachopia? *Human Neurobiology, 1,* 17–29.

Hess, R. F., Campbell, F. W., & Greenhalgh, T. (1978). On the nature of the neural abnormality in human amblyopia: Neural aberrations and neural sensitivity loss. *Pfluegers Archiv/ European Journal of Physiology, 377,* 201–207.

Hickey, T. L. (1981). The developing nervous system. *Trends in Neurosciences, 4,* 41–44.

Hilton, A. F. & Stanley, J. C. (1972). Pitfalls in testing children's vision by the Sheridan Gardiner single optotype method. *British Journal of Ophthalmology, 56,* 135–139.

Hoffman, K. P. (1979). Optokinetic nystagmus and single-cell responses in the nucleus tractus opticus after early monocular deprivation in the cat. In R. D. Freeman (ed.), *Developmental neurobiology of vision*. New York: Plenum Press.

Howland, H. C., Atkinson, J., Braddick, O., & French, J. (1978). Infant astigmatism measured by photorefraction. *Science, 202,* 331–333.

Humphrey, N. K. (1974). Vision in a monkey without striate cortex: A case study. *Perception, 3,* 241–256.

Jacobson, S. G., Mohindra, I., & Held, R. (1983). Monocular visual form deprivation in human infants. *Documenta Ophthalmologica, 55,* 199–211.

Julesz, B. (1980). Spatial nonlinearities in the instantaneous perception of textures with identical power spectra. In H. C. Longuet-Higgins & N. S. Sutherland (eds.), *The psychology of vision*. London: The Royal Society. (Pp. 83–94).

Julesz, B. (1981). Textons, the elements of texture perception, and their interactions, *Nature, 290,* 91–97.

Karmel, B. Z. & Maisel, E. B. (1975). A neuronal activity model for infant visual attention. In L. B. Cohen & P. Salapatek (eds), *Infant perception: From sensation to cognition*: Vol. I. New York: Academic Press. (Pp. 78–132).

Kleiner, K. A. (1987). Amplitude and phase spectra as indices of infants' pattern preferences. *Infant Behaviour and Development, 10,* 45–55.

Kleiner, K. A. & Banks, M. S. (1987). Stimulus energy does not account for 2-month olds' face preferences. *Journal of Experimental Psychology: Human Perception and Performance, 13,* 594–600.

Lawden, M. C., Hess, R. F., & Campbell, F. W. (1982). The discriminability of spatial phase relationships in amblyopia. *Vision Research, 22,* 1005–1016.

Lettvin, J. Y. (1976). On seeing sidelong. *The Sciences, 16*(4), 10–20.

MacFarlane, A., Harris, P., & Barnes, I (1976). Central and peripheral vision in early infancy. *Journal of Experimental Child Psychology 21,* 532–538.

McKenzie, B., & Day, R. H. (1976). Infants' attention to stationary and moving objects at different distances. *Australian Journal of Psychology, 28,* 45–51.

Marr, D. C. (1982). *Vision*. San Francisco: Freeman.

Maurer, D. & Lewis, T. L. (1979). A physiological explanation of infants' early visual development. *Canadian Journal of Psychology*, *33*, 232–252.

Maurer, D. & Martello, M. (1980). The discrimination of orientation by young infants. *Vision Research*, *20*, 201–204.

Miles, F. A. & Judge, S. J. (1982). Optically induced changes in the neural coupling between vergence eye movements and accommodation in human subjects. In G. Lennerstrand, D. S. Zee, & E. Keller (eds), *Functional basis of ocular motility disorders*. Oxford: Pergamon Press. (Pp. 93–96).

Milewski, A. E. (1976). Infants' discrimination of internal and external pattern elements. *Journal of Experimental Child Psychology*, *22*, 229–246.

Mitchell, D. E. (1981). Sensitive periods in visual development. In R. N. Aslin, J. R. Alberts, & M. R. Petersen (eds), *The development of perception: Psychobiological perspectives*: Vol. 2. *The visual system*. New York: Academic Press. (Pp. 3–43).

Mitchell, D. E., Freeman, R. D., Millodot, M., & Haegerstrom, G. (1973). Meridional amblyopia: Evidence for the modification of human visual system by early visual experience. *Vision Research*, *13*, 535–558.

Mitchell, D. E., Gifin, F., Wilkinson, F., Anderson, P., & Smith, M. L. (1976). Visual resolution in young kittens. *Vision Research*, *16*, 363–366.

Mohindra, I., Held, R., Gwiazda, J., & Brill, S. (1978). Astigmatism in infants. *Science*, *202*, 329–331.

Mollon, J. D. (1982). Color vision. *Annual Review of Psychology*, *33*, 41–85.

Movshon, J. A. & Van Sluyters, R. C. (1981). Visual neural development. *Annual Review of Psychology*, *32*, 477–522.

Norcia, A. M. & Tyler, C. W. (1985). Spatial frequency sweep VEP: Visual acuity during the first year of life. *Vision Research*, *25*, 1399–1408.

Peeples, D. & Teller, D. Y. (1978). White-adapted photopic spectral sensitivity in human infants. *Vision Research*, *18*, 49–53.

Pettigrew, J. D. (1974). The effect of visual experience on the development of disparity specificity by kitten cortical neurons. *Journal of Physiology*, *237*, 49–74.

Petrig, B., Julesz, B., Kropfl, W., Baumgartner, G., & Anliker, M. (1981). Development of stereopsis and cortical binocularity in human infants: Electrophysiological evidence. *Science*, *213*, 1402–1405.

Pipp, S. & Haith, M. M. (1984). Infant visual responses to pattern: Which metric predicts best? *Journal of Experimental Child Psychology*, *38*, 373–399.

Pulos, E., Teller, D. Y., & Buck, S. L. (1980). Infant color vision: A search for short-wave-sensitive mechanisms by means of chromatic adaptation. *Vision Research*, *18*, 1137–1147.

Rakic, P. (1977). Prenatal development of the visual system in the rhesus monkey. *Proceedings of the Royal Society of London*, *B 278*, 245–260.

Rauschecker, J. P. & Singer, W. (1981). The effects of early visual experience on the cat's visual cortex and their possible explanation by Hebb synapses. *Journal of Physiology*, *310*, 215–239.

Raviola, E. & Wiesel, T. N. (1978). Effect of dark rearing on experimental myopia in monkeys. *Investigative Ophthalmology and Visual Science*, *17*, 485–488.

Regal, D. (1981). Development of critical flicker frequency in human infants. *Vision Research*, *21*, 549–555.

Rentschler, I. & Treutwein, B. (1985). Loss of spatial phase relationships in extra-foveal vision. *Nature*, *313*, 307–310.

Salapatek, P. (1975). Pattern perception in early infancy. In L. B. Cohen and P. Salapatek (eds), *Infant perception: From sensation to cognition*: Vol I. New York: Academic Press.

Schiller, P. H. (1984). The superior colliculus and visual function. In I. Darian-Smith (ed.), *Handbook of physiology—the nervous system III. Sensory Processes, Part 1*. Bethesda, Md: American Physiological Society. (Ch. 11).

Shimojo, S., Bauer, J., O'Connell, K. M., & Held, R. (1986). Pre-stereoptic binocular vision in infants. *Vision Research, 26*, 501–510.

Slater, A. M. & Sykes, M. (1977). Newborn infants' responses to square-wave gratings. *Child Development, 48*, 545–553.

Stephenson, C. M. & Braddick, O. J. (1983). Discrimination of relative spatial phase in fovea and periphery. *Investigative Ophthalmology and Visual Science, 24*, (Suppl), 146.

Stromeyer, C. F. III & Klein, S. A. (1974). Spatial frequency channels in human vision as asymmetric (edge) mechanisms. *Vision Research, 14*, 1409–1420.

Teller, D. Y. & Bornstein, M. H. (1987). Infant color vision and color perception. In P. Salapatek & L. B. Cohen (eds), *Handbook of infant perception*. New York: Academic Press.

Teller, D. Y., Peeples, D. R., & Sekel, M. (1978). Discrimination of colored from white light by 2-month-old human infants. *Vision Research, 18*, 41–48.

Triesman, A. (1985). Preattentive processing in vision. *Computer Vision, Graphics, & Image Processing, 31*, 156–177.

Triesman, A. (1986). Features and objects in visual processing. *Scientific American, 255*(5), 106–115.

Tronick, E. (1972). Stimulus control and the growth of the infant's effective visual field. *Perception and Psychophysics, 11*, 373–375.

van Hof-van Duin, J. & Mohn, G. (1986). Visual field measurements, optokinetic nystagmus, and the visual threatening response: Normal and abnormal development. *Documenta Ophthalmologica Proceedings Series, 45*, 305–315.

Varner, D., Cook, J. E., Schneck, M. E., McDonald, M., & Teller, D. Y. (1985). Tritan discriminations by 1- and 2-month-old human infants. *Vision Research, 25*, 821–831.

Volbrecht, V. J. & Werner, J. S. (1987). Isolation of short-wavelength-sensitive cone photoreceptors in 4–6-week-old human infants. *Vision Research, 27*, 469–478.

Wattam-Bell, J., Braddick, O., Atkinson, J., & Day, J. (1987). Measures of infant binocularity in a group at risk for strabismus. *Clinical Vision Sciences, 1*, 327–336.

Weiskrantz, L. (1986). *Blindsight*. Oxford: Clarendon Press.

Werner, J. S. & Wooten, B. R. (1979). Human infant color vision and color perception. *Infant Behavior and Development, 2*, 241–274.

Wurtz, R. & Albano, J. E. (1980). Visual motor function of the primate superior colliculus. *Annual Review of Neuroscience, 3*, 189–226.

Youdelis, C. & Hendrickson, A. (1986). A qualitative and quantitative analysis of the human fovea during development. *Vision Research, 26*, 847–855.

Yonas, A. & Pick, H. (1975). An approach to the study of infant space perception. In L. B. Cohen and P. Salapatek (eds), *Infant perception: From sensation to cognition*: Vol. I. New York: Academic Press.

2

Visual Memory and Perception in Early Infancy

Alan Slater

Department of Psychology,
Washington Singer Laboratories,
University of Exeter,
Exeter EX4 4QG, U.K.

INTRODUCTION

For over three hundred years philosophers and visual scientists have speculated on the visual abilities of the infant and on the role of experience in visual development. Although there were few facts and little in the way of evidence, these speculations gave rise to one of the longest running debates in psychology, concerning the question of whether perception is innate or learned. The nativist view that perceptual abilities are unlearned and may be present at birth had fewer adherents than the opposing empiricist assertion that perception is exceptionally impoverished at birth and that its development is a consequence of learning.

Research conducted from the 1960s has not given support to either of these extreme assumptions. A useful model which avoids the oversimplification of the nativism–empiricism controversy is that described by Aslin and Pisoni (1980; see also Aslin, 1981) and shown in Fig. 1. In primates the onset of visual experience (the vertical dotted line in Fig. 1) coincides with birth, at which time a particular visual ability may be fully developed, partially developed, or undeveloped. Perceptual experience can play different roles, in part dependent upon the specific ability and its state of development at birth. For example, in terms of their dynamic aspects infants' saccadic eye movements display an adult-like maturity at birth, so that postnatal visual experience may act both to maintain their functioning and to improve their latency and accuracy (see Chapter 1); other types of eye movement, such as smooth pursuit and vergence movements, are not readily elicited from the

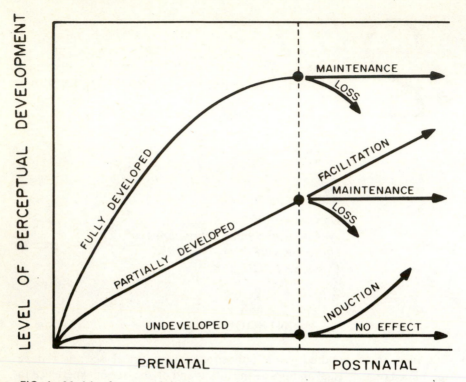

FIG. 1   Models of perceptual development. Aslin & Pisoni, (1980). *Child phonology: vol 2 PERCEPTION.*

new-born, so that visual experience may induce their development; visual acuity and contrast sensitivity are much poorer in the new-born than in the adult, and specific experiences, which can be thought of as serving a facilitating function, are necessary for their postnatal development.

THE NEW-BORN BABY'S WINDOW ON THE WORLD

Not surprisingly, the visual world of the new-born is quite different from that of the adult. One of the most obvious differences is that the visual information detected by the new-born is very impoverished. Sensitivity to contrast differences is poor. A black and white pattern gives a contrast approaching 100%, and under good viewing conditions adults can discriminate between shades of grey giving a contrast value less than 1%; a contrast of 30–40% is close to the new-born's threshold of detectability. Visual acuity is about 30 times poorer than in the adult; adult acuity is about

30 cycles per degree (c/deg.)—a value which corresponds to 20/20 or 6/6 vision—or better, whereas that for the new-born is about 1 c/deg. This resolving power allows the new-born to detect the presence of alternating black and white stripes, each one-tenth of an inch wide, shown at a distance of one foot from the eyes; narrower stripes are seen as a blur. This level of acuity for the new-born is, curiously, not too different from that for the adult cat (about 3 c/deg.), and the new-born's poor acuity allows for some degree of useful pattern vision. We might assume that movement will enhance the detectability of a visual stimulus, and in a later section the salience and role of movement in early visual perception is described.

It seems likely that the young infant's effective field of view is limited in spatial extent. New-borns will orient toward a stimulus that is presented 25–30° laterally, and 10° vertically (either up or down) from the line of sight, but not to more peripherally presented stimuli (Aslin & Salapatek, 1975; Harris & McFarlane, 1974). Infants under 5 months pay little visual attention to static objects located more than about 3 feet away, although this preference for near objects can be reduced or even eliminated if the farther object is moving (McKenzie & Day, 1972; 1976).

Much of the visual stimulation that is detected by the adult is simply not available to the young infant. For the new-born, high contrast, low spatial frequency patterns presented near to the line of regard, and one or two feet from the eyes, will be attended to, whereas stimuli outside of these ranges may not even be seen. It is likely that these perceptual limitations are an inevitable consequence of an immature visual system. However, it is tempting to speculate on the possible evolutionary significance of the new-born's limited "window on the world". The mother's face is three-dimensional (another aspect of stimulation that attracts attention), contains high contrast information, particularly the eyes, mouth and hairline, and when interacting with her baby is usually undergoing internal (mouth and eye), and perhaps external (back and forth) movement within the baby's limited field of view. This makes the human face one of the most attractive stimuli encountered by the new-born, and several researchers have argued that infants are born with a special predisposition to respond to faces. This is a claim that is investigated in a later section.

PREPAREDNESS FOR VISUAL PERCEPTION

Despite its immaturity the visual system is functional at birth. Haith (1980, p. 96) has described a number of dispositions or "rules" that determine visual activity in new-borns and which serve to get the infant started on the business of learning about the visual world. The first four of these "rules" are the following:

Rule 1: If awake and alert and light not too bright, open eyes;
Rule 2: If in darkness, maintain a controlled, detailed search;
Rule 3: If in light with no form, search for edges by relatively broad, jerky sweeps of the (visual) field;
Rule 4: If an edge is found, terminate the broad scan and stay in the general vicinity of that edge.

Many researchers would argue with the precise form of these "rules". Nevertheless, there is general agreement that the new-born is biologically prepared to explore the environment and is able actively to seek out and to attend to some forms of stimulation in preference to others. Most of the evidence which leads to this conclusion has come from studies in which infants' eye movements and eye fixations have been recorded or observed in the presence of various forms of visual stimulation. One very useful technique is the visual preference, or preferential looking (PL) method. In addition to its use in investigating sensitivity to visual contrast and visual acuity (see Chapter 1), PL has been used to show that infants will prefer to look at some types of patterned stimuli rather than others. Many such preferences have been found at birth, some of which have been alluded to earlier: New-borns will prefer moving to stationary, three-dimensional to two-dimensional, high contrast to low contrast stimuli (Morison & Slater, 1985; Slater, Morison, Town, & Rose, 1985; Slater, Rose, & Morison, 1983). They also have a tendency to prefer patterns which have curved rather than straight contours, a preference which is found in older infants (Fantz & Miranda, 1975).

The mechanisms that underlie preferences at a particular age, and those that mediate age-related changes in preferences, are by no means fully understood. However, there are several models whose aim is to describe and predict such preferences in terms of a small number of stimulus dimensions. Banks and Salapatek (1981) offer an approach using linear systems analysis and based on infants' contrast sensitivity functions (CFSs: see also Chapter 1). Their approach can be illustrated by describing a very powerful visual preference shown by new-borns. If a pair of high-contrast square-wave gratings (alternating black and white stripes) is constructed with different stripe widths, so that the larger stripes are 1-inch wide and the narrower 0.25 inch, and the pair is shown 1 foot from the baby's eyes, then a massive preference is found such that new-borns spend over 80% of the looking time viewing the wider stripes.

This finding is explained by Banks and Salapatek's approach as follows: New-born babies prefer to look at high-contrast gratings whose high amplitude spatial frequency components fall within their peak contrast sensitivity—the 1-inch stripe widths—when these are paired with high-contrast gratings whose high-amplitude components are outside of this range—the 0.25-inch stripes. The wider stripes are preferred simply because they are more readily detectable, that is, the babies see them more clearly.

According to this interpretation, if the contrast of the wider stripes is progressively reduced then this stimulus should become progressively less preferred if it remains paired with a high-contrast 0.25-inch striped pattern. This is the experiment we carried out, with precisely this result: When the contrast of the 1-inch grating was reduced it became progressively less preferred when paired with a high (95%) contrast 0.25-inch grating; when the contrast of the 1-inch grating dropped below 40% it attracted less than 20% of the total looking time (Morison & Slater, 1985).

The baby is born usually with the eyes wide open and actively searching for visual stimulation. As discussed above, much of this visual search can be described in terms of a few simple rules, and is profoundly, and predictably, affected by changes to low-order variables such as pattern detectability, movement, three dimensionality, contrast and spatial frequency. There is a paradox here. If new-born visual attention is so easily dominated by and described in terms of manipulations to low-order variables of stimulation, in what sense can it be said to be active and under the infant's volitional control? There are two major answers to this, both of which have some appeal. One is to suggest that rule-governed and mechanistic models of early visual activity inevitably underestimate both the flexibility of early visual attention and also the ways in which it can be readily modified by experience. The other is to deny active control to new-borns and to argue that there is a qualitative shift in the neural mechanisms underlying visual capabilities occurring some time in the second month from birth, a shift which brings with it a change from passive to active perception. The next two sections give evidence bearing on these issues.

VISUAL ACTIVITY AND MEMORY AT BIRTH

One commonly held view about visual behaviour in the new-born infant is that the baby is passive in his selection of visual stimuli, that he is "captured" by them: Stechler and Latz (1966) talked of the young infant's "obligatory attention" to stimuli. In fact, the evidence supports the view that in some situations the new-born is "passive" whereas in others we must consider him to be an active perceptual agent. Some support for the former position comes from the preferential looking literature mentioned earlier. Some new-born visual preferences are so powerful and predictable that every infant tested will spend longer looking at the preferred visual patterns. Haith (1980, p. 123), while emphasising that new-borns can be considered "dynamic" information seekers, suggested one limitation on their scanning which would also argue for visual "capture": "*Fact*: Very young infants tend to look at only one stimulus in a paired-stimulus array, whereas older infants look at both". However, we have not found this limitation in the hundreds of new-borns we have tested; in order to accumulate 40 seconds' looking at 2 paired stimuli new-borns typically shift attention from one to the other about 10 to 15 times. This frequent shifting of visual attention is found even if one of the patterns is strongly preferred. What happens in this instance is that the non-preferred pattern is looked at briefly each time it is fixated (compared with longer looks at the preferred pattern), but it continues to be glanced at regularly.

Figure 2 shows a new-born baby being tested in what might be a preferential looking study. The baby is presented two stimuli, in this case a triangle and a cross. An observer (not seen in the figure) who is positioned behind the screen, looks at the baby's eyes and records, with the help of a timer, which, if either, of the two stimuli the baby looks at. In this way a cumulative record of looking time is made as the trial progresses. Between these two stimuli no "natural" or unlearned preference exists, but it is often possible to create one temporarily by the use of habituation. Habituation has been used on innumerable occasions to study infants' discriminatory ability, and its usefulness was recognised several years ago: "Few behavioral phenomena rival habituation in usefulness as a measure of the infant's sensitivity and few have as many implications for theories of psychological development" (Kessen, Haith & Salapatek, 1970, p. 346).

Until recently there was some controversy concerning the youngest age at which an infant will habituate, and following habituation to one stimulus will display a preference for a novel stimulus, but it is now clear that this ability is present at birth. A great many varieties of habituation procedures are to be found in the literature. One of them, the so-called infant-controlled habituation procedure (Horowitz, Paden, Bhana, & Self, 1972; Slater, Morison, & Rose, 1983a; 1983b), works well with new-born babies, and the variation of it that we use can be illustrated by reference to Fig. 2. The habituating stimulus (perhaps the cross seen in Fig. 2) is presented by itself in the centre of the stimulus screen, and the first trial begins when the baby looks; the trial ends with a continuous look away from the stimulus of 2 seconds or more. The next trial begins when the baby looks again at the stimulus, and trials continue in this way until the total of any three consecutive trials, from the fourth trial on, is 50% or less than the total of the first three. Having reached this criterion of habituation, two test trials are then presented. On each of these the habituated stimulus (the cross) is paired with the novel stimulus (the triangle), and the trial continues until 20 seconds of looking has accumulated; the left/right positions of novel and familiar stimuli are reversed from trial 1 to trial 2 to prevent position bias (a tendency to look primarily to one side) from contaminating the results.

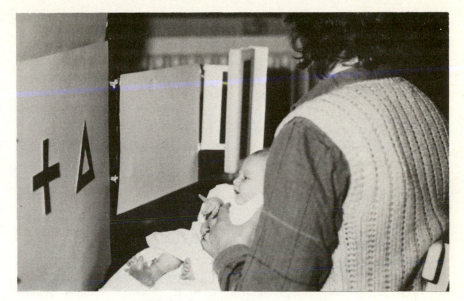

FIG. 2.   A new-born baby being tested.

Many aspects of this procedure are quite arbitrary, and variations in timing, habituation criteria, and novelty testing have been described. Nevertheless, the above variation is effective: During the post-habituation test trials new-born babies, if they are able to discriminate between the novel and familiar stimuli, will show a novelty preference, such that about two-thirds of the cumulative looking time is spent looking at the novel stimulus (Slater, Morison, & Rose, 1983b). The major advantage of the infant-controlled procedure is that it accommodates individual differences in the time needed to habituate to the "familiar" stimulus; such differences occur both within a cohort and across age. For example, new-borns average about 100 seconds to reach the criterion of habituation when presented simple geometric shapes such as the ones shown in Fig. 2, while 3- and 4-month-olds average, respectively, 50 and 40 seconds (Slater & Morison, 1985a).

In summary, new-born infants will reveal a variety of unlearned visual preferences when given paired stimulus presentation, findings which argue for passive selection of visual stimulation, or "visual capture". However, even when these preferences are very strong new-borns will regularly shift visual attention between the patterns. This finding indicates an active selection of stimulation rather than passive attentional capture. This active, volitional control is also evidenced by the way in which visual preferences for novel patterns can be produced by habituating infants to a "familiar" pattern.

NEURAL MECHANISMS UNDERLYING EARLY VISUAL CAPACITIES

Many neural mechanisms are required for normal visual function and it would not be surprising to find that the different mechanisms develop and mature at different times during ontogenesis. One major broad distinction which has implications for early visual development is between subcortical structures such as the superior colliculus in the midbrain, and cortical structures, in particular the visual or striate cortex.

The argument put forward by Bronson (1974) was that the visual abilities found in infants up to about 6 weeks are not dependent upon the cortex but are mediated entirely by subcortical pathways. Four broad lines of argument support Bronson's position (see Maurer & Lewis, 1979). First, the visual cortex is anatomically very immature at birth. Second, visually evoked responses appear to be mediated through the superior colliculus rather than through the cortex. Third, many of the visual abilities of normal infants under 2 months are similar to those of human infants, and other species, with lesions of the visual cortex (Dubowitz, Mushin, De Vries, & Arden, 1986). Fourth, there are changes in visual behaviours and visual responses emerging at about 6 weeks which are consistent with the view that the visual cortex becomes functional from that time.

This is an important issue because it affects the way in which we conceive the starting point of visual development: if the new-born is effectively visually decorticate then the beginnings of an intact visual system will only be found from 6 to 8 weeks from birth.

Several of the lines of evidence are given in Chapter 1 by Atkinson and Braddick. In this chapter, I will focus on three of them: The locus of habituation in the new-born, persistence of visual memory in the first few weeks, and orientation selectivity.

LOCUS OF HABITUATION IN THE NEW-BORN

Visual recognition memory is thought to require functional pathways to the visual cortex, and the reliable evidence for the presence of visual memory at birth weakens the claim that all visual behaviours displayed by the new-born are subcortically mediated. However, it is possible to claim that the apparently successful reports of habituation and dishabituation/novelty preferences are in fact attributable to retinal adaptation. This interpretation was offered by Bronson (1974) and suggests that the population of retinal cells that detect the stimulus undergoes adaptation during the course of the "habituation" trials. The recovery of visual attention which follows when the stimulus is changed (i.e. the novelty preference) results from the activation of a new population of retinal cells, which makes the novel stimulus more detectable than the familiar one.

Many effects are of known retinal origin. For example, if an observer stares at a red circle and then looks at a grey surface, a negative after-image of the complementary colour green will be seen. The two eyes work independently, so that if one eye only is adapted, the other does not see the after-image. This independence means that the experiment to test Bronson's model was quite simple: New-borns were habituated with one eye covered by a gauze patch and with the other eye as the "seeing" eye, and when they reached the criterion of habituation the other eye was covered, and paired presentation of novel and familiar stimuli followed. In two experiments we found significant preferences for a novel colour and for a novel shape (Slater, Morison & Rose, 1983a). These findings suggest that a retinal adaptation model can be ruled out, and that habituation in the new-born baby cannot be explained in terms of peripheral mechanisms.

PERSISTENCE OF VISUAL MEMORY

The novelty preferences described above give evidence of immediate visual recognition memory: Memory for the familiar stimulus needs only to last for seconds (at most a minute or two) beyond the habituation period.

The earliest age at which *delayed* recognition memory has been demonstrated is 5 weeks from birth. Bushnell, McCutcheon, Sinclair, and Tweedlie (1984) gave 3- and 7-week-old infants extensive familiarisation with a simple shape for 2 weeks. The shape varied from infant to infant: For one it might be a red circle, for another a blue cross, and so on. On the fourteenth day of familiarisation the stimulus was taken from the home and, after a delay of 24 hours, the babies gave evidence of memory for both colour and form, in that they looked more at a stimulus that was changed in both colour and form than at one that changed either in colour or form, and all three of these stimuli attracted more visual attention than the familiar one.

Adaptation, whether of retinal or cortical cells, or elsewhere in the visual system, would not persist over a delay of this length. In a study which is discussed in more detail later, Bushnell and Sai (1987) demonstrated recognition of the mother's face in 2-day-old babies after they had been separated from the mother by a minimum of 5 minutes, suggesting that durable memories are formed very shortly after birth.

ORIENTATION SELECTIVITY

A critical test of cortical functioning is discrimination of orientation: Orientation-selective neurones are found in cells of the visual cortex but not in subcortical parts of the visual system. While there is converging evidence, both behaviourally and from VEP studies, that 6-week-olds can discriminate mirror-image obliques, the evidence is less clear for younger infants (detailed treatment of this issue is given in Chapter 1 by Atkinson & Braddick). Braddick, Wattam-Bell, and Atkinson (1986), who used VEP testing of infants, could not find an orientation-specific response until 6 weeks. However, there is a clear gap in the research which was detailed by Atkinson and Braddick. The neural mechanisms which mediate VEPs may be different from those which mediate behavioural responses "but no-one has yet tested the younger infants who from the VEP results would be expected to fail" (Chapter 1, p. 13).

We carried out a study to do precisely this test. The four stimuli used are shown in Fig. 3. Each of 16 infants was habituated to one of the stimuli and was then tested with a phase-reversed grating in the familiar orientation paired with a grating in the novel orientation: For example, infants habituated to stimulus A were shown the paired stimuli C and D at test. In the test phase of the experiment a strong preference for the novel orientation was found. It is not clear as to why VEP and behavioural tests should give such different results, but this finding suggests that orientation selectivity is present at birth.

The several findings described give clear evidence for the storage of visual experience from birth. Infants from birth onwards seem to possess more active and durable memorial and representational capacities than can adequately be accounted for either by the selective adaptation of retinal (or other) cells or solely by the mediation of subcortical mechanisms. The evidence for orientation-selectivity at birth argues for at least some degree of visual cortical functioning. Although this may be the case it is clear that the arguments and uncertainties will continue: For example, why is it that VEP and behavioural studies tell different stories? The last word will be left with Ian Bushnell (1987, p. 10):

> Resorting to the claim that only subcortical processing is possible in young infants has been attempted repeatedly and there may well be some value in distinguishing between cortically and sub-cortically mediated processes, but unless we re-evaluate the subcortical system's capabilities (particularly as regards pattern processing and visual memory) a simplistic version of this approach seems doomed to founder on the rocks of a stubborn neonate who refuses to be relegated to the status of an involuntary, passive reactor.

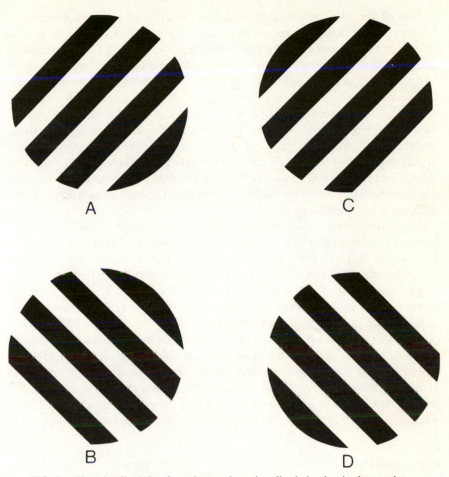

FIG. 3.   The stimuli used to investigate orientation discrimination in the new-born.

PERCEPTION OF FORM

The terms "figure", "shape", "pattern" and "form" are often used inter-changeably, and Zusne (1970, p. 1) commented that "Form, like love, is a many-splendored thing . . . there is no agreement on what is meant by form, in spite of the tacit agreement that there is". However, the most often used stimuli in studies of form perception are static, achromatic, two- or three-dimensional figures with readily perceived contours that can stand as figures in a figure–ground relationship, and it is primarily with reference to these that most theories of form perception have been concerned.

One of the most intractable issues in the area of infant perception is whether or not such figures or patterns are innately perceived as unified wholes or as elements or parts. For example, we know that new-born infants can discriminate between the outline shapes of a triangle, a square, a circle and a cross (Slater, Morison & Rose, 1983b), but the basis of the discrimination is unclear since any two of the shapes differ in a number of ways. For example, if the infant attends only to the bottom of the figures the square will have a line, but the cross will not. The stimuli differ along other dimensions: orientation of lines and angles, overall size, density of contour, curved versus linear, enclosed versus open, etc. These sorts of variables are detected by infants and it is therefore very difficult to eliminate the possibility that they are discriminating between configurations on the basis of such lower-order differences between them.

Two experiments which suggest that there is a change in the way form is perceived in early infancy are by Cohen and Younger (1984) and Slater and Morison (1987). The habituation and test stimuli used by Cohen and Younger are shown in Fig. 4. Each infant was habituated to one of the angles, and was then tested with the four test stimuli which varied along the dimensions of angle, size and orientation: test stimulus (1) is the same as the familiar stimulus; (2) differs in orientation from the familiar; (3) differs in angle; and (4) differs both in angle and orientation. Infants aged 6 and 14 weeks were tested and both groups responded identically, and predictably, to two of the test stimuli: Neither recovered attention to the familiar stimulus (1); both dishabituated to test stimulus (4). However, an interesting difference was found in attentional recovery to the other test stimuli: The 6-week-olds dishabituated to the change in orientation, stimulus (2), but not to

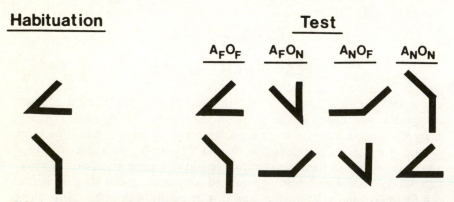

FIG. 4 Habituation and test stimuli used by Cohen, L. B & Younger, B. A (1984). Infant perception of angular relations. *Infant Behaviour & Development, 7,* p. 39. Half their infants were presented the stimuli shown on the top line, half the ones shown on the bottom line. Key: A = angle; O = orientation; F = familiar; N = novel.

the change in angle, stimulus (3); the 14-week-olds did the opposite, dishabituating only to a change in angle and not to a change in orientation.

These findings support the view that 2- to 4-month old infants are able to perceive angular relationships, which may be considered the basic elements or building blocks of shape perception, but they argue against the claim that this ability is innate. Instead they indicate that form perception in infants 6 weeks and younger may be dominated by attention to lower-order variables such as orientation. Note that our recent finding of orientation selectivity in new-borns is consistent with the views expressed by Cohen and Younger.

A rather different experimental procedure was used by Slater and Morison (1987). It is impossible to have two different shapes that are equated for all low-order variables, and so the only way to begin to establish true form perception is to *vary* them during familiarisation, making them irrelevant to the discriminations required in the test phase of the experiment. The stimuli used are shown in Fig. 5, and the question asked was quite simple, If infants are familiarised to a number of exemplars of the same shape (one of the four, triangle, square, cross, circle), will they extract the overall shape and learn to disregard the changes to the parts of the stimulus? If so, it was reasoned that they should show a novelty preference when a *different* exemplar of the same shape is paired on post-familiarisation trials with an examplar of a different shape.

New-born babies were compared with infants 3- to 5-months old. During the familiarisation phase of the experiment each baby was shown six exemplars of one stimulus shape. Following presentation of all 6 stimuli there were two post-familiarisation trials: These were paired presentation of a novel and familiar shape where, as mentioned earlier, the familiar shape was a different exemplar of the shape shown on the familiarisation trials.

The results produced a clear age difference. New-born babies did not give a preference for the novel stimulus on the post familiarisation trials, but the 3- to 5-month-olds did: the difference in novelty preference between the new-borns and the older infants was statistically reliable.

These are only two of the many experiments on infant form perception, but they illustrate the sorts of age changes that seem to occur. During the first two months infants can discriminate between shapes, but they probably do so on the basis of differences in low-order variables, such as orientation, contrast, spatial frequency, elements, and so on. Shortly after this something like true form perception begins and infants respond to higher-order variables of stimulation such as configurational invariance and form categories.

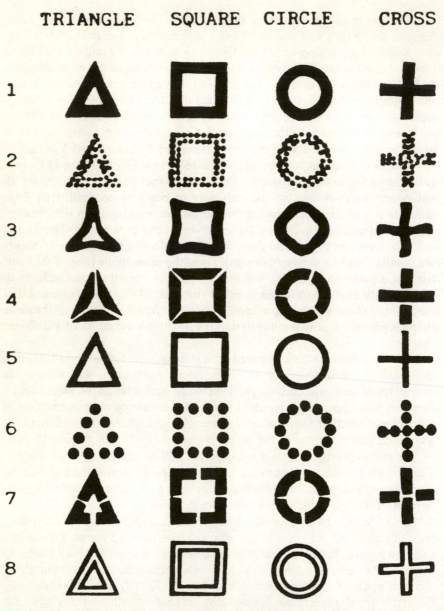

TRIANGLE	SQUARE	CIRCLE	CROSS

FIG. 5. The stimuli used by Slater and Morison (1987).

STATIC OR DYNAMIC STIMULI?

One theoretical issue has its links with, and implications for, the types of stimuli and stimulus events that are presented to babies. A great deal of the research that has been carried out on the development of visual perception, and almost all of the research described so far in this chapter, has involved showing static two-dimensional stimuli to infants. Preferential looking and much habituation research have used this form of stimulus presentation. While this research tradition remains a very active one, from the 1970s there has been a growing increase in the number of studies which have shown moving and changing "dynamic" stimuli to their infant subjects. Any creature, such as man, which has the ability to extract information about the world must be sensitive to stimulation that changes over time, and dynamic approaches to perception argue that visual perception is most meaningful, and is most meaningfully studied, under conditions of change, and not under conditions of static viewing. Dynamic approaches to perception are explored in detail in Chapter 3 by Butterworth.

The concept of "ecological validity" assumes importance here. Ecologically valid stimuli and events are those that bear relation to what the animal perceives in real life. A strong statement in support of the dynamic approach to visual perception has been made by von Hofsten (1983, pp. 243–244):

> If the infant has any preadapted means for extracting information about the environment, it is reasonable to believe that the information to be extracted is an ecologically relevant one for the infant. It seems less probable that the infant has any preadaptation for perceiving checkerboard patterns, stripes, or "bulls eyes". These patterns, so evidently deprived of any ecological relevance, have been the most popular stimuli for studying infant perception. It is quite remarkable that such patterns evoke any systematic reactions whatsoever in the infant. Obviously, they will have very little to do with the infant's ability to extract information about the environment. It might be useful to discuss the perception of such patterns in terms of number or density of contours but it is a terrible mistake to believe that such principles can be generalized to ordinary perception.

Butterworth argues that the presentation of static stimuli to infants coincides with a theoretical assumption "that visual perception depends upon the analysis of cues contained within a frozen retinal image" (Chapter 3). This need not necessarily be the case and one can argue that static visual stimulation is as ecologically valid as dynamic events. When an infant is shown a static stimulus what is perceived will most probably be richer than is suggested by the expression "a frozen retinal image". The baby will move his head and eyes in order to get different views of the same scene. Almost certainly these differences in perspective are integrated over time to give some sort of coherent view of the stimulus.

In the majority of visual surroundings there will be both dynamic and static forms of stimulation, and the infant will need to extract information from both. I would argue that investigations of responsiveness to both static and dynamic stimulation complement each other in increasing our understanding of perception and its development in infants: Much of the research described in the second part of this chapter focuses on infants' responses to three-dimensional, moving and ecologically valid stimuli.

PERCEPTION OF VISUAL SPACE

> For those of a creationist bent, one could note that God must have loved depth cues, for He made so many of them. (Yonas & Granrud, 1985, p. 45)

It might be supposed that the immediate visual input is that which impinges upon the flat, two-dimensional retinae, but neither adults nor infants perceive a two-dimensional world. Under normal viewing conditions the visual environment provides a sufficiently large number of depth cues that many are redundant. It is possible to carry out highly skilled activities requiring the use of depth information, even with the absence of many depth cues. For example, the Nawab of Pataudi batted for India in test matches with effective vision in only one eye; Joe Davis, undisputed world snooker champion for over 20 years, had good vision only in one eye. The depth cues that specify the spatial layout of the three-dimensional world can be broken down into three types: kinetic, binocular, and static monocular (pictoral). Yonas and Granrud (1985) argue that infants' sensitivity to these types of information appears in this sequence as infancy progresses.

Kinetic information is conveyed by motion, either of the observer or of the visual world. The retinal changes produced by motion can be very pronounced, i.e. as an object approaches an observer, or the observer moves around the visual world. Others involve fewer transformations but are nonetheless informative. When head movements, even very slight ones, are made when viewing a three-dimensional object, perspective variations are introduced in that nearer parts of the object will appear to move more than farther parts. This information is called motion parallax and even new-born babies are sensitive to it: New-borns will consistently fixate a three-dimensional object in preference to its photograph when they have one eye covered and the only differences between the two stimuli are provided by motion parallax (Slater, Rose, & Morison, 1983).

Sensitivity to binocular disparity is found at about 3 months (Atkinson and Braddick, Chapter 1). Atkinson and Braddick point out that the ability to distinguish retinal disparities does not mean that these specify *depth* to the infants, although of course it is possible that they do. Yonas and Granrud have demonstrated that infants as young as 5 months use binocular information to reach for the nearer of two objects. While preferential reaching can give compelling evidence of depth perception, the accuracy of reaching increases markedly beyond 5 months. One cannot therefore conclude (1985, p. 52): "...on the basis of the present evidence, that binocular depth sensitivity is absent in infants under 20 weeks of age". A reasonable, but as yet unconfirmed, hypothesis is that sensitivity to binocular disparity and detection of binocular depth information coincide in development and that both emerge at about 3 months.

Pictoral depth cues are the static monocular cues to be found in photographs. One such cue is relative size, the larger of two otherwise identical figures is usually perceived as the closer. An interesting experiment, described by Yonas, Cleaves, and Pettersen (1978), used the "Ames window", a trapezoidal window rotated around its vertical axis. When adults view the Ames window monocularly a powerful illusion is perceived of a slanted window with one side (the larger) closer than the other. Six-month-old infants wearing an eye patch (to remove binocular information) are twice as likely to reach for the larger side of the distorted window than for the smaller side. Yonas et al. (1978) describe additional control studies which make it likely that this differential reaching genuinely results from perceived size rather than from some other variable.

It is clear that sensitivity to a three-dimensional world is present at birth. Detection of some kinetic depth cues, including motion parallax, is present at birth, while sensitivity to binocular and pictoral depth cues appears later, the former probably between 3 and 5 months, the latter perhaps a little later.

MOVEMENT PERCEPTION

Movement is a powerful dimension of visual stimulation for the human infant. From birth infants prefer to scan or fixate moving rather than stationary stimuli, although there are preferences for certain types and speeds of movement. New-borns look more at a pattern rotating 90 degrees/second (one complete rotation every 4 seconds) than at one rotating at twice the speed, perhaps because the limits of their ability to process information are being reached at the faster speed. It seems likely that the preferred speed of movement changes with age (Burnham & Day, 1979; Slater, Morison, Town, & Rose, 1985).

If movement is a salient stimulus that is responded to in a way other than just as an automatic reflexive response, then we may expect infants to detect features of the stimulus other than movement, i.e. colour and form, and this is indeed the case. Habituation studies have shown that new-born and older infants can extract shape information from both stationary and moving stimuli, and can transfer what is learned both within and across the dimension of movement, i.e. from stationary to stationary or moving, and from moving to moving or stationary (Burnham & Day, 1979; Slater et al. 1985).

If the speed of movement is not too great it is clear that movement does not detract from infants' extraction of featural information, and Burnham (1987) argues that movement can in fact enhance object perception in infants. This it does in two ways. First, moving objects are detected and attended to at distances where stationary objects are not: 6- to 20-week-old infants' fixation of stationary objects decreases considerably as the viewing distance increases from 30cm to 10m, even if the far objects are larger to compensate for retinal size changes, whereas the same objects rotating attract the *same* attention as viewing distance increases (Ihsen & Day, 1981; McKenzie & Day, 1972; see also Burnham, 1987).

Second, movement can enhance the perception of the structure of certain objects. Different types of movement can be effective, depending upon the object structure. Rigid motion is where all surfaces, contours, and edges of the moving object maintain a constant relationship with each other. Ruff (1982) found that rigid translation of objects facilitated recognition of the objects by 6-month-old infants. The visual system handles more complex information than that specified by rigid motion, because it is able to extract stimulus invariants from non-rigid, deforming and biomechanical motion. Bower (Chapter 4) suggests that infants can detect the sex of toddlers from nothing more than the movement of spots of light attached to them.

THE VISUAL CONSTANCIES

Perhaps the major characteristic of perception, and one that applies to all the sensory modalities, is that it is organised. Infants' ability to perceive a three-dimensional world and to detect structure from stimulus movement presupposes some degree of organisation: With respect to visual perception we do not experience a world that consists of unrelated, random elements; rather we perceive objects that undergo change in a coherent fashion. An important organisation which would seem to be a necessary prerequisite for many other types of organisation is known as *perception constancy*. Brightness, size, shape, identity, and existence are examples of visual constancies. Brightness constancy is where we perceive a stimulus as being the same brightness, despite changes to levels of illumination. Size constancy refers to the fact that we see an object as the same size regardless of its distance from us: A person 60 feet away from us subtends an image on the retina that is one-sixth the size of that person 10 feet away, but we see the person as the same size. Bower (1966) was the first to test for size constancy in infants. He trained 2-month-old infants to respond with a head turn in the presence of a 1 foot cube located 3 feet away from them. Subsequently, the infants gave more head turns to the same size cube at a distance of 9 feet, whose retinal image was one-third the size of the training stimulus, than to a 3 foot cube at 9 feet, whose retinal image size was the same as the training stimulus. This response to the real, rather than retinal, size suggests that size constancy is present by 2 months. The data from more recent studies (Day & McKenzie, 1981; McKenzie, Tootell, & Day, 1980), using recovery from habituation as an index of size constancy, confirmed that the ability to perceive the true size of an object is present by 18 weeks (see also Day, 1987).

Shape constancy is perception of an object's real shape regardless of changes in orientation or slant relative to the observer. We used preferential looking (PL) and habituation/dishabituation procedures to investigate whether shape constancy is present at birth (Slater & Morison, 1985b). Using PL we found that stimulus slant affects the salience, or attractiveness, of one stimulus (the one used was a square) when paired with another (one of two trapeziums, see Fig. 6) in that the more it was oriented away from the fronto-parallel plane, the less time the babies spent looking at it. Slant changes of 15° caused reliable changes in new-borns' preferential looking, suggesting that new-borns are sensitive to fine variations in slant. In the second experiment, familiarisation trials were given with one stimulus (either a square or a trapezium), the stimulus being in a different slant from trial to trial. In each of these trials the stimulus in its particular slant was shown until the baby had looked at it for 25 seconds. Strictly speaking, therefore, these were not properly habituation trials, as we were not measuring a decline in looking over trials, and the stimulus changed on each trial: The aim was to make the babies familiar with the shape while at the same time desensitising them to the changes in slant. After this familiarisation period the square and the trapezium were shown for two paired test trials, with the familiarised stimulus in a different slant from any shown earlier. A similar procedure was used with 3-month-old infants by Caron, Caron, and Carlson (1979).

The stimulus slants used during familiarisation trials, and those shown on the novelty-testing trials, are shown in Fig. 6. The dependent variable of most interest is the time spent looking at novel and familiar stimuli on the post-familiarisation test trials, and every one of the 12 subjects tested spent more time looking at the novel shape in these trials.

These results suggest that new-born babies have the ability to extract the constant, real shape of an object that is rotated in the third dimension, i.e. they display shape constancy. An interesting parallel to this experiment was reported by Bornstein, Krinsky, and Benasich (1986), using 4-month-olds. They found that infants discriminated small orientation changes in the

ID—C*

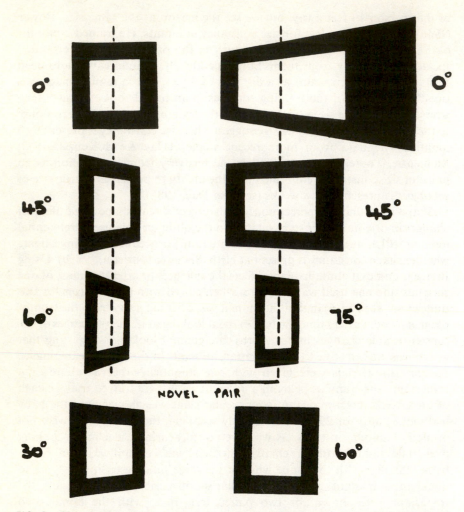

FIG. 6.   The stimulus slants presented during familiarisation and post-familiarisation (test) trials by Slater and Morison (1985b). The familiarisation stimulus (for half the infants the square, for half the trapezium) was shown in six slants; the ones shown here and their mirror images.

frontal plane, but were also able to extract the real shape of a stimulus regardless of orientation. Together, these studies point to the existence of two important perceptual abilities at birth: detection of transformations in orientation, whether in frontal plane or in depth, and the capacity to recognise object form independently of its orientation.

Other perceptual constancies include those of feature, identity, and existence. Feature constancy is the ability to recognise the invariant features of a stimulus across some detectable but irrelevant transformations, and this ability is present at birth. New-born infants perceive the features of moving and stationary stimuli and can transfer what is learned across the dimension of movement, i.e. having been habituated to a moving stimulus new-borns will show a novelty preference when shown the same stimulus paired with a novel shape when both are stationary. Feature constancy is a necessary prerequisite for identity constancy, which is the ability to recognise an object as being exactly the *same* object across some transformation. This ability is very difficult to demonstrate, and Burnham (1987, p. 15) argues that it is "difficult to envisage how such a conclusion (the presence of identity constancy) ... could ever be reached from the behaviour of preverbal infants". That is, how could we ever know that an infant perceives the unique identity of individual objects rather than simply being aware of featural similarities across transformations? One study that perhaps comes closest to demonstrating identity constancy was described by Bower (1971). Infants were seated in front of mirrors that could produce several images of the mother. Babies younger than 20 weeks happily smiled, cooed and waved their arms to each of the "multiple mothers", whereas older babies became quite upset at seeing more than one mother. This suggests that it is only the older babies who are aware that they have only one mother, and can therefore be said to have identity constancy.

Existence constancy refers to the belief that objects continue to exist even though they are no longer available to the senses. Several eminent researchers, among them Piaget, have claimed that the expression "out of sight, out of mind" literally captures the young infant's understanding of objects. An early expression of this view was by William James (1890):

> A baby's rattle drops out of his hand but the baby looks not for it. It has gone out for him as a candle flame goes out and it comes back when you replace it in his hand, as the flame comes back when relit. The idea of its being a thing whose permanent existence by itself he might interpolate between its successive apparitions, has evidently not occurred to him.

There is some uncertainty as to when existence constancy first appears in infancy. Bower (1971) has claimed that it is evident as early as 3 weeks of age. In Bower's experiment babies were seated in front of an object that was slowly occluded by a screen. The screen was moved away after one of several intervals (1.5, 3, 7.5, or 15 seconds) and on half the trials the object was still there, while in the other half it was not. At the shortest interval (but not the longer ones) 3-week-olds expressed "surprise" (as measured by heart rate changes) if the object failed to reappear: "In short, they expected the object still to be there" (p. 35).

However, there is other evidence which suggests that existence constancy appears later in development (Burnham, 1987). For example, Moore,

Borton, and Darby (1978) showed infants an object which moved laterally back and forth and either did or did not appear in a gap between two occluding screens. They reported that 9-month-olds tracked the object visually as if they believed that it continued to exist in the gap between the screens, while 5-month-olds did not.

The possibility remains, therefore, that identity and existence constancy make their appearance towards the middle of the first year of life, rather than earlier. Clearly, both of these constancies are more sophisticated than the other constancies described earlier, and Burnham (1987) raises the possibility that the object concept, of which identity and existence constancy are part, arises out of the "basic" constancies, such as size, shape, and feature.

PERCEPTION OF FACES

The human face is three-dimensional, contains areas of high contrast, provides visual and auditory stimulation, moves, and regulates its behaviour contingent upon the baby's activities. These characteristics combine to make the face probably the most interesting stimulus experienced by the young infant. Many theorists have gone beyond the truism that the face is highly attention-getting and attention-holding for infants, to claim that there is a predisposition to respond to the face other than as a collection of salient stimuli. The question then becomes: "Do infants have an innate perceptual knowledge of the face?"

There is no easy or definitive answer to this question: The answer depends upon both how it is asked, and who is asked. Kleiner (1987) and Kleiner and Banks (1987) compared new-borns' and 2-month-olds' preferences between two-dimensional face-like and abstract patterns, and they found a clear age difference. Kleiner, (1987, p. 49) found that new-borns preferred to look more at an abstract pattern whose high amplitude components were near to their peak contrast sensitivity rather than at a face-like pattern, suggesting that their "preferences for face-like patterns are governed primarily by stimulus energy and not by the familiarity or social significance of such patterns". On the other hand, the 2-month-olds looked more at the face-like patterns, suggesting the emergence of sensitivity to faces by this age. Dannemiller and Stephens (1988) reported a similar age-related trend: 3-month-olds showed a clear face preference, while 6-week-olds did not.

Melhuish (1982) showed pictures of the mother's face and female strangers' faces to 1-month-olds, one at a time for 30 second periods. He found no differential attention to the mother's versus the stranger's face, but there was one significant finding: The infants looked longest at the faces with the highest contrast. The important role of contrast in the early weeks is further indicated by an habituation study by Bushnell (1982), again looking for discrimination between mothers' and strangers' faces. The results suggested that infants as young as 5 weeks of age could discriminate between the photographed face of their mother and that of a female stranger, but it seemed probable that the basis for the discrimination was the outer boundary of the face, probably the hair-face outline, with internal features becoming important only from 4- to 5-months. Maurer and Barrera (1981) used both PL and habituation and could not show discrimination between natural and scrambled facial features in 1-month-olds, but 2-month-olds were able to make these discriminations.

These studies, using different procedures, PL, successive stimulus presentation, and habituation, combine to tell a coherent story. For the first 5 or 6 weeks infant attention is dominated by contrast and stimulus energy, and there is no response to faces, per se. When a response to faces does emerge the infant first discriminates among faces on the basis of contrast, with internal features assuming importance towards the middle of the first year.

However, if care is taken to equate the face-like stimuli for contrast, or in other ways make contrast irrelevant to the responses and discriminations required, a different story can be told. People are so important to the infant that it would not be surprising to find that neonates learn quickly to discriminate between them, and this is indeed the case. Within the first few days new-borns distinguish the odour of their mother's breast from odours belonging to other women, and they show a preference for the mother's voice compared with that of a female stranger (DeCasper & Fifer, 1980; Lipsitt, 1977). In a recent study Bushnell and Sai (1987) showed new-born infants (mean age 2 days, 5 hours) their mother's live face (i.e. not a photograph!) paired with that of a female stranger, the two being matched for overall brightness of the face and for hair colour (see Fig. 7). The infants reliably looked longer at the mother's face: Whereas the discriminate cues that babies were using cannot be specified, Bushnell and Sai's finding indicates a quickly learned visual preference for the mother's face.

Remarkable though this early learning may be, it is perhaps only a specific example of a more general learning ability, and we need to look elsewhere for convincing evidence of a special response to the human face. In a well-known study, Goren, Sarty, and Wu (1975) presented laterally moving stimuli to new-born infants. They reported that their subjects, who averaged only 9 *minutes* from birth at the time of testing, turned their heads and eyes significantly more to follow (i.e. track) a two-dimensional schematic face-like stimulus than either of two stimuli consisting of the same facial features in different arrangements. There were some methodological problems with this study, for example the observer who presented the stimuli was not "blind" as to which one was being shown. This, and other problems, was removed by Dziurawiec and Ellis (1986) who carried out a similarly heroic experiment in that their subjects, too, were less than an hour old at the time of testing. They

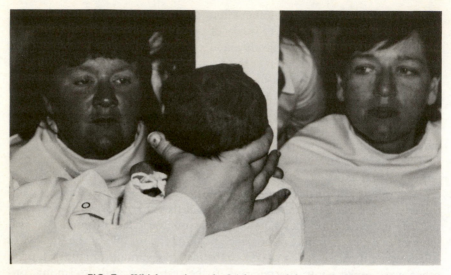

FIG. 7.   Which one is mother? (photograph by Ian Bushnell).

replicated this striking finding and their neonates "preferred" (i.e. followed more) the schematic face to a "scrambled" face, which in turn was preferred to a blank face which contained no internal detail.

Apparently, one of Piaget's co-workers, Maratsos, told him that new-borns would stick their tongues out if an adult produced this gesture within their field of view: Piaget's reply was "how rude!" Experimental evidence for neonatal imitation of various facial gestures has since appeared, the gestures involved being mouth opening, lip pursing, tongue protrusion, "happy", "sad", and "surprised" facial expressions (Field, Woodson, Greenberg, & Cohen, 1982; Meltzoff & Moore, 1977; 1983; see also Chapters 3 and 4 by Bower and Butterworth). These claims of precocious imitation are contro-versial and there is some disagreement, not only concerning which gestures new-borns will imitate, but also whether they will imitate *any* facial gestures (i.e. McKenzie & Over, 1983). If they are proven to be well-founded it would suggest that infants are innately endowed with a well-defined representa-tional system that allows them to translate adults' facial gestures to unseen facial gestures of their own: In short, the claim of innate, special responsive-ness to and recognition of the human face would be incontestable.

Finally, one set of intriguing findings that must spell gloom to many infants deserves mention. In a PL study, Samuels and Ewy (1985) showed pairs of black and white slides of same-gender faces (equal numbers of male and female faces were used) to 3- and 6-month-old infants. The slides were constructed so that each of the members of a pair were as similar as possible in gross physiognomic appearance, but they differed in attractiveness as rated by adults: Attractive and unattractive faces were paired together. Both age groups looked longest at the attractive faces, and this was true for all of the 12 facial pairings used: The preference was extremely strong with the attractive face eliciting 70% of the total looking. This finding was replicated with slightly younger infants (2- to 3-month olds) by Langlois et al. (1987) who used colour slides of female faces only. Whereas the infants in these studies would have had considerable exposure to faces, it is unlikely that they would have learned to prefer attractive ones. We do not as yet know on what basis the infants preferred the more attractive faces, but it may be that there is an unlearned aesthetic appreciation of faces: Whether infants are similarly discerning with respect to other aesthetic domains is an interesting question for future research.

The literature on infants' responses to faces and face-like stimuli is voluminous, complex, and belies easy generalisations. At birth, and for a few weeks afterwards, contrast and stimulus energy will easily swamp any specific responsiveness to facedness. Nevertheless, a growing body of converging evidence—early learning of and preference for the mother's face, visual following of face-like stimuli, imitation of facial gestures, aesthetic perception of faces—gives strong support to the claim that the human face has special, species-specific visual significance for the infant from birth onwards.

CONCLUSIONS

The new-born baby enters the world visually naïve but possessed of a number of means with which to make sense of the world. Certain predispositions, or as Haith terms them, "rules", guide the new-born's looking and the infant is clearly searching for and discriminating between visual stimulation. New-born visual attention is easily captured, and can be dominated, by low-order variables of stimulation such as size, contrast, and orientation. In this context we need to remember that the new-born baby's acuity is poor, as is contrast sensitivity: Low contrast and high spatial frequency stimuli are simply not seen. This means that a major problem confronting the new-born is actually seeing visual stimuli. It is perhaps not surprising, therefore, that the low-order stimulus variables that have the clearest and most predictable effects on new-born visual attention have to do with stimulus detectability: Those stimuli that are seen most clearly will attract the most attention. This effect is so powerful that if one has a pair of stimuli that are clearly different from each other, but where one is more detectable than the other, then no amount of familiarisation will shift this preference in favour of the least preferred one.

However, when stimuli are made equally detectable, or where contrast and spatial frequency are made irrelevant to the task, the new-born baby will begin to reveal those innate visual capabilities which already constitute an impressive list. At no point in development does the infant perceive simply a two-dimensional retinal image. The new-born distinguishes between two- and three-dimensional stimulation and seems to have some appreciation of the spatial layout of the three-dimensional world that goes beyond the mere detection of certain depth cues: Early in life infants perceive the real shape and size of objects, although it is not until 4–5 months that their reaching behaviour tells us that they are able to perceive their actual distances from them. Sensitivity to motion-carried information appears also to be a fundamental characteristic of the visual system from birth. Motion parallax is a salient cue available at birth and assists the new-born in detecting the spatial layout of a static three-dimensional world. Movement is a highly captivating stimulus and from birth infants will look at a moving stimulus in preference to a stationary one. Also from birth infants display feature constancy, that is, they recognise the shapes of moving and stationary stimuli and carry this recognition across the dimension of movement.

Many types of visual perceptual organisational abilities, including many of the visual constancies, are present at birth, so that it makes sense to claim that complex visual information processing may be evidenced during the first week of life, and that "the rules whereby information is extracted may be similar throughout infancy" (Antell & Keating, 1983, p. 699). It has also been claimed that "the manner in which the newborn baby views his world is (qualitatively) similar to that of the adult, although less differentiated" (Allik & Valsiner, 1980). However, we should be wary of attributing too much in the way of perceptual competence to the new-born. New-born babies do not appear to detect the similarity between an object and its photograph; while they discriminate between shapes they seem to do so on the basis of low-order variables of stimulation such as orientation rather than on differences in form. They do not seem to detect many important cues to depth; while they perceive objects as existing within three-dimensional visual space, their understanding of object coherence and unity is extremely limited (see Harris, Chapter 10).

By 3 months of age, many of these limitations have disappeared. Qualitative changes in visual processing have taken place so that higher order variables play a more significant role in perception.

One general ability which seems to underlie the qualitative changes in visual competence over the first few months is the ability to make perceptual inferences from visual input, an ability which allows the infant to become aware of higher-order variables of stimulation, to respond to stimulus equivalence, and to display increasing competence at forming concepts and classifying visual input. At present we are only part-way towards a description of the changes in visual competence in early infancy, and the causes of the changes are also poorly understool. New-borns are competent learners and some developments may be a consequence of perceptual experience; others may result from endogenous maturational processes, perhaps linked to the increasing involvement of the visual cortex.

REFERENCES

Allik, J. & Valsiner, J. (1980). Visual development in ontogenesis: Some re-evaluations. *Advances in Child Development and Behavior, 15*, 2–48.

Antell, S. A. & Keating, D. P. (1983). Perception of numerical invariance in neonates. *Child Development, 54*, 695–701.

Aslin, R. N. (1981). Experiential influences and sensitive periods in perceptual development: A unified model. In R. N. Aslin, J. R. Alberts & M. R. Petersen (eds), *Development of perception: Psychobiological perspectives*: Vol. 2. *The visual system*. New York: Academic Press.

Aslin, R. N. & Pisoni, D. B. (1980). Some developmental processes in speech perception. In G. H. Yeni-Komshian, J. Kavanagh, & C. A. Ferguson (eds), *Child phonology*: Vol. 2. *Perception*. New York: Academic Press.

Aslin, R. N. & Salapatek, P. (1975). Saccadic localization of visual targets by the very young human infant. *Perception and Psychophysics, 17*, 293–302.

Banks, M. S. & Salapatek, P. (1981). Infant pattern vision: A new approach based on the contrast sensitivity function. *Journal of Experimental Child Psychology, 31*, 1–45.

Bornstein, M. H., Krinsky, S. J., & Benasich, A. A. (1986). Fine orientation discrimination and shape constancy in young infants. *Journal of Experimental Child Psychology, 41*, 49–60.

Bower, T. G. R. (1966). The visual world of infants. *Scientific American, 215*, 80–92.

Bower, T. G. R. (1971). The object in the world of the infant. *Scientific American, 225*, 30–38.

Braddick, O., Wattam-Bell, J., & Atkinson, J. (1986). Orientation-specific cortical responses develop in early infancy. *Nature, 320*, 617–619.

Bronson, G. (1974). The postnatal growth of visual capacity. *Child Development, 45*, 873–890.

Burnham, D. K. (1987). The role of movement in object perception by infants. In B. E. McKenzie and R. H. Day (eds), *Perceptual development in early infancy: Problems and issues*. Hillsdale, N.J.: Lawrence Erlbaum Associates Inc.

Burnham, D. K. & Day, R. H. (1979). Detection of color in rotating objects by infants and its generalization over changes in velocity. *Journal of Experimental Child Psychology, 28*, 191–204.

Bushnell, I. W. R. (1982). Discrimination of faces by young infants. *Journal of Experimental Child Psychology, 33*, 298–308.

Bushnell, I. W. R., McCutcheon, E., Sinclair, J., & Tweedlie, M. E. (1984). Infants' delayed recognition memory for colour and form. *British Journal of Developmental Psychology, 2*, 11–17.

Bushnell, I. W. R. & Sai, F. (1987). Neonatal recognition of the mother's face. University of Glasgow Report, 87/1.

Caron, A. J., Caron, R. F., & Carlson, V. R. (1979). Infant perception of the invariant shape of objects varying in slant. *Child Development, 50*, 716–721.

Cohen, L. B. & Younger, B. A. (1984). Infant perception of angular relations. *Infant Behavior and Development, 7*, 37–47.

Dannemiller, J. L. & Stephens, B. R. (1988). A critical test of infant pattern preference models. *Child Development, 59*, 210–216.

Day, R. H. (1987). Visual size constancy in infancy. In B. E. McKenzie and R. H. Day (eds), *Perceptual development in early infancy: Problems and issues*. Hillsdale, N.J.: Lawrence Erlbaum Associates Inc.

Day, R. H. & McKenzie, B. E. (1981). Infant perception of the invariant size of approaching and receding objects. *Developmental Psychology*, *17*, 670–677.

DeCasper, A. J. & Fifer, W. P. (1980). Of human bonding: Newborns prefer their mothers' voices. *Science*, *208*, 1174–1176.

Dubowitz, L. M. S., Mushin, J., De Vries, L., & Arden, G. B. (1986, 17 May). Visual function in the newborn infant: Is it cortically mediated? *Lancet*, 1139–1141.

Dziurawiec, S. & Ellis, H. D. (1986, 19–22 September). Neonates' attention to face-like stimuli: Goren, Sarty & Wu (1975) revisited. Paper presented at the Annual Conference of the Developmental Section of the B.P.S, Exeter.

Fantz, R. L. & Miranda, S. B. (1975). Newborn infant attention to the form of contour. *Child Development*, *46*, 224–228.

Field, T. M., Woodson, R., Greenberg, R., & Cohen, D. (1982). Discrimination and imitation of facial expressions by neonates. *Science*, *218*, 179–181.

Goren, C. C., Sarty, M., & Wu, P. Y. K. (1975). Visual following and pattern discrimination of face-like stimuli by newborn infants. *Pediatrics*, *56*, 544–549.

Haith, M. M. (1980). *Rules that babies look by*. Hillsdale, N.J.: Lawrence Erlbaum Associates Inc.

Harris, P. L. & McFarlane, A. (1974). The growth of the effective visual field from birth to seven weeks. *Journal of Experimental Child Psychology*, *18*, 340–348.

Hofsten, C. von. (1983). Foundations for perceptual development. In L. P. Lipsitt & C. K. Rovee-Collier (eds), *Advances in infancy research*: Vol. 2. Norwood, N.J.: Ablex Publishing Corp.

Horowitz, F. D., Paden, L., Bhana, K., & Self, P. (1972). An infant-control procedure for studying infant visual fixations. *Developmental Psychology*, *7*, 90.

Ihsen, E. & Day, R. H. (1981). Infants' visual perception of moving objects at different distances. In A. R. Nesdale, C. Pratt, R. Grieve, J. Field, D. Illingworth, & J. Hogben (eds), *Advances in child development: Theory and research*. Perth, Australia: NCCD.

James, W. (1890). *Principles of psychology*. New York: Henry Holt.

Kessen, W., Haith, M. M., & Salapatek, P. H. (1970). Human infancy: A bibliography and guide. In P. Mussen (ed.), *Carmichael's manual of child psychology*, New York: Wiley.

Kleiner, K. A. (1987). Amplitude and phase spectra as indices of infants' pattern preferences. *Infant Behavior and Development*, *10*, 49–59.

Kleiner, K. A. & Banks, M. S. (1987). Stimulus energy does not account for 2-month-olds' face preferences. *Journal of Experimental Psychology*, *13*, 594–600.

Langlois, J. H., Roggman, L. A., Casey, R. J., Ritter, J. M., Rieser-Danner, L. A., & Jenkins, V. Y. (1987). Infant preferences for attractive faces: Rudiments of a stereotype? *Developmental Psychology*, *23*, 363–369.

Lipsitt, L. P. (1977). The study of sensory and learning process of the newborn. *Clinics in Perinatology*, *4*, 163–186.

Maurer, D. & Barrera, M. (1981). Infants' perception of natural and distorted arrangements of a schematic face. *Child Development*, *52*, 196–202.

Maurer, D. & Lewis, T. L. (1979). A physiological explanation of infants' early visual development. *Canadian Journal of Psychology*, *33*, 232–252.

McKenzie, B. E. & Day, R. H. (1972). Object distance as a determinant of visual fixation in early infancy. *Science*, *178*, 1108–1110.

McKenzie, B. E. & Day, R. H. (1976). Infants' attention to stationary and moving objects at different distances. *Australian Journal of Psychology*, *28*, 45–51.

McKenzie, B. E. & Over, R. (1983). Young infants fail to imitate facial and manual gestures. *Infant Behavior and Development*, *6*, 85–95.

McKenzie, B. E., Tootell, H. E., & Day, R. H. (1980). Development of visual size constancy during the 1st year of human infancy. *Developmental Psychology*, *16*, 163–174.

Melhuish, E. C. (1982). Visual attention to mother's and stranger's faces and facial contrast in 1-month-olds. *Developmental Psychology*, *18*, 299–331.

Meltzoff, A. N. & Moore, M. K. (1977). Imitation of facial and manual gestures by human neonates. *Science*, *198*, 75–78.

Meltzoff, A. N. & Moore, M. K. (1983). Newborn infants imitate adult facial gestures. *Child Development*, *54*, 702–709.

Moore, M. K., Borton, R., & Darby, B. (1978). Visual tracking in young infants: Evidence for object identity or object permanence? *Journal of Experimental Child Psychology*, *25*, 183–197.

Morison, V. & Slater, A. M. (1985). Contrast and spatial frequency components in new-born visual preferences. *Perception*, *14*, 345–348.

Ruff, H. A. (1982). The effect of object movement on infants' detection of object structure. *Developmental Psychology*, *18*, 462–472.

Samuels, C. A. & Ewy, R. (1985). Aesthetic perception of faces during infancy. *British Journal of Developmental Psychology*, *3*, 221–228.

Slater, A. M. & Morison, V. (1985a). Selective adaptation cannot account for early infant habituation: A response to Dannemiller and Banks (1983). *Merrill-Palmer Quarterly of Behavior and Development*, *31*, 99–103.

Slater, A. M. & Morison, V. (1985b). Shape constancy and slant perception at birth. *Perception*, *14*, 337–344.

Slater, A. M. & Morison, V. (1987). Lo sviluppo della percezione visiva nella prima infanzia. *Età Evolutiva*, *27*, 56–62.

Slater, A. M., Morison, V., & Rose, D. (1983a). Locus of habituation in the human newborn. *Perception*, *12*, 593–598.

Slater, A. M., Morison, V., & Rose, D. (1983b). Perception of shape by the new-born baby. *British Journal of Developmental Psychology*, *1*, 135–142.

Slater, A. M., Morison, V., Town, C., & Rose, D. (1985). Movement perception and identity constancy at birth. *British Journal of Developmental Psychology*, *3*, 211–220.

Slater, A. M., Rose, D., & Morison, V. (1983). New-born infants' perception of similarities and differences between two- and three-dimensional stimuli. *British Journal of Developmental Psychology*, *2*, 287–294.

Stechler, G. & Latz, E. (1966). Some observations on attention and arousal in the human infant. *Journal of the American Academy of Child Psychology*, *5*, 517–525.

Yonas, A., Cleaves, W., & Pettersen, L. (1978). Development of sensitivity to pictorial depth. *Science*, *200*, 77–79.

Yonas, A. & Granrud, C. E. (1985). Development of visual space perception in young infants. In J. Mehler and R. Fox (eds), *Neonate cognition: Beyond the blooming, buzzing confusion*. Hillsdale, N.J.: Lawrence Erlbaum Associates Inc.

Zusne, L. (1970). *Visual perception of form*. New York: Academic Press.

3 Events and Encounters in Infant Perception

George Butterworth

Department of Psychology,
University of Stirling,
Scotland

INTRODUCTION

Until the early 1970s much research on infant visual perception was carried out using static stimuli such as checkerboards, schematic faces, or geometric designs. A lot was learned from these studies about infants' visual acuity, preference for patterned over plain stimuli, colour vision, and other psychophysical parameters. Nevertheless, these studies imposed a particular theory of perception on the baby and ignored the fact that in the real world we must obtain information about the environment from an ever-changing, dynamic flux of stimulation that impinges on all the senses. "Frozen" perception in a single modality is the exception, not the rule in life and yet psychologists assumed that the static case was somehow the simplest and most appropriate for measuring the abilities of babies.

DYNAMIC APPROACHES TO PERCEPTION

There has been a strong tradition of "dynamic" perception in adult psychology, especially in the ecological psychology of James J. Gibson (1979) of Cornell University in the USA and Gunnar Johannson of Uppsala in Sweden. This approach is known as "event perception" (Johansson, Von Hofsten, & Jansson 1980). Johansson et al. (1980) point out that the shift from static to dynamic models of perception in the adult literature coincided with a move away from the assumption that visual perception depends upon the analysis of cues contained within a frozen retinal image towards an analysis of the flow of sensory stimulation. Information can be generated by the moving objects in the environment, by the movements of the perceiver, or by the interaction of movements of object and observer. On the dynamic theory visual perception occurs by means of information available in the flux of stimulation.

Within this flux certain transitions reliably specify events in the environment and others specify the actions of the perceiving organism. Recently, the theoretical rationale for this approach has been further elaborated and more formal definitions have been offered. Warren and Shaw (1985) distinguish between "events" and "encounters" in perception. "Events" are defined in terms of the minimum units of persistence and change contained within the flow of visual information at the retina that specify the objective properties of the environment and that do not involve the activities of the observer. For example, one object may occlude another through its own motion as it passes across a particular point of observation but the observer's own activities need not be involved in generating this sensory transformation in the visual array. "Encounters" on the other hand actively involve the observer, they are events that contain information derived from or implicated in the control of action (in Gibson's (1979) terminology such functional properties of sensory stimulation are called "affordances"). Hence the reference to "events" and "encounters" in the title of this chapter.

EVENTS IN INFANT PERCEPTION

The dynamic approach to infant perception has been pioneered by James Gibson's wife, Eleanor and her students at Cornell, by Claus von Hofsten in Sweden, and by Tom Bower at the University of Edinburgh in Scotland. A rapidly growing number of studies has shown that even the youngest infant reveals remarkable abilities once the investigator takes a dynamic approach to perception.

When we observe one object occlude another we experience the event as a temporary disappearance of the hidden object, rather than an annihilation of it. The "permanence" of the object is one of the fundamental outcomes of event perception; the perception of permanence ensures continuity and coherence of experience through the many vanishings and reappearances of things in the field of view.

Bower (1967) was the first to suggest that babies perceive permanence. Infants aged 7 weeks were conditioned to suck on a nipple in the presence of a large red ball. The ball was then made to disappear by slowly moving a screen in front of it. Babies continued to suck, evidence that they perceived the conditioned stimulus to be "present" but invisible. When the ball was made to vanish suddenly by an arrangement of mirrors, so that it appeared to have been annihilated, a condition that leads to the perception of impermanence among adults, then babies ceased to suck, as if the conditioned stimulus had ceased to exist. Thus, even very young babies may perceive that objects are permanent through the dynamic transitions in visual information that occur as one object occludes another.

Further evidence that infants extract information for permanence from the dynamic transitions in visual information obtained through movement has been obtained quite recently. Kellman and Spelke (1983) used the habituation method to investigate infants' perception of occlusion. Four-month-old babies were repeatedly shown a display that looked like a swinging pendulum with its centre covered but which actually comprised two separate elements in common motion behind a screen. The decline in their attention (habituation) over repeated trials was measured. Then the occluding screen was removed and babies were shown one of two displays, either the two separate objects in common motion or a complete pendulum. The results demonstrated that 4-month-old babies perceived the partially hidden display as a whole object moving behind the screen. When the occluding object at the centre was removed babies showed renewed interest in the display, as if they were not expecting to see two disconnected objects. In the control condition, where a single moving pendulum was revealed behind the screen, babies showed no recovery of attention. Their low level of attention to the unoccluded display showed that they had all along perceived the rod as complete and this was simply one further instance of the same event. The fact that dynamic information was responsible for perception of completion of the rod was demonstrated when the experiment was repeated with the same stimuli presented as stationary displays. Under these static conditions the babies showed no evidence of discriminating between the complete and incomplete rod. It appears that the rigid motion of the two parts leads the infant to perceive them as a single connected rod that is partially hidden.

A study by Granrud et al. (1984) with babies aged 5 months shows the importance of dynamic information for depth perception in the young baby. This study capitalised on the tendency of babies, when given a choice, to reach and touch the nearest of several objects or surfaces presented simultaneously. A randomly moving display of dots was generated by computer and shown on a television screen. By clever computer programming it was possible to create the appearance of depth at an edge by continuous deletion of one part of the visual texture by the remaining texture on the screen. That is, the picture on the TV screen gave the appearance of one moving surface sliding behind another and the position of the "uppermost" surface could be varied from the left to right or centre of the screen. Infants would reach to touch the part of the television screen where the moving surface appeared nearer to them, as specified by the occlusion of one textured surface by another. A similar study was carried out by Kaufmann-Hayoz and Kaufmann (1984) with babies aged 3 months. Displays were produced in which the figure and the background had a similar texture made up of randomly placed dots. When the figure is stationary it is invisible against the background. However, movement deletes texture in the background and immediately reveals the form of the figure. Babies easily discriminated a butterfly shape from a cross when both were in motion against the textured background. Furthermore, they were able to recognise the static form if it was placed on a white background when they had previously seen it in movement, as if the information about shape had been encoded in memory. Slater, Morrison, Town, and Rose (1985) have provided evidence that even new-born babies may perceive and encode shape from moving stimuli. It would appear that information derived from relative movement is fundamental in infant visual perception.

Evidence from older babies using other response indices is also consistent with this position. Babies of 4 months will reach for the nearer of two real objects so long as there is information available for relative motion of the nearer to the further object. Kellman and Spelke (1983), showed that babies use relative movement to derive depth information when a further object is made to move behind a nearer and they preferentially reach for the nearer object. With common movement of both foreground and background objects babies show no preference for the nearer part when they reach. Information from relative movement therefore informs the infant that objects are at different distances.

All these studies of event perception support the hypothesis that babies use dynamic information obtained from the relative movements of objects in the perception of a world of spatially connected, separately moveable, whole, permanent objects in the first 5 months of life.

BIOLOGICAL MOTION

A line of research originating in Johannson's laboratory in Uppsala concerns the perception of biological motion. Biological motions are mechanically complex, animate movements such as walking or the movements involved in emotional expression. Johannson developed a method of studying the dynamic visual information implicated in biological motion perception known as "point light walkers". Point light walkers are created by placing lights or luminous tape on the head, torso, and limb joints of a person dressed in black who is then filmed in the dark while traversing a path normal to the observer's line of sight. Adults viewing the filmed dots in motion report a compelling experience of seeing a human figure walking. In fact, adults can recognise the characteristic patterns of movement of their friends, and they can often tell the gender of the walking person, just from the moving points of light (Cutting & Proffitt, 1981). The same luminous points seen when stationary do not reveal anything to the perceiver (nor does a single frame of the film of the point light walker) which shows that the information is carried in the dynamic transitions of the moving display.

Recent evidence shows that babies of 4 to 6 months are sensitive to biomechanical motions specified by point light displays. Infants prefer to look at a display showing a walking motion than one in which the same number of dots simply move randomly (Fox & McDaniel 1982; Bertenthal, Proffitt, Spetner, & Thomas 1985). Additional detailed studies of infants' perception of computer-generated point light displays have been carried out (Bertenthal & Proffitt 1984). In these studies computer-generated "coherent" displays are produced in which the points of light mimic a person walking and are placed at the position of the major joints. In an "incoherent" condition the lights are positioned off the joints and move randomly. The authors demonstrated that babies of 3 months more rapidly encode "coherent" displays than "incoherent" displays. In another control experiment Bertenthal and Proffitt (1986) showed that infants do not discriminate an upside-down point light walker from random movement. Thus, it would appear that infants may be able to extract information about human movement from moving points of light, so long as the essential information for an upright, walking figure is retained in the computer generated display.

Bower (1982, p. 273, chapter 4) discusses an intriguing extension of this line of research. In a study of toddler's perception of point light walkers it was discovered that babies prefer to look at a point light walker display of a baby of their own gender than at a display of an infant of the opposite sex. The films were made in the standard way and showed a boy or girl toddler walking, bending, and picking up an object. Bower suggests that gender typical differences in skeletal articulation may underlie this preference for the same sex display. There does seem to be a tendency for little boys to bend and pick up objects from the waist, while little girls bend at the knees. Perhaps this sex difference in babies' selective attention to biomechanical movement is based on gender-typical movement patterns.

Eleanor Gibson and her students have also examined the potential of an event analysis for aspects of social perception. Walker et al. (1980) showed that babies can distinguish between elastic and rigid motions of an object early in the first year of life. They showed that babies perceive the difference between elastic deforming movements, as when a sponge is squeezed repeatedly and rigid movements of the same object as for example, when it rotates but is not deformed. The authors suggest that elastic motion may be discriminated from rigid motion because the external boundary and the interior texture of the object undergoes systematic deformation in the former case, whereas only the external boundary is transformed within the retinal array in the latter case. That is, information is available in the light projected to the retina for a discrimination between rigid and elastic objects and babies can make use of it. Taking this line of research even further, Kaufmann-Hayoz and Jager (1983) present evidence that infants may obtain sufficient information from point displays to perceive faces. In this study, white dots were placed on the face of a woman wearing black make-up. The adult was filmed while behaving as if interacting with a baby. The resulting film showed the dots in dynamic movement with no part of the face visible. Infants' habituation to this filmed display was compared with habituation to a film of random movements of a rubber mask that had been similarly prepared. The experimental data on habituation and emotional expressions during habituation suggested that infants discriminated the movements of the face from the elastic movements of the mask. Walker (1982) has gone on to demonstrate that babies under 6 months of age perceive the unity of visual and auditory expression of emotion using the preference method with simultaneous projection of a pair of films and a single sound track. The films showed an animate happy or sad face and the sound track was of an emotion appropriate to one of the films. Infants under 6-months-old prefer to look at the film which corresponds with the sound track. It could be said that the elastic motions of the face and the intonations of the voice jointly specify an emotional event to the baby.

Taken as a whole these results are consistent with the argument put forward by Bower (1974; 1982) and by Walker-Andrews and Gibson (1986) that what young infants first perceive are the superordinate aspects of perception. Faces, voices, emotional expression, and properties of skeletal articulation are perceived in the world to arise at a unified, embodied source. People behave in a coordinated fashion, in ways that yield information that has superordinate, common properties revealed by spatiotemporal patterning. Infants appear to be able to detect these commonalities, even in minimal form (as in point light displays). Early perception capture the essential, abstract, spatiotemporal transitions that yield a unified, coherent experience of persons and matter in motion.

INTERSENSORY EVENTS

As the previous examples show, not only do babies perceive events specified within a single modality, but there is also evidence that they are sensitive to intersensory information. One of the earliest studies to show intersensory coordination was by Wertheimer (1961) who showed that an infant only 8-minutes-old would turn her eyes toward a sound played softly in one ear or the other. This early demonstration of an innate link between vision and audition has since been supported by a wide variety of research (see

Butterworth, 1981 for a review) and again, a striking ability to extract information from the dynamic properties of sensory stimulation is revealed.

Kuhl and Meltzoff (1982) carried out a study in which 4-month-old babies were simultaneously presented with two video-recorded faces to left and right. One face was shown repeating the vowel "i" and the other repeated the vowel "a". However, the baby heard only one sound track, to correspond with one of the visually presented vowels, in a randomly counterbalanced experiment. It was found that babies preferred to look at the face that matched the sound track, suggesting that they detect an intersensory correspondence between the auditory and visual information for the vowel sound. In a related series of studies, Meltzoff and Moore (1977), Meltzoff (1981) and Vinter (1984) have carried out extremely interesting research on imitation in new-born babies that may also be implicated in mechanisms of speech perception and production. These authors have shown that neonates will selectively imitate mouth opening, tongue protrusion, and lip pursing movements. Imitation of "invisible" movements such as these may involve the same abilities as lip reading and this could be important in the acquisition of language. The dynamic approach shows that babies' speech perception may profitably be investigated as an inter-modal event.

Many further examples of infant event perception are reviewed by Gibson and Spelke (1983); just one further instance will be mentioned here. Spelke, Born, and Chu (1983) have carried out an extensive series of studies which reveal that babies are sensitive to the common rhythmic properties of events in vision and audition. Babies were simultaneously shown two films projected to left and right of the midline. In both films an object moved up and down in a rhythmic sequence with abrupt changes in the direction of movement. A single sound track was played of an abrupt noise. Babies prefer to look at the film where the sound track undergoes an abrupt transition at the same moment as the abrupt change in the visual direction of movement. That is, abrupt transitions in the patterning of auditory or visual stimulation are perceived as relating to the same event. The evidence suggests that event perception is not a modality specific process, rather it occurs by gathering of information from many sensory channels each attesting to the same external reality.

ENCOUNTERS IN INFANT PERCEPTION

An "encounter" is defined as an event that is particularly relevant to the perceiver's intentions or actions. Again, there is a great deal of evidence to show that even tiny babies are sensitive to the affordances of events. Some of the best-known examples come from the study of "looming" with new-born babies. Looming is produced by accelerated expansion of a delimited portion of the visual field, as when an object rapidly approaches toward an observer. For example, an object can be presented moving toward an infant on a collision course or so that it veers off to one side. When the looming object is on a collision course very young babies will raise their hands, move their heads backward and make "defensive" movements to the oncoming visual stimulus. When the looming object is on a miss path, the same babies simply sit and watch the object move by without making any defensive movements. Of course, no harm is allowed to befall the baby in these studies. That the response is specific to visual information has been shown by using a shadow caster to present the looming stimulus. Babies make defensive responses to the shadow so there can be little doubt that the response is to visually specified information rather than air movements, noise or other factors, (Bower, Broughton, & Moore, 1970).

In the looming studies, only a portion of the visual field expands in relation to the remainder and this specifies an impending collision. When the whole visual field is in motion another event is specified: Movement of the observer in a stable visual space. A number of studies have been carried out using the "moving room" technique, in which the whole visual environment is made to move in relation to the baby. Infants are tested inside a small room comprising three walls and a ceiling which can be moved above a rigid floor. Babies stand, sit, or are seated with support in the room which is then moved relative to the infant so that the end wall comes toward or away from the baby. This movement of the room produces a flow pattern of visual information that corresponds to that which would ordinarily occur if the baby sways backwards or forwards. Several studies have demonstrated that babies maintain a stable standing or sitting posture through sensitivity to the visual flow pattern. They lose balance when standing or sitting in the moving room and their loss of balance is always appropriate to the direction of instability specified by the misleading visual flow (Lee and Aronson, 1974; Butterworth and Cicchetti, 1978). In fact, this information may even be important in gaining head control, one of the earliest postures to be mastered by the infant. Pope (1984) showed that babies gain control of their heads with respect to the stable visual surroundings at least as early as the second month of life. Thus, dynamic transitions giving rise to a total flow of the visual array serve to specify the movement of self and babies use this dynamic information to gain control of the succession of postures and the motor milestones they achieve in the first 18 months of life.

Another example of the importance of dynamic information in the control of action comes from studies of the catching skills of very young babies. Von Hofsten (1982) reviews a series of studies in which he has shown that infants will manually intercept an object moving within reach on an elliptical trajectory. Babies will adapt the speed of their reach to the speed of the moving object. Even the new-born baby will attempt an interception, although obviously the very young infant is not as spectacularly successful in catching the moving target as the 9-month-old. This example of eye–hand coordination in the baby again shows that event perception is not modality specific. Visual information for object movement specifies the possibility of encountering the object on a conjoint kinaesthetically specified trajectory of the arm.

These examples show that visual perception is very important in the development and control of reaching and locomotion in the sighted baby. But what about the baby who cannot make use of this information through blindness? It is worth noting that theoretical advances stemming from the dynamic approach to perception offer the possibility of constructing prosthetic devices in which information that is unavailable through vision may nevertheless be substituted in another modality. Bower (1977) reported one such case in which a congenitally anophthalmic baby was equipped with a sonar device. The sonar was worn on the head and it projected a continuous stream of ultrasound onto the environment. Reflections of the sound were converted electronically to audible sounds which convey information about the properties of objects. For example, the texture of an object is reliably specified by the clarity of the echoed signal (a hard object produces a clear sound, a soft one a fuzzy sound), the amplitude of the signal specifies the size of the object (loud: big; soft: small), the direction of the object is given by differences in time of arrival of the stereo signal at the ears. After some practice in using this device the baby was able to reach and grasp objects, to place the arms as if to break a fall when lowered toward a surface, and would even play peek-a-boo with his mother with great pleasure as his head movements brought her in and out of the field of the sonic guide. The dynamic approach to infant perception not only helps us to understand better the abilities of the normal infant, but it also offers the possibility of developing new methods of helping those with sensory handicaps.

CONCLUSIONS

The study of infant perception has entered a new era. The move from static to dynamic theories of perception has revealed so much about the perceptual world of the very young baby that there is no going back to the old theory of limited perceptual abilities. No doubt, science proceeds by making simplifying assumptions and "static" perception may intuitively have seemed the appropriate way to study the naïve human. However, dynamic perception has proved to be the simpler case, as far as the developing infant is concerned. Johansson (1985) said that his own studies of event perception led him to the conclusion that sensory systems are most efficient under conditions that are exceedingly complex to describe mathematically. By the same token, we may conclude that early infant perception is most efficient in the complex dynamic case. The apparently simple, static, two-dimensional, visual stimulus is actually atypical of the spatiotemporal world to which the infant is biologically pre-adapted. The static case actually requires an analysis akin to that involved in explaining picture perception. Perception in the baby is not pre-adapted for comprehending pictures. Rather, it is based on events and encounters of adaptive significance from whatever modality the information is derived. It is from this dynamic spatiotemporal perspective on perception that exciting insights have come and which hold such promise for further study of the perceptual world of the young baby.

ACKNOWLEDGMENTS

A version of this paper has been published in *The New Psychologist*, Annual Journal of the Open University Psychology Society, May, 1986, 3–6.

REFERENCES

Bertenthal, B. I. & Proffitt, D. R. (1984). Infants encoding of kinetic displays varying in figural coherence. Paper presented at the International Conference on Infant Studies New York, 1984. *Abstract in Infant Behaviour and Development*, 7, 34.

Bertenthal, B. I. & Proffitt, D. R. (1986). The extraction of structure from motion: Implementation of basic processing constraints. Paper presented at the International Conference on Infant Studies, Los Angeles, 1986. *Abstract in Infant Behaviour and Development*, 9, 36.

Bertenthal, B. I., Proffitt, D. R., Spetner, N. B., & Thomas, M. A. (1985). The development of infant sensitivity to biomechanical motions. *Child Development*, 56, 531–543.

Bower, T. G. R. (1967). The development of object permanence: Some studies of existence constancy. *Perception and Psychophysics*, 2, 411–418.

Bower, T. G. R. (1977, February). Blind babies see with their ears. *New Scientist*, 255–257.

Bower, T. G. R. (1974, 1982). Development in Infancy (2nd ed.). San Francisco: Freeman.

Bowen, T. G. R., Broughton, J., & Moore, M. K. (1970). Infant responses to approaching objects: An indicator of response to distal variables. *Perception and Psychophysics*, 9, 193–196.

Butterworth, G. E. (1981). The origins of auditory–visual perception and visual proprioception in human infancy. In R. D. Walk and H. L. Pick, Jr (eds), *Intersensory perception and sensory integration*. New York: Plenum Press. (Pp. 37–70).

Butterworth, G. E. & Cicchetti, D. (1978). Visual calibration of posture in normal and motor retarded Down's syndrome infants. *Perception*, 7, 513–525.

Cutting, J. E. & Proffitt, D. R. (1981). Gait perception as an example of how we may perceive events. In R. D. Walk and H. L. Pick, Jr (eds), *Intersensory perception and sensory integration*. New York: Plenum Press. (Pp. 249–279).

Fox, R. & McDaniel, C. (1982). The perception of biological motion by human infants. *Science*, 218, 486–487.

Gibson, J. J. (1979). *The ecological approach to visual perception*. Boston: Houghton-Mifflin.

Gibson, E. J. & Spelke, E. (1983). The development of perception. In J. H. Flavell and E.

Markman (eds), *Cognitive development*: Vol. 3 of P. Mussen (ed.), *Handbook of child psychology*. New York: Wiley.

Granrud, C. E., Yonas, A., Smith, I. M., Arterberry, M. E., Glicksman, M. L., & Sorkness, A. C. (1984). Infants sensitivity to accretion and deletion of texture as information for depth at an edge. *Child Development*, *55*, 1630–1636.

Johansson, G. (1985). About visual event perception. In R. E. Shaw & W. H. Warren (eds), *Persistence and change*. Hillsdale, N.J.: Lawrence Erlbaum Associates Inc.

Johansson, G., Von Hofsten, C., & Jansson, G. (1980). Event perception. In M. R. Rosenzweig and L. W. Porter (eds), *Annual review of psychology*. Palo Alto, Calif: Annual Reviews Inc. (Pp. 27–63).

Kaufman-Hayoz, R. & Kaufman, F. (1984). Kinetic contour information in infant's form perception. Paper presented at the International Conference on Infant Studies, New York, 1984. *Abstract in Infant Behaviour and Development*, *7*, 185.

Kaufman-Hayoz, R. & Jager, B. (1983). Infant's perception of a face revealed through motion. Paper presented at a meeting of the Society for Research in Child Development, Detroit.

Kellman, P. J. & Spelke, E. S. (1983). Perception of partly occluded objects in infancy. *Cognitive Psychology*, *15*, 483–524.

Kuhl, P. K. & Meltzoff, A. N. (1982). The bimodal perception of speech in infancy. *Science*, *218*, 1138–1141.

Lee, D. and Aronson, E. (1974). Visual proprioceptive control of standing in human infants. *Perception and Psychophysics*, *15*, 529–532.

Meltzoff, A. N. (1981). Imitation, intermodal coordination and representation in early infancy. In G. E. Butterworth (ed.), *Infancy and epistemology: an evaluation of Piaget's theory*. Brighton: Harvester Press.

Meltzoff, A. N. & Moore, M. K. (1977). Imitation of facial and manual gestures by human neonates. *Science*, *198*, 75–78.

Pope, M. J. (1984). *Visual proprioception in infant postural development*. Unpublished Ph.D. thesis, University of Southampton.

Slater, A., Morison, V., Town, C., & Rose, D. (1985). Movement perception and identity constancy in the newborn baby. *British Journal of Developmental Psychology*, *3*, 211–220.

Spelke, E. S., Born, W. S., & Chu, F., (1983). Perception of moving, sounding objects by four month old infants. *Perception*, *12*, 719–732.

Vinter, A. (1984). *Imitation, representation et mouvement dans les premieres mois de la vie*. Unpublished Ph.D. thesis, University of Geneva.

Von Hofsten, C. (1983). Foundations for perceptual development. In L. Lipsitt and C. K. Rovee-Collier (eds), *Advances in infancy research*: Vol. 2. New Jersey: Ablex Publishing Corp. (Pp. 241–261).

Walker, A., (1982). Intermodal perception of expressive behaviour by human infants. *Journal of Experimental Child Psychology*, *33*, 514–535.

Walker, A., Owsley, C. J., Megaw-Nyce, J., Gibson, E. J., & Bahrick, E. (1980). Detection of elasticity as an invariant property of objects by young infants. *Perception*, *9*, 713–718.

Walker-Andrews, A. & Gibson, E. (1986). What develops in bimodal perception? In L. Lipsitt and C. Rovee-Collier (eds), *Advances in infancy research*: Vol. 4. New Jersey: Ablex Publishing Corp. (Pp. 171–181).

Warren, W. H. & Shaw, R. E. (1985). Events and encounters as units of analysis for ecological psychology. In R. E. Shaw and W. H. Warren (eds), *Persistence and change*. Hillsdale, N.J.: Lawrence Erlbaum Associates Inc.

Wertheimer, M. (1961). Psychomotor coordination of auditory and visual space at birth. *Science*, *134*, 1692.

4 The Perceptual World of the New-Born Child

Tom Bower

School of Human Development,
University of Texas at Dallas,
P.O. Box 830688,
Mail Station GR41,
Richardson,
Texas, U.S.A.

INTRODUCTION

The topic of this paper is perceptual development. We adults are all aware of the perceptual world we live in. We can describe it in public terms, with little disagreement. Where there is disagreement is over the developmental paths by which we reach our rich, public perceptual world. The starting point for disagreement is the starting point for development, the perceptual world of the new-born child. Historically there have been many descriptions of that unknown world. Currently there are rather fewer. Extreme nativism, for example, the belief that the new-born's world is the same as our own, would find few present-day adherents, save perhaps among the dwindling band of behaviourists. Historically and currently I suppose the most popular account of the new-born's perceptual world is some version of sensory atomism. Unlike ourselves, who live in a world of objects and events related in space and time, the new-born is supposed to live in a world of isolated sensory experiences, sounds, touches, lights, with no given connection in space or time. Extreme proponents of this view, as I was 20 years ago, have even argued that the components of a single object are seen in isolation, as separate fragments (Bower, 1966; Cohen & Gelber, 1975). Some theorists (e.g. Werner, 1948) have wished to complicate this already confusing world by endowing the new-born child with synaesthesis, so that sounds will elicit hallucinatory visual, etc. experiences as well as the proper auditory responses.

ID—D

My own current view of the new-born's perceptual world is very different. I would argue that the new-born does not respond to sensory experiences as such, indeed is probably unaware of the sensory qualities of stimulation; instead, I would maintain, the new-born responds to the formal, abstract properties of stimulation, properties which are independent of any specific sense, what Gibson (1950) called higher-order variables. The simplest example of such a variable is provided by those inputs that specify the radial direction of a source of stimulation. Consider a sound source. If straight ahead, a sound source produces exactly the same stimulation at each ear; if it is to the right, the right ear is stimulated earlier and more intensely than the left ear; if it is to the left, the opposite happens. In this case symmetry of stimulation equals "straight ahead", asymmetry "off-straight ahead". At a formal level the same system operates for detection of an olfactory source, a vibratory source, and, I have argued, for a visual source. Symmetry–asymmetry of stimulation is independent of any specific modality; it is thus a genuine high-order variable. I am proposing that the new-born responds to these formal, high-order properties of stimulation, not the sensory inputs which mediate them.

THE SONIC GUIDE

Whereas there is certainly evidence that new-borns do pick up and respond to symmetry–asymmetry, the most compelling evidence I know of response to formal properties of stimulation utilises an artificial sensory surrogate, the sonic guide. Its main features are summarised in Fig. 1. As can be seen there, the machine, at a formal level, can present the same information as vision, through a different modality. The signal I wish to focus on is that generated by an approaching object. An approaching object to the eye generates the optical expansion pattern (Fig. 2), a purely visual signal. That signal, however, can be looked at as a change pattern over time (Lee & Lishman, 1977) because the intensity of stimulation increases rapidly as the object approaches the eyes. This pattern of change at a formal level can be mimicked precisely by the sonic guide. The question is, can the young infant detect and respond to the form of stimulation? The experiments we did (Aitken & Bower, see Aitken, 1981) aimed to answer this question and also to look at the role of learning in response to approaching objects. The apparatus used is shown in Fig 3. It allowed us to vary the sonic guide signal independent of "reality". The infants were run in darkness. The information presented was thus confined to the sonic guide signal and the air displacement produced by the moving object, ending in slight contact with the baby's face. In one condition these two signals were consonant, both indicating approach or withdrawal; in the other they were dissonant, the sonic guide indicating approach whereas in reality the object receded from the baby's

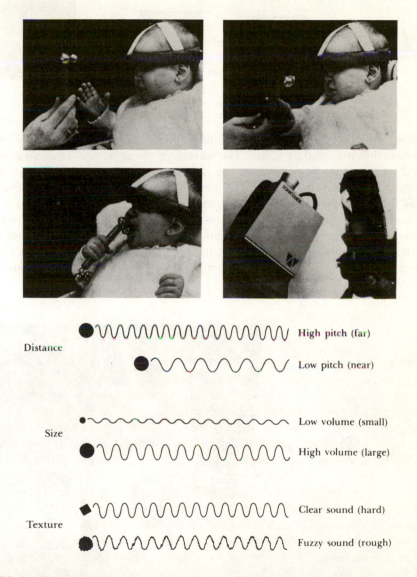

FIG. 1.   The sonic guide emits an ultrasonic pulse. The ultrasonic echo is transformed to give audible information about direction, distance, size, shape, and composition.

face and vice versa. The dependent measure taken was backward head-pressure (Dunkeld & Bower, 1980). The results indicated that the sonic guide signal was more important than contact in determining head retraction. It is important to remember that the sonic guide provides a signal to the infant that, at a sensory level, is novel in the experience of the individual and,

FIG. 2.   The optical expansion pattern.

indeed, of the species. The form of stimulation however, is the same familiar form as that provided by vision. The efficacy of the sonic guide information surely attests that young infants are sensitive to the form of stimulation rather than its sensory content, the formal properties of stimulation rather than the fragments of sense-data whose arrangement constitutes that form.

I must also point out that these formal properties of stimulation are quite sufficient to support normal perceptual–motor development. I have worked with a number of congenitally blind babies. If they are provided with the sonic guide when they are young enough, they grow like sighted children,

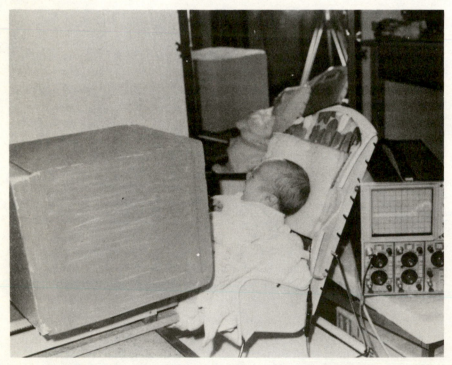

FIG. 3.   The "looming object" apparatus used by Aitken and Bower.

showing none of the lesions of development that usually characterise the blind child. One child began using the guide when she was about 6 months old. She is totally blind, but not only is she not motorically retarded, she is actually precocious. She shows none of the terrified immobility customarily seen in blind children. Cognitively she is advanced, by 22 months of age having solved all of the Piagetian tasks that would normally occupy the first 2 years of a sighted child's life. In language even before age 2 she was using prepositions correctly, unusual in a sighted child, unheard of in a blind child. Formal, abstract higher-order variables, variables whose sensory content is novel to us as a species, can thus support a normal programme of development, evidence surely that these variables *are* the starting point for development.

NEW-BORN REACHING

The most compelling evidence that the new-born elaborates his view of the world on the basis of formal properties comes from an experiment on reaching in the new-born period (Aitken, 1981). The new-born's ability to reach was a subject of controversy following the initial publication of positive results by Bower, Broughton, and Moore (1970). However, there are now enough positive replications around for the presence of the ability to be beyond doubt. One of the most interesting of these was carried out by Scania de Schonen (1980). She studied the reaching of infants aged 3, 4, 5, and 6 days of age. In full-term infants of 5 and 6 days, born without anaesthesia, reaching was observed. It was not observed in 3- or 4-day-old subjects. In other words, it appeared that four days' experience in the world was necessary for this primitive visual–motor coordination to appear. I say experience rather than post-natal maturation because of some results obtained by Aitken (1981) with premature infants. These premature babies, all tested before they had reached full term, could all reach at least as successfully as term infants of 7 days. It appears then that, after birth, the infant elaborates the visual–motor coordination we call reaching and that this elaboration depends on experience. Is the coordination truly visual–motor, implying an elaboration from a specific sensory base, or is it perceptual–motor, implying that the base is the higher-order modality free from the form of stimulation? One way to test this is to look at the infant's behaviour with a completely novel sensory input which retains the form of the information given by vision. This is what we did, using the sonic guide described above. The infants were all in the second week of life, and thus had the requisite experience for reaching to seen objects. How would they do with the sensorily novel but perceptually familiar information provided by the guide? They did extremely well, performing in the dark with the sonic guide, even *better* than with vision in light, as shown in Table 1. To ensure that neither result stemmed from simple excitement, we ran another study with another stimulus, in this case a sound-emitting object presented in darkness. This sound-emitting, unseen toy could not, as the other two conditions could, give information about distance. On an excitement hypothesis this should not matter. However, as Table 2 shows, distance and the availability of even sensorily novel information about distance were important. The information was used where it was available.

It seems to me that the successful transfer of an elaborated perceptual–motor coordination to a completely new sensory input system is clear evidence that the elaboration was not based on specific sensory inputs but on the formal, perceptual properties of stimulation.

NEW-BORN IMITATION

In a previous publication (Bower, 1978) I wrote that the strongest contrary evidence to the view I have been outlining here, was provided by two of its strongest supporters, Meltzoff and Moore (1977) who have shown that new-born infants, infants whose age can be measured in hours or even minutes, can in fact imitate facial expressions. Imitation, it seemed to me, required a

TABLE 1
Results from 2-Week-Old Infants Reaching in the Light or with the Sonic Guide in Darkness

	Vision in Light	Sonic Guide in Darkness
Mean No. of Reaches	190	161
No. of Contacts	110	131
Percent Success	58	81

TABLE 2
Infants Reaching with and without Distance Information

	Condition	No. of Reaches
Vision	Within reach	11
	Out of reach	3
Sonic Guide	Within reach	17
	Out of reach	4
Sound-Emitting Toy	Within reach	15
	Out of reach	11

degree of sensory specificity. I would now incline to the view that perhaps it does not. Perhaps, for example, the opening mouth of another is perceived directly as an act of mouth opening, just as is the opening mouth of the baby himself. The input from the outside world maps into the same perceptual structures as the input from the baby's own muscles. If they have the same form, and why should they not, new-born imitation would be an act of what Michotte (1962) has called empathetic perception, an example of the pick-up of formal, perceptual information in the context of the social world rather than the physical world.

PERCEPTION OF "PURE" HUMAN MOVEMENT

I will elaborate slightly. What can be happening in imitation? The new-born is presented with a face, part of which moves. Does the new-born see the face or the movement? I am arguing that the new-born sees the movement. Movement is an intermodal variable. The baby can *see* the movement of another and *feel* the movements of his own face. On this view imitation is simply the intermodal mapping of movement. If this view is correct, one should be able to elicit imitation by presenting pure movement. How to do this? We have used a technique derived from Johansson (1973) that reduces a face to a pattern of spots of light. As Fig. 4 shows, the dots are meaningless to us, and to babies. But when the dots move the gestures are easily seen by adults and new-borns. The gestures we have used are eye-opening and closing, mouth opening and closing, and mouth protrusion. Babies in the new-born period can imitate films of this kind. The youngest baby I have thus far tested with this kind of presentation was 3 days old. There was no difference between his imitation of such dot patterns and his imitation of his mother's face. He imitated both with equal fluency, surely evidence that higher-order intermodal information, that specifies movement, is the basis for imitation (Kujawski, 1985).

The next example of intermodal perception that I am going to discuss is perhaps different from the last one, or from most of the others I have mentioned, in that, viewed as a skill, it is a skill in which babies far surpass adults.

Some years ago Lewis and Brooks (1975) showed that 12-month-olds can identify the gender of other infants from slides. If shown a slide of a boy side by side with a slide of a girl, boys will look more at the slide of a boy and girls more at the slide of a girl. There is thus not only differentiation but also "like me" identification. What are the bases of these important social perceptions? The most obvious seemed to be those that are under cultural control, hair length, style and colour of clothing, and perhaps the associated toys. There have been some studies indicating that these variables are important (Aitken,

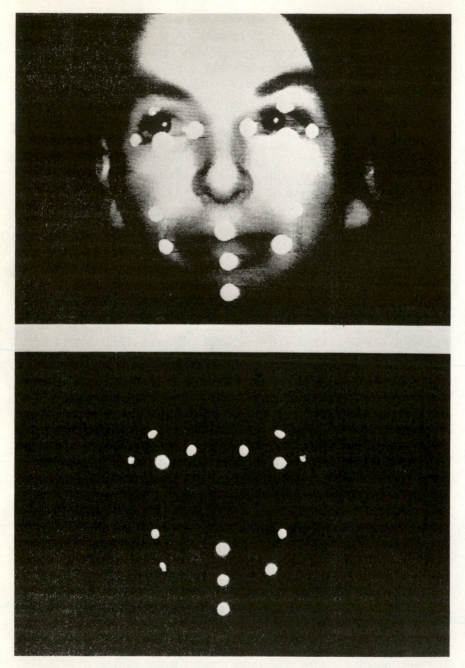

FIG. 4   Light spots attached to face (above) result in a pattern of spots (below).

1977). Aitken, for example, dressed up boy models in frilly dresses and photographed them holding a doll; his girl models were dressed in dark coloured dungarees and were in the act of banging a drum (Fig. 5). When shown pairs of slides like this, boys looked more at the girls dressed as boys, and girls more at the boys dressed as girls. In other words gender identification seemed to be based on low-order, culturally based, empirical cues. A rather different picture emerged when movies were substituted for slides. Here once more boys looked at boys, even though dressed as girls. It thus appeared that the patterning of movement could be more significant than the low-order cues described above. The next stage in the research was to look at the effect of movement pattern per se, with all other cues to gender, or even "humanness" removed. This was done by using the techniques of Johansson (1973), mentioned above. A light was attached to the joints of a baby, one at each shoulder, elbow, wrist, hip, knee, and ankle joint. With appropriate film technique nothing is visible in the developed print except these 12 lights. In a still frame the result is not recognisable as a human, much less a male or female baby (Fig. 6). Nevertheless, when the films were set in motion babies had no trouble in identifying the gender of the babies who had modelled the display, 12-month-old boy babies looking more at the pattern generated by a baby boy, girl babies more at the pattern generated by a girl baby. These patterns, in sensory terms, are completely abstract, completely novel to the baby, and yet they yield even better discrimination of gender than a full-scale colour film: the mean duration of the first look at the same-sex infant was

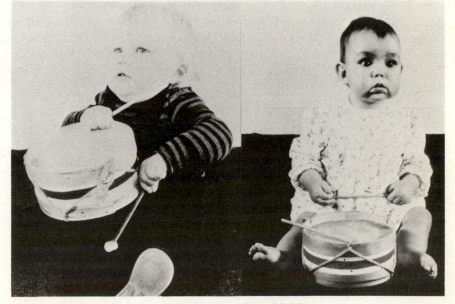

FIG. 5.   Two cross-dressed babies.

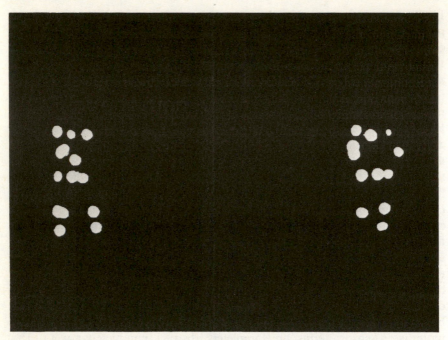

FIG. 6.   Still patterns of lights that, in movement, can define a human.

5.29 seconds, while that for the opposite-sex infant was 2.88 seconds. Thus, even at the advanced age of 12 months perceptual identifications are still elaborated on the basis of the higher-order, formal properties of stimulation, rather than the simple, sensory qualities that might seem more obvious. The subjects in this experiment had never in their lives before seen a display like the one used, if we define the display in terms of the simple, sensory qualities that it provides.

CONCLUSIONS

We can also now offer a definition of what constitutes the perceptual world of the new-born, and what stimuli from the worlds of physics and anatomy will be registered in the psychological world of the new-born. I would propose that those events that *can* be specified in a common form to two or more modalities will be registered as events in the psychological world of the new-born. The application of this principle to physical stimuli is obvious. More intriguing, I think, it explains the high degree of interest the baby takes in the stimuli coming from people. The baby has been rehearsing a wide variety of movements, including facial movements, from well before birth. Suddenly there is an external match for these internally known stimuli. If familiarity is important, then the new-born has far more familiarity with the information generated by his own movements than he could have with any other type of stimulus. In all probability the most familiar stimuli are those that specify changes in the face, and we know how interested in faces are new-borns.

Perception of course will develop from this starting point, and development from such a starting point can only be a process of differentiation and specification. A very large part of this will be accounted for by restriction of the range of possible stimuli the baby is set to attend to. Thirty years after the widespread popularisation of information theory, many psychologists find it strange still that *potential* stimuli are a major component of information load. The new-born must be preset for many stimuli that are never actually encountered. As the presentation set is defined in experience, there will be more information processing space freed for analysis of the stimuli that actually occur. No change within the baby is actually required. However, in addition, there will be changes in the baby, actual growth, that will permit differentiation, although their role is, I feel, minor. No processes beyond these are at all necessary to account for any perceptual changes that may occur after birth.

The world of the new-born has been described in a memorable phrase as blooming, buzzing confusion. If my speculations have any validity, it is far from that. My new-born's perceptual world is form without content, a structure of places and events, without the rich sensory bloom which characterises our own perceptual world. The nearest we can get to understanding that world is to subject ourselves to a classic experiment on intermodal perception. In that experiment there are three sensory events, a flash of light, a single sound and a touch, each in a different place. What we adults perceive is movement between three locations; we do not see the movement, we do not hear the movement nor do we feel it. We perceive it, an experience as close to pure perception as we adults can attain, an experience, I would say, like all of the experience of the new-born child.

REFERENCES

Aitken, S. (1977). Psychological sex differentiation as related to the emergence of a self-concept in infancy. Unpublished Honours thesis, 1977, Department of Psychology, University of Edinburgh.

Aitken, S. (1981). Differentiation theory and the study of intersensory substitution using the sonic guide. Unpublished Ph.D. thesis (1966), University of Edinburgh.

Bower, T. G. R. (1966) Heterogeneous summation in human infants. *Animal Behaviour, 14,* 395–398.

Bower, T. G. R, (1978). Perceptual developement: Object and space. In C. Carterette & M. Friedman (eds), *Handbook of perception*: Vol. VIII. *Perceptual coding*. New York: Academic Press.

Bower, T. G. R., Broughton, J. M. & Moore, M. K. (1970). Demonstration of intention in the reaching behaviour of neonate humans. *Nature, 228*, 697–681.

Cohen, L. B. & Gelber, E. R. Infant visual memory. In L. B. Cohen & P. Salapatek (eds), *Infant perception: From sensation to cognition: Basic visual processes:* (Vol. 1). New York: Academic Press.

Dunkeld, J. & Bower, T. G. R. (1980). Infant response to impending optical collision. *Perception, 9*, 549–554.

Gibson, J. J. (1950). The perception of the visual world. Boston, Mass.: Houghton Mifflin.

Johansson, G. (1973). Visual perception of biological motion and a model for its analysis. *Perception and Psychophysics, 14*(2), 201–211.

Kujawski, J. (1985). The origins of gender identity. Unpublished Ph.D. thesis, 1985, University of Edinburgh.

Lee, D. N. & Lishman, R. (1977). Visual control of locomotion. *Scandinavian Journal of Psychology, 18*, 224–230.

Lewis, M. & Brooks, J. (1975). Infants social perception: A constructivist view. In L. B. Cohen & P. Salapatek (eds). *Infant perception: From sensation to cognition*: Vol. II. New York: Academic Press.

Meltzoff, A. N. & Moore, M. K. (1977). Imitation of facial and manual gestures by human neonates. *Science, 198*, 75–78.

Michotte, A. (1962). *Causalite permanence et realite phenomenales*, Louvain, Belgium: Publications Universitaires.

de Schonen, S. (1980). Developpement de la coordination visuo-manuelle et de la lateralisation manuelle des conduites d'atteinte et de prise d'objet. Travaux du Centre Étude des Processus Cognitifs et du Language, Laboratoire de Psychologie, CNRS, Paris.

Werner, H. (1948). *Comparative psychology of mental development*. Chicago: Follett.

2 Cognitive Development

Cognitive Development: Introduction

Gavin Bremner

As was indicated in the introduction to the section on perceptual development, it is often not at all easy to draw a clear distinction between perception and cognition. However, the conventional view is that such a distinction, however difficult, is certainly valid. Underlying this assumption is the notion that perception does not supply objective information about reality; instead objective understanding comes only through the construction of cognitive structures that interpret perception. Piaget put this view forward strongly in his work on infancy, claiming, for instance, that it was one thing to perceive and respond in accordance with a set of physical principles, but quite another to understand them as such. And for Piaget, one of the hallmarks of cognition was the ability to represent reality even when it was not present to the senses.

As a number of chapters in the preceding section have indicated, however, this position is meeting an ever increasing challenge. On a theoretical level, proponents of Gibson's theory of direct perception question the need for the development of cognitive structures to interpret perception they would have it that objective reality is directly perceived and requires no interpretation. On an empirical level, evidence discussed in earlier chapters is beginning to point more and more clearly to the presence of objective perception at a very much earlier age than we could reasonably expect if such perception had to wait upon the development of interpreting cognitive structures. Admittedly, Gibsonian theory does not produce all the answers here, because we still need to reach an understanding of the complex structure of the young infant's mind that makes these impressive abilities possible. The main point, however, is that they are there and need to be incorporated in any view that we construct about the nature of development in infancy.

Such a position, if accepted, could lead us to the conclusion that the phrase "infant cognition" is a bit of a misnomer: If all information is supplied by perception, already interpreted, then maybe we need not look for a development of cognitive structures that interpret reality. However, another look at the literature shows that this is far from the case. Although impressive new-born abilities are uncovered almost daily, these mainly occur under well-structured laboratory conditions, and the fact remains that infants do not show that they can use these "abilities" to guide their spontaneous behaviour until a good deal later. Consequently, there is an important role for developmental theory in explaining how early "potential" comes under voluntary control, to appear in everyday purposive behaviour. In addition, there is an urgent need for good accounts of how infants develop increasingly complex strategies for dealing with the problems that they encounter in the world. These strategies are certainly not innate.

With these considerations in mind, this section contains a selection of contributions that re-evaluate infants' cognitive development in the light of what we now know about their early perceptual abilities.

In the first chapter in Part 2, Harris presents a re-evaluation of the object permanence literature in the light of recent research. He sets the scene by indicating the fundamental opposition between the Piagetian viewpoint, in which objective reality is laboriously constructed during development from subjective perception, and the Gibsonian view, in which objective reality extending even to the permanence of objects is considered to be directly perceived. As so often happens when two views appear in extreme opposition, an intermediate view emerges as a more plausible alternative, and Harris presents Spelke's approach as an example. Spelke prefers to argue that perception is interpreted by innate principles, and presents supporting evidence from studies with quite young infants: evidence that shows how infants detect violations of spatial principles even when these are not directly perceived, such as when a screen rotates "through" the position occupied by the object that it hides.

Harris then moves on to deal with the question that has dogged recent research. Why, if young infants have knowledge of object permanence, do they initially fail to search for hidden objects and later show errors in search? After reviewing various contemporary interpretations of these phenomena, Harris presents a memory-deficit account, suggesting that the infant's problem is not conceptual, but arises because of limitations to their short-term storage span. This limitation means that under many circumstances search errors occur because infants rely on long-term memory of past location rather than new information about object position that is coded in short-term memory alone. The general message here is that phenomena long interpreted as indicators of conceptual immaturity are in reality symptoms of information processing limitations that gradually reduce as the infant gets older.

The second chapter surveys recent research on infant spatial abilities. Again, using Piagetian search phenomena as his point of depature, Bremner goes on to look at a range of evidence on spatial orientation in infancy, evidence derived from tasks in which infants have to manually relocate an object or visually relocate an event after they have been moved to a new location. Two main points emerge from this literature. First, younger infants show a fairly heavy reliance on spatial landmarks, a reliance that gradually wanes as they develop. Secondly, a number of indicators point to a link between the development of spatial awareness and the onset of locomotion. Bremner suggests that it is possible to extend the second point, tracing links between earlier developments in spatial awareness and the development of postural control leading to the infant's sitting up unsupported. The notion being advanced is not so much that these postural and motor developments lead to a better tuned space perception, rather that what we see are infants adapting their newly aquired activities to the perceptual world. Thus, rather than constructing an objective awareness of space, infants are seen as constructing ways of organising space that allow them to adapt their emerging action systems to surrounding reality.

In the final chapter in the section, Willatts looks at cognitive development in a more general way than either of the preceding chapters. Rather than focusing on a specific area such as object permanence or spatial awareness, he starts from the background of problem-solving literature, to analyse infant cognition as intentional, goal-directed behaviour. Again, this necessitates a temporary return to Piaget's theory, according to which the development of intentionality and means–ends differentiation is a central aspect of cognitive development. However, Willatts indicates a number of shortcomings of Piaget's account, pointing among other things to evidence that newborn infants have the ability to separate means from ends, an ability that Piaget only fully credited to the 9-month-old.

The outcome of this analysis is a model of infant problem-solving composed of three principal components, what infants know about the world, what they are capable of doing in the world, and the methods they use to coordinate the two. The first two abilities may often be out of balance. For instance, infants' levels of task analysis may often be in advance of their level of skill, and so will not be reflected in everyday behaviour. The very existence of these sorts of imbalance makes the third ability the central one with regard to problem-solving, since the ability to adopt appropriate strategies that coordinate current knowledge and existing levels of skill is particularly important for an organism whose information processing capacity and level of skill is severely limited. Willatts indicates how the strategies available to infants change with age, beginning with heuristic solutions right at birth and progressing to properly planned solutions by the end of the first year.

Finally, it is interesting to note that Willatts analyses the Piagetian Stage IV search error as a failure of error-inhibition in problem-solving. At first sight, this appears at variance with Harris's analysis in terms of a short-term memory deficit. It may well be, however, that the two accounts are complementary, since it could be said that Harris has described the information-processing deficit, while Willatts has described the problem-solving skills the infant will require to surmount it.

5 Object Permanence in Infancy

Paul Harris

Department of Experimental Psychology,
University of Oxford

INTRODUCTION

Watching a new-born baby or even a baby of several months of age, I waver between two contradictory reactions. On the one hand, very young babies are clearly immature. So different are they in physical appearance from adult members of the species, so clumsy in their movements, and so restricted in their communication, that one is prepared to believe that their phenomenal world, the world they perceive and remember, is radically different from ours. On the other hand, such helplessness might be quite misleading. It guarantees our care and attention, but perhaps it hides a surprisingly mature perceptual and intellectual competence. Swayed in this direction, I am prepared to believe that the baby must surely see the same world of people and objects that adults see.

Until about 15–20 years ago, there was very little research that could answer the question that I have sketched above: To what extent does the baby perceive the world in the same way as an adult? There was, however, a set of remarkable books by Piaget (Piaget, 1952; 1954) that on the basis of detailed observation of Piaget's own three infants came down firmly in favour of a radical discontinuity. According to Piaget, the baby's universe is fundamentally different from ours in the sense that conceptions that we take for granted—the existence of three-dimensional objects that endure over time even when they cannot be seen—are quite absent from the infant's mind.

Perhaps the most persuasive and intriguing aspect of Piaget's account of infancy is his account of object permanence—the baby's conception of enduring objects. As adults, we assume that an object that we have just seen that is either covered up or moves behind some obstacle, continues to exist and can be found again if we look under the cloth or behind the screen. Piaget claims on the other hand, that young babies have no such conception of an enduring object that can be recovered; they have no idea that the object continues to exist when it leaves their view. Gradually, by dint at first of chance recovery of the object and then more systematic search, the baby comes to abandon this naïve picture of the world and to adopt instead a hypothesis that we adults take for granted, namely that objects can be recovered provided one searches in the right place for them.

An important theme in Piaget's writing is that the world offers only a series of perceptual snapshots to the baby from birth. These snapshots are a rather poor guide to the underlying reality. Consider an object which suddenly disappears from sight. We adults know that this visual loss should not be taken to indicate the annihilation of the object—lift the cover and it is still there. The baby, on the other hand, is misled by the visual loss into thinking that the object is no longer available. Only when the baby is able to explore the world, and reinterpret such misleading experiences will an accurate view of the world be constructed. In this respect, the story of development for Piaget is very much the triumph of thought over perception. Perceptual appearances are not to be trusted and must be reinterpreted in the light of slowly constructed hypotheses about the underlying reality.

To appreciate just how much this epistemological stance imbues Piaget's developmental account, we may look at the writings of James and Eleanor Gibson who have sharply different views about the nature of development. The Gibsons start from the assumption that, for the most part, the way in which the world looks is the way it is. Or to put the point more cautiously, the way the world looks to us is very similar to the way we think it is. Take, for example, the disappearing object which is gradually hidden from view bit by bit as it moves behind a screen; the Gibsons point out that so long as we confine our analysis to the moment of complete disappearance, there is indeed nothing to tell us where the object is nor whether it exists. In this respect, the available perceptual information is at best uninformative, and at worst misleading, as Piaget argues. Yet such a narrow analysis is highly artificial. Just prior to its disappearance, we see the object moving in a particular direction, and we see first its leading edge covered by the screen and then an increasingly large portion of its area covered by the screen until it is totally invisible. Consider, in contrast, what would have happened had the object been annihilated. We would see it one moment, only to see it implode, explode, or instantaneously disappear. This is visibly different from the gradual occlusion that we see during a normal disappearance. So, argue the Gibsons, visible appearances or disappearances are not misleading. Information is available to tell the infant whether and where to search for the disappearing object. Of course, infants may not notice this information or they may notice it and not know what to make of it, but this does not mean that perceptual information is misleading as Piaget argues.

Finally, let us turn to a third position which is being actively pursued by several investigators at the moment, particularly Spelke (1985) and her colleagues. They grant that at any given moment we cannot see what things are really like. In particular, we live in a cluttered environment where one object will conceal another. Consider, for example, what we see when a horse gallops past. At any given moment, part of one leg will obscure our view of part of another leg. Yet we do not hesitate to credit the horse with four complete legs, and indeed we see the moving limbs as belonging to a single animal, although they move to some extent independently from one another. Where does this perception of unity come from? It might be a principle that arises from specifically sensory mechanisms which automatically connect up edges and surfaces that move together in the same direction. Spelke herself favours a different possibility. She argues that the perception of unity results from a conception of objects that the baby is born with and which guides its sensory mechanisms. Whichever possibility is favoured, both assume that the baby imposes a principle of unity on incoming sensory data, the data themselves being too fragmentary and indeterminate to clearly indicate where one object ends and another begins.

Notice that Spelke (1985) agrees in part with both Piaget and the Gibsons but also disagrees with them. So far as Piaget is concerned, she agrees that appearances can be uninformative: We cannot literally see that the horse has four complete legs. She claims that appearances are reinterpreted, however, not by some hypothesis that we laboriously construct in the course of our infancy, but in the light of innate principles, be they sensory or conceptual in origin.

So far as the Gibsons are concerned, she agrees that the perceptual system, even that of the infant, probably produces a useful and valid picture of reality, but she disagrees with the Gibsons as to how that comes about. It is not available—out there—for direct inspection. The visible world is too cluttered to allow such uninterrupted inspection. Gaps have to be filled in by the use of organising principles that are imposed on fragmentary data.

To sum up then, the three positions that I have described disagree about what we might call the problem of missing data. Gibson says there is no such problem. The data are out there if you look hard enough. Piaget says that there is a very real problem but it can be solved by a willingness to invent hypotheses and revise them in the light of one's mistakes. A third group of investigators also say that there is a problem but they think that babies are born with innate principles or rules for filling in missing data.

THE OBJECT HIDDEN BY A SCREEN

We saw in the preceding section that Piaget made two claims about young babies: At first, they do not believe that objects continue to exist when they are covered up; gradually, by exploring the world and by finding objects, they revise this mistaken belief. Piaget made various observations that support these claims. At about 4–5 months, the infant who has been playing with a toy and then seen an adult cover it with a cloth will do very little to recover the object. Even if a portion of the toy is left visible, sticking out from under the cloth, the baby will not lift the cloth. Two or three months later, the infant has progressed: if the object is fully covered, the infant will do nothing, but if it remains partially visible, then the cloth will be removed, and the object recovered. Finally, at about 8–9 months, the baby spontaneously lifts the cloth even if the object is completely covered.

For Piaget, these three stages illustrate the gradual construction of the idea of object permanence by the babies—in the first stage it is entirely absent, in the next stage, a reconstruction of the whole can be imagined on the basis of the parts that are visible, and finally in the third stage, the babies appreciate that the object can be recovered by their actions on the cloth, even if the cloth has rendered it entirely invisible.

Bower (1967) was one of the first investigators to attack this claim. Like the Gibsons, he took as his point of departure the fact that there is a very distinctive pattern of events whenever an object is occluded by a screen: The object's leading edge is covered bit by bit as it moves behind (or underneath) the cover. Babies were presented with disappearances that took place in this standard way. They were also shown various non-standard types of disappearance. For example, using an arrangement of mirrors, Bower was able to present a display in which the object disappeared instantaneously behind the screen rather than gradually. In another display, the object disappeared instantaneously but there was no screen there to occlude it. The results showed that the baby reacted differently when they watched these various types of disappearance as measured by a conditioned response (sucking for a reward). However, these results, interesting though they are, remain inconclusive. They tell us that that baby notices a difference between a standard and a non-standard disappearance, but they do not tell us what the baby believes about the hidden object. In particular, because the baby was not required to search for the disappearing object, they do not show that the baby thinks it continues to exist when it fully disappears behind the screen.

A later and more successful attack on Piaget's claims was made by Kellman and Spelke (1983). They did tackle the thorny but crucial question: When an object or part of an object is invisible does the baby nevertheless assume that it is there? Kellman and Spelke (1983) showed babies of $3\frac{1}{2}$–$4\frac{1}{2}$ months a block of wood behind which they saw a rod moved from side to

Habituation   Display

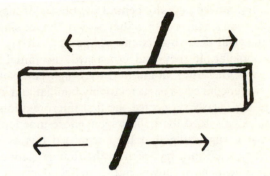

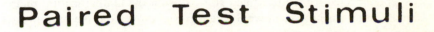

Paired   Test   Stimuli

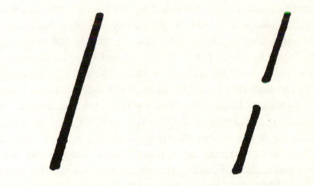

FIG. 1.   Habituation display and paired test stimili used by Kellman and Spelke (1983).

side (see top half of Fig. 1). During this familiarisation phase of the experiment the ends of the rod protruded above and below the block, so that as the rod was moved laterally, these two ends could be seen by the baby moving from side to side, but the middle portion of the rod was invisible being hidden by the block. How did the babies perceive this display: As two unconnected bits of rod that happened to move from side to side at the same time, and at the same speed, or as a single rod connected by an invisible portion? To answer this question Kellman and Spelke subsequently gave the babies two test displays to look at: One consisted of a single complete rod, the other of two unconnected parts, a top part and a bottom part (see bottom half of Fig. 1). They reasoned (on the basis of countless other experiments) that the babies would want to look at the display that appeared relatively different or novel, as compared to what they had been shown immediately before (i.e. the rod moved laterally behind the block). If they had construed this latter display as a single rod, then they would find the single complete rod relatively familiar and the two unconnected parts relatively novel and more interesting to look at. If they had construed the initial display as two unconnected parts, then they would find the single complete rod relatively novel and the two unconnected parts relatively familiar and less interesting to look at. The results clearly supported the first interpretation. When the two test displays were presented the babies spent more time looking at the two unconnected parts, suggesting that they regarded this as the more novel display, relative to what they had seen in the familiarisation phase.

Further experiments have shown that this effect depends on the presence of two critical factors in the familiarisation phase. The rod has to move behind the block; the baby does not seem disposed to perceive the visible parts as connected if they remained static during the familiarisation phase. Second, both parts have to move: If the top part moves and the bottom part remains stationary, again the baby does not seem disposed to perceive them as connected. On the other hand, provided the two parts move in the same direction, it does not seem to matter which direction they move in. Thus, Kellman, Spelke, and Short (1986) have shown that if the rod is moved backwards away from the block (and the baby) and then forwards towards the block (and the baby) a connected rod is seen. The same thing happens if the rod is moved up and down rather than from side to side. This latter demonstration is especially important because it shows that even if the two parts look different (i.e. during a downward motion, the upper visible portion shrinks, as the lower visible portion expands, and vice versa during an upward motion) they are perceived as connected so long as the two parts move in a common direction. Finally, the effect depends on the age of the baby. When Slater, Morison, and Somers (1987) tested new-born babies, they found a preference for the connected rod rather than the two unconnected parts. The implication of these findings is that new-born babies stick fairly rigidly to the visible evidence. They do not fill in the missing parts of the rod when they see it moving behind the block of wood, so that they are surprised to see a complete rod in the final test display, and treat the unconnected parts as familiar.

Overall, these results do not fit neatly into any of the three theoretical positions described earlier. The 4-month-old appears to be adept at filling in the data that are missing in a cluttered environment. For Piaget such filling-in depends on active manual exploration, yet 4-month-olds are quite clumsy in picking up an object, let alone in picking up a cloth so as to retrieve an object underneath it. For the Gibsons such filling in does not occur because the visible environment is usually informative in and of itself, especially when an object is seen to move out of sight. If filling in did not occur, however, we would expect 4-month-old babies to treat the unconnected display as the familiar display in the test phase, in conformity with what they actually saw during the familiarisation period. Recall that they never saw the hidden part of the rod at any point in the experiment, only the two protruding ends. Finally, although the behaviour of the 4-month-olds gives strong support to the suggestions made by Spelke and her colleagues that babies perceive objects in the light of fundamental conceptual principles such as the unity of parts that move together, the fact that new-born babies do not exhibit the filling-in effect, strongly suggests that such principles are not innate.

The results, so far, concern partially occluded objects only. They do not speak to the question of whether young babies acknowledge the continued presence of a completely invisible object. Baillargeon, Spelke, and Wasserman (1985) have recently reported a study which does address that issue. The babies were somewhat older—5 months—but still considerably younger than the age that Piaget thought was necessary to cope with complete invisibility. The babies first watched a screen that started out laying flat on the table and then rotated upwards and backwards like a drawbridge; it continued on through an arc of 180° until it ended up lying flat on the table again. After the baby was thoroughly familiar with this display, it saw one of two different test displays: the same 180° rotation, or a truncated version of the original movement, i.e. a 120° rotation. Under normal circumstances we would expect the baby to look more at the relatively novel, truncated movement, and less at the relatively familiar 180° movement.

However, between the familiarisation phase of the experiment and the test phase, the babies saw the experimenter place a block behind the screen in the location where it would usually end up after its 180° rotation. The block was solid and should effectively have prevented the screen or drawbridge travelling through its full arc: In fact, the screen would be forced to stop its movement at about 120°. If babies appreciate that the block remains in position and constitutes an impassable obstacle, even when the screen has been raised so as to hide it from view, they should be surprised at the full "impossible" 180° rotation, and relatively unperturbed by the truncated 120° rotation (see Fig. 2).

This was, in fact, the result that was obtained. The babies spent more time watching the "impossible" complete 180° rotation even though they had seen it several times before, during the familiarisation phase, as compared to the 120° rotation, suggesting that they were puzzled about how the screen could pass through a solid obstacle. One possible alternative to this interpretation is that the babies were not thinking about the block at all, they were concentrating on the moving screen and, not surprisingly therefore, spending

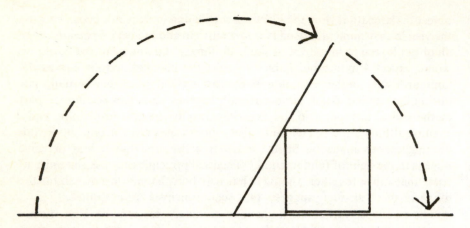

FIG. 2.   Side-view of rotating screen with wooden block preventing full 180° rotation, as used by Baillargeon, Spelke, and Wasserman (1985).

more time watching it if it travelled through a longer arc. To check this interpretation, Baillargeon and her colleagues used a control condition, in which the block was placed to one side of the rotating screen, out of its path, and fully visible throughout. Under these circumstances the infants looked at the screen for an equally long time whether it rotated through 180° or 120°.

These results go a good deal further than those reported earlier. First, the baby's acknowledgement of the continued presence of the invisible block does not depend upon its movement. Movement seemed to be crucial, it will be remembered, to the results described above by Kellman and his colleagues. Second, the baby is acknowledging the continued presence of an object that is completely invisible, not just one that is partially visible. Third, and perhaps most surprising of all, the baby appears to appreciate not just that the block remains behind the rotating screen but that its solid presence in a particular position constitutes an obstacle to the screen.

Baillargeon (1986) reports some further results which are just as surprising. In this study, the critical comparison was again between a possible event and an impossible event. Babies aged 6 and 8 months first saw a toy car roll down a hill and continue along a flat track, disappearing momentarily behind a screen standing in front of part of the track. Once they had seen this event several times and become used to it, the screen was lifted so that the entire track was visible. A box was placed either on top of the track, or beside it. The screen was then lowered so that the box was invisible, but babies with object permanence ought presumably to remember that it was still there, and conceivably might also remember its position, particularly whether it was on top of the track or beside it. The car rolled down the hill once more and continued along the track, again disappearing momentarily behind the screen. The babies tended to be more surprised (looked longer) at the movement of the car when the box had been placed on top of the track rather than beside it suggesting that they were puzzled, just as you or I might be, about how the car had managed to continue along the track, apparently unimpeded by the box standing on the track. Such puzzlement implies that the infants could understand that: (1) the box continued to exist, and remained on top of the track; (2) that the car continued to exist and would continue along the track even when it was invisible behind the screen; and (3) that the car could not travel through the box.

The experiments carried out by Baillargeon and her colleagues are clever and ingenious, but they are also complicated. A fairly lengthy chain of linked assumptions—three in the formulation that I have set out above—is needed to interpret the baby's puzzlement. It is reassuring, therefore, to find support for Baillargeon's claims in a different laboratory, using relatively simple techniques. Hood and Willatts (1986) presented 5-month-old babies with an object either to their left or right. They were restrained from reaching for it until the room lights had gone off, and the object was invisible. Nevertheless, the babies reached out in the dark and they reached more to the appropriate side (where the object had been seen), as compared to the wrong side.

These experiments with completely invisible objects provide a major challenge to Piaget's account. They strongly suggest that 5- to 6-month-old infants can both understand and remember the continued existence and indeed the location of a hidden object. To what extent do the experiments provide support for the position adopted by the Gibsons or by Spelke and her colleagues? The Gibsons emphasise the richness of perceptual information and the fact that it is rarely misleading. However, if we examine the set-up used by Baillargeon and her colleagues, it is the paucity of visible information that is striking. The baby can admittedly see a difference between a box that sits on top of the track and one that sits beside it, but for the baby to show puzzlement in the former case some additional complicated assumptions must be made by the baby about invisible solid obstacles. The baby seems to be exhibiting some understanding of the underlying physics that govern the situation, not attuning to visible information. Nor can the recent results be easily explained by the notion that infants fill in missing data by means of some automatic perceptual process that unifies moving parts into a coherent whole. Whether the baby is puzzling over a movement through a hidden block or box, or reaching for an object in the dark, there are no moving parts of the object that are visible. At present, then, it looks as if babies do understand object permanence several months earlier than Piaget suggested. It is too early to say whether we should adopt the position favoured by Spelke (1985), namely that babies begin life with a conception of the underlying unity and persistence of objects, but certainly recent experiments have shown that such a conception is available quite early in the first year.

SEARCH UNDER A CLOTH

As I noted earlier, the baby searches for an object that is completely hidden by a cloth at about 8–9 months. Even at this point, however, the baby continues to search inaccurately. For example, if the experimenter hides the object two or three times under the same cloth A and then on the next trial hides the object under a different cloth B, the baby often makes what Piaget (1954) regarded as a very revealing error: The baby watches as the object is being hidden under the new cloth B but once it has disappeared, turns away, and searches at the cloth where the object was hidden on the initial trials, apparently expecting to find the object there. Occasionally, the baby will correctly approach the new cloth, but if the object is not immediately discovered there will promptly revert back to the old cloth. This type of perseverative error has come to be called the AB̄ error (i.e. A not B error).

Piaget's explanation of these errors is to deny that the baby has a full understanding of permanence even at 9 months of age. The baby will certainly look underneath a cloth and presumably expects to find the object there, but this does not show that the baby thinks of the object as enduring throughout its invisibility, according to Piaget. The baby might think that the object comes back into existence when the cloth is lifted. In fact, Piaget puts forward precisely this interpretation. He argues that the baby egocentrically believes that it is the action of lifting the cloth which brings the object back into existence. Accordingly, when the object is shifted to a new location, there is no need to alter the response. The object is thought to remain at the disposal of the first response and so this is simply repeated. Such egocentric responding is, according to Piaget, the result of the baby's discovery that certain actions such as turning to look in a particular direction or groping in a given place, have the result of bringing an object which has just disappeared back into view. Such actions are repeated and extended without the baby fully appreciating how they actually succeed in restoring the object to visibility. Search for an object that is fully hidden by a cloth is simply an extension of such actions and should not be interpreted, according to Piaget, as reflecting any full belief in permanence.

The results described earlier obviously call this entire account into question. It certainly looks as if babies of 8–9 months have two fundamental ideas: If an object is partially occluded, assume nevertheless that its visible parts are connected up; if an object is fully occluded, assume nevertheless that it can remain an obstacle to other objects. The availability of these ideas from about 5 months is scarcely compatible with Piaget's claim that the baby has no idea of object permanence at 5 months, and even lacks a full understanding at 9 months.

If we accept that the baby already understands object permanence at 5 months, however, we still have to explain why the baby makes perseverative errors. After all, the baby's accurate search at A clearly shows that it has the necessary motor and conceptual skills to make things visible. Why should it make a mistake at B, where presumably exactly the same skills are needed? Indeed, in trying to explain this puzzling asymmetry between accurate search on A trials and perseverative search on B trials, investigators, including myself, have taken various twists and turns.

A reasonable starting point is an experiment that I carried out several years ago, which suggested that it might be harder for the baby to remember the hiding of an object on B trials as compared to A trials (Harris, 1973). Infants were required to search at A several times and then at B, in the manner described by Piaget. On B trials, however, the infants were sometimes permitted to search straight away, as soon as the object was covered at B; and they were sometimes made to wait by their mothers who restrained them from reaching forward for 5 seconds. The results were quite clear. Babies who were allowed to search immediately at B did not go back to A, despite what Piaget predicted, whereas those who were made to wait often did so. My interpretation was as follows: The baby sees and understands that the object is underneath B; if the baby can search immediately there is no difficulty in remembering that information, and search at B is executed accurately. Memory for this new hiding-place, however, is fragile; so fragile, in fact, that if the baby is made to wait and happens to catch sight of A, the new information is disrupted and replaced by the information that was stored on the earlier A trials, i.e. that the object is at A. In short, the baby is vulnerable to what is called proactive interference in memory: The displacement of new information by old information. This interpretation was attractive because it allowed one to argue that babies understand object permanence on the one hand but to explain how they might also get into a muddle in trying to find an object on B trials. It is still an attractive line of explanation because it is compatible with all the evidence I reported in the previous section.

I abandoned it, however, because of some later findings. Butterworth (1977) asked what would happen if the opaque covers at A and B were replaced by transparent covers so that the object could be covered but remain visible. He found that perseverative errors to A still occurred even though the object was visible at B. This result was very difficult to explain in terms of a memory deficit. If the object is visible at B, the baby does not have to remember where it is, so why does the baby turn away and search at A? There is a possible line of defence for the memory-based interpretation. Let us suppose that the baby watches as the object is placed underneath or behind a transparent cover at B. As in the experiment reported earlier, the baby is made to wait for a few seconds before being allowed to search. Conceivably, during this short wait, the baby turns away from B, looks around, and effectively renders the object temporarily invisible. At this point, a memory problem could arise, especially if the baby caught sight of A and was reminded of previous trials. Some further work was carried out to evaluate this possibility (Harris, 1974). Babies were tested with transparent doors, as in the study by Butterworth (1977), but two changes were made. First, they were not made to wait even on B trials, but second, the covers at A and B were fixed in positions so that they could not be moved. As expected, because there was no delay, the majority of the infants approached B correctly when the object was placed there. They found, however, that the cover at B could not be moved, and the object could not be retrieved. At that point, many of the infants turned away from B, even though the object was visible there, and immediately searched at A even though A was visibly empty. These results strongly suggest that whatever the problem is, it is not a memory problem because the infants had noted and approached the object located at B. It looked, instead, as if Piaget was partially right: They really did think that the act of searching at A would render an otherwise unattainable object attainable. Nor could the results be attributed to some diffuse reaction to frustration. A control group of infants saw the object placed at A, but when they failed to move the cover at A, which was also fixed in position, they almost never turned away from A to search at B.

These findings strongly suggested that a memory-based explanation was a dead-end. I retreated back to a more conceptually-oriented explanation. Like Piaget, I concluded that the baby did have a naïve and incorrect understanding of objects. However, whereas he had focused on the baby's apparent difficulties with disappearance and permanence, I suggested instead that the baby did not understand the movement of an object from an old place to a new place (Harris, 1975; 1983). As adults, when we see such a movement we realise immediately that because the object can only be in one place at a time it can no longer be in the old place. Suppose, however, that babies of 8 or 9 months do not realise that an object can only be in one place at a time. When they see the object shifted to B they will fail to delete A as a possible location for the object. They will search at A or B depending on how salient or negotiable each location happens to be in a given experiment. For example, if they are allowed to search straightaway at B, while they are still staring at it after seeing the object hidden there, they will search correctly at B. If they are frustrated at B, or turn away from it during an enforced delay, then they are likely to spot A and search there. This interpretation, like the memory difficulty hypothesis, is compatible with the idea that babies understand the concealment or occlusion of an object at a single location. It implies that the infant's difficulty only arises when it tries to keep track of an object that moved from one location to another.

Recently, however, an experiment has been published which suggests that the idea of some sort of difficulty in processing information, possibly a vulnerability to proactive interference, remains a useful one, whereas an interpretation that is exclusively couched in terms of the baby's conceptual *naïveté* is almost certainly inadequate. This is just one example of the unexpected twists that research on object permanence has taken. The experiment in question was a longitudinal study of infants from 7–12 months carried out by Diamond (1985). She used several criteria to define an AB̄ error pattern: The infant had to make more than one error in the session but to make no more than a single error on A trials. The delay level needed to elicit this pattern steadily increased between 7 and 12 months. A delay of approximately 3 seconds was required at 8 months and of approximately 10 seconds at 12 months. In fact, the duration of delay necessary for error increased continuously by about 2 seconds per month. If delays were shorter than the appropriate level for the AB̄ error, the babies tended to produce accurate performance at both A and B, whereas if they were longer, they tended to produce errors at both A and B. So the AB̄ pattern appears to mark an intermediate level of performance, one which is partially but not wholly accurate.

These very orderly data create a problem for any purely conceptual or cognitive interpretation. Consider, for example, the idea I proposed earlier, namely that the infant does not appreciate that an object can be in only one place at a time, and fails to rule out A as a possible hiding place. Are we to say that the 8-month-old baby can rule out A for 3 seconds but no longer, the 9-month-old for 5 seconds but no longer, and so forth? If the baby has come to understand that an object can only be in one place, why does it not apply this knowledge to delays of any length? Of course, one could begin to elaborate the conceptual deficiency I have proposed. One could suppose that the new information about B does not delete the old information about A, but rather that it exceeds it in strength for a period that increases in length with age. Yet as soon as we talk in these terms, we are beginning to talk about the efficiency with which the baby processes information, rather than simply proposing conceptual rules that the baby either understands or does not understand. We are admitting, at the very least, that a purely conceptual interpretation will not work.

Diamond herself has proposed an interpretation that relies neither on conceptual nor on memory difficulties. Her idea is a very intriguing one and it boils down to the suggestion that babies sometimes err through sheer force of habit even when they know better. She argues that B trials set up a competition between two potential guidelines for action. On the one hand, there is information about the new hiding at B which is presumably stored in some type of short-term memory. On the other hand, there is the habit (which hitherto has led to success) of going to A. If the new information about B has to be held in short-term memory for too long, it is not strong enough to override the habit of going to A and perseveration occurs.

In some respects, this interpretation echoes the earlier notion of proactive interference which also postulated competition between old and new information. However, Diamond introduces a crucial and distinct idea, namely that the new information about B is not forgotten or lost in the face of the old information. Rather, it remains available but loses its ability to guide the motor system. The implication of this claim is that babies may perseverate even when they remember that the object is hidden at B. Evidence for this claim comes from Webb, Massar, and Nadolny (1972) who found that given an opportunity babies could correct themselves after an error. Thus they would first approach A, and then correct themselves by going to B, ignoring a third empty location such as C. This interpretation is also compatible with the finding that babies perseverate even when the object is visible at B, especially if they approach the cover at B, and find that it cannot be removed. The visible information about the new location may quickly lose its power to guide action, and perseverative reaching toward A ensues.

In summary, Diamond's ideas suggest that the idea of proactive interference is not such a dead end after all. True, we cannot postulate proactive interference in memory, but competition between old and new information certainly seems a vital element in any explanation of perseverative errors. A final experiment by Horobin and Acredolo (1986) suggests, however, that Diamond's explanation is still not completely adequate. They compared three different tasks: A so-called close-pair task in which A and B were placed quite close together in the usual way; a far-pair task in which A and B were placed at a considerable distance from one another; and a six-location task in which A and B were again placed far apart but four other hiding places identical in appearance to A and B were arranged in a line between A and B. The results were quite clear cut: Very few errors occurred in the far-pair condition. When A was close to B (as in the close-pair task) or when hiding-places resembling A were close to B (as in the six-location task), errors were much more frequent. This result is obviously difficult for Diamond (1985) to explain. Why should the habit of returning to A be any less potent if A is at some distance from B?

The following explanation borrows concepts freely but even-handedly from the various investigators whose results have been described. The explanation rests on two mechanisms. First, there is a mechanism for the long-term coding of spatial position. Such coding specifies those positions where the object has reappeared in a more less distinctive, but not an exclusive, fashion. Thus, once the object has reappeared at A, information about A is stored in long-term memory. The same happens for B, once the object has reappeared there, but long-term memory for B does not preclude long-term memory for A. Thus, when the object moves from A to B, the baby does not delete A from memory. The other mechanism is a short-term store which holds information about the direction in which an object was most recently seen. This memory provides for a short period only a point of focus for the baby's postural system. So long as it lasts it can guide the baby's fixation or re-fixation of the B location. In addition to these two storage systems, we may make one further developmental assumption: The short-term store, which guides the baby's posture, lasts longer in older babies.

The AB̄ error can now be explained as follows. When the object disappears for the first time at A, the short-term memory for the object's most recent visible location keeps the baby oriented toward A. If the object is successfully found on the first A trial, this information about A is entered into long-term memory. Search at A will usually be accurate on A trials. On the first A trial, the baby must rely on the short-term store, but there is no competitive long-term memory if that fades. On subsequent A trials, the baby can rely on either short- or long-term memory for A.

On the first B trial, the B location is initially registered in the short-term store only. The object has not yet reappeared at B, so there is no information about B in long-term store. Nevertheless, the short-term memory ensures that, for a brief period, the baby will remain oriented to B; during this brief period, there will be few reminders of A and little competition between A and B. If, however, the baby turns away from B there is an increased likelihood of seeing A, retrieving information about A from long-term memory, and searching there. This will happen if the delay is increased so that the short-term memory no longer guides the baby's orientation. This analysis makes the following predictions: So long as the infant remains oriented to B, search will be accurately directed toward B (Diamond, 1985; Horobin and Acre-dolo, 1986). If the delay is increased, the chance of turning away from B, seeing A and searching at A is increased (Diamond, 1985; Gratch et al., 1974; Harris, 1973). Indeed, at long delay intervals the infant should rely more or less exclusively on long-term memory, and search predominantly at A. The length of delay needed to produce this latter effect is longer in older babies (Diamond, 1985); if the baby is frustrated at B, for example by finding it impossible to move the cover there or find the object, then it will again be likely to turn away from B, notice A and search there (Harris, 1974); if, however, A is placed at some distance from B, it will rarely be noticed, and perseveration will be unlikely (Horobin and Acredolo, 1986); once the short-term memory has ceased to control the baby's direction of gaze, and the infant is forced to rely on long-term memory, locations that look like A will attract search depending on the probability of their being seen, which will in turn depend on their distance from B. Thus, locations close to B that look like A may attract more errors than A itself (Bjork and Cummings, 1984; Horobin and Acredolo, 1986).

This explanation obviously draws on concepts that have been advanced by other investigators. Following my earlier proposals (Harris, 1983) the explanation assumes that infants lack any kind of conceptual rule to indicate that A and B are mutually exclusive alternatives. As distinct from that account however, a temporary instruction is postulated, that keeps the baby oriented toward B to the exclusion of A for increasingly longer periods with age. In line with the proposal made by Diamond (1985) it is assumed that both short- and long-term information is available but whereas Diamond envisaged competition between a short-term information and a conditioned habit for control of the motor system, the present account assumes that short-term information temporarily inhibits retrieval from long-term memory by influencing the postural orientation of the baby: Short-term information does not compete directly with long-term memory for control of the motor system.

One test of any new account is the extent to which it leads to novel predictions. The account developed above makes several predictions about changes in the baby's postural orientation during the delay period following an A or B hiding. The probability of looking away will increase as the delay length increases. The probability will increase more rapidly for younger babies than older babies; and it will increase with equal rapidity for A and B trials. Diamond (1986) would make the first two predictions but not the third, because previous habits should intrude on B hidings but not A hidings, particularly as the delay increases.

This line of explanation can also be extended to other difficulties that babies of 6–12 months show in retrieving objects. Diamond (1988) describes how babies below 8 months try to reach directly, along the line of sight, for an object placed in a Perspex (Plexiglass) box. They repeatedly strike the top of the box rather than reaching through an opening at the side or front. Somewhat older babies can adopt the strategy of first looking down or from the side in order to see the object through the opening; they then return to their normal upright viewing position, and reach through the opening rather than along their line of sight. This development can be explained by postulating that the younger infants have no short-memory for the location of the object as seen through the opening, so that they reach exclusively along their line of sight. Older babies can retain such short-term information and use it to guide their reaching; they do not need to rely on the directional information that is provided by the object when they assume their normal posture.

In the above sections, I have deliberately concentrated on a small number of studies which have been especially influential for my own thinking about the AB̄ error. There are a large number of studies that I have ignored. Does this mean that a biased picture has been presented, one that highlights variables that may appear important in one study but prove less important in other studies? It is rarely the case in developmental psychology that one can answer questions about bias. Fortunately, in the case of the AB̄ error, a quantitative answer is available. Wellman and his colleagues have carried out a meta-analysis by pooling a large number of studies of the AB̄ error to find out which variables have a measurable effect on the proportion of babies who perseverate to A (Wellman, Cross, & Bartsch, 1986). In general, their survey confirms the picture presented above. They find that the probability of perseverative error increases with longer delays. Thus, at delays of 3–5 seconds, 9-month-old babies make significantly more errors to A than would be expected by chance. Second, the probability of perseveration declines with age. Third, a single A trial is just as likely to elicit perseveration as several A trials. This pattern of results can be easily explained by the proposals made earlier: At longer intervals the baby is no longer guided by information in short-term store about the object's most recent location, but by long-term information about where the object has been previously found. Such short-term information lasts longer in older babies so that perseveration is avoided. Finally, assuming that a single successful trial at A is needed to enter information about A in long-term memory, it is not surprising that more trials at A do not increase perseveration.

In one respect, the meta-analysis does not fit the picture I have presented. Wellman and his colleagues report that correct search at B is more probable, not when A and B are widely separated as I have argued, but when the space between A and B is occupied by additional hiding places. So, for example, if there are 5 hiding places as opposed to two, search at B will be more accurate. However, this conclusion appears to emerge only when several studies are pooled (Harris, 1986). When individual studies are examined (Bjork & Cummings, 1984; Horobin & Acredolo, 1986), the number of correct searches at B increases if A is placed at a distance from B, but not if there are several other hiding places close by. The exact role of distance and number of hiding places clearly needs more research.

CONCLUSIONS

At the beginning of the Chapter, I asked whether the young baby perceives a fundamentally different universe from the one that we perceive as adults. The evidence is beginning to suggest that babies may share some of our basic convictions from an early age. By 4–5 months, they see objects as unified even when parts of them are hidden, and as continuing to exist even when they are entirely hidden. In this respect, the baby is much more sophisticated than Piaget (1954) admitted. Still, the baby does exhibit some puzzling and intriguing difficulties. In particular, the baby gets muddled when an object is hidden first in one and then in a second hiding place. A possible explanation for this difficulty is that the baby starts off in life with a fairly sophisticated perceptual apparatus for dealing with the world as it appears right now, and also with a long-term memory for remembering places where objects have been previously found, but it is not equipped for dealing with short-term shifts in object position. Since objects are typically located either where they can be seen or where they were last found, the baby's problem only occasionally shows itself.

REFERENCES

Baillargeon, R. (1986). Representing the existence and the location of hidden objects: Object permanence in 6- and 8-month-old infants. *Cognition*, *23*, 21–41.

Baillargeon, R., Spelke, E. S., & Wasserman, S. (1985). Object permanence in 5-month-old infants. *Cognition*, *20*, 191–208.

Bjork, E. L. & Cummings, E. M. (1984). Infant search errors: Stage of concept development or stage of memory development? *Memory and Cognition*, *12*, 1–19.

Bower, T. G. R. (1967). The development of object permanence: some studies of existence constancy. *Perception and Psychophysics*, *2*, 411–418.

Butterworth, G. E. (1977). Object disappearance and error in Piaget's stage IV task. *Journal of Experimental Child Psychology*, *23*, 391–401.

Diamond, A. (1985). Development of the ability to use recall to guide action, as indicated by infants' performance on AB. *Child Development*, *56*, 868–883.

Diamond, A. (1988). Differences between adult and infant cognition: Is the crucial variable presence or absence of language? In L. Weiskrantz (ed.), *Thought without language*. Oxford: Oxford University Press.

Gratch, G., Appel, K. J., Evans, W. F., LeCompte, G. K., & Wright, N. A. (1974). Piaget's Stage IV object concept error: Evidence of forgetting or object conception? *Child Development*, *42*, 359–372.

Harris, P. L. (1973). Perseverative errors in search by young children. *Child Development*, *44*, 28–33.

Harris, P. L. (1974). Perseverative search at a visibly empty place by young infants. *Journal of Experimental Child Psychology*, *18*, 535–542.

Harris, P. L. (1975). Development of search and object permanence during infancy. *Psychological Bulletin*, *82*, 332–344.

Harris, P. L. (1983). Infant cognition. In P. H. Mussen (ed.), *Handbook of child psychology* (4th ed., Vol. 2), New York: Wiley.

Harris, P. L. (1986). Bringing order to the A-not-B error. *Society for Research in Child Development Monographs*, *51* (3, Serial No 214).

Hood, B. & Willatts, P. (1986). Reaching in the dark to an object's remembered position: Evidence for object-permanence in 5-month-old infants. *British Journal of Developmental Psychology*, *4*, 57–66.

Horobin, K. & Acredolo, L. (1986). The role of attentiveness, mobility history, and separation of hiding sites on stage IV search behavior. *Journal of Experimental Child Psychology*, *41*, 114–127.

Kellman, P. J. & Spelke, E. R. (1983). Perception of partly occluded objects in infancy. *Cognitive Psychology*, *15*, 483–524.

Kellman, P. J., Spelke, E. R., & Short, K. R. (1986). Infant perception of object unity from translatory motion in depth and vertical translation. *Child Development*, *57*, 72–86.

Piaget, J. (1952). *The origins of intelligence in children*. New York: International University Press.

Piaget, J. (1954). *The construction of reality in the child*. New York: Basic Books.

Spelke, E. S. (1985). Perception of unity, persistence, and Identity: Thoughts on infants' conceptions of objects. In J. Mehler and R. Fox (eds), *Neonate cognition: Beyond the blooming, buzzing confusion*. London: Lawrence Erlbaum Associates Ltd.

Slater, A., Morison, V., & Somers, M. (1987). Infants' understanding of objects. Paper presented at the British Psychological Society Developmental Section Meeting, York, 11–14 September.

Webb, R. A., Massar, B., & Nadolny, I. (1972). Information and strategy in the young child's search for hidden objects. *Child Development*, *43*, 91–104.

Wellman, H. M., Cross, D., & Bartsch, K. (1986). A meta-analysis of research on stage 4 object permanence: The A-not-B error. *Society for Research in Child Development Monographs, 51* (3, Serial No 214).

6 Development of Spatial Awareness in Infancy

Gavin Bremner

University of Lancaster,
Department of Psychology,
Bailrigg,
Lancaster LA1 4YF

INTRODUCTION: PIAGET, OBJECTS AND SPACE

It would be quite easy to borrow most of the phenomena discussed by Paul Harris in the previous chapter, and use them as indicators of the quality of infants' spatial awareness. A full knowledge of object permanence involves not just the knowledge that an object continues to exist, but that it exists as a physical body in a place defined in terms of spatial relationships to other physical bodies. In particular, the infant needs to be able to understand the relationship between hidden object and occluder in order to understand the spatial principles that allow it both to exist in a known place and not be visible.

This is very much the rationale behind Piaget's approach. In *The Construction of Reality in the Child* (1954), he writes in successive chapters about the infant's concepts of objects, space, causality, and time. But instead of using different phenomena to illuminate development in each of these areas, he economically re-uses the evidence from prior chapters, simply re-interpreting it in terms of its implications for the new conceptual domain. Prime examples are the object search phenomena on which Piaget hangs much of his account of the development of object permanence. The onset of object search is indication of an important step forward in the development of permanence, but it can also be interpreted in spatial terms. This is not just a matter of good empirical fortune, since Piaget sees the two concepts as inseparably linked. As he puts it (1954, p. 98): "Space . . . is not at all perceived as a container but rather as that which it contains, that is, objects themselves." More specifically, he claims that infants only begin to be aware of object permanence once they start to understand spatial relationships in an objective fashion. Prior to the onset of search, infants understand relations between specific objects and self (that is, in *egocentric* terms), but have no understanding of relationships between objects. The onset of search is taken as evidence for the beginning of understanding of inter-object relationships, a step that carries with it the beginnings of knowledge that objects are enduring solid forms that exist in an external space.

These claims relate to the general theme of infantile egocentrism which runs through Piaget's writing. Infants are born with no awareness of the distinction between self and surrounding world, and a major part of their developmental task is the construction of an objective world in which they are themselves situated like every other object. It is often assumed that the implication here is that infants are aware of self and nothing else, however Piaget argues that they are neither aware of self *nor* external reality; they are only aware of a set of sensations or "pictures" that accompany action. Only as early concepts are constructed does egocentrism gradually wane as these images begin to act as indicators of an objective reality separate from the sensations themselves. Even once this process is well advanced, the self is maintained as a sort of spatial "centre of the universe", and a full awareness of self as an object situated within external reality comes as the final step in sensory-motor development.

Given the evidence on early perception reviewed in some of the earlier chapters of this book, the reader should be rightly sceptical about some of Piaget's more pessimistic claims about the young infant's state of awareness. Many workers now claim that perception of the world is objective from the very beginning, marshalling an impressive array of evidence in their support, findings that at very least call for important modifications to the starting-points of his theory. But I want to lay aside questions about Piaget's theory until later in the chapter. First we need to look at ways of diagnosing spatial awareness in infancy, and whatever we may decide about his theory, Piaget's observations provide a rich source of methodology that it would be perverse to overlook as a possible starting point. Indeed, modified versions of his object search tasks have been widely used to test the infant's spatial ability.

POSITION CODING AND SPATIAL ORIENTATION

Using Search for Objects as a Measure

I have already noted how Piaget interprets the onset of search during stage IV as indication that infants' spatial coding is no longer entirely self-related: They are beginning to relate objects to each other (in this case, hidden object and occluder) and not just *egocentrically* in relation to self. In addition, there is the peculiar search error of this stage, in which infants search successfully for an object until it is moved to a new location, whereupon they search again at the old location. In this case, the infant has no problem searching; the error concerns the place of search, and this fact has led some workers to seek a spatial basis for the phenomenon. For instance, Butterworth, Jarrett, and Hicks (1982) argue that infants have problems in updating their spatial coding of the object's position as it moves, and consequently fail to recognise its identity over the move (for a fuller review of this literature, see Bremner, 1985).

My view some years back was that although we had to reserve judgement on the reason for the error, it was a convenient phenomenon on which to base investigation of the infant's methods of coding space (Bremner, 1980). Given that 9-month-old infants show a marked tendency to search at only one place, it seemed possible to manipulate the task in ways that would allow us to find out how they defined that place. Returning to the issue of egocentrism, we asked whether infants coded positions egocentrically, in relation to self, or whether they used some form of external coding, relating its position to landmarks in the surrounding space (Bremner & Bryant, 1977; Bremner, 1978a). There were no clear indicators on this from Piaget' work, since although he stressed the egocentric nature of young infant's notions of space, he also noted that the onset of search marked the beginning of non-egocentric coding of inter-object relationships.

The problem with the conventional stage IV task is that an object consistently hidden in a fixed place relative to the infant is also hidden in a fixed place relative to all other stable external reference systems that the infant might use. In other words, self-referent and external systems are confounded, a situation which is only resolved by moving the infant to a new location during the task. As Fig. 1 shows, if the infant is moved to the opposide side of an array consisting of two hiding locations, the position say to the left of the infant becomes the opposite position within the external space. Bremner and Bryant (1977) employed this technique, starting with the usual series of search trials at one place, but moving the infant to the opposite side of the table before recommencing search trials, either at the same place on the table (and hence at the opposite side relative to the infant) or at the opposite position on the table (and hence at the same place relative to the infant). The results were very clear. Despite the fact that the two positions were clearly differentiated, lying on different backgrounds, infants, once moved, showed a strong tendency to search at the same position relative to self as had been correct prior to the move.

This suggested that 9-month-olds had little or no ability to define positions relative to external referents. However, it still seemed possible that they might perform differently if stronger position cues were supplied. In a

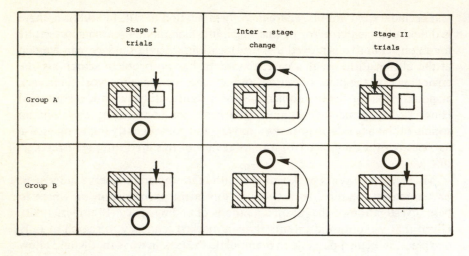

	Stage I trials	Inter - stage change	Stage II trials
Group A			
Group B			

↓ -- object position   ◯ -- infant

FIG. 1.   The task used by Bremner and Bryant (1977) to separate self-referent and external codings of position.

follow-up (Bremner, 1978a) I repeated the study, this time using differently coloured covers instead of different backgrounds. This minor alteration led to a dramatic change in performance; infants in this study searched correctly after movement, wherever the object was hidden.

This result certainly indicated that infants were capable of using external position cues, provided they were strong enough, but it also yielded an interpretative problem. Provision of stronger cues did not simply lead to a shift from self-referent to external coding of position, since this would have led to a reversal in the error pattern, with infants only searching correctly after the move when the object was hidden under the same cover as before (and hence in the opposite position relative to self). But infants made few errors under either condition. In other words, they were no longer making the search error on which the spatial analysis depended. The conclusion was that a new task was needed, one that would yield less ambiguous indications about the infant's spatial coding. The problem with the modified stage IV task was that infants could use information from prior to movement or information following movement to decide where to search, and the cover cue study indicated that we could not rely on the assumption that they did not use the latter information. The solution was to adapt the task further, this time hiding the object but preventing search until after the infant had been moved to the new location. In order to make the movement with minimal distraction, a turntable was constructed so that the infant could be smoothly rotated to the opposite side of the table.

This study (Bremner, 1978b) was run under two cue conditions, background differentiation and cover differentiation. In addition, comparable conditions were run in which the table rather than the infant was rotated after the object had been hidden (see Fig. 2). Two clear effects emerged. Once again, performance was better when cover cues were used. But also, performance was better in infant-rotation conditions than in table-rotation conditions. This second finding confirmed results from the earlier studies, in which table-rotation conditions were included, and was something of a surprise in light of the fact that rotation of the infant was often a source of distraction.

There are two ways in which infants might have succeeded at this task. Either they might have used the available cues as a means of defining the

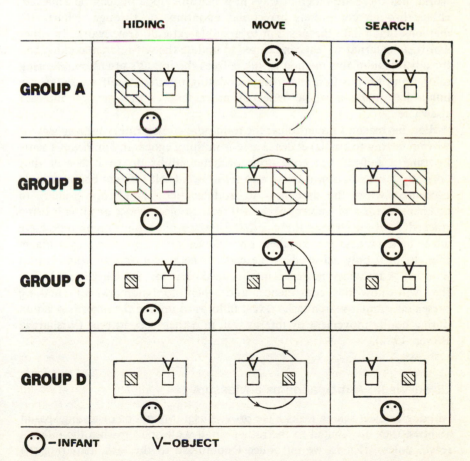

FIG. 2.   The conditions used by Bremner (1978b) to investigate infants' position coding.

place at which the object had disappeared (e.g. as "under the black cover"), or they might have used these cues as an aid to fixation of the location as they moved around. The second alternative seemed likely, since it was those infants who successfully fixated the correct location during the full movement that were more likely to search correctly. So maybe rather than invoking a different method of position coding, these cues acted as aids for the infant in updating a self-referent coding during movement.

Here we can see a reformulation of the question taking place in the light of new findings. Initially the issue was whether infants used self-referent or external spatial systems. Now it has more to do with whether they are capable of updating their self-referent definition of a position during a movement. Indeed, if we think it through, a self-referent coding of position is always a necessary part of maintaining the relationship between self and world. But there are different ways in which this updating can be achieved, either through continuous perceptual updating, or through "short-cut" methods that relate the position to a stable external framework. In other words, an external system can be used to update the self-referent coding, and the advantage of this method is that it frees the infant's attention, allowing relocation of a position and instant updating relative to self even after the infant has made a whole series of movements with attention directed elsewhere.

For this reason I prefer to use the term *self-referent* rather than *egocentric* when referring to spatial codes. There is nothing egocentric in Piaget's sense in using a self-referent code appropriately; adults do so whenever they correctly locate an object relative to self. Use of self-referent coding is only egocentric when the user fails to update the coding appropriately to compensate for a movement of the self or the object whose position is being tracked. And the striking thing is that 9-month-old infants seem to be quite adept at compensating for their own movements, something that Piaget thought they only achieved at the end of the sensory-motor stage (18–24 months). Admittedly, however, infants need very obvious spatial cues before they will show this competence, and when no landmarks or cues are presented, similar search tasks reveal failures to update the object's position during bodily movement by infants well into their second year (Wishart & Bower, 1982).

Using Visual Anticipation as a Measure

Although object search tasks have proved useful methods of testing spatial abilities, they are limited to the rather small-scale space within the infant's reach, unless, that is, we introduce locomotion to the task, requiring the infant to crawl or walk to find the object. This would be a reasonable strategy, but has the limitation that only infants of crawling age can be tested. As we shall see, the onset of crawling may itself be an important factor in development of spatial abilities, so it is important to be able to test infants both before and after they begin to crawl.

The solution to this problem came from Acredolo (1978) who developed an ingenious method for testing infant's orientation within a room-sized space. The procedure is illustrated in Fig. 3. Instead of manual search, she used visual anticipation as her dependent measure. Infants were trained to anticipate the appearance of an experimenter at one of two windows in the walls to their left and right. On each trial, a central buzzer was sounded, followed by the appearance of the experimenter at the chosen window. These trials were continued until the infant reliably anticipated the event with a head turn to the correct window, whereupon the infant was moved around to the opposite side of the room, facing in the opposite direction. Then the crucial trial followed; the buzzer was sounded again and the infant's response was measured. If infants had updated the location during their movement they should turn in the opposite direction to locate the correct window, whereas if they had failed to do this they should make the same direction of head turn as before, locating the wrong window in the process.

Acredolo presented this task to 6-, 11- and 16-month-olds under two conditions. In the "landmark" condition a large star surrounded the correct window, whereas in the "no-landmark" condition no features were provided to differentiate the windows. At 6 months the majority of infants in both conditions failed to update, responding to the same self-referent position as prior to the move. The same happened with the 11-month-olds in the "no-landmark" condition, but at this age only half of the infants in the "landmark" condition made an error. So here we seem to have a result in keeping with my findings with 9-month-olds in search tasks, that is, reasonable performance when spatial cues are present. Finally, at 16 months,

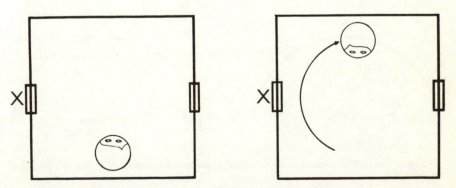

FIG. 3.   The task used by Acredolo (1978) to investigate infants' position coding.

few infants in either condition made an error, so by that age updating ability appears to be well enough established to be successful without the aid of landmarks. In a subsequent study (Acredolo & Evans, 1980) using an even more salient landmark (stripes and flashing lights around the correct window) 9- and 11-month-olds showed near perfect performance. Although one might worry that infants were simply drawn by the extreme salience of the landmark in this study, Acredolo and Evans dismiss this possibility, pointing out that anticipation training took as long in the "landmark" condition as in the "no-landmark" condition, something we would not expect if infants were simply being drawn to the landmark.

The advantage of this technique over object search tasks is that we can use it with infants who have not begun to search for hidden objects or who are rather unreliable in this respect. A number of workers have successfully used the anticipation technique with infants as young as 6 months old, this time, however, testing infants' ability to take account of bodily rotations (Cornell & Heth, 1979; McKenzie, Day, & Ihsen, 1984; Rieser, 1979). The technique used by McKenzie et al. (1984) is shown in Fig. 4. As in Acredolo's work, infants were trained to anticipate an event at a particular locus. However, McKenzie et al. (1984) were concerned that this sort of training might lead to response preservation which might conceal infants' true spatial ability. So rather than carrying out training with the infant in a single orientation, a series of blocks of trials were administered with the infant oriented either to the left or the right of the target. For instance, a particular infant might be trained first while oriented 30° to the left of target, and then trained while oriented 60° to the right of target, and finally while oriented in each direction at random. This procedure ensured that preservation of a single response did not develop during training.

Test trials were carried out with the infant in a totally new orientation, in the above example, 60° to the left of target. Six- and eight-month-olds showed ability to fixate the correct location from this new orientation,

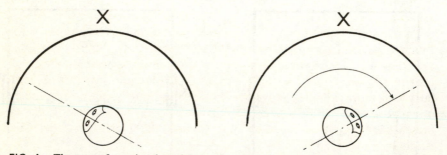

FIG. 4. The type of rotational spatial transformation investigated by McKenzie, Day, and Ihsen (1984).

indicating that they could re-orient to the original place through a response that had never been correct during training.

Other work suggested that there might be the limit of their ability. Cornell and Heth (1979) found that infants of this age do not appear to be able to take account of 180° rotations. However, this study involved training with the infant in a single orientation, so it is possible that an ability was concealed by response preservation. More recently, Keating, McKenzie, and Day (1986) found that 8-month-olds showed limited ability to re-orient from a position 180° from one of the training orientations and 45° from the other, a response that demanded 90° head turn.

In all these studies, infants could solve the problem by fixating the correct locus as they are rotated into the test position, and any immediate environmental cues might help them to do this by giving them structure to "lock onto". However, Meuwissen and McKenzie (1987) found that 8-month-olds still showed some success at relocating the target when they were turned so that they faced away from it during rotation. Clearly, then, continuous visual contact with the locus is not crucial. But Meuwissen and McKenzie only obtained convincing evidence of relocation in a condition in which the target locus was marked by a landmark. It is possible that infants do use continuous visual updating when it is possible, but are still capable of using landmarks when visual fixation is prevented. There is a good deal more to be done in this area, but again visual landmarks emerge as important contributors to accurate orientation. It is also interesting to note that the general visual structure of the surround may serve such a purpose, even for infants of this age. Keating et al. (1986) found that when no landmark was placed at the target locus, infants performed better in a square room than in a circular one. Presumably the visual structure provided by the corners of the room helped them to keep track of the location of the target. It seems likely, however, that this is a fairly subtle effect that may only appear in the simpler bodily-rotation tasks. If this were not the case, we would have expected better performance at all ages in Acredolo's "no landmark" condition, since testing was in all cases carried out in a rectangular room with well-defined corners.

In summary, infants of 6 months are capable of taking account of bodily rotations, as long as they are not too large. By 8 months, they are capable of updating over larger rotations, and when landmarks are present they do not need to have the target constantly in view during rotation. But the ability to deal with more complex movements involving both displacement and re-orientation seems to be a later development, appearing at 9 months in the presence of strong spatial cues or landmarks, and at 18 months when landmarks are absent.

ACTIVE MOVEMENT, POSTURAL CONTROL AND SPATIAL ORIENTATION

The proposal that active movement has an important part to play in development crops up in one guise or another in a number of notable developmental theories. Piaget saw it as a crucial factor in development; according to him it was only through action on the world that the infant constructed an objective understanding of it. More recently, Gibson (1979) pointed out that perception is an active process which occurs as the organism moves through its habitat. If that is so, then the organism's ability to extract perceptual information from the environment should be closely related to its ability to orient and move in that environment.

The notion also appears in slightly different form in some classic work on perceptual development by Held and Hein (1963). They were developing the idea that perceptual development depended on the visual experiences that accompany active movement. Although babies and young animals are exposed to a whole set of perceptual experiences even when they themselves are stationary, the hypothesis was that it was primarily the experiences that resulted from their own movements that led to perceptual development. This seemed a sensible hypothesis, since visually guided behaviour involves an intimate coordination between perception and action, a coordination which, if not innate, cannot be extracted from passive perception or from action in the dark.

Held and Hein used the method illustrated in Fig. 5 to test this hypothesis. Kittens were reared in the dark until they were able to walk, whereupon they were placed in the apparatus for a 3-hour period each day. One kitten was permitted active experience and was free to move at will. The other kitten, being boxed in, was unable to initiate bodily displacements. But the ingenious part of the arrangement was that every movement made by the active kitten was imparted to the passive one. Hence, both kittens received the same perceptual input, but only for one did this experience relate to its actions. After a number of sessions in this device, kittens were tested on a range of behaviours. Although their motor development was normal, they showed impairments in visually guided behaviour. For example, they showed poor visual placing (extension of the paws as the animal is lowered towards a surface). In addition, they showed impairment on the visual cliff, a method of measuring depth perception developed around that time by Gibson and Walk (1960).

The visual cliff task provides us with a link back to human development, since it has been used to test the depth perception of human infants as well as young animals. The apparatus consists of a long platform with sheets of strong glass on either side. On one side there is a solid surface immediately below the glass. whereas on the other there is a drop of several feet. Gibson

FIG. 5. Held and Hein's (1963) method of giving kittens passive experience. The kitten in the basket cannot bring about its own movements, but every move of the active kitten is reproduced for the passive one.

and Walk found that the young of a range of animal species avoided the deep side but walked freely on the shallow side, and it was this avoidance that Held and Hein's passive kittens failed to show.

Gibson and Walk concluded that depth perception was innate, a conclusion which at first sight appears to be falsified by Held and Hein's results. However, there is one snag in interpreting the basis for their passive kittens' deficit. It was a transitory problem that disappeared after a short period of normal active experience, and it is possible that innate spatial perception had been interfered with by the passive experience itself. The kittens might have adapted to a situation in which there was no relationship between action and perception, thereby temporarily losing any innate visual–manual coordination.

Gibson and Walk also found strong visual cliff avoidance in human infants. However, due to the fact that subjects had to be able to crawl, these infants were at least 6-months-old when they were tested. This means that although we know that this age group perceive the drop and are wary of it, we cannot say whether the ability is innate or acquired in the months prior to testing. This is a particularly important issue, since if there is anything in Held and Hein's argument, the onset of crawling may itself lead to development of spatial perception.

Subsequent modification of the visual cliff technique has permitted its use with younger pre-locomotor infants. Instead of measuring active avoidance, Schwartz, Campos, and Baisel (1973) used changes in infants' heart rate as an indicator of their reaction to the drop, finding that pre-locomotor 5-month-olds showed a deceleration in heart rate on being lowered onto the deep side (relative to a baseline rate when lowered onto the shallow side), whereas 9-month-olds showed an increase. A reduction in heart rate is generally taken as an indicator of increased attention, and Schwartz et al. conclude that the younger infants perceive the difference between deep and shallow sides, showing greater interest in the deep side. In contrast, they interpret the acceleration shown by older infants as indication that they both detect the drop and are wary of it. It is tempting to conclude that perception does not change between these ages, but that the older infants have learned to interpret perception in terms of its implications for their safety.

Of course, this study does not show that there is a definite link between crawling experience and this change in infants' reactions to vertical drops. And although the proposal that the onset of crawling leads to developments in spatial awareness is quite straightforward, investigating a direct causal link of this sort is a good deal more difficult than one might think. The major confounding in the study by Schwartz et al. (1973) is between age and mobility status. The mobile group was older than the immobile group and so would be likely to be more advanced cognitively as well as motorically. This is an important problem, since it is possible that understanding of vertical drops results from general cognitive development rather than from experiences resulting from locomotion. Svejda and Schmid (1979) surmounted this particular difficulty by gathering two groups of infants who differed in whether or not they could crawl but whose average age was the same. They found that even with age held constant, those infants with crawling experience showed evidence of wariness on the visual cliff (on the heart rate measure), whereas those who were still immobile did not.

But even in this study there is an interpretative problem. As Campos, Svejda, Campos, and Bertenthal (1982) point out, infants who crawl early may do so because they are generally more advanced, cognitively as well as motorically. Indeed, the direction of causality could even be in the opposite direction, with crawling onset motivated by cognitive advance rather than permitted by motor developments. This means that simply holding test age constant is no guarantee of controlling all relevant factors other than mobility. This is a good example of the general problem that crops up when we rely on semi-naturalistic studies in which none of the potentially important variables is actually manipulated by the experimenter.

Other evidence does point to crawling as a causal factor. Campos et al. (1978) tested infants on the visual cliff immediately after they began to crawl, and found that it took a few sessions before they began to avoid the deep side. Apparently, some experience of crawling was needed before wariness developed. Temporal lags of this sort are often taken as indices of the direction of causality.

Stronger evidence for a causal link comes from a study by Campos et al. (1981), who manipulated crawling experience by supplying one group of infants with baby-walkers during their fifth month, subsequently comparing their responses on the visual cliff to a control group who had not been given this mobility advantage. Even looking at those infants who were not crawling by the time of testing, those given early locomotor experience were more likely than control subjects to show wariness on the deep side of the visual cliff. Consequently, it looks as if there is a causal relationship between experience of locomotion and wariness of drops.

Some further evidence suggests that this causal link may be complicated by other factors, however. Richards and Rader (1981) obtained results that seem to run entirely against prediction; infants who crawled before 6.5 months often failed to show visual cliff avoidance in comparison with a later crawling group who did. However, this does not mean that we must abandon the causal model above; instead we may just need to include another factor in it. Rader, Bausano, and Richards (1980) suggest that early crawlers are directed more by tactile than by visual input, a difference which may persist into later crawling. Consequently, they may not just fail to benefit from the visual experiences early in crawling, but they may also fail to do so later, when they have achieved the cognitive sophistication to do so but are still "locked into" a tactual mode of locomotion guidance.

These findings may only apply to very early crawlers, however, and a fair number of other studies lend support to the notion that for most infants understanding of depth emerges partly as a result of experiences gained through locomotion. If this is true in the case of awareness of vertical depth, it should be doubly true in the case of the sort of spatial orientation measured by the object search and visual anticipation tasks reviewed in the previous section. It is rather far-fetched to assume that crawling results in most infants directly experiencing the dangers of large vertical drops. Given the elaborate precautions taken by most parents, falling large distances through careless locomotion can only be the experience of a minority. In contrast, every time the infant crawls, visual transformations occur of just the sort that take place in spatial orientation tasks.

Given this fact, it is rather surprising that direct research on crawling and spatial orientation has taken such a time to flourish. However, a start has now been made along two slightly different lines. Two studies have investigated whether accuracy of spatial orientation is affected by whether the infant moves actively or passively within the task itself (Acredolo, Adams, & Goodwyn, 1984; Benson & Uzgiris, 1985). In both studies, the two-position object search task was adapted by placing screens on three sides of the array. Infants watched the object hidden through the screen, with the unscreened side opposite. Thus, to search for the object, they had to crawl around to the opposite side in order to get through the screen. This ingenious method is successful in inducing infants to execute the displacement which other studies have carried out on the infant's behalf, and both Acredolo et al. (1984) and Benson and Uzgiris (1985) found that infants who made the movement themselves were more accurate at relocating the object than a comparison group who were moved passively. This is a striking finding, since the active group perform better despite the fact that their attention must be partly directed to executing the detour.

Other workers have taken the same approach as much of the visual cliff work, trying to show a relationship between amount of crawling experience and spatial orientation. So far, there is little work of this nature, and what there is is contradictory. McComas and Field (1984) found no relationship between amount of crawling experience and spatial orientation in a task much like that used by Acredolo (1978). However, they did not hold test age or crawling onset age constant, and they compared infants with different degrees of crawling experience rather than comparing crawlers to non-crawlers, so there are a number of possible reasons for their negative result. On the other hand, Bertenthal (1985) showed a positive relationship between crawling experience and spatial orientation on both Acredolo's and Bremner's tasks. More work is needed in this area before a clear conclusion can be drawn, but given the evidence from visual cliff studies, it would be surprising if a clear relationship between crawling onset and spatial orientation did not emerge in the long run.

Probably we should not limit our attention to the onset of locomotion, since it may well be the case that infants find out a good deal about the relationship between self and environment through simpler sorts of active movement. In this respect, the relatively mundane achievement of sitting up unaided may be very important. Young infants lack the postural control to support themselves, and the sort of support supplied from without by baby chairs or the floor generally acts to impede the infant's head and body movements further. In contrast, once the infant achieves the sitting posture, a new degree of control can be exercised over bodily movements. At this point, infants are capable of exercising reasonably fine control over rotational movements of head, and later the trunk, movements of just the sort that are produced for the infant in the spatial rotation studies carried out by McKenzie and her colleagues.

There is a striking chronological agreement here which seems unlikely to be a coincidence. On average, infants sit unaided at 6 months, and begin to execute rotational movements of the trunk about a month later (Illingworth, 1973). This matches up nicely with the finding that 6-month-olds were capable of taking account of relatively limited rotational movements

(McKenzie et al. 1984), while 8-month-olds extended this ability to larger rotations (Keating et al. 1986).

Such an analysis has some interesting implications for the development of spatial reference systems. Once infants can sit unaided, control over head movements precedes control over movements of the trunk. This leads to the possibility that we may need to distinguish between position relative to the body, position relative to the head, and position in the external world, since while infants are only capable of head movements, the relation between body and world remains fixed (as far as actively achieved changes are concerned). Thus the body-centred system is confounded with any stable external system. On the other hand, position relative to the head is dissociated from position in an external system whenever a head movement is executed. If active movements of this sort have an important effect on spatial competence, the prediction is that infants should quite early be able to dissociate position defined by a head-based system from position in the external world, but that they should take longer to dissociate a body-centred system from external systems.

An important further prediction here is that since manual responses are coordinated within the body system, externally defined place and response are only dissociated if the body is moved. On the other hand, since head movements are already under the infant's control, a dissociation between particular head movements and particular places in space has already been formed. This could mean that tasks like those of McKenzie and her colleagues, in which the response is a head movement, may tap a higher level ability than would appear at 6 months if the response were an arm movement.

As a final note, it should be pointed out that we can take this analysis a step further back to the stage before infants gain good control over head movements, to recognise the fact that they have good control over eye movements at this point. Hence, the full sequence of dissociation between bodily and external systems should proceed from eye-centred, through head-centred, to body centred systems.

CONCLUSION: A MODEL OF SPATIAL DEVELOPMENT

A good deal of ground has been covered since we took Piaget's account as our point of departure, and it is work summarising the account and putting it in a more general theoretical framework. The assumption implicit in the material covered later in the chapter is that active movements of various sorts have had an important part in the development of spatial awareness. More specifically, I have pointed to two landmarks in motor development that are likely to be important in this respect. At around 6 months, infants achieve the sitting posture, an achievement that gives them better control over head movements and hence the opportunity to sample the relationship between perception and that form of rotational movement. Later, this movement is extended by the addition of controlled trunk movements. The prediction is that the ability to deal with rotational transformations that alter the relation between environment and head should emerge at about 6 months, and that the dissociation between place and manual response should come some time later with the onset of control over trunk movements. Here there is a chance that this dissociation is actually delayed because of prior knowledge. Infants who do not yet have trunk control know that although the relation between head and external place changes, the relation between place and manual response remains constant. Once they achieve control over trunk movements the resultant visual changes differ only in degree, so there may be no direct evidence from visual sources that the assumption of a constant relation between manual response and place is no longer valid.

The second motor landmark is the one discussed at most length in earlier sections. Once infants begin to crawl they gain access to the relationship between visual events and their own actions involving both bodily rotation and displacement. Up to this point, they may have learned how to update their self-referent coding of positions to take account of bodily rotations, but they may not have achieved this in the case of movements involving rotation and displacement. However, once they start to crawl, they will quickly be confronted with situations in which such updating is required, and it may not take them long to realise that self-referent position codings that are not updated are particularly unreliable following a bodily displacement; a realisation that may generalise to passive movements as well.

The development of the sitting posture may have another less direct effect on the infant's developing spatial awareness. Before infants can sit up, their parents probably put them in relatively few places such as their chair, cot, or changing mat, which are designed specifically for their support. Other places are relatively inappropriate, and if used are unlikely to give infants a clear view of the surroundings. On the other hand, the achievement of the sitting posture means that infants are now self-supporting, with the implication that they can be placed on almost any sort of relatively flat surface. So we can supplement the developmental account as follows. Infants may at first be limited to a few relatively static views of the world: ones that they may well not integrate to form an overall scene. Once they can sit up, however, the number of views of the world increases dramatically. This, in itself, may lead to partial integration of these scenes, a process that may be further advanced by the self-initiated transformations of one scene into another that occur once the infant begins to crawl.

Finally, how does this sort of account fit in with Piaget's constructivist theory on the one hand, and theories of direct perception on the other? My hope is that it is harmonious with both, and may be the sort of account that could reconcile what are on the face of it, totally opposed views. First of all, the assumption is that the infant does construct knowledge through action in the world, and so the account developed here has much in common with Piaget's theory. But at the same time, we cannot ignore the evidence from the earlier chapters of this book that shows that the young infant is much more perceptually sophisticated than Piaget admitted. Consequently, we have to revise our notions about the sort of knowledge that is being developed through activity. Infants appear to be able to perceive an objective world from very early on, even from birth, so that sort of knowledge does not have to be constructed. However, the claim is that they do have to construct relationships between perception and the new activities that they acquire during development. This needs to be done at the direct level of constructing spatial reference systems which allow them to adapt their activities to the perceptual world. And it also needs to be done at a level once removed, in which infants come to realise what certain types of perceptual information mean in relation to newly developed motor abilities. For example, they need to learn that vertical drops take on a particular danger value once they begin to crawl. In this case, they are learning about the implications of perceptual information rather than learning to perceive.

There is some evidence that there may be a social component to the construction process here. Sorce, Emde, Campos, and Klinnert (1981) found that faced with an intermediate height of drop on the visual cliff, infants' decision on whether to cross was determined by the mothers' expression. When a fearful expression was produced, they refused to cross, but if an encouraging expression was used, they crossed. So some aspects of knowledge, in this case those relating to the danger of certain spatial features, may be constructed largely through a social process in which the infant draws on parent's emotional reactions in developing wariness.

Thus, if we take cognitive development in infancy to be very much to do with construction of relations between perception and action, there is scope for allowing the better parts of Piagetian constructionism to live in harmony with more recent theories of direct perception. Also, if a social dimension is included in the construction process, the field of cognitive development can be reconciled with approaches that recognise the infant's considerable social awareness as a potent factor in cognitive development as well as social development.

REFERENCES

Acredolo, L. P. (1978). Development of spatial orientation in infancy. *Developmental Psychology, 14,* 224–234.

Acredolo, L. P., Adams, A., & Goodwyn, S. W. (1984). The role of self-produced movement and visual tracking in infant spatial orientation. *Journal of Experimental Child Psychology, 38,* 312–327.

Acredolo, L. P. & Evans, D. (1980). Developmental changes in the effects of landmarks on infant spatial behavior. *Developmental Psychology, 16,* 312–318.

Benson, J. B. & Uzgiris, I. C. (1985). Effect of self-initated locomotion on infant search activity. *Developmental Psychology, 21,* 923–931.

Bertenthal, B. I. (1985). *Some indirect effects of early crawling experience on perceptual, cognitive, and affective development.* Paper presented at the 8th Biennial Meeting of The International Society for the Study of Behavioural Development, Tours, France.

Bremner, J. G. (1978a). Spatial errors made by infants: inadequate spatial cues or evidence for egocentrism? *British Journal of Psychology, 69,* 77–84.

Bremner, J. G. (1978b). Egocentric versus allocentric coding in nine-month-old infants: Factors influencing the choice of code. *Developmental Psychology, 14,* 346–355.

Bremner, J. G. (1980). The infant's understanding of space. In M. V. Cox (ed.) *Are young children egocentric?* London: *Batsford Academic.*

Bremner, J. G. (1985). Object tracking and search in infancy: A review of data and a theoretical evaluation. *Developmental Review, 5,* 371–396.

Bremner, J. G. & Bryant, P. E. (1977). Place versus response as the basis of spatial errors made by young infants. *Journal of Experimental Child Psychology, 23,* 162–171.

Butterworth, G., Jarrett, N., & Hicks, L. (1982). Spatio-temporal identity in infancy: Perceptual competence or conceptual deficit. *Developmental Psychology, 18,* 435–449.

Campos, J., Hiatt, S., Ramsay, D., Henderson, C., & Svejda, M. (1978). The emergence of fear on the visual cliff. In M. Lewis & L. Rosenbloom (eds), *The development of affect.* New York: Plenum Press.

Campos, J., Svejda, M., Bertenthal, B., Benson, N., & Schmid, D. (1981). *Self-produced locomotion and wariness of heights: New evidence from training studies.* Paper presented at the meeting of the Society for Research in Child Development, Boston, Mass.

Campos, J. J., Svejda, M. J., Campos, R. G., & Bertenthal, B. (1982). The emergence of self-produced locomotion: Its importance for psychological development in infancy. In D. Bricker (ed.), *Intervention with at-risk and handicapped infants.* Baltimore: University Park Press.

Cornell, E. H. & Heth, C. D. (1979). Response versus place learning by human infants. *Journal of Experimental Psychology: Human Learning & Memory, 5,* 188–196.

Gibson, E. J. & Walk, R. D. (1960). The 'visual cliff'. *Scientific American, 202,* 64–71.

Gibson, J. J. (1979). *The ecological approach to visual perception.* Boston, Mass.: Houghton Mifflin.

Held, R. & Hein, A. (1963). Movement produced stimulation in the development of visually guided behavior. *Journal of Comparative & Physiological Psychology, 56,* 872–876.

Illingworth, R. S. (1973). *Basic developmental screening: 0–2 years.* Oxford: Blackwell Scientific.

Keating, M. B., McKenzie, B. E., & Day, R. H. (1986). Spatial localization in infancy: Position constancy in a square and circular room with and without a landmark. *Child Development, 57,* 115–124.

McComas, J. & Field, J. (1984). *Does crawling experience affect infants' emerging spatial orientation abilities?* Paper presented at the Fourth International Conference on Infant Studies, New York.

McKenzie, B. E., Day, R. H., & Ihsen, E. (1984). Localization of events in space: Young infants are not always egocentric. *British Journal of Developmental Psychology*, 2, 1–9.

Meuwissen, I. & McKenzie, B. E. (1987). Localization of an event by young infants: The effect of visual and body movement information. *British Journal of Developmental Psychology*, 5, 1–8.

Piaget, J. (1954). *The construction of reality in the child* (trans. M. Cook). New York: Basic Books (originally published in French, 1936).

Rader, N., Bausano, M., & Richards, J. E. (1980). On the nature of the visual cliff avoidance response in human infants. *Child Development*, 51, 61–68.

Richards, J. E. & Rader, N. (1981). Crawling-onset age predicts visual cliff avoidance in infants. *Journal of Experimental Psychology: Human Perception & Performance*, 7, 382–387.

Rieser, J. (1979). References systems and the spatial orientation of six month old infants. *Child Development*, 50, 1078–1087.

Schwartz, A., Campos, J. &, Baisel, E. (1973). The visual cliff: Cardiac and behavioral correlates on the deep and shallow sides at five and nine months of age. *Journal of Experimental Child Psychology*, 15, 86–99.

Sorce, J., Emde, R. N., Campos, J. J., & Klinnert, M. (1981). *Maternal emotional signaling: Its effect on the visual cliff behavior of one-year-olds*. Paper presented at the Meeting of the Society for Research in Child Development, Boston, Mass.

Svejda, M. & Schmid, D. (1979). *The role of self-produced locomotion in the onset of fear of heights on the visual cliff*. Paper presented at the Meeting of the Society for Research in Child Development, San Francisco.

Wishart, J. G. & Bower, T. G. R. (1982). The development of spatial understanding in infancy. *Journal of Experimental Child Psychology*, 33, 363–385.

7 Development of Problem-solving in Infancy

Peter Willatts

Department of Psychology,
University of Dundee,
Dundee DD1 4HN, U.K.

PROBLEM SOLVING BEHAVIOUR

Any parent who has had to fit "child-proof" locks to cupboard doors knows that during the first 2 years infants become very competent at finding ways of overcoming obstacles to attain a goal. By the end of the sensory–motor period, children possess a range of abilities that make them effective, though sometimes frustrated, problem-solvers. They are better able to keep a goal in mind and are not so easily distracted. They have a wide range of skills and knowledge which can be applied to tasks. Emerging abilities in language and communication allow children to make requests for help and to benefit from the assistance provided by another person. The use of strategies becomes more effective, with the result that children can often plan their problem-solving and work out a solution without always having to go through the tedious process of trial-and-error.

Throughout their development, infants are always coming up against problems for which they have no ready solution. A 4-month-old who is just learning how to reach struggles to grasp an object. An 8-month-old who is already holding an object in each hand tries to pick up another. A 12-month-old, captive inside a playpen, wants a toy that is on the other side of the bars, and a 2-year-old, while playing with a teaset, notices that the teapot is missing. In each situation the infant can find some way to overcome the difficulty, but the method will vary markedly with the child's age and the nature of the task. The 4-month-old may lack control over arm movements and can do little else but try again and hope for better luck next time. The 8-

month-old, having fumbled and dropped both objects, discovers that you have to let go of one in order to pick up another. The infant in the playpen unsuccessfully tries to reach through the bars or climb over the top before calling out to its mother for help. The 2-year-old, noticing that the teapot is missing, immediately sets about searching all the likely places until it is found.

These examples are typical of the changes that occur during the first 2 years (Piaget, 1953; Bruner, 1970; Uzgiris & Hunt, 1975). There appears to be a gradual advance from reliance on accident and luck by the younger infant to the more controlled, directed approach of the older infant. However, this diversity makes it difficult to know whether all of these activities should be regarded as problem-solving, and we therefore need to consider the criteria for judging whether a baby has solved a problem or not. According to Newell and Simon (1972, p. 72), "a person is confronted with a problem when he wants something but does not know immediately what series of actions to perform to get it". From this definition we can extract three main characteristics: There is a goal which is desired, direct access to the goal is blocked, and the problem-solver will try to do something to achieve the goal. This may seem quite obvious, but we cannot be certain that, for young infants at least, any activity which follows from the perception that access to a goal is blocked will necessarily be carried out with the intention of achieving the goal.

Problem-solving is intentional and should be distinguished from other activities, such as exploration, which may not be carried out with a specific goal in mind. A baby who is attracted to the buttons on a television set and discovers how to switch it on may have learned a new contingency, but has not solved any problem. Identifying intentionality on behavioural criteria alone is not easy, but there is agreement among authors such as Piaget (1953), Bruner (1973; 1981), Wellman (1977), and Harding (1982) that intention is shown when an infant persists in trying to achieve a goal, selects from among alternative actions those which are appropriate to the goal, corrects for errors, and stops when the goal is attained.

Bruner (1970; 1973) noted that intention provides two sources of information about the status of performance. First, recognition that the goal has been achieved supplies the necessary stop-rule to prevent further activity. Second, when an error occurs, the discrepancy between what was intended and what was achieved may assist in directing future attempts. These two ways of regulating behaviour, referred to by Rutkowska (1985) as "goal terminated" and "goal directed" respectively, are seen by Bruner as the hallmarks of intentional behaviour. In each of the above examples achievement of the goal causes the infant to break off further activity and begin something else. The young infant finally grasps the object and puts it in his mouth, and the older child finds the teapot and resumes her game. Goal-directedness is also evident but varies considerably. The oldest child only searches those places where the missing object is likely to be found, and carefully eliminates each in turn. The infant in the playpen tries out a series of possible methods before finding a way of getting the toy. Even the 4-month-old shows a rudimentary form of goal-directedness in the form of persistent repetition. Thus, there are some features which are common to each performance.

This analysis suggests that we should be prepared to look for evidence of problem-solving whenever infants are capable of organising intentional behaviour. This is not to say that all intentional behaviour should be regarded as problem-solving because in many instances the infant knows how to attain the desired goal. However, it does mean that we should not restrict the study of problem-solving to a narrow range of situations such as tasks requiring the use of objects as tools or intermediaries. For example, Bruner has argued convincingly that early skilled performance is regulated by goals, and thus the acquisition of new skills requires the application of problem-solving strategies. Skill acquisition and problem-solving can be regarded as equivalent because both entail finding a sequence of actions for transforming the initial state into the goal state. The strategies involved in skill acquisition map onto the strategies involved in problem-solving, and "the competence involved in the combinatorial performance of skill is . . . homologous to the competence observable in directed problem solving" (Bruner, 1972, p. 124). In the next section we consider the range of strategies that might be available to infants.

PROBLEM-SOLVING STRATEGIES

Two main types of strategy have been described in the problem-solving literature. The first is forward search in which a sequence of actions is tried out one at a time until eventually the goal is reached (Nilsson, 1971; Winston, 1984). For example, you could find a route through a maze by walking to a junction, choosing an exit path, walking to the next junction, choosing another path, and so on. If you come to a dead-end, you return to the previous junction and take a different path. This kind of search will eventually lead to the goal, but can be a slow and laborious process. One difficulty is remembering what has been tried already, and quite simple problems can make substantial demands on memory. Efficiency can be improved by using some form of heuristic information to select which step to try out next. If you had an idea of the direction in which the end of the maze lay, you might choose to explore paths that went roughly in that direction and ignore those that appeared to lead away.

Heuristic search does not guarantee that in every case the goal will be reached quickly or even at all, but generally the number of steps that need to be considered will be reduced. There are many different kinds of heuristic search which vary with regard to the overall structure of the search (e.g. depth-first or breadth-first), the quality of the heuristic information, and the way the information is applied. At one extreme is random search where no information is used to select candidate actions, while at the other are algorithms which can find the shortest path to a goal as efficiently as possible (Nilsson, 1971). However, despite the differences, all of these methods share a basic set of common procedures.

The second type of strategy is problem-reduction or subgoaling of which the best known example is means–ends analysis. With this approach, you identify a difference between the current state and the goal state and then consider a possible means for reducing this difference. The problem may be solved immediately if you can act directly to reduce the difference, but if the action is blocked or inappropriate, further problem-solving will be needed. This can result in a lengthy sequence of subgoals, each of which must be achieved before the difference can be reduced and the goal attained. For example, suppose someone spills an ashtray at the office party and you want to clean it up before the boss arrives. The difference between what you have and what you want is the location of the pile of ash. What would change it is a suction cleaner. The cleaner is in the janitor's cupboard which is locked. The difference between what you want and what you have is the state of the cupboard door. A key would change this, but you have to find it, and so on until eventually the mess is removed. With this strategy, a plan of action is assembled in which the initial problem is gradually redefined as a series of further subproblems. When at some stage it becomes possible to take a direct action, this sets in train a sequence that leads to the goal.

Search and problem-reduction strategies have certain features in common. Both make demands on memory. In the case of forward search, the problem-solver must retain information about which steps have already been tried and their outcome. With problem-reduction, the whole plan must be remembered until the goal has been achieved. Both strategies will therefore be more effective if the problem-solver can carry out a relevant task analysis to identify actions which are appropriate and thus avoid getting sidetracked down blind alleys. However, random methods may also be used with each strategy. If heuristic information or inspection of differences fails to identify one action as the most promising, then a random choice may be the only way of proceeding. Although there is nothing inherently wrong with random choice, it does require careful monitoring. If any information is forgotten, it might not be possible to retrace the original sequence of steps because a different random selection could be made on a subsequent attempt.

Search and problem-reduction strategies also differ in several ways. Each strategy is suited to a particular kind of problem. Search is appropriate when there is a restricted set of alternative actions to consider at each step, but can become unmanageable if the set is extensive. Problem-reduction is appropriate when the range of actions is undefined and potentially very large. The classic "monkey and bananas" problem is a good example (Köhler, 1925). The chimp, faced with the task of retrieving a basket of fruit which is hanging from the ceiling, could select almost any behaviour from the entire chimp repertoire, but a stepwise search through this domain would be unfeasible. Problem-reduction narrows the range of choice by focusing attention on specific subgoals that are likely to lead to a solution. If the chimp identified the height of the fruit above the floor as a difference to reduce, then methods such as jumping and climbing might be considered.

Another difference concerns whether the strategy has to be carried out in a planning mode. By planning, I have in mind the definition of Wellman, Fabricius, and Sophian (1985) which stresses looking beyond the first step to consider further steps in the sequence. Thus, *planned* solutions should be distinguished from *planful* solutions which may only entail consideration of a single step. Forward search does not need to be planned because each step can be tried, the outcome noted, and a decision taken about the next step on the basis of the information gained, a method which Wellman *et al.* (1985) termed "sighting". However, if the effects of actions can be anticipated, forward search may be implemented by planning. In contrast, problem-reduction must be planned in advance because no action can be performed until the sequence of subgoals has been established.

The importance of this discussion of strategies for our understanding of infant problem-solving is twofold. First, we can see that even a simple strategy such as unplanned, random search has a relationship with other more advanced methods. This opens up the possibility of an underlying continuity in the strategies involved in skill acquisition and problem-solving throughout infancy. The implication for a developmental account is that we may not be faced with the task of explaining how strategies appear when previously there was none, but instead, of explaining how existing strategies become transformed. Second, we can identify several cognitive factors such as effective task analysis and memory capacity, and speculate about their impact on problem-solving ability. In particular, strategies involving planning would require a basic capacity for representation. The infant must be able to recall procedures for actions, anticipate their effects, and coordinate them into coherent sequences without information supplied through overt action. This is one of the issues addressed by Piaget's theory which presents an account of the development of these strategies in infancy.

PIAGET'S THEORY

Piaget's (1953) theory of the development of problem-solving during the first 2 years of life makes two major claims. The first is that the emergence of strategies is linked to sensory–motor stages with changes occurring only when there is an advance to the next stage. The second is that there is a sequence in the appearance of strategies. Although Piaget did not carry out a formal analysis of problem-solving strategies, it is possible to interpret his descriptions in terms of the strategies presented in the previous section. The first to appear in stage IV is a simple form of unplanned forward search which is followed in stage V by more complex methods of search guided by heuristic information. Last to appear in stage VI are strategies based on planning, and Piaget ruled out the possibility of planning occurring any earlier because of his claim that mental representation is only achieved at the very end of the sensory–motor period.

Stages I–III

Piaget, like Bruner, viewed intentionality as essential for problem-solving, but did not identify any problem-solving activity in stages I and II because he saw no evidence that actions could be carried out with the intention of achieving a goal. Early behaviour is restricted to the exercise of single sensory–motor schemes, and the infant is unable to comprehend the relations between its own activity and the effects which are produced. However, with the onset of secondary circular reactions in stage III, infants start to coordinate independent sensory–motor schemes and thus acquire structures which might support intentional behaviour. For example, the infant can discover how to shake a rattle that hangs above her cot and is tied to her arm by a piece of string. The initial discovery that an arm movement will shake the rattle is made accidentally, but the infant quickly learns to repeat the movements and demonstrates a coordination of schemes for controlling arm movements, looking, and hearing (Piaget, 1953, obs. 97).

Piaget did not regard these secondary circular reactions as evidence for early goal-directed problem-solving. It was not necessary to credit the infant as setting out with the intention of making the rattle move; instead, it might simply be a repetition of a familiar action with no expectations about the result. It is almost inevitable that an arm movement would shake the rattle, thus the structure of the situation rather than the implementation of any strategy could account for performance. The infant at this stage regards the effect of an action as a part of the action itself and fails to make any distinction between means and ends. These early schemes are not "mobile": That is, the infant is unable to access their components independently of the situation in which they were originally coordinated. Piaget concluded that in stage III, "means and ends are inseparable from one another and, consequently, produced in the same entity" (Piaget, 1953, p. 208). The infant has merely learned that two schemes can co-occur, but does not understand the causal relation between its own actions and the effects of those actions. Studies showing that it is possible to elicit the activity from infants by presentation of the effect of the activity alone lend some support to Piaget's interpretation (Cavanagh & Davidson, 1977; Rovee-Collier et al. 1980; Davis & Rovee-Collier, 1983).

Having said this, Piaget did offer two intriguing pieces of evidence in favour of an intentional account of the acquisition of secondary circular reactions. The first was his observation that behaviour might generalise to new situations. Jacqueline showed this after watching the movement of a new object presented at some distance from her cot. When the movement had stopped, she pulled on the string in an apparent attempt to restart it, though there was no effect because the string and object were not joined (Piaget, 1953, obs. 113). Attempts to replicate this observation have not met with much success (Rovee-Collier & Sullivan, 1980; Fagen, 1984), although the amount of generalisation has been shown to be related to the degree of similarity between the stimuli (Fagen, Rovee, & Kaplan, 1976). However, a more recent study by Fagen, Morrongiello, Rovee-Collier, and Gekoski (1984) showed that generalisation does occur, but is highly sensitive to the effects of context. Infants generalised their behaviour if they had prior experience at controlling several different mobiles, but not if their experience had been restricted to a single mobile.

The second piece of evidence comes from Piaget's account of the way that some secondary circular reactions became established. For example, Laurent at 4.5 months accidentally set a toy swinging with a stick. Instead of continuing to wave the stick about, he stopped, moved it nearer to the toy, then away a little, and finally struck the toy. This was repeated several times with the stick always kept close to the toy and the movements becoming increasingly faster (Piaget, 1953, obs. 105). This suggests that not only did Laurent have the goal of making the toy move, but that he was also showing goal-directedness in the regulation of his behaviour. It is tempting to conclude that Laurent used a forward search strategy which included heuristic information of the sort, "keep the stick near to the toy". Piaget certainly saw this as a possibility, and went so far as to suggest that "there is almost an articulation of the response-pattern into a means (reconstructed afterwards) and an end (adopted afterwards)" (Piaget, 1950, p. 102).

Stage IV

Planful means–ends behaviour first appears in stage IV. Familiar action schemes achieve a greater level of independence or mobility, and can be combined so that simple barrier problems may be solved (Woodward, 1971). Infants in stage IV are able to search for hidden objects, push aside obstacles, and use supports or strings to retrieve distant objects. The strategy by which these problems are solved is one of unplanned forward search with solutions often emerging by accident in the course of trying out several familiar activities.

Piaget's (1955) description of the development of search behaviour is a good example. At first the infant shows interest in a visible object, but does not attempt to remove a cover when the object is hidden. Instead, attention is redirected towards the cover, and the infant may run through a series of activities such as scratching, striking, and pushing, each of which has previously appeared in a different context. Although these efforts may displace the cover, Piaget did not believe they are always performed with the intention of regaining the toy. He showed that variations in the method of hiding could disrupt behaviour, and even when the cover was removed, the infant might not look for the object and could appear surprised when it was eventually seen (Piaget, 1955, obs. 38).

The criteria Piaget used to identify intentional search were that the infant should remove the barrier and not treat it as a plaything, look for the toy, and retrieve it quickly once it became accessible. These criteria are not achieved all at once, and there is a transitional period in which the infant's activity only gradually becomes influenced by an intended outcome. Eventually the infant's performance gets reorganised and becomes smoother, faster, and more efficient. Irrelevant activities, such as scratching, drop out, and the infant starts to pick up the screen while looking for the hidden toy. Thus, there are three steps in the development of this sort of means–ends problem-solving. An initial phase in which the infant makes little or no effort (stage III), a transitional phase in which a variety of familiar actions are tried out with the possibility of some goal in mind, and an intentional phase in which performance is clearly goal-oriented and efficient. At this point the infant is distinguishing means from ends, and Piaget regarded such achievements as among the first genuine acts of intelligence.

Stage IV problem-solving is limited in several ways. Infants can solve problems if a method is present in their repertoire, but are unable to generate new methods. This is a consequence of problem-solving at this level being more goal-terminated than goal-directed. The infant simply aims for a direct result and is unable to use heuristic information to organise and modify a series of attempts with reference to the goal. An illustration is provided by

Piaget's observations of the difficulties his children experienced in trying to use a stick to retrieve distant objects. The infant may touch the object with the stick, but fails to notice which movements bring the object nearer, and which move it further away.

There are also difficulties in modifying a successful performance to cope with changes in tasks, particularly those involving spatial arrangements. The typical reaction is persistence which appears in the form of repetition of the original performance. Probably the best known example is the A not-B error where infants who have previously found an object at place A return to search at the original place when the object is subsequently hidden at place B (see Chapter 5 by Harris). Similarly, Piaget found that infants who were able to pull a support to retrieve an object that was resting upon it persisted in pulling the support when the object was held above or placed alongside. Other examples of persistence arise in switching from pulling on a horizontal string to a vertical string which is attached to a toy (Uzgiris & Hunt, 1975), and changing the direction of locomotor detours (McKenzie & Bigelow, 1986) or manual detours (Willatts, 1987; Jarrett, 1988). This lack of flexibility also shows up when a method is tried which would normally be successful but is no longer appropriate. A good example is reaching around a transparent screen to retrieve a toy (Bruner, 1970; Diamond, 1988; Jarrett, 1988). Stage IV infants who can search competently will nevertheless fail this task by persistently trying to reach directly through the screen, and rarely discover how to make the necessary detour reach.

Stages V and VI

These two limitations, lack of flexibility and inability to generate new methods, are overcome in stage V because infants begin to deliberately introduce variations in their behaviour. Bath-time provides a rich setting for observing this new competence. When exploring the effects of dropping objects into water or holding them beneath the surface and letting go, the infant is not content merely to repeat the same actions but alters the height or depth at which the object is released and notices the way that the water splashes when struck (Piaget, 1953, obs. 147). The impact of this "experimentation" on infants' knowledge is considerable. Instead of simply learning that action A leads to effect B, the infant establishes a whole range of parameters for actions and effects and coordinates this information systematically. For example, infants of 14 months begin to relate variations in the size of objects with variations in weight, and can predict an object's weight from its size (Mounoud & Hauert, 1982).

This gives rise to the strategy which Piaget termed "directed groping". A stage V infant may find a way of using a stick to rake in a distant object by a procedure of deliberate experimentation. Having seen that the stick can make the object move, the infant conducts a controlled investigation of the relationship between the movements of the stick and of the object, and discovers how to rake in the object (Piaget, 1953, obs. 157–161). These solutions do not appear to be planned in advance and may take a considerable time to emerge. However, the activity is not random trial-and-error, but is guided by the information gained from successive attempts. Thus, the infant will come to select a stick which is appropriate in length, and holds it in whichever hand is more suitable for dealing with an object presented in a variety of different positions (McCrickard, 1982). Piaget's description of this "directed groping" strategy corresponds to unplanned forward search guided by heuristic information. Greater flexibility is shown, and infants are able to modify methods that initially were unsuccessful. The range of problems that can now be solved includes many that defeated the limited strategy of stage IV, such as retrieval of elongated objects through the bars of a playpen, rotation of platforms or levers, and the insertion of blocks into shape sorters.

However, stage V infants lack a capacity for mental representation which means that all problem-solving is unplanned. The infant may produce a greater range of behaviour, but the effects of a sequence of actions can only be discovered by trying them out and observing the result. The ability to solve new problems without the need for overt activity first appears in stage VI. Piaget (1953, obs. 179) reported a nice example when Lucienne, having failed three times to fit a long chain into a small box, paused, placed the chain on the flat surface beside the box, rolled it into a ball, and then succeeded in putting it in the box. This performance contrasts with the clumsy attempts at stage V in which the infant may eventually achieve the same method, but only after a lengthy series of trials (Piaget counted over 22 for Jacqueline). Similar planned solutions were reported for other tasks such as the use of a stick and the retrieval of an object from a partially open box.

The source of these planned solutions lies in the emerging capacity of stage VI infants to coordinate schemes in the absence of overt action. Piaget suggested three schemes that might contribute to the solution of rolling the chain into a ball. One was squeezing material to make it smaller, another was putting an object into a large opening, and the third was orienting an object to pass it through a narrow opening. None of these alone provided a method for solving the task, but this emerged when they were coordinated with each other (Piaget, 1953, p. 346). This interpretation of Lucienne's strategy reads exactly like an account of means–ends analysis. The length of the chain and the size of the box provided the difference to be reduced, making an object smaller was one method, and rolling up the chain was an appropriate action.

Summary

Piaget has offered an elegant account of the way that problem-solving strategies might be bootstrapped into existence. The sequence is plausible because there appears to be a progression in the complexity of strategies and there is a basis for continuity. Random forward search can be readily converted into a more powerful method with the inclusion of heuristic information to evaluate the outcome of each successive attempt. The shift from stage IV to stage V could therefore occur simply by the addition of a new stage-linked component to an existing problem-solving procedure. Equally, the onset of representation in stage VI would generate a new way of implementing search strategies, and could promote the use of new problem-reduction methods.

However, it should be noted that these strategies are neutral with regard to the issue of development. The sequence that Piaget described is not derived from any characteristics intrinsic to the strategies themselves, but from the supposed changes brought about by advance through successive sensory–motor stages. Random search, heuristic search, and problem-reduction are alternative methods, and there is no particular reason why one should take developmental precedence over the other.

PROBLEMS WITH PIAGET'S THEORY

While other areas of Piaget's sensory–motor theory have come under attack (see Chapter 5 by Harris, for criticisms of Piaget's account of object concept development), the theory of problem-solving has remained intact and is still widely accepted (Lamb & Bornstein, 1987). However, it is becoming clear that there are a number of difficulties. Piaget's own account contains inconsistencies, and some of the interpretations he made of certain key observations can be challenged. In addition, the findings of more recent research point to some very different conclusions.

Stages I–III

It has already been pointed out that Piaget himself expressed doubts about the absence of means–ends separation and intention prior to stage IV, and there is now much evidence to show that structures which could support intentional behaviour are innate. Many of the coordinations that Piaget argued took several months to establish are already present in some form at birth. Infants of 2 months or younger will turn and look in the direction of a sound (Muir & Field, 1979; Zelazo, Brody, & Chaika, 1984), imitate facial expressions they have seen modelled by an adult (Field, Woodson, Greenberg, & Cohen, 1982; Metlzoff & Moore, 1983), transfer information across modalities (Metlzoff & Borton, 1979; Gibson & Walker, 1984; Streri, 1987); and direct arm movements towards seen objects (Bower, Broughton & Moore, 1970a; von Hofsten, 1984). Very young infants can also learn how to control events through their own activity. Examples are sucking to hear a voice (DeCasper & Carstens, 1981) or to produce a visual display (Milewski, 1976), and moving limbs to activate a mobile (Rovee-Collier, 1983). Thus some of the coordinations Piaget identified as stage III achievements are even shown by new-borns.

It is important in these situations to know whether the infant is acting intentionally to make the event happen, or merely expecting an outcome. If young infants can only acquire expectancies, then Piaget's general view of development up to the age of 6 months would be supported, though the boundaries between the first three stages would become blurred. One technique to distinguish expectancy from intention is to observe reactions to disruption of the normal outcome. If the infant had only an expectation, then he or she might indicate this in some way, but would do nothing else. If the infant had been acting intentionally, then we should expect to see some attempt to make the intended event happen.

Disruption or violation of expectancy studies have been reported for several types of situation. In face-to-face interaction between infants and adults it is clear that young infants notice when their partner is not responding as normal. Infants typically show distress and disorganised behaviour when confronted by a still-face (Tronick et al., 1978; Field, Vega-Lahr, Scafidi, & Goldstein, 1986), or a videorecording of the parent (Trevarthen, 1983). This disruption may show that infants have expectancies about the normal course of such interactions, but there is as yet no clear evidence for intentionality in early face-to-face exchanges (Kaye, 1982; Sylvester-Bradley, 1985). Indeed, it has been suggested that differential reactions to responsive and unresponsive facial displays may simply reflect the fact that an unresponsive facial display is less interesting and therefore produces more boredom (Lamb, Morrison, & Malkin, 1987).

Less ambiguous evidence for the emergence of social expectancies in the early months comes from studies of distress–relief situations. Gekoski, Rovee-Collier, and Carulli-Rabinowitz (1983) reported a marked increase at around 4 months in the anticipatory quieting of crying infants to the approach of an adult. Quieting occurred to the approach of either the infant's mother or a stranger and was not mediated by the perceived familiarity of the adult.

Where claims for the occurrence of intentional behaviour have been made, it may take some months to develop. One example is a longitudinal study by Lamb and Malkin (1986) of infants' reactions to disruption of distress–relief sequences. The typical sequence of events is that the infant cries, the parent enters the room, picks up the infant, and the crying stops. Infants as young as 1 month began to quieten before being picked up, but it was only at 5 months that a marked increase in protesting occurred when infants were not picked up. Protest was rather loosely defined as an increase in intensity of distress which, given the distress scale adopted in the study, could have been indicated by a rather modest shift from pleasurable vocalisation to weak fussing, or a more extreme shift from quiet to screaming. The increase in protest was also accompanied by a concurrent increase in turning away and avoidance of the adult. In addition, infants showed more protest to disruption by the mother than by an unfamiliar adult, suggesting that specific expectations had been acquired of the mother's behaviour.

Lamb and Malkin concluded that a cognitive change occurs at around 5 months such that infants not only show expectancies but also understand something of the relationships between their own behaviour and external events. The finding that infants protest when their expectation is violated might be an early sign of intention to achieve a desired outcome. However, the earlier criticism of studies of face-to-face interaction can also be made of this interpretation. Protest when the adult does not pick up the infant may simply occur because the baby is reacting to a situation which is less interesting and not because the infant is trying to achieve a goal. The fact that there was less protest when the adult was unfamiliar fits with this differential interest explanation. However, these observations of Lamb and Malkin do suggest one context in which intentional behaviour may first appear, and 5 months is close to the age predicted by Piagetian theory.

A comparable pattern has been found in studies of early reaching. Bower, Broughton, and Moore (1970b) presented infants as young as 6 days with an illusory "virtual" object produced by a stereoscopic shadow-caster. Infants became distressed when they were unable to make contact with the virtual object, but there was an increase with age in the number of repeated attempts to grasp the object. At 5 months, infants produced a whole range of exploratory tactile behaviours. Thus younger infants showed an expectancy to touch a seen object, but only older infants displayed persistent behaviour in an attempt to produce that outcome.

Another disruption study that also shows intention in the reaching behaviour of 5-month-olds was carried out by Bruce Hood and myself (Hood & Willatts, 1986). Infants were presented with an object at one side, but were prevented from reaching by the mother. The room lights were turned out, and the infant's behaviour recorded with an infra-red video system. Before the mother released the infant's hands, the object was removed to avoid any risk of chance contacts in the darkness. We found that infants reached more to the place where the object had been seen than to the control place on the opposite side where no object had been presented (Fig. 1). This reaching for an object in the dark is evidence that infants will try to

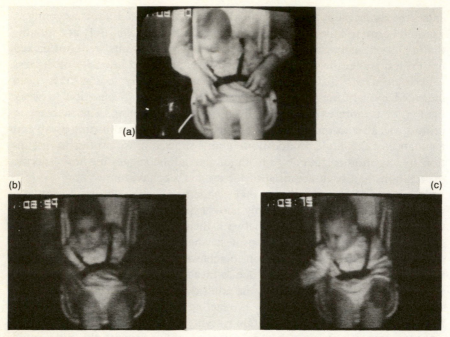

FIG. 1.   A 5-month-old infant reaching in the dark. The infant (a) looks at the object; (b) looks away when the light goes out; (c) reaches to the object's remembered position. (From Hood & Willatts (1986), *British Journal of Developmental Psychology*, *4*, 62. © The British Psychological Society. Reprinted by permission.)

attain a remembered goal, and persist in their attempts when that goal is not achieved.

These studies all confirm that infants have expectancies very early on, but that the distinction between merely expecting something to happen and intending it to happen may not be made until about 5 months. However, there is some evidence that intentional behaviour might occur much earlier. Butterworth and Hopkins (1988) recorded the spontaneous arm movements of new-borns and noted that about 32% of these movements carried the infant's hand to its mouth. In many instances the mouth was open before the arm moved, suggesting that infants were anticipating the arrival of the hand. Even more surprising was the observation that when the hand had missed the target and arrived at another part of the infant's face, the infant was often able to get it directly to the mouth without needing to start all over again from scratch. These corrective movements suggest that Butterworth and Hopkins may have observed a very early form of guided or heuristic search for a goal.

A similar conclusion comes from a quite different set of studies of conditioned learning reported by Papousek and Bernstein (1969). Infants as young as 3 months were taught to produce complex series of head turns such as two to the left and two to the right to receive a reward. Many infants appeared to follow a strategy to learn these tasks, such as turning to the other side if no reward was obtained. As in the Butterworth study, chance mechanisms did not seem to be operating, and Papousek and Bernstein concluded that "correcting operations were being organised that involved the mobilization of orienting or experimenting behaviours" (Papousek & Bernstein, 1969, p. 246).

It will be recalled that some of Piaget's own observations led him to suggest that secondary-circular reactions may be intentional and goal-directed. Clear support for this account is reported in a study by Fagen and Rovee (1976). Three-month-old infants were trained to kick in order to move a mobile with six components. When the number of components was reduced to two, the rate of kicking increased rapidly, which may be viewed as "a strategy by which the infant conserves the amount of stimulus change in the moving mobile" (Rovee-Collier, 1983, p. 79). This interpretation of kicking rate as goal-directed is reinforced by the further observation of Fagen and Rovee that infants who underwent a shift from ten components to two also increased their rate of kicking, but soon gave up and started to cry, presumably because their goal of maintaining the original level of stimulation was unattainable. This finding, which has been replicated by Mast, Fagen, Rovee-Collier, and Sullivan (1980), provides compelling evidence that early contingency learning is goal-oriented. However, I know of no other studies which have examined the strategies involved in the acquisition of secondary circular reactions, and there is a clear need for microanalytic studies of performance on a range of different tasks.

These observations are sufficient to raise doubts about Piaget's account. In two quite different situations we have evidence that even new-borns may conduct some form of guided, heuristic search to attain a goal, long before they enter stage V. However, it is also clear that we must have further, more detailed studies of young infants to confirm these important claims.

Stage IV

While intentional problem-solving may occur much earlier than predicted by Piagetian theory, means–ends separation in manual tasks does appear to develop only gradually. The series of steps in the development of intentional search has been confirmed by one of my own studies (Willatts, 1984a). Infants were tested at 6, 7, and 8 months on tasks in which either a toy was hidden behind a single screen, or the screen alone was presented with no toy. Intention was rated by considering what the infant did with the screen, where he or she looked, and whether the toy was retrieved. The infant's first activity with the screen was scored as intentional if it was picked up but not examined or played with. Fixation was scored as intentional if the infant looked for the hidden toy and did not look away after the screen had been moved. Behaviour with the toy was scored as intentional if it was retrieved.

Although there were no differences with age in success at retrieving the toy, there were changes in the organisation of behaviour. At 6 months, search took the form of a sequence of unrelated acts in which the infant first picked up the screen, played with it, noticed the toy, and picked that up as well (Fig. 2). The infant did not appear to have a goal of retrieving the toy because activity with the screen and fixation were the same regardless of whether a toy had been hidden or not. Intentionality increased steadily across the following 2 months, and by 8 months, most infants were showing intention on all three measures. Of particular interest was the finding that the 7-month-olds, who were producing a transitional level of performance, were nevertheless goal-oriented because scores for intention were significantly higher on the task in which a toy was hidden.

These changes are not restricted to the development of search. A further study examined the appearance of skills for using supports to retrieve distant objects (Willatts, 1985a). Again, infants were tested at 6, 7, and 8 months on a task in which an object was presented out of reach but on a cloth. Several

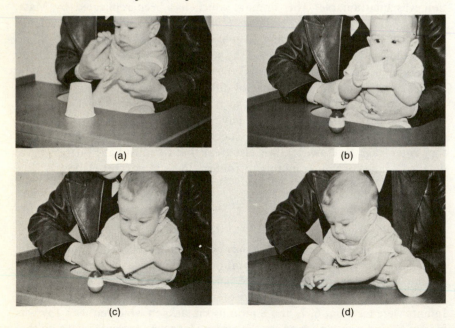

FIG. 2.   Search at 6 months is a sequence of independent actions. (a) Infant reaches for the cup; (b) takes the cup to his mouth and looks away; (c) notices the toy; (d) reaches for the toy. (Photographs by Peter Willatts.)

components of intentional performance were identified: The infant should pull the support and not play with it, should maintain attention to the task and not lose interest, and retrieve the toy. Once more, there was no change with age in success at retrieving the toy, but a marked change in method. At 6 months, infants often played with the cloth in some way. They scratched at it, shook it, or put it in their mouth, and quite often broke off completely for a while before resuming again. In the course of this activity, the toy gradually moved nearer until it came within reach, at which point the infant picked it up. As with search, 6-month-olds achieved success by performance of a series of apparently independent activities (Fig. 3). By eight months, these ir-relevant activities had dropped out, and performance was much faster, more efficient, and direct. The cloth was pulled immediately, and often the infant would hold out its other hand in anticipation of the toy.

Two interesting questions arise in connection with these early achieve-ments. The first concerns the means by which infants come to select actions to try out. Piaget suggested that the infant merely runs through a series of available schemes until something is found which works (Piaget, 1953, obs. 120). However, things may not be quite so straightforward, and it is possible that the infant does carry out some task analysis to identify actions that might be suitable. We have very little information about this sort of procedure, but a study by Kaye (1979) suggests that infants do need to perceive the relevance of an activity to the goal before it is used. Kaye tested 6-month-old infants on a detour task in which they had to reach around a Perspex screen for an object that was visible behind it. One group of infants received no pre-training, but a second group was taught by their mothers how to reach around the edge of the screen with no object present. This group learned to reach around the screen, and therefore acquired an appropriate means, but had no opportunity to utilise it for attaining the goal.

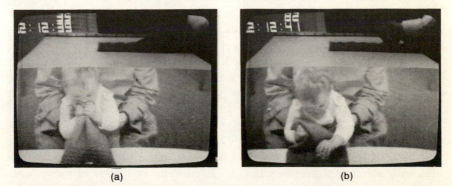

(a)   (b)

FIG. 3.   A 6-month-old using a cloth to retrieve an object; (a) he first puts the cloth in his mouth; (b) then he grasps the toy when it is within reach. The infant does not appear to pull the cloth with the intention of retrieving the toy. (Photographs by Peter Willatts.)

When tested on the detour task with an object present, the training gave no advantage. Infants were unable to apply the effective method, and both groups attempted to reach through the screen for the object. This is an ingenious paradigm, and is worth pursuing on other tasks to examine some of the factors determining the infant's selection of actions.

The second issue concerns the way that infants gradually alter their performance. With both search and the use of supports, infants do not simply repeat their initial method for retrieving the object, but progressively alter and reorganise the procedure. Picking up the screen or support in order to play with it gives way to moving the screen aside or pulling the cloth which are activities that are quite distinct from those that appeared originally. Piaget has little to say about these changes except that they arise from the mutual assimilation of schemes and differentiation through accommodation, which, as Klahr (1982, p. 80) pointed out, still remain "mysterious and shadowy forces". As an alternative, Klahr has suggested that there might exist innate procedures for detecting consistent sequences and eliminating redundancies in processing (Klahr & Wallace, 1976; Klahr, 1984). Detection of the sequence, "pick up screen, play with screen, pick up toy" might lead to elimination of the redundant activity "play with screen" to produce a more efficient procedure. Similarly, Karmiloff-Smith (1979) proposed that once children have achieved an adequate performance, spontaneous reorganisations will occur so that the same result is achieved with the minimum of effort. If procedures of this sort are operating, then the strategies used by young infants may be far more complex than has previously been imagined.

If young infants do use information about the goal to select suitable actions to try out and do restructure the sequence to achieve maximum efficiency, it is also possible that heuristic information plays a part in early means–ends problem solving. We have already seen some evidence for this with newborns, but there has been little study of this topic with infants between 6 and 12 months. However, some observations of imitation by Kaye and Marcus (1978; 1981) are relevant. Six-month-old infants were given a demonstration by an adult of a series of actions such as opening and closing a mouth five times. This was repeated after each attempt by the infant to imitate the activity, with up to as many as 40 presentations in a session. Although young infants are usually poor at imitating movements of such complexity (Piaget, 1951; Uzgiris, 1972), repeated viewing of the target behaviour led to considerable success. Imitation did not occur immediately, but there was a gradual "working-up" of performance over a series of trials. The infant might respond at first by opening its mouth only once and follow this with a burst of arm movements. Eventually the burst of movements would shift from the arm to the mouth, and the infant would eventually assemble a good copy of the target behaviour. This performance reveals a surprising capacity for early, goal-directed search for a solution in which random trial-and-error seems totally absent.

One other prediction of Piaget's theory is that stage IV problem-solving lacks flexibility and that infants are unable to adapt means–ends coordinations. Some support for this account was provided by a study of Frye (1980) on the A not-B search error. Frye argued that it should be possible to eliminate search errors by presenting an intervening task that could disrupt the original coordinated scheme for searching at A. By eliminating the coordination at A, infants would be free to establish a new coordination at place B. Some infants were given an intervening task involving a new means–ends coordination such as searching for the object at place C or retrieving the object on a support. For others, the task involved no new coordination, and they were simply distracted with a new object, or given a partial-hiding task that did not require a means–ends coordination. The results showed that only those infants who received intervening means–ends tasks did make significantly fewer errors on the B trial.

If Frye is correct, then it should be possible to obtain similar errors on other kinds of means–ends tasks. However, the findings of studies using support tasks lead to very different conclusions. In one study (Willatts, 1985b), 9-month-old infants were tested on a standard A not-B search task, and an equivalent support task. Two cloths were laid out in front of the infant, and an object either hidden under one of them for the A trials (search), or placed on top of one (support). On the B trials, the object was hidden under or placed on top of the other cloth. While many errors were made when infants searched on B trials, very few occurred with the support task. This difference emerged on the very first B trial, and infants were able to switch from pulling one cloth to pulling the other. Of course, it might be argued that 9-month-old infants do not regard an object on a support as two separate objects, but as a single unit. Given that infants can adjust their reaching to changes in an object's position from as early as five months (Willatts, 1979), performance on the support task would not tell us much about means–ends skills. However, studies of infants' reactions to objects placed on platforms and supports have shown that by 6 months, the two are regarded as separate and distinct (Bresson, Maury, Pieraut Le-Bonniec, & de Schönen, 1977; Wishart & Bower, 1984). Further, when goal object and tool do look perceptually similar and resemble a single unit, means–ends problem-solving is actually impaired (Bates, Carlson-Luden, & Bretherton, 1980). It is also unlikely that infants were simply trying to reach directly for the object, touched the cloth, and came to pull it by accident. Infants do not attempt to reach for objects that are too distant (Field, 1976; 1977), and direct reaching rarely occurs on these means–ends tasks (Richardson, 1932; Willatts, 1982).

One further support task which also shows effective adjustment by 7- and 8-month-olds was reported by Willatts (1985a). Infants were given a long, single cloth on which a toy was placed beyond reach, at either the centre of the cloth (near condition), or twice as far away at the end (far condition). Each infant received three trials with the toy at one distance, followed by three more trials at the other distance. It was predicted that a failure to adapt performance to a change in the distance of the toy would show up in two ways. Infants who could successfully retrieve the toy in the near condition would do so by pulling the cloth only a short distance. If this method was repeated in the far condition, then the toy would not be brought within reach, and the infant would pause and have to pull the cloth again. Performance would therefore be slower and less efficient. For infants receiving the far condition first, success would occur after a long pull on the cloth. If this was repeated in the near condition, the toy would be carried over the edge of the table and fall on the floor. Neither of these predicted effects occurred, and infants showed an immediate adjustment in their method of retrieval when the distance of the object was changed (Fig. 4). Hardly any objects were pulled off the edge of the table, and while retrieval of the object

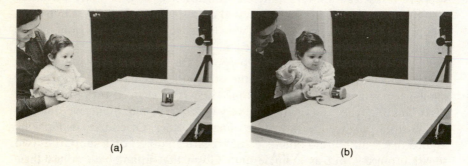

(a)   (b)

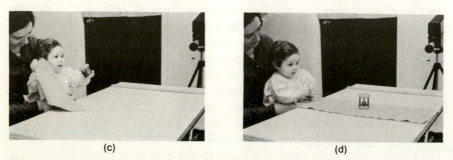

(c)   (d)

FIG. 4.   An 8-month-old showing efficient use of a cloth as a means for retrieving an out-of-reach object. (a) The toy is presented in the far condition; (b & c) the infant pulls the cloth in a single, uninterrupted movement; (d) when presented with the near condition, the infant was equally successful and adapted her pull to the changed distance of the object. (Photographs by Peter Willatts.)

in the far condition was slower and less efficient than in the near condition, the order of tasks had no effect.

Clearly infants have none of the difficulties in adjusting to changes in support tasks that they appear to experience with search. They switch from pulling one support to pulling another, and readily alter the style of pulling to cope with variations in the object's distance. Frye might have obtained his results, not because the intervening means–ends tasks disrupted an inflexible coordination, but because they were complex and demanding and resulted in infants simply forgetting the A trial experience (Bremner, 1985). Indeed, recent research with the classic A not-B task has shown a whole range of situations in which infants can adjust their search to take account of new hiding places. Failure to adapt may arise more from the characteristics of tasks than from the characteristics of infants (Corrigan & Fischer, 1985).

Stages V and VI

Although Piaget demonstrated that during the second year infants could solve increasingly complex problems, his claim that many solutions were planned or "invented" can be challenged. First, Piaget did not report a single example of a stage VI solution that occurred without some form of overt activity which initially failed. Recall that Lucienne did try to put the chain into the box before coming up with the method of rolling it into a ball. Similarly, when tackling the problem of removing the chain through a narrow opening in a box, she first attempted to grasp it before pulling the drawer to enlarge the gap (Piaget, 1953, obs. 180). Thus, the crucial performance that ought to distinguish stage VI solutions from those of earlier stages did not actually occur. In addition, Piaget's infants often had considerable prior experience with the tasks and the materials. Laurent finally produced a "stage VI" solution with the stick after having used it on at least 8 separate occasions from the age of 4 months, and while Lucienne managed to put the chain into the box with apparently no experience at all of the task, she had for several months played extensively with both items.

Second, Piaget frequently used other criteria such as speed and success in attaining the goal to identify a planned solution. The methods of stages IV and V were often described as being slow and resulting in failure (e.g. Piaget, 1953, obs. 178). These criteria are unsatisfactory because planned solutions may be just as fast or as slow as unplanned solutions, and differences in speed may have more to do with level of skill than with strategy. Further, planning does not necessarily guarantee success, and an infant who planned a method which was inappropriate and failed would not have been identified as having used a stage VI strategy.

Third, a younger child may fail to plan because the materials are novel and their possible functions unknown. Laurent may have made little progress with the stick because he simply did not know what to do with it. Planning may not be evident because an initial period of examination or play might naturally lead into a solution through heuristic search, or the infant could become so engrossed that the original goal is ignored (Koslowski & Bruner, 1972). Variations in materials are known to affect success at problem-solving with 10-month-olds (Bates et al., 1980) and with older children (Kopp, O'Connor, & Finger, 1975; McKechnie, 1987; Willatts & Cupolillo, 1988), and familiarity with the materials increases the chances that older children will solve means–ends tasks (Sylva, Bruner, & Genova, 1976; Smith & Dutton, 1979). Poorer performance by younger infants may not reflect a difference in the strategies they can use, but simply a difference in their knowledge.

These criticisms lead to two opposite conclusions. One is that Piaget did not observe any planning in stage VI, but instead a more efficient form of heuristic search. Planning may not be a method that is available at all in the sensory–motor period, but appears later when representational skills are more firmly established (Klahr & Robinson, 1981; Wellman et al., 1985). The alternative is that planning occurs much earlier, but has not been identified because of poor task design or because infants may adopt a mixture of strategies and thus planning has been obscured.

There have been very few studies of planning in infancy, but there is evidence to suggest that the strategy appears sooner than Piaget claimed. Lockman (1984) reported that infants began to make manual detours at about 10 months, somewhat earlier than has been found in other studies (Bruner, 1970; Butterworth, 1983; Jarrett, 1988). However, Lockman only recorded whether his infants successfully retrieved an object from behind a screen, and did not report the method they used. The screen was narrow and allowed the infant to make a detour around either side. If infants were using trial-and-error methods, this would have effectively doubled their chances of getting around. In some recent studies of my own, 12-month-old infants did not plan their detours, but discovered how to reach around a barrier after first having tried to reach through it. These infants also had difficulties in adapting to a change in the position of the screen, so that an infant who made a detour with its left hand continued to use the same hand and tried to reach through the screen when it was moved to the opposite side (Willatts, 1987). A similar conclusion comes from a study by Jarrett (1988) who reported that 67% of 12- to 14-month-olds, and even 50% of 16- to 18-month-olds first attempted a direct reach for an object behind a transparent barrier. Comparable findings with infants of the same age were obtained by McKenzie and Bigelow (1986) in a study of locomotor detours, suggesting that detours are not planned at 12 months.

Other studies have shown that young locomotor infants can select the shortest route to a goal (Cornell & Heth, 1983; Lockman & Pick, 1984;

Rieser & Heiman, 1982), but again the design of these studies does not reveal whether these detour routes are planned. The infants may have made a mental comparison of alternative routes, or they may have been responding directly to some feature in the array. However, evidence that infants as young as 13 months may be able to make simple inferences and coordinate schemes mentally comes from studies of search. Sophian and Sage (1983) showed that infants demonstrated some competence at inferring the location of a hidden object by taking into account information about where the experimenter moved her hand, and whether the hand contained an object or not. More recently, Sophian and Adams (1987) demonstrated that children aged 14 to 28 months were able to infer which of two locations concealed more objects after the number had been transformed by an insertion or a deletion. Similar findings were obtained with 15-month-olds by Haake and Somerville (1985) who argued that infants were solving invisible hiding tasks by inferring the location of a hidden toy from both spatial and temporal information. Either source alone would have been insufficient to solve the task.

One study that indicates planning may occur as early as 9 months was reported by Willatts (1984b). The task required infants to retrieve a toy by first removing a barrier and then pulling a support on which the toy was placed. A large block of foam was used for the barrier and a cloth for the support. Two groups were tested on different versions of the task. For each, the barrier was in front of the cloth, but the position of the toy differed. For the experimental group, it was placed on the cloth, but for the control group, it was placed alongside the cloth and could not be retrieved. If infants are unable to plan a solution, they would have to work through these tasks one step at a time with no difference in performance until the final step when the toy is either retrieved or not. Alternatively, if infants could use their knowledge of support relations to plan a solution, differences should be apparent because only one of the tasks can be solved. The results supported a planning interpretation. The experimental group removed the barrier, did not play with it, but quickly went on to pull the cloth and retrieve the toy. The control group also picked up the barrier, but played with it for a long time and on many trials completely ignored the cloth (Fig. 5). These differences were present on the very first trial and did not emerge through a process of learning over a series of attempts. Thus, the infants' first activity with the barrier was not determined by the characteristics of the foam block, but by what they intended to do next.

Although this study suggests that infants may have planned how to retrieve the toy, Wellman et al. (1985) offered an alternative interpretation. It is possible that the experimental group did not really care that the toy and cloth were separate and simply regarded the two as a combined cloth–toy object. The task would then have been a more straightforward means–ends problem of removing a barrier to obtain a goal, and the differences in

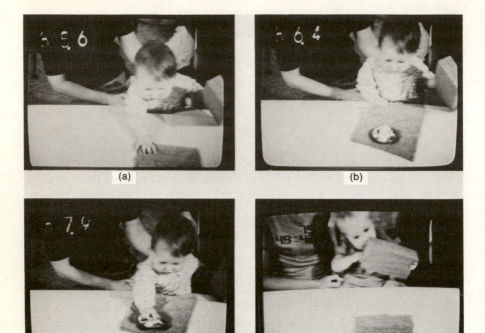

FIG. 5.   A 9-month-old uses her knowledge of support relations to plan how to retrieve the toy. (a) She removes the block of foam; (b) then pulls the cloth; (c) and grasps the toy. (d) In contrast, an infant in the control condition ignores the cloth and plays with the block of foam. (Photographs by Peter Willatts.)

performance could have arisen from the greater attractiveness of the cloth–toy in contrast to the less interesting cloth on its own. The decision to pull the support and retrieve the toy might have been taken *after* the barrier was removed and not *before*. If this is what happened, then infants were only showing goal-directedness and were not planning a series of actions.

The finding of this study is not as clear as we would wish, but a further study by Willatts and Rosie (1988) provides more convincing evidence for planning by infants of less than one year. A group of 10- to 12-month-olds was tested on two forms of an extended version of the planning task requiring 3 steps for solution. In the experimental condition, a barrier (block of foam) was positioned in front of a long support cloth on the far end of which was a string. An attractive toy was fastened to the other end of the string, but was some distance from the cloth and resting on the table. In order to retrieve the toy, infants had to remove the barrier, pull the cloth, recover the string, and pull it. In the control condition, infants were presented with the same arrangement of barrier, cloth, and string, but the toy was visibly separate from the string and could not be retrieved.

There are two main features of this new task. One is that the appearance of the cloth is equivalent in the two conditions so that differential attractiveness could no longer provide the basis for any difference in performance. The other is that in both conditions, achievement of the first step (removing the barrier) provides access to the same combination of support and string. However, in the experimental condition the string is a means for obtaining the toy, whereas in the control condition it has no such function. Even if infants regarded the cloth and string as a combined object, any evidence for a more rapid or direct approach to the cloth in the experimental condition would indicate an appreciation of the function of both cloth and string as intermediaries and would show that infants had planned what to do.

Each infant was tested on both conditions with order of the tasks counterbalanced. In the experimental condition, infants were far more likely to remove the barrier without playing with it, and were much quicker to get it out of the way and to contact the cloth than in the control condition. In addition, the string was retrieved more often and there were fewer refusals to contact the barrier in the experimental condition. Finally, performance was altered as soon as the condition was changed and regardless of which had come first.

These findings demonstrate that infants of about 12 months are capable of planning a series of actions to obtain a goal. When the string was fastened to the toy they were more likely to approach the barrier, were quicker to get it out of the way and contact the cloth, and were less likely to ignore the string. The more rapid approach to the cloth in the experimental condition could not have been a response to a more attractive appearance because the support was presented with an identical string in both conditions. It is not possible to say with certainty just how much of the sequence was planned in advance. The infants must have considered at least two steps and planned to remove the barrier in order to pull the cloth and retrieve the string in the experimental condition. Whether they also included the final step of pulling the string in the plan, or thought about it after they had grasped the support remains unclear. However, these results do show that infants of about one year can think beyond the first step of a compound means–ends problem.

Summary

These findings do not fit well with Piaget's theory. There is evidence that heuristically guided search occurs throughout infancy, appearing in the hand-to-mouth activity of the new-born, imitation at 6 months, and tool-use at around 12 months. It is not therefore a strategy which develops towards the end of the first year in stage V, but appears to be a feature of infant cognition at all periods. Of course, the use of the strategy will become more effective with the inclusion of more powerful heuristics, but the basic procedures will be independent of any stages. The finding that planning occurs as early as stage IV challenges Piaget's claim that representation is the final achievement of sensory–motor development. Instead, this observation may be added to the growing body of evidence for the existence of a representational capacity throughout infancy and across a variety of domains which include imitation (Meltzoff & Moore, 1977; Meltzoff, 1988), recall memory (Mandler, 1984), object permanence (Baillargeon, Spelke, & Wasserman, 1985; Hood & Willatts, 1986), and knowledge of causal relations (Leslie, 1982).

DEVELOPMENTAL INFLUENCES ON PROBLEM-SOLVING

Problem-solving is not a single skill, but an activity that draws on a variety of separate abilities, each of which may develop independently of others. Although infants may use strategies at all ages, changes in problem-solving may come about through developments in at least five possible areas: error detection and diagnosis; error inhibition; persistence; processing constraints; and representation of solutions. Although we have very little information on most of these topics, I will give some indications in this final section of the way that each might affect problem-solving.

Error Detection and Diagnosis

The nature of the infant's goal will play a significant role in the detection of errors, and performance may vary markedly when children pursue different goals. A good example was reported in a recent study of early seriation skills by DeLoache, Sugarman, and Brown (1985). Children were required to arrange sets of objects in order of size. One set consisted of nested cups which could be inserted inside each other, and the other was a collection of rings which were to be stacked on an upright rod. With the cups, it was clear that children had the goal of trying to arrange them in order to size, because any cup that was too big to enter another led to some attempt to correct the error. However, the goal with the rings appeared to be that of merely getting them all onto the rod, regardless of their order. Once a ring had been placed it was left alone, and nothing was done to alter the arrangement. As DeLoache et al. (1985, p. 937) commented, "whether children will detect and attempt to correct their own errors depends on the extent to which the task informs them that they have erred". Thus, changes in performance may not reflect changes in problem-solving ability, but changes in the structure of goals.

The differences in goals may be quite subtle. In a study of memory-based searching (DeLoache and Brown, 1984), 18- to 30-month-old children watched as a toy was hidden in a room. On some trials, while the child waited outside for few minutes, the toy was secretly removed from its hiding place. Most children searched where the toy was expected to be found, and the older children went on to search other related locations when the toy was not discovered. Occasionally, a child would make an error and begin by searching at the wrong place. On these trials, failure to find the toy did not tend to produce an extensive search of other related locations. This difference, at least for the older children, suggests that the organisation of search was determined by how certain the child was of the accuracy of the initial search.

The ability to diagnose the cause of errors will be influenced by the infant's general and task-specific knowledge. One example of general knowledge is the understanding of causal relations in event sequences. An infant who failed to differentiate between the effects of her own actions and the effects of independent agents would not consider using other people as a means to help solve a problem. Harding and Golinkoff (1979) found that only those infants who could look for external causes of events stopped trying to retrieve an object from a sealed container and attempted to enlist the help of the mother. An example of specific knowledge is knowing that a lid is a special part of an object that usually can be removed. It is not difficult to see that a lack of either sort of knowledge will constrain the infant's ability to understand the reason for failure.

Error Inhibition

When an error occurs, the infant must somehow prevent the action that led to error from being re-selected in order to allow other possibilities to be tried out. This is less of a problem if selection is random because other actions have an equal chance of being considered, but error inhibition is an essential feature of heuristic search. This means that infants who are unable to inhibit errors would have difficulties in engaging in any strategy other than random search. The procedure would need to be sensitive to context because an action that leads to error at one step may be correct later on. For example, a direct reach for a toy at the end of a rotating lever will be ineffective when the toy is too far away. The infant must abandon that method and rotate the lever to bring it nearer. At this point, a direct reach would now be appropriate, but the problem would not be solved if error-inhibition completely eliminated direct reaching from any further consideration (Koslowski & Bruner, 1972; McKechnie, 1987).

We know little of the memory processes that must underpin this ability, but sufficient to be confident that they do develop. Studies of search for hidden objects on the A not-B task suggest that infants do not forget the original place of hiding but retain information about both A and B locations (Harris, 1987 and Chapter 5 this volume). To find the object on B-trials, the infant must search at B and at the same time inhibit an approach to A. Sophian (1984) reported a series of studies that examined the ability of children to inhibit prior information and attend to recent information. This "selectivity" was shown by infants of 9 months when both sorts of information were in conflict, but the performance was fragile and easily disrupted (Sophian & Sage, 1983). The tendency to select prior information shows a marked decline during infancy, although it can still appear as late as 4 years of age. Another factor that may determine the infant's ability to search accurately is delay. This was examined by Diamond (1985) who found that all infants between 7 and 12 months could inhibit search errors, but that the duration of inhibition changed from only a second or two at the youngest ages to about 12 seconds at one year. Diamond suggested that this increase reflected a change in the ability to use recall to guide behaviour while overcoming the tendency to be guided by habit.

A further study by Diamond (1988) showed that improvements occurred between 6 and 12 months in the ability to inhibit inappropriate actions on a task which did not require the use of recall memory. Infants were seen longitudinally and presented with an attractive toy that was covered by a transparent box with an opening in one side. The infants' efforts at retrieving the toy went through four distinct phases. The youngest (6–7 months) reached persistently along the line of sight and failed to grasp the toy, just as the youngest infants in Diamond's (1985) persistently reached to place A after a minimal delay. They seemed unable to modify their approach in any way, and as Diamond reported, "no clue, no coaxing, no amount of failure could persuade infants of this age to try anything other than reaching straight to where they saw the toy" Diamond (1988, p. 32). In the second phase (7–8 months), the infants began to shift their line of sight by bending down or leaning over in order to see the toy through the open side of the box. The original method of reaching along the line sight was still employed, but now the toy was frequently retrieved because the line of sight had shifted. In the third phase (10 months), the infants would look at the toy through the opening, but then sat up and reached around through the open side. For this level of performance, the infants reached along the remembered line of sight, and ignored the current one. In the final stage (12 months), the infants retrieved the toy without any need for shifting their position to look through the opening.

Further evidence for developmental changes in error inhibition comes from two studies reported by McKechnie (1987). In one, the performance of infants aged between 12 and 24 months on lever rotation tasks was examined over a series of trials. Individual attempts to solve the tasks were rated on a scale devised originally by Koslowski and Bruner (1972), and ranged from simple methods such as reaching directly for the goal, to more advanced methods such as partially rotating the lever. McKechnie found a trial by age interaction with the youngest infants (12–14 months) using simpler methods and showing no advance over trials. In contrast, older infants showed a clear improvement and used more advanced methods on later trials. In a second study, McKechnie tested the same infants on a variety of bent-wire barrier tasks (Whitecraft, Cobb, & Davis, 1959; Hollis, 1962; Davis, 1974). Infants were presented with bent-wire shapes on which were suspended brightly coloured objects. A hole in the centre of each object was large enough to allow it to be manipulated around the bends in the wire. The task for the infant was to discover how to remove the object from the wire. Again, simpler methods such as hitting or spinning the object dominated the performance of the youngest infants. Older infants also tried such methods, but changed to more appropriate ones such as moving the object to and fro along the wire when their initial attempts produced no success. On both types of task all infants tried simple methods at first, but only older infants were able to discard them and move on to something else.

While these observations do suggest that a change may occur in infants' ability to inhibit one action while performing another, we should be cautious about assuming that this is a general capacity which will influence performance on all tasks, or is dependent on the age of the infant. In a number of studies of means–ends problem-solving on support tasks, I have not found any indication that infants have difficulty with inhibiting actions that were previously successful but are no longer appropriate (Willatts, 1985a; 1985b). In addition, there is some evidence that infants as young as 2 and 3 months are capable of inhibiting unsuccessful actions in the context of contingency learning. In one study, Kalnins and Bruner (1973) investigated the ability of infants to control their rate of sucking when the focus of a visual stimulus was contingent upon sucking rate. There was a rapid increase in sucking when this produced a sharp picture, and the rate decreased when the contingency was altered and sucking produced a blurred picture. However, Kalnins and Bruner did note an asymmetry in their results. Infants were better able to increase their sucking than they were to inhibit sucking in order to achieve the same result.

Response inhibition has also been observed in studies of contingent leg kicking. Rovee-Collier, Morrongiello, Aron, and Kupersmidt (1978) trained 3-month-olds to kick one leg in order to activate a mobile. When the mobile was attached to the infant's other leg, the rate of kicking with the original leg decreased, while the rate for the attached leg increased. This result is particularly interesting because it is not necessary for the infant to stop kicking the unattached leg in order to move the mobile; the same result would have been obtained regardless of whether the infant kicked both legs or only the one which was attached. The fact that a reduction in kicking with the non-attached leg did occur demonstrates both that young infants can inhibit previous actions, and that they are sensitive to very subtle differences in contingencies.

Error-inhibition requires careful regulation when infants generate multiple attempts at a solution. If it is difficult to inhibit a single inappropriate method, then it is likely to be even more difficult when there are several. Unfortunately, we have little information on the development of skills at monitoring progress towards a solution. Koslowski and Bruner (1972) reported that those children who tried more than one method to solve a lever-rotation task did so by attempting a primitive method first and more complex methods later. Ordering attempts from simple to complex might be one way of easing the load on memory, and clearer evidence for this structuring on similar tasks was obtained by Willatts and Domminney (1987). They reported a progression in the complexity of methods used by 2-year-olds with the simplest methods being tried first, intermediate ones next, and the most complex last of all, although 40% of attempts were repetitions of previously unsuccessful methods. Studies of search by children aged 2 years and older have revealed a steady improvement in the ability to search non-redundantly and look in each place only once (Wellman et al., 1984; DeLoache & Brown, 1984). By 2 years, children can structure their sequence of attempts and show some ability to reject inappropriate methods from further consideration.

Persistence

How long should the infant continue with one method before it is rejected, and when should all attempts be abandoned? Infants may reject a method too soon and before they have properly identified the reason for the error. For example, an object may fail to drop into a hole in a shape-sorter because it was misaligned, but not because it was the wrong shape. An infant who gave up at this point and switched to a new object or a different hole would not gain a realistic understanding of the basis for error.

There is also the question of when to abandon all attempts at solving a problem. Infants who generally persist for longer periods will have more opportunity to discover an effective method and will be more likely to find a solution. Significant correlations between persistence and success on means–ends tasks have been reported in a number of studies (Jennings et al., 1979;

Yarrow et al., 1983; Jennings, Yarrow, & Martin, 1984), but it is unclear whether persistence is a cause or a consequence of competence on problem-solving tasks. Persistence on search tasks shows a considerable increase during the second year (Bertenthal & Fischer, 1983), and many toddlers will continue working at a task until they achieve success (Matas, Arend, & Sroufe, 1978; Willatts & Domminney, 1987; Wellman et al., 1984).

Persistence or mastery motivation is influenced by quality of the home environment and parental style of care-giving such as level and quality of stimulation (Yarrow et al., 1984). This suggests a causal link between parental style, persistence, and problem-solving competence, but the nature of the link remains uncertain (although see Chapter 10 by Lock, Service, Brito, and Chandler, in this volume). Infants who show more persistence may elicit different kinds of stimulation from parents, and it is not difficult to imagine a situation where an infant who tends to try harder will generate more encouragement and assistance from a parent. Nevertheless, these relationships are very interesting and suggest a plausible way in which problem-solving abilities might be affected by more general aspects of the infant's personality and environment.

Processing Constraints

A further influence on problem-solving are those constraints which limit cognitive processes. Bruner (1973) suggested that infants deliberately restrict the degrees of freedom for action when attempting to solve a problem or master a new skill. This allows the infant to focus on certain components of the task, and avoid becoming overwhelmed by complexity. As each component is mastered, the restriction on degrees of freedom can be progressively relaxed, and new methods will emerge. Developmental sequences in mastery of increasingly complex tasks may be explained, not by the appearance of more elaborate strategies, but by the operation of the same strategies in more complex domains which are determined by the infant itself. Studies by Bruner (1970) of tasks requiring infants to negotiate detours or coordinate the use of both hands to take possession of objects and remove covers provide evidence that infants do progress by gradually incorporating more components. In one of my own studies, 6-month-old infants who were learning to handle two objects simultaneously showed clear evidence for a reduction in the degrees of freedom for action by producing a level of bimanual activity below that expected by chance (Willatts, 1986). This sort of restriction would exert a powerful influence on problem-solving, and Bushnell (1985) has argued that the gradual appearance of means–ends ability on manual tasks may be determined by the mastery of visually guided reaching and the consequent release of attentional capacity.

A similar account has been offered by Fischer (1980) who proposed that infants' skills develop through a sequence of levels. At any time, there is an upper limit on the complexity of skills that the infant can control, but this limit increases at regular intervals. At the first level, the infant can control only a single sensory–motor skill. At the second level, the infant can control relations between individual sensory–motor skills, while at the third level the infant controls two or more second-level skills to produce a system. At the final sensory–motor level, the infant can control two or more systems simultaneously.

A demonstration of the change from Level 3 to Level 4 problem-solving was provided by Goldfield (1983). A group of infants was tested at 16, 18, and 20 months on a task which required the use of a stick to retrieve a cookie from within a transparent tube. At 16 months, infants controlled independent systems for handling the stick and the tube, and most did not attempt to touch the tube with the stick. At 18 months they began to contact the tube with the stick, but it was only at 20 months that many were able to orient the stick in order to insert it into the tube. This sequence of changes in mastery of control over complementary systems was mirrored by corresponding changes on a picture-showing task which required infants to show a picture to another person (Lempers, Flavell, & Flavell, 1977). At 16 months, the response was to give the picture to the other person, but at 18 months, the infants did attempt to show the picture though without orienting it correctly. At 20 months, the picture was held up so that it could be viewed by the other person, an accomplishment which required the coordination of one system for holding the picture and another system for taking into account the other person's viewpoint. This correspondence in progression between two very different tasks lends weight to Fischer's claim that these levels impose a restriction on all skills.

Within each level, new skills may be constructed by combining or modifying existing skills in a variety of ways. The gradual emergence of intentional search may be explained as the coordination of simpler Level 2 skills to produce a new Level 2 skill (Corrigan & Fischer, 1985), and the ability to plan to remove a barrier, pull a cloth, and retrieve a toy would be a skill compounded from two such Level 2 skills.

Representation of Solutions

Finally, we might expect that infants who solve a problem will benefit from the achievement and be able to incorporate the new method in their repertoire. This presupposes several accomplishments. The solution may have emerged from a succession of false starts and dead ends, and it would be inefficient to record the whole sequence and reproduce it all when the same problem is encountered again. An infant who reaches directly for an object behind a transparent screen, fumbles, discovers the edge of the screen, and reaches around it would be better off disregarding the initial direct reach and remembering only the detour. However, this presumes that the infant can decompose the whole solution into task-relevant and task-irrelevant segments. Although we have already touched on this issue in connection with the development of means–ends performance on search and support tasks, little is known about the development of skills that would support such segmentation. One technique which might reveal them is to model a solution with the inclusion of actions that are both relevant and irrelevant to the task. In a study which used this method, Harnick (1979) found that infants between 12 and 24 months could ignore irrelevant actions if the task was easy for them, but would imitate these actions if the task was of moderate difficulty. The finding that this difference often occurred on the first trial before the infant had attempted the task suggests that this could be a very informative technique for identifying the infant's capacity for effective task-analysis.

There is also the question of whether a solution is retained in a form that is specific to the context in which the problem was presented, or in some general form with a wider range of application. Koslowski and Bruner (1972) argued that transfer was built into the solution of a lever-rotation task, but offered no evidence to support their claim. Willatts and Domminney (1987) found that 2-year-olds could readily transfer their solution from one form of the task (a lever) to another (a rotating tray), but this level of transfer is not always apparent on other tasks. It has already been mentioned that 12-month-olds do not immediately transfer their detour skills to changes in the position of a barrier (McKenzie & Bigelow, 1986; Willatts, 1987; Jarrett, 1988), and 2- and 3-year-olds may need assistance to promote the transfer of problem-solving skills (Crisafi & Brown, 1986). Yet 8- and 9-month-olds are able to search in a wide range of different settings such as under cloths and cups, in containers, behind screens, and even after crawling across the floor. Recall that Piaget himself observed that string-pulling could occur in novel situations, and he thought that such behaviour "surely constitutes an early form of true generalization". Virtually nothing is known about the processes by which infants come to represent the solution to a problem, although it seems fairly safe to conclude that generalisation and transfer does occur at all ages.

CONCLUSIONS

As infants grow older, they are able to tackle a wider range of tasks and find solutions when previously they could do nothing. What is it that develops?

We can be certain that it is not some "general problem-solving ability" because there is no such entity. Problem-solving is a complex mixture of processes and in this chapter I have discussed three main components.

First, there is what the infant can do. This concerns the actions, skills, or operators (Newell & Simon, 1972) that combine to transform the initial state into the goal state. The problems an infant can solve will, in part, be determined by the skills that are available. You could hardly expect a 5-month-old who is just learning how to pick up objects to make much progress with a shape-sorter task. Yet surprisingly, this obvious fact seems often to have been overlooked with the result that infants' problem-solving abilities have been underestimated. This criticism can be made of a number of Piaget's observations where the behaviour may have occurred because the children were trying to discover what to do rather than how to attain the goal. When care is taken to ensure that infants do possess the necessary skills, we often come away with a very different picture of their abilities (e.g. Kaye & Marcus, 1978; Willatts, 1984b; Butterworth & Hopkins, 1988).

Second, there is what the infant knows. The capacity for carrying out an effective task-analysis will not only suggest appropriate methods for solving a problem, but will cut down the range of choice and thereby reduce the strain on limited cognitive resources. Sometimes the infant's task-analysis will outstrip his or her level of skill, as in the case of the 4-month-old who struggles to grasp an attractive toy in order to carry it to the mouth (Bruner, 1981), but in general, the expansion of knowledge during infancy will equip the child with an increasingly more powerful problem-solving capacity.

Third, there is how the infant organises what it knows and what it does. This is the question of strategy, which in many respects is central to our understanding of problem-solving. We see this clearly on puzzles such as the Tower-of-Hanoi (Klahr & Robinson, 1981) where the level of motor skill is trivial, but progress can only be made when a strategy has been formulated for organising complex sequences of moves. Strategy is important for knowing not just what to do, but when to do it, and provides a crucial way of overcoming the limitations of the human information processing system. Given that infants are far more limited in their processing capacity than adults, the possibility of operating with a strategy may be a critical factor in early development.

For many years we have had only Piaget's theory to guide our understanding of problem-solving in infancy. This theory is now showing signs of strain, and is beginning to crack under the weight of a considerable body of recent research. Heuristic search, which should only appear after a sequence of five stages, is present at birth, and planning, which should mark the end-point of sensory–motor development, is available towards the end of the first year. Instead of a gradual series of advances throughout infancy, it now seems more likely that from quite an early age, infants have the choice of a range of different problem-solving methods.

Development of problem-solving in infancy does not seem to come about through the appearance of radically new strategies, but through the development of new abilities which increase the power of existing strategies. In the final section of this chapter, I have tried to indicate some of these abilities which would allow infants to use their problem solving skills to a greater advantage. However, it is obvious that there are still many gaps in our understanding, and that the search for solutions to our problems will continue as we watch infants searching for solutions to theirs.

REFERENCES

Baillargeon, R., Spelke, E. S., & Wasserman, S. (1985). Object permanence in five-month-old infants. *Cognition, 20*, 191–208.

Bates, E., Carlson-Luden, V., & Bretherton, I. (1980). Perceptual aspects of tool using in infancy. *Infant Behavior and Development, 3*, 127–140.

Bertenthal, B. I. & Fischer, K. W. (1983). The development of representation in search: A social-cognitive analysis. *Child Development, 54*, 846–857.

Bower, T. G. R., Broughton, J. M., & Moore, K. M. (1970a). Demonstration of intention in the reaching behaviour of neonate humans. *Nature, 228*, 679–681.

Bower, T. G. R., Broughton, J. M., & Moore, K. M. (1970b). The coordination of visual and tactual input in infants. *Perception and Psychophysics, 8*, 51–53.

Bremner, J. G. (1985). Object tracking and search in infancy: A review of data and a theoretical evaluation. *Developmental Review, 5*, 371–396.

Bresson, F., Maury, L., Pieraut Le-Bonniec, G., & de Schönen, S. (1977). Organization and lateralization of reaching in infants: An instance of asymmetric functions in hands collaboration. *Neuropsychologia, 15*, 311–320.

Bruner, J. S. (1970). The growth and structure of skill. In K. Connolly (ed.), *Mechanisms of motor skill development*. London: Academic Press.

Bruner, J. S. (1972). Origins of problem solving strategies. In R. Rudner & I. Scheffler (eds), *Logic and art: Essays in honour of Nelson Goodman*. New York: Bobbs-Merrill.

Bruner, J. S. (1973). Organization of early skilled action. *Child Development, 44*, 1–11.

Bruner, J. S. (1981). Intention in the structure of action and interaction. In L. P. Lipsitt (ed.), *Advances in infancy research*: Vol. 1. Norwood, N. J.: Ablex Publishing Corp.

Bushnell, E. W. (1985). The decline of visually guided reaching during infancy. *Infant Behavior and Development, 8*, 139–155.

Butterworth, G. (1983). Structure of the mind in human infancy. In L. P. Lipsitt & C. K. Rovee-Collier (eds), *Advances in infancy research:* Vol. 2. Norwood, N.J.: Ablex Publishing Corp.

Butterworth, G. E. & Hopkins, N. (1988). Hand–mouth coordination in the new-born baby. *British Journal of Developmental Psychology, 6*, 303–314.

Cavanagh, P. & Davidson, M. L. (1977). The secondary circular reaction and response elicitation in the operant learning of 6-month-old infants. *Developmental Psychology, 13*, 371–376.

Cornell, E. H. & Heth, C. D. (1983). Spatial cognition: Gathering strategies used by preschool children. *Journal of Experimental Child Psychology, 35*, 93–110.

Corrigan, R. & Fischer, K. W. (1985). Controlling sources of variation in search tasks: A skill theory approach. In H. M. Wellman (ed.), *Children's searching: The development of search skill and spatial representation*. Hillsdale, N.J.: Lawrence Erlbaum Associates Inc.

Crisafi, M. A. & Brown, A. L. (1986). Analogical transfer in very young children: Combining two separately learned solutions to reach a goal. *Child Development, 57*, 953–968.

Davis, R. T. (1974). *Primate behaviour: Development in field and laboratory research*: Vol. 3. *Monkeys as perceivers*. London: Academic Press.

Davis, J. M. & Rovee-Collier, C. K. (1983). Alleviated forgetting of a learned contingency in 8-week-old infants. *Developmental Psychology, 19*, 353–365.

DeCasper, A. J. & Carstens, A. A. (1981). Contingencies of stimulation: Effects on learning and emotion in neonates. *Infant Behavior and Development, 4*, 19–35.

DeLoache, J. S. & Brown, A. L. (1984). Where do I go next?: Intelligent searching by very young children. *Developmental Psychology, 20*, 37–44.

DeLoache, J. S., Sugarman, S., & Brown, A. L. (1985). The development of error correction strategies in young children's manipulated play. *Child Development, 56*, 928–939.

Diamond, A. (1988). *Retrieval of an object from an open box: The development of visual–tactile control of reaching in the first year of life*. Manuscript submitted for publication.

Diamond, A. (1985). Development of the ability to use recall to guide action, as indicated by infants' performance on AB. *Child Development, 56*, 868–883.

Fagen, J. W. (1984). Infants' long-term memory for stimulus color. *Developmental Psychology, 20*, 435–440.

Fagen, J. W., Morrongiello, B. A., Rovee-Collier, C., & Gekoski, M. J. (1984). Expectancies and memory retrieval in three-month-old infants. *Child Development, 55*, 936–943.

Fagen, J. W. & Rovee, C. K. (1976). Effects of quantitative shifts in a visual reinforcer on the instrumental response of infants. *Journal of Experimental Child Psychology, 22*, 349–360.

Fagen, J. W., Rovee, C. K., & Kaplan, M. G. (1976). Psychophysical scaling of stimulus similarity in 3-month-old infants and adults. *Journal of Experimental Child Psychology, 22*, 272–281.

Field, J. (1976). The adjustment of reaching behavior to object distance in early infancy. *Child Development, 47*, 304–320.

Field, J. (1977). Coordination of vision and prehension in young infants. *Child Development, 48*, 97–103.

Field, T. M., Woodson, R., Greenberg, R., & Cohen, D. (1982). Discrimination and imitation of facial expressions by neonates. *Science, 218*, 179–181.

Field, T., Vega-Lahr, N., Scafidi, F., & Goldstein, S. (1986). Effects of maternal unavailability on mother–infant interactions. *Infant Behavior and Development, 9*, 473–478.

Fischer, K. (1980). A theory of cognitive development: The control and construction of hierarchies of skills. *Psychological Review, 87*, 477–531.

Frye, D. (1980). Stages of development: The stage IV error. *Infant Behavior and Development, 3*, 115–126.

Gekoski, M. J., Rovee-Collier, C. K., & Carulli-Rabinowitz, V. (1983). A longitudinal analysis of infant distress: The origins of social expectations? *Infant Behavior and Development, 6*, 339–351.

Gibson, E. J. & Walker, A. S. (1984). Development of knowledge of visual–tactual affordances of substance. *Child Development, 55*, 453–460.

Goldfield, E. C. (1983). The development of control over complementary systems during the second year. *Infant Behavior and Development, 6*, 257–262.

Haake, R. & Somerville, S. (1985). The development of logical search skills in infancy. *Developmental Psychology, 21*, 176–186.

Harding, C. G. (1982). The development of the intention to communicate. *Human Development, 25*, 140–151.

Harding, C. G. & Golinkoff, R. M. (1979). The origins of intentional vocalizations in prelinguistic infants. *Child Development, 50*, 33–40.

Harnick, F. S. (1979). The relationship between ability level and task difficulty in producing imitation in infants. *Child Development, 49*, 209–212.

Harris, P. L. (1987). Object perception and permanence. In P. Salapatek & L. B. Cohen (eds), *Handbook of infant perception: Vol 2. From perception to cognition*. London: Academic Press.

von Hofsten, C. (1984). Developmental changes in the organization of prereaching movements. *Developmental Psychology, 20*, 378–388.

Hollis, J. H. (1962). Solution of bent-wire problems by severely retarded children. *American Journal of Mental Deficiency, 67*, 463–472.

Hood, B. & Willatts, P. (1986). Reaching in the dark to an object's remembered position: Evidence for object permanence in 5-month-old infants. *British Journal of Developmental Psychology, 4*, 57–65.

Jarrett, N. L. M. (1988). *The origins of detour problem solving in human infants*. Unpublished M.Phil. thesis, University of Southampton.

Jennings, K. D., Harmon, R. J., Morgan, G. A., Gaiter, J. L., & Yarrow, L. J. (1979). Exploratory play as an index of mastery motivation: Relationships to persistence, cognitive functioning, and environmental measures. *Developmental Psychology, 15*, 386–394.

Jennings, K. D., Yarrow, L. J., & Martin, P. P. (1984). Mastery motivation and cognitive development: A longitudinal study from infancy to 3½ years of age. *International Journal of Behavioural Development, 7*, 441–461.

Kalnins, I. V. & Bruner, J. S. (1973). The coordination of visual observation and instrumental behavior in early infancy. *Perception, 2*, 307–314.

Karmiloff-Smith, A. (1979). Micro- and macro-developmental changes in language acquisition and other representational systems. *Cognitive Science, 3*, 91–118.

Kaye, K. (1979). The development of skills. In G. Whitehurst & B. Zimmerman (eds), *The functions of language and cognition*. New York: Academic Press.

Kaye, K. (1982). *The mental and social life of babies*. Chicago: University of Chicago Press.

Kaye, K. & Marcus, J. (1978). Imitation over a series of trials without feedback: Age six months. *Infant Behavior and Development, 1*, 141–155.

Kaye, K. & Marcus, J. (1981). Infant imitation: The sensory–motor agenda. *Developmental Psychology, 17*, 258–265.

Klahr, D. (1982). Nonmonotone assessment of monotone development: An information processing analysis. In S. Strauss (ed.), *U-shaped behavioral growth*. London: Academic Press.

Klahr, D. (1984). Transition processes in quantitative development. In R. J. Sternberg (ed.), *Mechanisms of cognitive development*. New York: Freeman.

Klahr, D. & Robinson, M. (1981). Formal assessment of problem-solving and planning processes in preschool children. *Cognitive Psychology, 13*, 113–148.

Klahr, D. & Wallace, J. G. (1976). *Cognitive development: An information-processing view*. Hillsdale, N.J.: Lawrence Erlbaum Associates Inc.

Köhler, W. (1925). *The mentality of apes*. New York: Harcourt Brace.

Kopp, C. B., O'Connor, M. J., & Finger, I. (1975). Task characteristics and a Stage 6 sensorimotor problem. *Child Development, 46*, 569–573.

Koslowski, B. & Bruner, J. S. (1972). Learning to use a lever. *Child Development, 43*, 790–799.

Lamb, M. E. & Bornstein, M. H. (1987). *Development in infancy: An introduction (2nd ed)*. New York: Random House.

Lamb, M. E. & Malkin, C. M. (1986). The development of social expectations in distress-relief sequences: A longitudinal study. *International Journal of Behavioural Development, 9*, 235–249.

Lamb, M. E., Morrison, D. C., & Malkin, C. M. (1987). The development of infant social expectations in face-to-face interaction: A longitudinal study. *Merrill-Palmer Quarterly, 33*, 241–254.

Lempers, J., Flavell, E. R., & Flavell, J. (1977). The development in very young children of tacit knowledge concerning visual perception. *Genetic Psychology Monographs, 95*, 3–53.

Leslie, A. M. (1982). Discursive representation in infancy. In B. de Gelder (ed.), *Knowledge and representation*. London: Routledge & Kegan Paul.

Lockman, J. J. (1984). The development of detour ability in infancy. *Child Development, 55*, 482–491.

Lockman, J. J. & Pick, H. L. (1984). Problems of scale in spatial development. In C. Sophian (ed.), *Origins of cognitive skills*. Hillsdale, N.J.: Lawrence Erlbaum Associates Inc.

Mandler, J. M. (1984). Representation and recall in infancy. In M. Moscovitch (ed.), *Infant memory: Its relation to normal and pathological memory in humans and other animals*. London: Plenum Press.

Mast V. K., Fagen, J. W., Rovee-Collier, C. K., & Sullivan, M. W. (1980). Immediate and long-term memory for reinforcement context: The development of learned expectancies in early infancy. *Child Development, 51*, 700–707.

Matas, L., Arend, R. A., & Srouge, L. A. (1978). Continuity of adaptation in the second year of life: The relationship between quality of attachment and later competence. *Child Development, 49*, 547–556.

McCrickard, D. (1982). *Some aspects of tool use in infancy*. Unpublished M.Ed. dissertation, Department of Psychology, University of Dundee.

McKechnie, J. (1987). *Problem solving in infancy: A study of infants' performance on tasks of spatial manipulation*. Unpublished Ph.D. thesis, University of Stirling.

McKenzie, B. E. & Bigelow, E. (1986). Detour behaviour in young human infants. *British Journal of Developmental Psychology, 4*, 139–148.

Meltzoff, A. N. (1988). Infant imitation and memory: Nine-month-olds in immediate and deferred tests. *Child Development, 59*, 217–225.

Meltzoff, A. N. & Borton, R. W. (1979). Intermodal matching by human neonates. *Nature, 282*, 403–404.

Meltzoff, A. N. & Moore, M. K. (1977). Imitation of facial and manual gestures by human neonates. *Science, 198*, 75–78.

Meltzoff, A. N. & Moore, M. K. (1983). Newborn infants imitate adult facial gestures. *Child Development, 54*, 702–709.

Milewski, A. E. (1976). Infants' discrimination of internal and external pattern elements. *Journal of Experimental Child Psychology, 22*, 229–246.

Mounoud, P. & Hauert, C. A. (1982). Development of sensorimotor organization in young children: Grasping and lifting objects. In G. E. Forman (ed.), *Action and thought: From sensorimotor schemes to symbolic operations*. London: Academic Press.

Muir, D. & Field, J. (1979). Newborn infants orient to sounds. *Child Development, 50*, 431–436.

Newell, A. & Simon, H. A. (1972). *Human problem solving*. Englewood-Cliffs, N.J.: Prentice-Hall.

Nilsson, N. J. (1971). *Problem-solving methods in artificial intelligence*. London: McGraw-Hill.

Papousek, H. & Bernstein, P. (1969). The functions of conditioning stimulation in human neonates and infants. In A. Ambrose (ed.), *Stimulation in early infancy*. London: Academic Press.

Piaget, J. (1950). *The psychology of intelligence*. London: Routledge & Kegan Paul.

Piaget, J. (1951). *Play, dreams, and imitation in childhood*. London: Heinemann.

Piaget, J. (1953). *The origin of intelligence in the child*. London: Routledge & Kegan Paul.

Piaget, J. (1955). *The construction of reality in the child*. London: Routledge & Kegan Paul.

Richardson, H. M. (1932). The growth of adaptive behavior in infants: An experimental study at seven age levels. *Genetic Psychology Monographs, 12*, 195–357.

Rieser, J. & Hieman, M. L. (1982). Spatial self-reference systems and shortest route behavior in toddlers. *Child Development*, *53*, 524–533.

Rovee-Collier, C. K. (1983). Infants as problem-solvers: A psychobiological perspective. In M. D. Zeiler & P. Harzem (eds), *Advances in analysis of behavior*: Vol. 3. London: Wiley.

Rovee-Collier, C. K., Morrongiello, B. A., Aron, M., & Kupersmidt, J. (1978). Topographical response differentiation and reversal in 3-month-old infants. *Infant Behavior and Development*, *1*, 323–333.

Rovee-Collier, C. K., & Sullivan, M. W. (1980). Organization of infant memory. *Journal of Experimental Psychology: Human Learning and Memory*, *6*, 798–807.

Rovee-Collier, C. K., Sullivan, M. W., Enright, M., Lucas, D., & Fagen, J. W. (1980). Reactivation of infant memory. *Science*, *208*, 1159–1161.

Rutkowska, J. C. (1985). *A computational alternative to Piaget's theory of infant knowledge: Action is non-trivially representational.* Unpublished manuscript, Cognitive Studies Programme, School of Social Sciences, University of Sussex.

Smith, P. K. & Dutton, S. (1979). Play and training on direct and innovative problem solving. *Child Development*, *50*, 830–836.

Sophian, C. (1984). Developing search skills in infancy and early childhood. In C. Sophian (ed.), *Origins of cognitive skills*. Hillsdale, N.J.: Lawrence Erlbaum Associates Inc.

Sophian, C. & Adams, N. (1987). Infants' understanding of numerical transformations. *British Journal of Developmental Psychology*, *5*, 257–264.

Sophian, C. & Sage, S. (1983). Developments in infants' search for displaced objects. *Journal of Experimental Child Psychology*, *35*, 143–160.

Steri, A. (1987). Tactile discrimination of shape and intermodal transfer in 2- to 3-months old infants. *British Journal of Development Psychology*, *5*, 213–220.

Sylva, K., Bruner, J. S., & Genova, P. (1976). The role of play on the problem-solving of children 3–5 years old. In J. S. Bruner, A. Jolly, & K. Sylva (eds), *Play: Its role in development and evolution*. Harmondsworth: Penguin.

Sylvester-Bradley, B. (1985). Failure to distinguish between people and things in early infancy. *British Journal of Developmental Psychology*, *3*, 281–292.

Trevarthen, C. B. (1983). Interpersonal abilities of infants as generators for transmission of language and culture. In A. Oliverio & M. Zappella (eds), *The behavior of human infants*. New York: Plenum Press.

Tronick, E., Als, H., Adamson, L., Wise, S., & Brazelton, T. B. (1978). The infant's response to entrapment between contradictory messages in face-to-face interaction. *Journal of the American Academy of Child Psychiatry*, *17*, 1–13.

Uzgiris, I. C. (1972). Patterns of vocal and gestural imitation in infants. In F. Monks, W. Hartup, & J. deWit (eds), *Determinants of behavioral development*. New York: Academic Press.

Uzgiris, I. C. & Hunt, J. McV. (1975). *Assessment in infancy: Ordinal scales of psychological development*. London: University of Illinois Press.

Wellman, H. M. (1977). The early development of intentional memory behavior. *Human Development*, *20*, 86–101.

Wellman, H. M., Fabricius, W. V., & Sophian, C. (1985). The early development of planning. In H. M. Wellman (ed.), *Children's searching: The development of search skill and spatial representation*. Hillsdale, N.J.: Lawrence Erlbaum Associates Inc.

Wellman, H. M., Somerville, S. C., Revelle, G. L., Haake, R. J., & Sophian, C. (1984). The development of comprehensive search skills. *Child Development*, *55*, 472–481.

Whitecraft, R. A., Cobb, H. V., & Davis, R. T. (1959). Supplementary Report: Solution of bent-wire detour problems by preschool children. *Psychological Reports*, *5*, 609–611.

Willatts, P. (1979). Adjustment of reaching to change in object position by young infants. *Child Development*, *50*, 911–913.

Willatts, P. (1982, September). *Adjustment of means–ends coordination by "Stage IV" infants on tasks involving the use of supports.* Paper presented at the British Psychological Society Developmental Section Conference, Durham.

Willatts, P. (1984a). Stages in the development of intentional search by young infants. *Developmental Psychology, 20*, 389–396.

Willatts, P. (1984b). The Stage IV infant's solution of problems requiring the use of supports. *Infant Behavior and Development, 7*, 125–134.

Willatts, P. (1985a, July). *Development and rapid adjustment of means–ends behavior in infants aged six to eight months.* Paper presented at the Biennial Meeting of the International Society for the Study of Behavioral Development, Tours.

Willatts, P. (1985b). Adjustment of means–ends coordination and the representation of spatial relations in the production of search errors by infants. *British Journal of Developmental Psychology, 3*, 259–272.

Willatts, P. (1986, April). *Learning to do two things at once: Development of bimanual skill in young infants.* Paper presented at the Fifth International Conference on Infant Studies, Los Angeles.

Willatts, P. (1987). *Development of infants' manual detour skills.* Unpublished manuscript, Department of Psychology, University of Dundee.

Willatts, P. & Cupolillo, M. (1988, September). *Transfer in problem solving by preschool children.* Paper presented at the British Psychological Society Developmental Section Conference, Harlech.

Willatts, P. & Domminney, C. (1987, September). *Analogical transfer in problem solving by two-year-olds.* Paper presented at the British Psychological Society Developmental Section Conference, York.

Willatts, P. & Rosie, K. (1988, September). *Planning by 12-month-old infants.* Paper presented at the British Psychological Society Developmental Section Conference, Harlech.

Winston, P. H. (1984). *Artificial intelligence* (2nd ed.). London: Addison-Wesley.

Wishart, J. G. & Bower, T. G. R. (1984). Spatial relations and the object concept: A normative study. In L. P. Lipsitt & C. K. Rovee-Collier (eds), *Advances in infancy research*: Vol. 3. Norwood, N.J.: Ablex Publishing Corp.

Woodward, W. M. (1971). *The development of behaviour.* Harmondsworth: Penguin.

Yarrow, L. J., McQuiston, S., MacTurk, R. H., McCarthy, M. E., Klein, R. P., & Vietze, P. M. (1983). Assessment of mastery motivation during the first year of life: Contemporaneous and cross-age relationships. *Developmental Psychology, 19*, 159–171.

Yarrow, L. J., MacTurk, R. H., Vietze, P. M., McCarthy, M. E., Klein, R. P., & McQuiston, S. (1984). Developmental course of parental stimulation and its relationship to mastery motivation during infancy. *Developmental Psychology, 20*, 492–503.

Zelazo, P. R., Brody, L. R., & Chaika, H. (1984). Neonatal habituation and dishabituation of head turning to rattle sounds. *Infant Behavior and Development, 7*, 311–321.

3

SOCIAL INTERACTION, EARLY LANGUAGE, AND EMOTION

Social Interaction, Early Language, and Emotion: Introduction

Gavin Bremner and Alan Slater

Part 3 is a tricky one to attach a simple label to, since none of the chapters in it considers social or emotional development alone, each instead extending its analysis to look in one way or another at how infants' development within a social world either affects or is affected by developments in cognition or perception. To many readers social interaction probably seems an obvious vehicle for cognitive development, yet such an assumption is largely absent from much of the contemporary work on cognitive development, and it is only relatively recently that workers have begun to do serious research on this direction of causality.

The chapters in Part 3 confront this issue directly through a rich mix of arguments pointing to the interdependences between areas conventionally kept fairly separate. Indeed, rather than viewing this section as dealing with a separate aspect of infant development, it is better to consider at least some of the contributions here as radical rethinks of the conventional psychological view of the infant as an individual developing individual abilities in an apparent social vacuum. This radical component, however, means that the reader will encounter a wider diversity of styles of argument and supporting data than in the previous chapters.

In the first chapter, Schaffer reviews our knowledge on the development of social interaction, and presents a stage model of its development in which progress relies heavily on developments in perceptual, cognitive, and attentional ability. However, he stresses that while developments in the latter areas may provide the infant with propensities for new forms of social functioning, these propensities cannot become actualities without the support of parents within the social interaction itself. Here we see an important argument about the role of social interaction in producing development, and Schaffer does not limit it to the case of social development itself, arguing that important cognitive developments like object permanence are likely to be influenced by the experiences that parents present to infants. It is just this argument that is later taken up and expanded fully by Lock, Service, Brito, and Chandler (see Chapter 10).

In considering the development of attachment, Schaffer points out how infants' representations of people become increasingly complex as they get older. Again, it is tempting to fall back on the old view that what we are seeing is a socio-emotional change driven by developments in cognition. However, it is reasonable to wonder how much the infant's emotional needs drive forward the development of more sophisticated representations of persons, resulting in parallel changes in object representation.

In the second chapter, Barrett changes the focus to early language development, tracing the infant through the period from first words to the two-word stage. He notes how the infant's first words are context bound, being produced only in specific situations or during particular activities. The explanation offered for this phenomenon shows immediately that there are again strong links identified with cognitive development. Barrett argues that around this time infants have formed event representations that are global rather than composed of separate objects or elements. First words are associated with these event representations, and are not used to refer to particular objects or aspects of a situation. From this starting point, development in word use is viewed as a gradual decontextualisation, in which words come to be used across different contexts in which they are appropriate. It is suggested that this happens as a result of the infant's partitioning the original global representations into their elements and attaching the word to the relevant core element.

Toward the end of the chapter, Barrett focuses on individual differences in language development, pointing out that infants can often be classified in one of two ways. Referential infants acquire many object names, and proceed to the two-word stage through fitting single words together. Expressive infants retain context-bound word use for longer and go on to produce multi-word formulae that appear to be treated as unanalysed wholes, until later when they are analysed into their separate semantic components.

This focus on individual differences sets the scene well for Lock et al. (Chapter 10), since one of their goals is the developmet of an explanation of differences in developmental style in terms of a theory of social construction of reality. This account draws on the work of Vygotsky, Macmurray, and Mead, and is based on the notion that knowledge is constructed by infant and parent in interaction rather than through the infant's individual efforts. But this is not just an argument for social influences on the development of knowledge. It is more radical than that, since knowledge is conceptualised as initially possessed by the partners in the interaction and only later by the infant as an individual. At first, the infant cannot be said to know things outside the support provided by the parents' analysis of the situation. Within this model it is inevitable that the parental style of analysis will influence the infant's style, and so Lock et al. go on to investigate correlations between parental interactional styles and differences in infants' cognitive styles. They present very impressive relationships, finding that parents who mark and break down events have infants who perform better on tests that require analytic skill. In conclusion, they suggest that parents (particularly the marking ones) have an important guiding role in the development of attention. In addition, they argue that the infant's perception is reorganised by the structuring actions of the parent. Thus in every way, parents provide the initial structure for the infant's knowledge, a structure that eventually comes to be possessed by the infant as an individual.

The final chapter by Urwin is at least as radical in theoretical style, and is presented as a very different way of thinking about many of the well-established phenomena in cognitive development. Urwin points out that the infant's emotional world is largely left out of mainstream infancy research. However, her aim is not just to review work on emotional development and its links with cognition. Instead she reinterprets cognitive development in psychoanalytic terms. This sort of analysis yields quite different ways of conceptualising development. For instance, Freud argued that conscious cognition develops for the purpose of satisfying the infant's primary emotional needs, needs that cannot be satisfied without being geared to a proper representation of reality.

However, there are also some themes that find echoes in the literature on cognitive development. For instance, the Freudian notion that an important part of emotional development involves testing reality and progressively distinguishing it from the internal world of imagination has its parallel in Piaget's view of the infant as initially unaware of any physical distinction between self and world, but progressing towards an increasing differentiation between self and world. There are enough common themes here to make it likely that a continued dialogue between developmental psychology and psychoanalysis would be profitable. Whatever the nature of the theory that emerges, it seems hard to deny emotion an important place in general development.

8

Early Social Development

Rudolph Schaffer

*Department of Psychology,
University of Strathclyde,
155 George St.,
Glasgow G1 1RD*

INTRODUCTION

Research on early social development has a short history, confined to just the last 30 years or so. Yet even in this brief period there have been marked changes in the way the subject has been thought about, in the methods adopted to investigate it, and especially in the questions being asked in order to further our knowledge. These changes involve a progressive widening of the focus of interest which one can best represent in terms of three stages, concerned respectively with the *individual*, the *dyad*, and the *polyad* as the unit of study.

Initially social behaviour was seen as a class of *individual* behaviour. Thus questions were asked about the first appearance of particular social patterns in children (the first smile, the onset of attachments, the beginnings of cooperative play, etc.), or about the incidence of certain forms of behaviour (e.g. the amount of fear of strangers under various conditions, the amount of aggressive behaviour in boys as opposed to girls, the amount of social play at different ages, etc.). In all these cases behaviour was thought of as describing the characteristics of individuals; their activity may have been observed in the presence of other people, but the behaviour of these others was not taken into account.

In the early 1970s this changed; the focus became increasingly fixed on the *dyad* as the unit of study. The to-and-fro between child and social partner was now of primary interest. Interactions, rather than individuals interacting, became the main topic of research. The questions asked concerned

ID—G*

such problems as how interactions are established at different ages, how they are maintained and developed over time, and in what ways the roles played respectively by child and adult interlock (see Schaffer, 1977, for some illustrative studies). We have learned a lot from this dyadic approach: for instance, about the abilities children of different ages bring to social interaction and how they use them, about the techniques adults adopt to support these abilities, and about the nature of interpersonal synchronisation and how that is accomplished.

However, very recently a new approach has emerged, which I shall refer to as the *polyadic* approach (a fuller treatment is provided in Schaffer, 1984). It is based on the recognition that children live in a multi-person world; dyadic interactions occur but do so in the context of other interactions and relationships that the individual has with persons outside the dyad. What is more, how the child interacts with the group may well require different skills compared with those used in interacting with one other individual. Indeed it could be that a set of quite different concepts are needed to explain polyadic interaction compared with those in use for dyadic interactions.

We thus have three different levels at which social development has been studied. It should be emphasised that any one is not necessarily "better" than any other; each is valid in its own right, each useful for answering certain questions distinctive from those found at the other levels. However, in so far as most of the recent work on early social development has been carried out with the dyad as the basic unit of study I shall confine myself primarily to the body of knowledge generated at that level.

SOME CONCEPTUAL GUIDELINES

Let us first consider the nature of psychological development in general. It has become increasingly apparent that such development is best conceived of in terms of sequential reorganisation rather than steady quantitative accretion. The child's mental life, that is, will periodically and relatively suddenly show transitions to new psychological levels that, in certain respects at least, are *qualitatively* different from preceding levels. As Piaget above all has shown, new sets of capacities emerge from time to time which drastically alter the child's mode of adaptation to the environment and which thus reveal major changes in psychological organisation. Whether these take the across-the-board form which Piaget described or whether they apply to much more specific functions as Fischer (1980) argued remains to be settled. In the early years in particular, however, it is apparent that major transition points can be located when such realignments are evident and various attempts have recently been made to list these (e.g. by Emde, Gaensbauer, & Harmon, 1976; McCall, Eichorn, & Hogarty 1977; Fischer, 1980). In each case development is conceived of as a step-like course, where progression to qualitatively different modes of behaviour occurs from time to time, bringing about new modes of adaptation on the part of the child. Each break represents a period of instability when, conceivably, the child is particularly vulnerable; each new phase requires the consolidation of whatever achievements were ushered in at the point of transition.

The following has been put forward (Schaffer, 1984) as a developmental scheme that is particulary useful in considering infants' social behaviour and the progressive changes that take place therein during the first 2 years:

1. *The immediate post-birth period.* At that time the most urgent developmental task for the parent–child couple is to regularise the infant's basic biological processes such as feeding and waking–sleeping states and to harmonise these with environmental requirements.

2. *From 2 months on.* At the age of 2 months a marked increase in attentiveness to the external world takes place, with particular reference to other people. As a result the regulation of responsiveness in face-to-face interactions then becomes a central theme for infant and care-taker.

3. *From 5 months on.* Largely as a result of newly emerging manipulative abilities a shift of attention from people to objects is found at this transition point. Increasingly, encounters with social partners occur around objects. How to incorporate objects in such encounters and thus ensure topic sharing becomes the new developmental task confronting infant and partner.

4. *From 8 months on.* A number of profound changes take place at this age, in particular the emergence of the ability to interrelate diverse environmental features and to produce coordinated activity to more than one aspect at a time. As a result the infant's behaviour becomes much more flexible; reciprocity and intentionality come to characterise social exchanges and the relationship with the care-taker thus becomes a more symmetrical one.

5. *From the middle of the second year.* At this point the capacity for symbolic representation gradually emerges. Social interactions increasingly incorporate verbal aspects and growing self-awareness leads the infant to reflect more on its and on other people's behaviour and to guide its actions accordingly.

Social development in infancy may thus be thought of as constituting a sequence of changes, heralded by various perceptual, motor, and cognitive events taking place in species-typical fashion. But whatever powerful inherent push may be responsible in the first place for the emergence of new capabilities and new levels of functioning, a propensity cannot become reality unless the infant's care-taker supports, maintains, completes, and furthers the child's efforts. All psychological functions develop in a social context; the younger the child the more important it is to regard it as part of a unit which inevitably includes the care-taker as a vital complement to the child's state of immaturity. The intimate dependence of human development on the rearing environment must be acknowledged; each stage brings with it particular developmental tasks that can only be tackled by child and care-taker jointly. Thus changes in the child's psychological organisation have implications not just for the child alone but also for its relationship with others and for the role that these others need to adopt. After every transition point the parent must be prepared to help the child deal with new tasks and offer new forms of support; only if this is done successfully can the child progress to the next level. Appropriate input from social partners must therefore be added to the list of perceptual, motor, and cognitive factors that enable children to pass through the various developmental phases.

Thus, two conceptual guidelines should be borne in mind when examining the course of early social behaviour:

1. Development occurs through a series of sequential reorganisations.
2. Development is a joint enterprise involving the efforts of both child and adult care-taker.

Our account of some of the themes which arise from an examination of social behaviour in infancy will be based on these two general guidelines.

SOCIAL PRE-ADAPTATION

The new-born is not a formless blob of clay, devoid of all psychological organisation. On the contrary, it comes into the world with certain predispositions—certain tendencies, that is, selectively to attend to particular kinds of stimuli and to structure its responses in particular ways. What is especially striking is the way in which both perceptual and response tendencies are pre-adapted to mediate the infant's interaction with the social environment.

Perceptual Organisation

It has become apparent that from the early days of life on, infants have surprisingly good perceptual capacities (see Chapters 2 and 3 of this book). But it has also become apparent that these capacities are selective in nature, and that the types of stimuli to which they are particularly attuned are those generally associated with other people, such as their faces and voices.

The topic of face perception has attracted a great deal of attention (see Sherrod 1981, for a detailed review). Most studies on this subject use one of two methodologies: The *visual preference technique*, whereby the amount of attention paid by an infant to each of a pair of stimuli is ascertained, and the *operant sucking technique,* which examines the amount of effort exerted by an infant to produce a particular stimulus (such as the picture of a human face) by sucking for it. It is now generally agreed that initially it is not "faceness" as such that attracts infants' attention but rather a set of more primitive qualities that are inherent in human faces such as contour density, complexity, three-dimensionality, and mobility. Each of these characteristics alone is attention-worthy; when combined (as they are in "real" faces) they ensure that the social partner is a highly salient source of stimulation. This is particularly so as the optimal visual fixation point is initially confined to a distance of about 8 inches—a distance at which mothers quite naturally place their faces when interacting with a young infant. On the basis of this initial attraction infants can then in due course begin to pay attention to other features of the social partner, in particular those distinguishing one person from another, and thus become capable of differentiating familiar and unfamiliar people.

A *matching* process is thus evident between, on the one hand, the visual capacities of infants that are available to them from birth and, on the other hand, the stimulus qualities of those aspects of the environment that are biologically of greatest importance to them, i.e. other people. The same applies to auditory responsiveness: here too there is evidence (Hutt et al., 1968; Molfese & Molfese, 1980) that human speech-like noises have a particular potency for young infants not possessed by other auditory stimuli. Thus the structure of the auditory apparatus at birth is such as to ensure that the voice of other people is a particularly attention-worthy stimulus. Taken in conjunction with demonstrations that infants appear to have a pre-adapted capacity to make meaningful phonemic distinctions within speech long before they themselves begin to speak (Eimas, 1975), it appears that on the auditory as on the visual side infants arrive in the world especially attuned to the kind of stimulation provided by other people.

Response organisation

As well as such perceptual sensitivities infants demonstrate a number of behaviour patterns specifically designed to bring them into contact with people. Of these, smiling, crying, rooting, and sucking are the best known and most closely studied. Their survival value during the initial period of helplessness is evident; each is linked to a set of highly specific stimulus conditions and operates at first along somewhat stereotyped lines before assuming more complex, flexible, and intentional form towards the end of the first year (Bowlby, 1969).

One particular attribute of early response organisation to which we must draw attention is its temporal structure, for in this respect too there are implications for social interaction. They may best be illustrated by reference to the feeding situation—one of the earliest contexts in which an infant encounters another person. The infant's sucking response has been shown (e.g. by Wolff, 1968) to be a high-frequency micro-rhythm that is organised as a burst-pause pattern—i.e. bursts of sucks are followed by pauses, the length of each component varying somewhat according to a number of conditions. As Kaye (1977) has shown, this temporal patterning is highly suited for incorporating feeding into a more general social interaction sequence, for mothers tend to interact with their infants in precise synchrony with the burst–pause pattern. Thus during bursts they are generally quiet and inactive; during pauses, on the other hand, they jiggle, stroke, and talk to the baby. The mother, that is, fits in with the baby's natural sucking rhythm, responds to its signals such as ceasing to suck, accepts the opportunity to intervene offered by pauses, and in this way sets up a turn-taking pattern which, as we shall see, is typical of many other forms of early interaction. The infant's behaviour is thus structured in such a way as to facilitate coordination with the partner's behaviour; the to-and-fro which characterises most dyadic exchanges among human beings is therefore evident from the beginning, and in this respect too we may consequently conclude that social pre-adaptation determines the nature of the infant's initial encounters with other people.

THE CHANGING NATURE OF SOCIAL INTERACTION

A suitable way of viewing infants' development of social competence is to adopt a *modular model*, similar to that proposed for the acquisition of sensory–motor skills (e.g. by Bruner, 1973). According to this model individual units of action (so-called subroutines) are learned first, each being practiced to the point where it can occur with minimal conscious attention, leaving the child free to attend to those action units not yet mastered. The various components can then be combined into organised wholes, thus forming new, more complex, higher-order patterns which are constituted by the totality of the individual modules but in which the separate existence of the modules is no longer acknowledged. The acquisition of social interactive skills in infancy goes through such a process. Initially (during the period 2 – 5 months approximately) infants are absorbed in the task of learning about their care-takers: Direct face-to-face encounters are the principal contexts for social interaction and enable infants to become acquainted with the physical characteristics of the adults and perfect the art of fitting their own behavioural flow to theirs. Around the age of 5 months, coinciding with the onset of manipulative competence, infants turn abruptly away from a preoccupation with faces to a similarly intense preoccupation with the world of things: Attention is now taken up by the newly acquired ability to act upon objects and during the next few months priority is given to becoming competent in this sphere. Eventually, sometime around the age of 8 months, there are indications that infants become capable of putting together these separate accomplishments: Instead of attending to only one thing at a time (person *or* object) the infant can now integrate these diverse features and interact with other people via objects and other such external topics. Let us consider the various phases of this developmental timetable.

Face-to-face Interaction

The most urgent requirement during the first few weeks is to regulate the infant's basic biological processes of feeding, sleeping, and arousal, i.e. to stabilise these and to establish a timetable that not only conforms with the infant's requirements but also with those of its care-takers. Mutual adjustment thus takes place round the infant's endogenous functions. From about 2 months, however, infants turn increasingly to their outer environment—in large part, no doubt, due to a sharp increase in visual efficiency (Bronson, 1974). As a result their behaviour towards other people changes: Direct eye contact is made with the partner, periods of prolonged gaze ensue, and the first externally elicited smiles appear. Social interactions thus occur primarily in the context of face-to-face encounters, and the main developmental theme for adult and child becomes the regulation of mutual attention and responsiveness.

Such regulation takes various forms. Take the way in which mother and infant establish mutual gazing. Among adult dyads such gazing is mostly symmetrical in nature: The on–off looking patterns of the two individuals tend to have the same characteristics and the initiation and termination of mutual gaze episodes are determined by both to a similar extent. Not so in mother–infant pairs, where asymmetry of looking patterns is much more typical. The mother, that is, looks at the infant for extremely long periods, constantly ready to respond to any sign of attention on the infant's part and to adjust her behaviour to the child's. She thus provides a "frame" (as Fogel, 1977, has described it) within which the infant's gazing may cycle to and fro. These gazes are much briefer than the mother's; they are originally constrained by biologically determined limits which regulate the alternation of gazing-at and gazing-away periods (Stern, 1974) and show none of the flexibility and intentionality that characterise looking patterns in older individuals. Responsibility for initiation and termination is thus also unequally distributed: It is far more likely that the mother will be the first to look and the infant the first to look away. The mother, that is, appears to be almost constantly ready for interaction, but it is up to the infant as to whether that interaction in fact takes place. It may well be that prolonged gazing at the mother would be too arousing an experience in the early months, and looking away by the infant therefore serves to modulate the level of its arousal. Certainly mothers can be observed continually to adjust the timing, nature, and intensity of the stimulation they provide during such episodes, using the infant's gaze at their face as a cue to begin stimulation and the gaze away as a cue to cease stimulation, thereby helping the infant to maintain optimal arousal.

A similar picture of early interaction is provided when we turn to another feature of social encounters, namely vocal interchange. In adult conversations mutual adjustment is essential: If both members of a dyad were to talk simultaneously the communication of information would be virtually impossible. A turn-taking pattern is therefore required, involving the sequential integration of the two participants' individual contributions as well as knowledge of the rules whereby speaker and listener exchange roles. Such knowledge can hardly be attributed to young infants, yet vocal interactions with mothers are already marked by a turn taking pattern. Just how prevalent that pattern is (as opposed to "coaction", i.e. a pattern marked by simultaneous vocalisation) has been subject to some debate (see Schaffer, 1984, for a more detailed review); suffice it to say that precise turn-taking can occur already during the early months and certainly long before the onset of formal speech. Let us stress, however, that turn taking is a dyadic phenomenon and that it tells us nothing about the "abilities" of infants to take turns. It seems in fact more likely that it is brought about by the mother's action in skillfully inserting her contributions in the pauses between bursts of vocalisations produced by the infant. As we have already seen, mothers are highly attentive to their infants in face-to-face encounters and can therefore time their vocal interventions in such a way as not to interrupt the baby. The mother, that is, allows herself to be paced by the infant and thereby takes the responsibility for converting the encounter into a dialogue that, in certain formal respects, has all the hallmarks of a conversation. The difference when compared with adult dialogues is, however, that only one of the partners knows the rules; from that point of view the exchange is more accurately labelled a "pseudo-dialogue". Nevertheless we can speculate that by involving infants in such mature interaction formats from an early age on mothers facilitate children's acquisition of the necessary skills to participate eventually in social exchanges as "full" partners.

Mutual gazing and vocal interchange are two examples of early face-to-face interactions. They point to some common features, but above all to the fact that there is already a "smoothness" in the dyadic encounters of infant with adult that suggest a mutually satisfying meshing of the two sets of individual contributions.

Topic Sharing

With the onset of manipulative abilities around the age of 5 months infants turn increasingly to the world of things. Not that they are any less responsive to people when directly confronted by another person; it is rather that they have now discovered a new sphere of interest, i.e. objects on which they can directly act and produce effects upon. Attentional capacity is as yet limited; being unable to incorporate two different environmental features into their activity infants will attend to an object *or* a person but not to both. The exclusive fascination with faces typifying the earlier months is replaced by the new function pleasure derived from the mastery of toys and other objects to handle. No wonder that Kaye and Fogel (1980), in a longitudinal study of face-to-face interactions, found a drop in visual attention to the mother from 70% of total session time at 6 weeks of age to 33% at 26 weeks; the mothers, moreover, reported that they no longer felt the direct face-to-face situation to be appropriate at the older age and that instead their task was now to share with the child reactions to external events.

Every social interaction has a topic to which the participants address themselves, but whereas during the face-to-face encounters in the early months the topic arose from within the dyad itself it now refers to some external focus that comes to be incorporated in the interaction. At this stage, however, given the infant's attentional limitations, it is entirely due to the adult's initiative that such incorporation takes place. The mother, that is, uses a variety of procedures to share with the infant the objects that interest it and so converts an *infant–object* situation into an *infant–object–mother* situation.

Take the phenomenon of "visual coorientation"—a term used to indicate the joint attention of two or more people to some common focus in the environment. In a study of mothers and infants who were confronted by a display of toys along the wall of a playroom (Collis & Schaffer, 1975), several things became apparent from an analysis of videorecordings obtained of their behaviour. In the first place, there was a strong tendency for both mother and infant to be attending to the same toy at the same time—the phenomenon of visual coorientation. In the second place, when examining how this was brought about it emerged that almost invariably it was the infant that took the lead by spontaneously looking from one toy to another while the mother, closely monitoring the baby's gaze direction, immediately followed and looked at the same toy. Mutual reference to an external topic was thus brought about, thanks to the powerful effect which the infant's direction of gaze appeared to exert on the mother. And in the third place, such topic sharing was rarely an end in its own right; more often, having established joint attention, the mother used that topic in order to further the course of the interaction with the infant, e.g. she would elaborate on it by pointing to the toy, labelling it, commenting on it, and taking other steps to incorporate it in the exchange with the infant.

There are indications that infants do not become capable of following another person's gaze until 8 months or so (Collis, 1977). Even then they can do so only under certain situational conditions, such as the need for the target to be located within the periphery of the infant's visual field (Butterworth & Cochrane, 1980). It does appear, however, that by the end of the first year another person's gaze direction has become a meaningful signal to the infant, and that the onus for topic sharing therefore no longer rests exclusively with the mother.

Somewhat similar conclusions arise from studies of another means of achieving topic sharing, namely by gestures such as pointing. As Murphy and Messer (1977) have shown, infants aged less than 9 months are mostly unable to follow the direction of a pointing finger: They look at the finger itself rather than at the object indicated. Thereafter they follow correctly, but only under "easy" conditions as defined by the spatial relationships of infant, finger, and target (in particular, when the latter two are in the same sector of the visual field). Infants' own use of pointing does not emerge until the very end of the first year; when it does, however, it appears first in the form of "pointing-for-self", i.e. the infant points to the object but without checking whether the other person is following the gesture. This, according to Werner and Kaplan (1963), shows pointing initially to be an attentional mechanism which merely indicates that the infant is now able to distinguish self from object. "Pointing-for-others", as a communicative phenomenon indicative of the infant's desire to share the object with another person, emerges later.

The third principal means of topic sharing, one which comes to assume great importance in the post-infancy period, is referential speech. People share topics, that is, by verbally referring to them and thus one of the child's tasks is to acquire labels which can be used in communicative situations. Yet curiously, long before children become verbally competent, adults use speech when interacting with them—indeed from the neonatal period on (Rheingold & Adams, 1980) language appears to be a natural means of relating to an infant, despite the fact that the infant may still be many months away from comprehending what is said. But the nature and timing of the speech used is far from arbitrary—on the contrary, it is carefully geared to infants' attentional capacities (being high-pitched in delivery, repetitive, chunked in brief phrases, and plentifully accompanied by facial distortions and hand gestures, Snow, 1977). It is also precisely synchronised with the infant's ongoing behaviour at the time, as illustrated in a study by Messer (1978) based on observations of mother–infant couples during a joint play session. The great majority of the mothers' verbal references to particular toys turned out to co-occur with either the infant's or the mother's manipulation of that toy. The mothers, that is, showed the watchfulness so typical of many of their interactions with young children and thus were able closely to synchronise their speech with ongoing manipulative activities. Labels were therefore supplied to the infant at a point where its attention was focused on the relevant object; language, that is, was closely tied to the non-verbal context as defined by the child's own behaviour.

Person–object integration

At about 8 months a new developmental achievement becomes apparent in infants' behaviour. It is marked by the onset of relational abilities, i.e. infants now become capable of interrelating diverse events and combining them into one coordinated activity. Whereas previously an infant would play with the mother *or* with a ball it is now able to play ball *with* the mother; similarly it can request an object from another person or point out an interesting toy to someone else. In short, the infant now starts to coordinate multiple activities that could previously be performed only separately and thus to combine person-directed actions with object-directed actions.

It has been suggested that the coordination achieved at that time is *specific* to integrating objects with people and that there is an earlier stage where acts can be combined within the two realms of objects and people respectively but not across them (Sugarman-Bell, 1978). This is not so (see Schaffer, 1984 and 1986 for further details); there is considerable evidence that the growth of coordination applies to *any* set of actions directed at multiple stimuli and that it can just as well be observed *within* the social and *within* the object sphere. Take the "social referencing" phenomenon (Feinman, 1982): up to the third quarter of the first year infants tend to relate to one individual at a time, e.g. to the mother *or* to a stranger; from then on, however, infants can regulate their reaction to a stranger by affective signals from the mother, thus relating the characteristics of one person to those of another. Or take studies of play (Fenson, Kagan, Kearsley, & Zelazo, 1976): up to 8 months or so infants typically play with one object at a time; thus, if offered a toy while holding another they are likely to drop the latter before taking the former. Simple relational actions like banging one object with another or manipulating two objects simultaneously emerge only subsequently.

One implication of the new-found ability is that social interactions become more reciprocal and less one-sided. This is particularly well illustrated by some of the games which are such a marked feature of the daily lives of infants and parents. Take Bruner's (1977) description of the development of give-and-take games. Up to 8 months the infant's participation is limited to "take": The mother offers the toy, the infant takes it, and the sequence ends with the child dropping the toy. After that age the game ceases to be so one-sided: Infant begins to initiate the sequence by showing or offering the toy to the mother; they may also now hand it to her at her request. The exchanges are still hesitant, with the infant constantly checking between object and mother as though not sure of the procedure; by the end of the first year, however, the game has definitely become established as a set of routines, the infant having learned the basic rule, i.e. that the roles of giver and taker are reciprocal and also exchangeable.

Of all the developmental transitions to be found in the early years of life that taking place around 8 months of age is probably the most far reaching (Schaffer, 1986). The consequences for behaviour are considerable and the list of new achievements a lengthy one (Trevarthen & Hubley, 1978), but they add up to the fact that behaviour becomes vastly more flexible, more coordinated and more integrative, that the infant is less reactive and more proactive, and that it can now begin to monitor its own activity and adjust its reactions according to the perceived effects on the environment. The consequences for social behaviour are considerable: Instead of being tied to separate, here-and-now events involving other people the infant becomes increasingly capable of welding together interactive sequences out of series of individual responses; more and more these sequences assume an intentional character in that infants begin to anticipate future goals and to plan their behaviour accordingly; and other people come to be represented as individuals in their own right, with a permanent existence independent of the infant's own existence.

ATTACHMENT

Many of the issues outlined above have been investigated under the rubric of attachment development. The ability to form focused, permanent, and emotionally meaningful relationships with specific others is one of the most important acquisitions of the infancy period; how this is achieved, the timing of the various steps involved, the choice of attachment objects, the influence of such extraneous factors on the relationship as maternal employment and day-care and the implications of that first bond with another person for relationships formed in future years—these have been the main issues to which research has addressed itself ever since the topic first surfaced in the 1950s. The relevant literature is thus considerable; here we can only touch briefly on some of the main conclusions.

There is general agreement regarding the developmental course of attachment formation. Once again the third quarter of the first year is pinpointed as the crucial period for drastic change; it is then that the first indications are given that the infant has focused its attachment behaviour on specific individuals. Up to that point infants are by and large indiscriminate; caretakers are interchangeable and are not missed in their absence. This does not mean that familiar people cannot be recognised and distinguished from strangers; this accomplishment is achieved quite early, certainly by 3 months of age (Schaffer, 1971). However, such perceptual distinction is only a necessary but not a sufficient condition for the development of permanent attachment bonds; the infant, that is, may recognise a person as unfamiliar and yet accept care from her as readily as from the mother. It is only from 7 or 8 months on that there is, as it were, a parting of the ways: On the one hand the infant now seeks the proximity of just certain individuals and becomes distressed by being separated from them (Schaffer & Emerson, 1964), and on the other hand proximity avoidance is shown to other, unfamiliar people and fear of strangers first emerges (Schaffer, 1966). Thus the developmental course of attachment formation takes place over a quite prolonged period, though the actual onset of discriminative relationships (as given by such indices as separation upset and stranger fear) is usually quite rapid, occurring suddenly in a step-wise fashion.

Bowlby's Theory

The most comprehensive theoretical account of attachment formation has been provided by John Bowlby (1969). It is heavily influenced both by psychoanalysis and by ethology and has become the most widely used conceptual framework within which research on attachments has been conducted in recent years.

According to Bowlby, attachment is based on a number of species-specific action patterns (such as sucking, crying, and smiling) that have emerged in the course of evolution because they afforded survival advantage in the "environment of evolutionary adaptedness". Each of these initially functions like a fixed action pattern, i.e. it is activated by certain quite specific stimulus conditions and then runs its course in a more or less mechanical fashion until terminated by further specific stimulus conditions. The function of these patterns is to promote proximity to and interaction with the care-taker; the fact that they share this function entitles one to classify them together as "attachment responses" and to regard them as constituting a behavioural system.

In the course of development several changes occur in this system. Two are particularly notable. The first refers to the progressive narrowing down that occurs in the range of eliciting and terminating stimuli. For instance, smiling is initially elicited by nothing more than two dots—a primitive sign–stimulus that triggers the smile in the same way that the red dot on the herring gull's beak triggers the pecking response of the young bird. In time the dots must become more and more eye-like in shape to have that effect; subsequently they must be accompanied by more and more facial features until the face as a whole is required as the sufficient stimulus, and finally it is no longer *any* face that has that effect but only that of certain familiar individuals (Sherrod, 1981). This means that the fixed action patterns are no longer independent of each other but have now become integrated by being focused on one individual, usually the mother. The second noteworthy development is that the attachment system becomes an organised whole which increasingly functions in a "goal-corrected" manner. Thus the young baby does not vary its cry according to whether the mother is far or near or whether she is coming or going; the older infant, on the other hand, is capable of continually adjusting its behaviour in the light of prevailing circumstances, taking note of the discrepancy between stimulus conditions and thus making use of feedback information to control its own behaviour. Its actions thus become flexible and purposive, organised in accordance with "plans".

The attachment system is, of course, not the only behavioural system in the infant; it is antithetically related to such other systems as exploration and stimulus seeking, and a child's behaviour at any one time is the outcome of the interplay of these various systems. In so far as the set-goal of attachment is the maintenance of proximity it will be activated by any conditions that interfere with the goal: separation, insecurity, fear, and so forth. The knowledge that the attachment figure is available provides the child with security: She constitutes a safe haven and a base from which the child can explore. Any conditions that activate attachment behaviour will result in cessation of exploration; the appearance of a stranger, for instance, may well stop the child in its tracks and cause it to scuttle back to the mother for reassurance and security.

There are certain features of Bowlby's account that have attracted criticism. One example is his concept of "monotropism", i.e. the notion that infants are initially unable to form attachments with more than one person, and that all other attachments are only formed subsequently and will be of minor significance compared with the basic one. This has not been borne out (Schaffer & Emerson, 1964): Infants are capable of forming multiple (yet still discriminative) relationships and individuals such as fathers, siblings, and day-care personnel may thus also assume importance in the child's emotional life. And another point which has not found universal acceptance is Bowlby's suggestion that the biological function of attachment is protection against predators, i.e. that such behaviour evolved in order to ensure that helpless infants remain with protective care-takers and are not prey to hostile attacks from others. This is, of course, speculative and quite impossible to verify; it does seem worthwhile, however, to point out that attachment serves so many useful functions that to single this one out as the biological basis seems somewhat far-fetched. Nevertheless, the theory as a whole is a most imaginative one; it is a great advance on previous accounts derived from psychoanalysis and learning theory (Gewirtz, 1972), and in particular so because it does justice to the planned, purposive, and intentional nature of behaviour which emerges later in infancy. Thus the infant is seen not just as an organism driven by inner needs or outer stimuli in some blind and mechanical fashion; it is described instead as quickly evolving its own intentions and plans and so becoming capable of steering its own course.

The "Strange Situation"

In order to highlight individual differences in infants' attachment Ainsworth evolved a procedure (known as the "strange situation") that, when applied around the end of the first year, is said reliably to elicit behaviour indicative of such differences (Ainsworth, Blehar, Waters, & Wall, 1978). It consists of a series of standardised episodes that take place in an unfamiliar laboratory playroom and that include being confronted by a strange adult, being left by the mother with the stranger, and being left entirely alone. According to Ainsworth three main groups of children can be distinguished on the basis of their behaviour in the "strange situation", with particular emphasis laid on their response to the mother on reunion following two brief separation episodes:

1.   *Group A infants* are conspicuous by their avoidance of the mother after reunion; they are judged to be insecurely attached.
2.   *Group B infants* actively seek contact with the mother after the separation episode and show little or no avoidant behaviour; they are thus said to be securely attached.
3.   *Group C infants* are ambivalent, in that they seek contact with the mother on reunion but mingle this with resistant behaviour towards her; they too are regarded as insecurely attached.

According to most studies of American children, approximately one-quarter to one-third fall into Groups A and C, these being the groups that are generally evaluated negatively from the point of view of social adjustment and mental health. The classification is said to be stable over time: A child allocated to Group A at age 12 months is likely still to be assessed as a Group A child at age 18 months, though the avoidant behaviour which was the main criterion for such a judgement may well take quite different forms at the two ages due to motor and other developmental changes (Waters, 1978). However, such consistency is only found when the environment remains stable: Vaughn, England, Sroufe, and Waters (1979) tested 100 economically disadvantaged infants at both 12 and 18 months and found that changes in classification were related to changes in family circumstances. One further claim relates to the predictive power of the tripartite classification with respect to other spheres of behaviour: Thus securely attached infants are said to develop greater competence in play, less fear of strangers, and more positive and confident peer relationships than insecure infants (Ainsworth et al., 1978).

Most of the attachment research conducted in recent years has been carried out within the "strange situation" paradigm, examining individual differences rather than the nomothetic trends outlined by Bowlby. The great advantage of this paradigm has been to highlight the fact that these differences need to be expressed in terms of *patterns* rather than by means of single responses; the latter generally change in the course of development but the former are organisational properties which are more likely to endure. However, the technique does bring with it considerable methodological problems (Lamb et al., 1984), and of these special mention must be made of the highly artificial nature of the assessment situation, the failure to take into account the effects of the mother's behaviour in the "strange situation", and the extraordinarily narrow data base (i.e. the two reunion episodes, each lasting no more than a few seconds) on which assessment depends. Additional techniques for evaluating infants' social competence are clearly required.

Cognitive Processes

The interrelationship of social and cognitive development is a complex one— far more so than past accounts have led us to believe. These have generally considered cognitive changes as "causing" changes in social behaviour: A unidirectional conception that does little justice to the difficulties involved in disentangling the two sets of processes. Take the onset of focused attachments, which has been explained as emerging because around the same age (of 8 months) infants first become capable of object permanence (Schaffer & Emerson, 1964). Just as a child can now search for a missing object and thereby show that it no longer functions on the basis of "out of sight, out of mind", so now the appearance of separation upset indicates that it is capable of remaining oriented towards a missing mother and that permanent social bonds can now be formed. The assumption is that a basic cognitive restructuring occurs which then has implications, *inter alia*, for social behaviour. Such a conception is to a large extent due to Piaget's almost wholly a-social account of early development—an account which disregards the social context in which children are reared and which thus tends to explain developmental change entirely in terms of processes *within* the child. In so far as phenomena such as separation upset and fear of strangers make their first appearance at virtually the same age across a wide range of cultures and child-rearing practices (Konner, 1982) there may well be a temptation to consider this as evidence (as Kagan, 1984, has put it) "that these talents follow orderly changes in the central nervous system", i.e. that the transition is solely dependent on a biologically determined timetable. There are indications, however (further explained in Schaffer, 1986), that the social context does matter and that the child's experience with other people may have a crucial influence, jointly with inherent forces, on developmental transitions. Piaget's description of object permanence concentrated entirely on the infant–object relationship, yet let us consider as one example the hiding games that mothers play with young infants—how they teasingly cover the toy again and again for a second or two at a time, how they make it disappear very slowly to ensure the child's attention is properly focused on the hiding place, or how they leave it half exposed to tempt it to recover it. Similarly with peek-a-boo games that mothers play with their infants (Bruner & Sherwood, 1976), in which hiding is again carried out in a manner carefully adapted to the child's present capacities yet at the same time challenging it to further achievements. Thus in the period preceding object permanence the child is involved in a series of many experiences, set up and flexibly managed by other people, that would appear to be highly relevant to the acquisition process. Taken in conjunction with the fact that under conditions of severe social deprivation, separation upset and fear of strangers fail to emerge (Schaffer, 1986), it is apparent that interpersonal experiences are intimately involved in bringing about psychological reorganisation which will then in turn have implications for both cognitive and social functioning.

The later course of attachments draws attention to one very important cognitive development, namely the role of central representations. As Bowlby (1969) pointed out, children come to construct internal working models of their attachment figures; these evolve out of experienced relationships but are no passive reflections of such events in that the child actively construes its experience and acts on the basis of the meaning attached to that experience. Most past research on attachments has concerned itself with infants' overt behaviour, and the adoption of techniques such as the "strange situation" was therefore appropriate. As attachment work comes to be carried forward beyond the infancy period, and in particular from the middle of the second year on when representative abilities emerge in more marked form, it becomes increasingly important to find new methods that do justice to the child's cognitively more sophisticated status and that can adequately describe the nature of the increasingly complex working models formed of other people (see Bretherton & Waters, 1985, for some examples). How children come to construe attachment figures, how these representations relate to representations of the self, and how they influence overt behaviour are problems to which research must turn if the development of social behaviour from late infancy onward is to be understood.

THE RESPECTIVE ROLES OF INFANT AND PARENT

It is characteristic of human development that the child's functioning needs to be supplemented by the parent. This is particularly evident early on in life; the precise form which this supplement takes, however, varies from one stage to another. Parent and child may be regarded as a mutually accommodative interactive system, but how that accommodation is achieved at any one stage varies according to the particular circumstances prevailing at that time, with special reference to the child's current competencies. Thus each of the transition points found during early development heralds a new *interactive issue*, i.e. the task confronting parent and child to which they must jointly address themselves changes with the mastery of previous developmental challenges and the advent of new ones. At each phase the parent is required to play a complementary role that in certain respects is different from that played at earlier phases.

Interaction with Peers

The respective roles of parent and infant are highlighted by comparing parent–child with peer–child interactions. In the latter we can observe participants of equal psychological status; unlike the former, the two partners are not likely to fill in for each other and the ways in which care-takers make up for their children's deficiencies and foster their development thus become apparent.

According to Sylva, Roy, and Painter (1980) the creativity of pre-school children's play tends to be lowest when the child is on its own, rather greater when with other children and greatest when in the company of an interested adult. The effectiveness of adult intervention can already be observed in the play of babies as young as 6 months, according to a report by Bakeman and Adamson (1984): when babies played together with their mothers they were capable of operating at a higher cognitive level in certain respects than when another baby of the same age was present. It seems that joint involvement episodes of adult and child provide a setting in which one can obtain optimal performance from a child and where one can assume that learning and the acquisition of skills are fostered to an extent that does not happen when the child is either alone or in the company of a child of similar developmental status.

Precisely what it is that the adult contributes needs to be specified. Vygotsky (1978) long ago drew attention to the fact that development occurs in social contexts and that it proceeds from an interpersonal to an intra-personal level; his concept of the "zone of proximal development" stresses that children's performance varies according to the type of support given by a sympathetic adult. Similarly Bruner (1982) used the notion of "scaffolding" in order to emphasise the supportive role which the adult plays in compensating for the child's deficiencies, and Kaye's (1982) concept of "apprenticeship" also stresses the need for the young child to acquire skills and knowledge with the help of a sensitive adult. Let us note, however, that terms such as zone of proximal development, scaffolding, and apprenticeship by themselves have no explanatory value. They serve to draw our attention to the fact that much of early learning is essentially of a social nature; we need to go one step further, however, and specify precisely what it is that an adult provides which enables the young child to perform competently. As yet our knowledge in this respect is very limited.

Parental Sensitivity

What is apparent is that if the adult is to have any effect on the child it is essential that she must be closely attuned to that child—she must, that is, be highly sensitive to the child's interests, abilities, and skills as they unfold themselves from one moment to the next in the course of the interaction and thus be able constantly to use feedback information from the child in order to judge what kinds of support are appropriate at any given point.

Sensitive responsiveness has recently emerged as a dimension of particular interest to those attempting to understand parental behaviour and the implications of that behaviour for children's psychological functioning (see Schaffer & Collis, 1986). Essentially, the term refers to adults' awareness of children as individual in their own right. It is a continuum: At one end are the optimally sensitive adults who are able to see things from the child's point of view, are alert to the child's signals and communications, can interpret these correctly, and then respond promptly and appropriately. At the other end are the adults who cannot see the child at all as a separate individual, who distort the child's communications in the light of their own needs, and who interact with the child on the basis of their own wishes rather than the child's. Whether these characteristics refer to a unitary dimension or whether the term is merely an umbrella for a lot of different aspects has not yet been established; it is possible, for instance, that there are at least three distinct components, namely responding promptly, responding consistently, and responding appropriately.

However this may be, variations in this set of parental qualities are believed to be associated with variations in children's psychological functioning. Two aspects in particular have been mentioned: the infant's attachment security and its developmental progress. As to the first, it has been suggested (Ainsworth et al., 1978) that the security of an infant's attachment to the mother depends on the sensitivity with which the mother has treated the child in the past. When a mother answers the child promptly and predictably the child will built up a set of expectations about her from which it derives security; by learning that it can affect the environment by its behaviour the child will in due course develop a sense of personal effectiveness and confidence. This does not occur with an insensitive mother who conveys that she is not interested in the child's needs and an anxious, insecure personality will thus be fostered.

The second effect, that concerned with the child's developmental progress, has been investigated mainly in relation to language acquisition. It is now well estalished that it is not so much the quantity of talk directed to children that fosters the beginnings of language development but rather the meaningfulness of that talk. Thus what the adult says should be related to the child's interests, attentional focus and actions at that moment. The mother therefore needs to be attuned to the child and tie in her own comments with the child's concerns as well as with its abilities to process what she says. There are indications (Nelson, 1973; Moerk, 1975; Cross, 1978) that under such circumstances language development proceeds more quickly than when the adult imposes her own ideas on the child and talks about these; similarly when she takes little note of the child's current processing skills she is likely to provide an input that is too meaningless for the child to profit from it.

It must be emphasised that there are no grounds as yet for making cause-and-effect statements involving parental practices and child outcomes. We cannot be certain that the parents' speech is directly responsible for the nature of the child's language progress, any more than we know for sure that a mother's sensitive treatment is a determinant of the child's security. It is at least plausible that the cause-and-effect sequence goes in the opposite direction, from child to adult; it is even more plausible that parent and child exert a *mutual* set of influences on each other that in practice is far from easy to unravel. In general, our knowledge of early social development is soundest on the descriptive side, i.e. *how* infants and their care-takers behave toward each other at different ages and stages. When it comes to stipulating the *mechanisms* of that development, and in particular the part played by adults in bringing about change in the child, we are still extraordinarily ignorant. Much of what happens during the first 2 years or so can be considered in terms of a gradual progression from being largely *other-controlled* to becoming increasingly *self-controlled*; how this is brought about is one of the major challenges for future research.

REFERENCES

Ainsworth, M. D. S., Blehar, M. C., Waters, E., & Wall, S. (1978). *Patterns of attachment.* Hillsdale, N.J.: Lawrence Erlbaum Associates Inc.

Bakeman, R. & Adamson, L. R. (1984). Coordinating attention to people and objects in mother–infant and peer–infant interaction. *Child Development, 22,* 1278–1289.

Bowlby, J. (1969). *Attachment and loss*: Vol. 1 *Attachment*. London: Hogarth Press.

Bretherton, I. & Waters, E. (eds) (1985). Growing points of attachment theory and research. *Monographs of the Society for Research in Child Development*, *50* 1–2 (Serial No. 209).

Bronson, G. (1974). The postnatal growth of visual capacity. *Child Development*, *45*, 873–890.

Bruner, J. S. (1973). Organization of early skilled action. *Child Development*, *44*, 1–11.

Bruner, J. S. (1977). Early social interaction and language acquisition. In H. R. Schaffer (ed.), *Studies in mother–infant interaction*. London: Academic Press.

Bruner, J. S. (1982). The organization of action and the nature of adult–infant transaction. In M. von Cranach & R. Harre (eds), *The analysis of action*. Cambridge: Cambridge University Press.

Bruner, J. S. & Sherwood, V. (1976). Early rule structure: The case of "peekaboo". In R. Harre (ed.), *Life sentences*. London: Wiley.

Butterworth, G. E. & Cochran, E. (1980). Towards a mechanism of joint visual attention in human infancy. *International Journal of Behavioural Development*, *4*, 253–272.

Collis, G. M. (1977). Visual coorientation and maternal speech. In H. R. Schaffer (ed.), *Studies in mother–infant interaction*. London: Academic Press.

Collis, G. M. & Schaffer, H. R. (1975). Synchronization of visual attention in mother–infant pairs. *Journal of Child Psychology & Psychiatry*, *16*, 315–320.

Cross, T. (1978). Mothers' speech and its association with rate of linguistic development in young children. In N. Waterson & C. Snow (eds), *The development of communication*. Chichester: Wiley.

Eimas, P. D. (1975). Speech perception in early infancy. In L. B. Cohen & P. Salapatek (eds), *Infant perception: from sensation to cognition*: Vol. 2. New York: Academic Press.

Emde, R. N., Gaensbauer, T. J., & Harmon, R. J. (1976). Emotional expression in infancy: A behavioural study. *Psychological Issues*, *10* (1, Whole No. 37).

Feinman, S. (1982). Social referencing in infancy. *Merrill–Palmer Quarterly*, *28*, 445–470.

Fenson, L., Kagan, J., Kearsley, R. B., & Zelazo, P. R. (1976). The developmental progression of manipulative play in the first two years. *Child Development*, *47*, 232–236.

Fischer, K. W. (1980). A theory of cognitive development: The control and construction of hierarchies of skills. *Psychological Review*, *87*, 477–531.

Fogel, A. (1977). Temporal organization in mother–infant face-to-face interaction. In H. R. Schaffer (ed.), *Studies in mother–infant interaction*. London: Academic Press.

Gewirtz, J. L. (ed.) (1972). *Attachment and dependency*. New York: Wiley.

Hutt, S. J., Hutt, C., Lenard, H. G., Bernuth, H. V., & Muntjewerll, W. J. (1968). Auditory responsivity in the human neonate. *Nature*, *218*, 880–890.

Kagan, J. (1984). *The nature of the child*. New York: Basic Books.

Kaye, K. (1977). Toward the origin of dialogue. In H. R. Schaffer (ed.), *Studies in mother–infant interaction*. London: Academic Press.

Kaye, K. (1982). *The mental and social life of babies*. London: Methuen.

Kaye, K. & Fogel, A. (1980). The temporal structure of face-to-face communication between mothers and infants. *Developmental Psychology*, *16*, 454–464.

Konner, M. (1982). Biological aspects of the mother–infant bond. In R. N. Emde & R. J. Harmon (eds), *The development of attachment and affiliative systems*. New York: Plenum Press.

Lamb, M. E., Thompson, R. M., Gardner, W., Charnov, E. L., & Estes, D. (1984). Security of infantile attachment as assessed in the "Strange Situation": Its study and biological interpretation. *Behavioral and Brain Sciences*, *7*, 127–171.

McCall, R. B., Eichorn, D. H., & Hogarty, P. S. (1977). Transitions in early development. *Monographs of the Society for Research in Child Development*, *42* (No. 3., Serial No. 171).

Messer, D. J. (1978). The integration of mother's referential speech with joint play. *Child Development*, *49*, 781–787.

Moerk, E. (1975). Verbal interaction between children and their mothers during the preschool years. *Developmental Psychology*, *11*, 788–794.

Molfese, D. L. & Molfese, V. J. (1980). Cortical responses of preterm infants to phonetic and nonphonetic speech stimuli. *Developmental Psychology*, *16*, 574–581.

Murphy, C. M. & Messer, D. J. (1977). Mothers, infants and pointing: A study of a gesture. In H. R. Schaffer (ed.), *Studies in mother–infant interaction*. London: Academic Press.

Nelson, K. (1973). Structure and strategy in learning to talk. *Monographs of the Society for Research in Child Development*, *38* (Serial No. 149).

Rheingold, H. L. & Adams, J. L. (1980). The significance of speech to newborns. *Developmental Psychology*, *16*, 397–403.

Schaffer, H. R. (1966). The onset of fear of strangers and the incongruity hypothesis. *Journal of Child Psychology and Psychiatry*, *7*, 95–106.

Schaffer, H. R. (1971). *The growth of sociability* pp. 81–105. Harmondsworth: Penguin.

Schaffer, H. R. (ed.) (1977). *Studies in mother–infant interaction*. London: Academic Press.

Schaffer, H. R. (1984). *The child's entry into a social world*. London: Academic Press.

Schaffer, H. R. (1986). Psychobiological development in a social context. In H. Rauh & H. C. Steinhausen (eds), *Psychobiology and early development*. Amsterdam: North Holland/ Elsevier.

Schaffer, H. R. & Collis, G. M. (1986). Parental responsiveness and child behaviour. In W. Sluckin & M. Herbert (eds), *Parental behaviour in animals and humans*. Oxford: Blackwell.

Schaffer, H. R. & Emerson, P. E. (1964). The development of social attachments in infancy. *Monographs of the Society for Research in Child Development*, *29* (3, Whole No. 94).

Sherrod, L. R. (1981). Issues in cognitive–perceptual development: The special case of social stimuli. In M. E. Lamb & L. R. Sherrod (eds), *Infant social cognition: Empirical and theoretical considerations*. Hillsdale, N.J.: Lawrence Erlbaum Associates Inc.

Snow, C. E. (1977). The development of conversation between mothers and babies. *Journal of Child Language*, *4*, 1–22.

Stern, D. N. (1974). Mother and infant at play: The dyadic interaction involving facial, vocal and gaze behavior. In M. Lewis & L. A. Rosenblum (eds), *The effect of the infant on its caregiver*. New York: Wiley.

Sugarman-Bell, S. (1978). Some organizational aspects of pre-verbal communication. In I. Markova (ed.), *The social context of language*. Chichester: Wiley.

Sylva, K., Roy, C., & Painter, M. (1980). *Childwatching at playgroup and nursery school*. London: Grant McIntyre.

Trevarthen, C. & Hubley, P. (1978). Secondary intersubjectivity: Confidence, confiding and acts of meaning in the first year. In A. Lock (ed.), *Action, gesture and symbol*. London: Academic Press.

Vaughn, B., Engeland, B., Sroufe, A. L., & Waters, E. (1979). Individual differences in infant–mother attachment at twelve and eighteen months: Stability and change in families under stress. *Child Development*, *50*, 971–975.

Vygotsky, L. S. (1978). *Mind in society*. Cambridge, Mass.: MIT Press.

Waters, E. (1978). The reliability and stability of individual differences in infant–mother attachment. *Child Development*, *49*, 483–494.

Werner, H. & Kaplan, B. (1963). *Symbolic formation: An organismic–developmental approach to language and the expression of thought*, pp. 77–84. New York: Wiley Hillsdale, N.J.: Lawrence Erlbaum Associates Inc.

Wolff, P. H. (1968). The serial organization of sucking in the young infant. *Pediatrics*, *42*, 943–956.

9 Early Language Development

Martyn Barrett

Department of Psychology,
Royal Holloway and Bedford New College, University of London,
Egham Hill,
Egham,
Surrey TW20 0EX

INTRODUCTION

The word *infant* is derived from the Latin word *infans,* which means literally "unable to speak". Consequently, the acquisition of speech is often regarded as marking the end of infancy. However, deciding precisely when speech has appeared (and hence, when infancy has ended) is not an easy matter. This is because the early development of language takes place very gradually. Thus, during the months which follow the production of the first word, the infant might learn to produce only one, two or three new words per month (Benedict, 1979; Nelson, 1973). Consequently, during these early months of language development, the infant still relies much more heavily upon cries, actions, and gestures rather than speech for the purposes of communication (Lock, 1978, 1980; Lock, Service, Brito, & Chandler, Chapter 10, this volume; Schaffer, 1977, chapter 8, this volume; Zinober & Martlew, 1985a, 1985b). And even after the infant has come to rely upon words as a major medium of communication, that infant might still not be able to combine words together to form simple two-word utterances with any degree of regularity until several more months have passed (Bloom, 1973; Garman, 1979).

The present chapter describes these various linguistic developments which gradually draw the period of infancy to a close. The chapter is divided into three parts. The first part considers the first words which infants acquire, whereas the second part describes the subsequent linguistic developments that occur during the period of single-word speech. The third part considers how infants make the final transition into the multi-word speech of early childhood.

THE FIRST WORDS OF THE INFANT

There is considerable variability in the age at which infants produce their very first word. While some infants may produce their first word at 9 months of age (Bates et al., 1979), other may not do so until they are 16 months old (Barrett, Harris, Jones & Brookes, 1986a). Similarly, infants vary considerably in the age at which they achieve a productive vocabulary of 10 different words: Nelson (1973) found that this can occur anywhere between 13 and 19 months of age (the average age being 15 months).

The Context-bound Nature of the First Words

As far as the first 10 words are concerned, it has recently been argued by several different observers that these very early words are not used by the infant referentially to name particular objects and actions (see, for example, Barrett, 1986; Bates et al., 1979; Dore, 1985; Nelson & Lucariello, 1985). Instead, it has been proposed that the infant's earliest words are usually context-bound in nature, their predominant characteristic being that they are produced only in very limited and specific situations or contexts in which particular actions or events occur. To give some examples which might help to clarify this notion, Bloom (1973) reports the case of one infant who initially began to use the word *car* at 9 months of age only while she was looking out of the living room window at cars moving on the street below. She did not use this word at this early age in any other contexts which might suggest that she was able to use it referentially: for example, she did not use it to refer to stationary cars, to refer to pictures of cars, or while she was actually sitting in a car. Similarly, Bates et al. (1979) report that one of their infant subjects only ever produced the word *bye*, when it was first acquired, while that infant was putting a telephone receiver down. Further instances of context-bound word use are reported in Barrett (1986) and in Barrett et al. (1986a) and Barrett, Harris, Jones, & Brookes (1986b); for example, one infant I observed first began to produce the word *duck* only while he was hitting a toy duck off the edge of the bath, and never in any other contexts at this initial stage. Observations such as these (see Table 1 for a summary of these and other similar examples) have therefore led to the proposal that the infant's first words are usually context-bound in nature, with referential word-usage being a later phenomenon that does not emerge until a later point in development.

TABLE 1
Examples of the Types of Context within which Infants Produce Their First 10 words

Word	Context of Use	Source
car	While infant looks out of living room window at cars moving on street below.	Bloom (1973)
bye	While infant puts telephone receiver down.	Bates et al. (1979)
papa	When infant hears the doorbell.	Bates et al. (1979)
see	While infant points, and turns to the listener for eye contact.	Bates et al. (1979)
duck	While infant hits toy duck off the edge of the bath.	Barrett (1986)
boo	While infant hides behind curtain.	Barrett et al. (1986a)
go	While infant takes mother to door or stands by door with mother.	Barrett et al. (1986a)
no	While infant is rejecting an object.	Barrett et al. (1986a)

The examples which are shown in Table 1 illustrate several further characteristics of these very early context-bound words. Firstly, although in many cases these words are produced while the infant is engaged in performing a particular action, this is not always the case. For example, the words *car* and *papa* were both produced when the infant merely perceived a particular type of event occurring; in these instances, the infant was not an active participant in the events that elicited the use of the words but only a percipient of those events. Thus, it would be a mistake to characterise these words as always being tied to the motor activities of the infant. Instead, it would seem more appropriate to describe them as being tied to the occurrence of particular events, events which often (but not always) involve motor activity by the infant.

Secondly, although the contexts for the production of these words are rather heterogeneous, it is nevertheless possible to identify certain types of event which often characterise these contexts. In many cases, the event consists simply of an action which the infant regularly performs in the course of free play with a particular object (e.g. *bye* and *duck*). In other cases, the event consists of a specific behaviour drawn from a frequently performed social–interactional routine such as picture-book reading or peekaboo (e.g. *see* and *boo*). In a third type of context, the event involves a behaviour which is produced regularly by the infant to express a particular desire, want or need (e.g. *go* and *no*). And finally, in those instances which do not involve any motor activity by the infant, the context contains a perceptually salient event which the infant has frequently experienced (e.g. *car* and *papa*). The important point to notice here is that in all of these cases, the context is characterised by a frequently occurring event; furthermore, the behaviours which comprise these events have often acquired a standardised and ritualised format by the time the first words are produced (Bruner, 1983).

In order to explain these findings, Barrett (1983a; 1983b; 1986) and Nelson (1983, 1985; Nelson & Lucariello, 1985) have proposed that by the time the first words are acquired, the infant has already acquired mental representations of certain types of event. In particular, they hypothesise that the pre-linguistic infant acquires a knowledge of frequently recurring events; thus, the pre-linguistic infant would acquire mental representations of precisely those events which occur regularly in free play, in social–interactive routines, and in recurrent episodes of expressive behaviour, and of those perceptually salient events which are repeatedly experienced by the infant. In addition it is postulated that, when a context-bound word is initially acquired, that word is linked with a particular event representation. The word is subsequently produced when the infant recognises the occurrence of that particular event, the infant simply treating the occurrence of this event as providing an appropriate context for the production of the word. Thus, the word is produced in a context-bound manner (without the infant yet understanding that it could perhaps be used referentially as the name of a particular object or action).

Affect Expressions

However, although many of the earliest words do appear to be context-bound, it is also clear from the available studies that infants sometimes produce another type of very early word which displays rather different characteristics; some examples of this second type of word are shown in Table 2. Notice that these words can be used in a variety of different behavioural contexts, unlike the context-bound words in Table 1. However, an invariant still exists across all the different contexts in which each word is produced, namely a particular type of affect state which the infant seems to be expressing by means of that word. Thus, these words are also used only in a limited range of situations; however, this range is defined not in terms of an external event, but in terms of a particular internal affect state of the infant.

It has been suggested that the use of these affect expressions (which are often phonetically idiosyncratic) tends to precede the use of context-bound words (see Dore, 1985). However, the evidence from the studies by Barrett et al. (1986a; 1986b) and Bates et al. (1979) does not support this suggestion, indicating instead that, if affect expressions are acquired by an infant (which

TABLE 2
Examples of the Affect Expressions Sometimes Included within Infants' Very Early Vocabularies

Word	Contexts of Use	Source
[ae::]	While infant looks at a puppet, plays with hats, rocks on a horse, walks round a room with a cup in her mouth: on all occasions, pleasurable affect is apparent.	Dore et al. (1976)
[ubiba]	While infant plays with a peg, a crayon, a puppet, and a jack-in-a-box: always with an expression of mild frustration.	Dore et al. (1976)
dada	When infant is happy.	Bates et al. (1979)
mama	While infant cries in anger.	Bates et al. (1979)

is not always the case), they are usually acquired contemporaneously with context-bound words

The Communicative Functions of the First Words

Some recent findings concerning the pragmatic characteristics of the infant's first words can also be illustrated by reference to the examples shown in Tables 1 and 2. As we have already seen, context-bound words are used simply as accompaniments to the occurrence of particular actions or events. Consequently, many of these words do not seem to serve a communicative purpose as such. Instead, they appear to function as pure "performatives" (in the sense that their utterance is more like the performance of a ritualised action rather than the expression of a lexical meaning to an addressee: see Barrett, 1983a, and Greenfield & Smith, 1976). Nevertheless, it is usually possible to attribute a communicative function to some of the infant's very early words. In particular, it has been argued that some first words are used for expressive and directive functions (see, for example, Griffiths, 1985; Halliday, 1973, 1975). The expressive function is the use of language to express internal states such as affect states (e.g. pleasure, distress, etc.) and reactions to objects (e.g. surprise, recognition, rejection, etc.) The word *no* in Table 1, and all of the words in Table 2, could therefore be interpreted as serving expressive functions. By contrast, the directive function is the use of language to direct the actions and behaviour of other people. It includes issuing orders, requesting objects, obtaining attention, and directing the attention of others to objects in the environment. The words *see* and *go* in Table 1 could thus be interpreted as serving directive functions.

In this connection, it is interesting to note that studies into the gestures which infants use to communicate with other people prior to the acquisition of language (see, for example, Lock, 1978, 1980; Lock et al., Chapter 10, this volume; Zinober & Martlew, 1985a, 1985b) have revealed that these pre-linguistic gestures are also used for both expressive and directive communicative functions (e.g. arm waving, hand flapping, and object rejection are often used in the pre-linguistic period to express internal states, while open-handed reaching, arm raising, pointing, and direct physical contact are often used pre-linguistically to direct the behaviour of other people). Thus, there would appear to be considerable functional continuity between pre-linguistic and very early linguistic communication, with the transition from the former to the latter consisting, at the pragmatic level, of the acquisition of new means for fulfilling existing communicative functions, rather than any substantial extension of those established functions.

A Divergent Finding

Before leaving this topic of the infant's first words, there is one further finding which ought to be mentioned here. As we have already seen, in most recent studies (e.g. Barrett, 1986; Bates et al., 1979; Dore, 1985) it has been found that the infant's very early words are not used referentially when they are initially acquired. However, in the study by Barrett et al. (1986a; 1986b), it was found that, although the majority of the first words which were observed were indeed context-bound, there was also a substantial minority of these words which were not context-bound. Furthermore, most of these contextually flexible words appeared to be functioning referentially as the names of objects (i.e. nominally) right from the outset, with just a few functioning as non-nominals instead (see Table 3 for examples). However, the infants who were studied differed considerably from one another in terms of how many of their first 10 words were used in this contextually flexible manner: the number here ranged from 2 to 7.

The findings of this study (as well as the differences between these findings and the findings of previous studies) suggest that individual differences probably exist in the way in which infants begin to use their first 10 words. We will return to this issue later on. In addition, these findings indicate that infants' first words can sometimes be referential in nature, contrary to the conclusions of many recent studies. The explanation of how infants acquire these referential words will be examined in the following section, when we consider how all infants eventually acquire such words.

TABLE 3
Examples of the Contextually Flexible First Words Reported by Barrett et al. (1986a, 1986b)

Word	Initial Contexts of Use	Word Type
teddy	While infant looks at, points to, touches, plays with, a big toy teddy.	nominal
shoes	While infant looks at pictures of shoes in a book, points at her own shoes, holds toy shoes.	nominal
car	While infant plays with a toy car, looks through window of house at cars outside, stands outside house looking at a car turning into the road, looks at a toy car, points at a toy car.	nominal
more	While infant holds out an empty bowl, brings an empty bottle to her mother and leads her into the kitchen, reaches for her drinking cup before having another drink, reaches into a toybox and takes out more bricks.	non-nominal

LINGUISTIC DEVELOPMENTS DURING THE PERIOD OF SINGLE-WORD SPEECH

As we have already seen, the first 10 words are acquired very slowly at the rate of 1 – 3 new words per month, with the tenth word being acquired at 15 months of age on average. From this time onwards, the acquisition rate begins to accelerate sharply. Nelson (1973) found that the infants in her sample had acquired 50 words by the time they were 19 months old, with the acquisition rate increasing very rapidly towards the end of this period to well over 25 new words per month (all the figures here are means: considerable individual variation exists). This sudden increase in the rate of acquisition of new words is called the "vocabulary explosion" or "vocabulary spurt" (see Barrett, 1985; Bloom, 1973; Halliday, 1975). Despite this major development, the infant's utterances throughout this period still consist only of single words which are articulated separately from one another: the first utterances to contain two words enclosed within a single intonation contour are not usually produced until a month or two after the vocabulary explosion has occurred (see Garman, 1979). In this section, I will consider the lexical and pragmatic development of the infant prior to the production of these first two-word utterances.

LEXICAL DEVELOPMENT IN THE SINGLE-WORD PERIOD

Close examination of the vocabularies which are acquired during the period of single-word speech reveals that there are in fact several distinct phenomena which characterise the lexical development of the infant during this period. Firstly, the infant continues to acquire further context-bound words (Barrett, 1983a; 1986). Secondly, some of the context-bound words which the infant has already acquired are decontextualised (that is, their production is dissociated from the occurrence of just one particular type of event, and they begin to be used much more flexibly in a variety of different behavioural contexts: see Barrett, 1983a, 1986; Bates et al., 1979; Lock, 1980). Thirdly, the infant acquires referential words for labelling objects and actions; these words are used in a contextually flexible manner from the outset (Barrett, 1986; Bowerman, 1978). And finally, the infant acquires a variety of other non-nominal words which are also used in a contextually flexible manner (see Barrett, 1983a, 1983b; Bloom, 1973; Gopnik, 1982; Gopnik & Meltzoff, 1986; McCune-Nicolich, 1981). I will discuss each of these four phenomena in turn.

Context-bound Words

To begin with the issue of context-bound words, it is clear from recent studies that, during the course of the single-word period, the infant continues to acquire such words. For example, I have previously documented how words as varied as *catch, off, inside, chuff-chuff* and *dog* have all been acquired as context-bound words during the course of the single-word period (see Barrett, 1983a, 1986). As we shall see, most context-bound words are soon decontextualised; however, a few may continue to be used in a context-bound manner for many more years (for example, the words *ta* and *hello*, which are often acquired as context-bound items at this age, may remain tied to the occurrence of particular interactional events for some considerable time after infancy).

Decontextualisation

Despite this continued acquisition of context-bound words, however, the infant does begin to decontextualise many of these words as the single-word period progresses. Some examples of decontextualisation are shown in Table 4. In each case, the infant initially used the word for a substantial period of time only in one particular behavioural context; subsequently, however, the

TABLE 4
Examples of the Decontextualisation of Context-Bound Words

Word	Initial Context of Use	Subsequent Contexts of Use	Source
catch	While infant throws an object to another person.	While infant sees another person throwing an object, before infant throws an object, to request another person to throw an object which they are holding (common reference: the action of throwing).	Barrett (1983a)
off	While infant removes an item of clothing from either her own or her mother's body	When infant sees another person remove an item of clothing, while infant tries to pull away from her mother, while infant pulls a toy cat out of a carry cot, to refer to getting off a train (common reference: the separation of objects which have previously been in contact).	Barrett (1983a)
duck	While infant hits a toy duck off the edge of the bath.	While infant plays with a toy duck in any situation, after infant is asked "What's that?" in reference to a toy duck, when infant sees a toy duck lying on the floor (common reference: a toy duck).	Barrett (1986)
choo-choo	While infant pushes a toy train along the floor.	While infant looks at a picture of a train in a book, while infant puts a teddy into a carriage of a toy train, while infant pulls a toy steam roller out of a toybox, while infant pushes a toy steam roller along the floor (common reference: a wheeled vehicle).	Barrett et al. (1986a)

infant began to produce the word not only in that initial context but also in several additional contexts.

There are two important points to note about this process. Firstly, decontextualisation involves a shift from using a word only when one particular event occurs to using that same word to refer to a particular object or action in a variety of different situations (see Table 4). Furthermore, the object or action which comes to form the reference of the word after decontextualisation has occurred seems to derive directly from one of the core elements in the event which had previously been eliciting the initial context-bound use of that word. This suggests that decontextualisation occurs as a consequence of the infant partitioning the original event representation that was governing the initial context-bound use of the word into its constituent parts, identifying one core element in that event representation, and then using that element to derive a specification of the type of object or action that can be referred to by means of that word (cf. Barrett, 1983a, 1986; and Nelson, 1983, 1985).

The second point to note about decontextualisation is that the various context-bound words in the child's vocabulary are not decontextualised simultaneously. Instead, decontextualisation occurs at different times for different words. Indeed, one infant whom I observed first began to decontextualise some of his earliest words when he was only 12½ months of age, very soon after these words had been acquired; however, he did not decontextualise other words until he was 21 months of age and even older (see Barrett, 1986).

Referential Words

In addition to the decontextualisation of context-bound words, the infant also acquires, during the course of the single-word period, many new referential words for labelling objects and actions, words which are used immediately in a decontextualised manner. Many examples of such words have been reported in the literature. To give just a few examples here, Bowerman (1978) reports the acquisition of the word *ball*, which was used by one infant right from the outset for referring to any rounded object of a size suitable for handling and throwing; Bates et al. (1979) report the acquisition of the word *dog*, which was used immediately for referring to both toy and real dogs; and Barrett (1986) reports the acquisition of the words *tick-tock* (for referring to clocks and watches) and *cut* (for referring to the action of cutting), both of these words being used by one infant in a variety of different behavioural contexts right from the outset. The acquisition of these words shows that infants are able to establish a specification of the type of object or action which can be referred to by means of a particular word, without first having to use that word in a context-bound manner for a while. And as we saw earlier (see Table 3), some infants do so right at the beginning of the single-word period, when they are still acquiring their first 10 words.

It has been proposed by several authors (e.g. Dore, 1978, 1985; Kamhi, 1986; McShane, 1979, 1980; Nelson, 1983; Nelson & Lucariello, 1985) that there is a sharp discontinuity in lexical development during the single-word period. These authors have suggested that, during the first part of this period, the infant does not understand that words can be used referentially as the names of particular objects or actions; as a consequence, the infant at this stage of development can only use words in the context of particular interactive or communicative situations (i.e. in a context-bound manner). Mid-way through the single-word period, it is proposed, infants acquire a fundamental insight into the symbolic properties of words: that words can be used in order to name particular objects and actions. And as a consequence of this realisation, existing words are decontextualised and many new referential words are suddenly acquired.

However, the observations which have been noted above would seem to cast some doubt upon the notion that all infants only acquire the naming insight mid-way through the single-word period. In particular, the finding that the very first words of some infants are used in a variety of different behavioural contexts in a referential manner (Barrett et al., 1986a, 1986b) implies that at least some infants acquire the naming insight before they begin to produce their very first words. The hypothesis that the naming insight is a sudden acquisition occurring mid-way through the single-word period would seem to be further undermined by the fact that decontextualisation does not always begin mid-way through the single-word period, affecting simultaneously all of the context-bound words which are in the infant's vocabulary. Instead, the decontextualisation of context-bound words may begin at a very early age, just after the acquisition of the very first words, and may then continue gradually, word-by-word, for many more months (Barrett, 1986). Finally, the fact that words which could potentially be used referentially may continue to be acquired and used initially only as context-bound words, even towards the end of the single-word period, well after the time when the acquisition of the naming insight is supposed to have occurred (Barrett, 1983a), would also seem to mitigate against the notion that a sharp discontinuity in lexical development occurs mid-way through the single-word period.

Nevertheless, it is possible that different infants acquire the naming insight at different points in their development. Thus, it is possible that the infants who were studied by Barrett et al. (1986a; 1986b) acquired this insight at a comparatively early age, with the consequence that some of their very first words were used referentially right from the outset. By contrast, the two infants who were studied by Dore (1985) and by Kamhi (1986), and who arguably provide the strongest evidence for a discontinuity in early lexical development, many not have acquired the naming insight until a much later point in their development; this would indeed explain why all of their earliest words were context-bound, and why their use of referential words commenced rather suddenly mid-way through the single-word period.

Thus, the exact point in development at which infants first begin to use words referentially probably varies. The precise way in which infants use referential words, once they have been acquired, has also been investigated in detail in several recent studies (see, for example, Anglin, 1977, 1986; Barrett, 1978, 1982a, 1983b; Bowerman, 1978; Clark, 1973, 1983; Gruendel, 1977;

Rescorla, 1980). These studies have revealed that infants often underextend referential words when they first begin to use them; that is, they often use these words to name only a subset of the full range of objects or actions which are properly labelled with those words in the adult language. An example of underextension is shown in Table 4: the word *duck* was used immediately after decontextualisation to refer to toy ducks but not to refer to real ducks. In addition, some referential words may be subsequently overextended by the infant; that is, these words may be used eventually not only to refer to all of the objects or actions which are properly labelled with those words in the adult language, but also to refer to some further objects or actions as well. Thus, the infant who used the word *duck* gradually extended its use such that he eventually used it to label not only toy ducks but also real ducks, pictures of ducks, swans, geese, and a picture of a quail (see Barrett, 1986). In addition to underextension and overextension, infants' referential words may occasionally display a mismatch with the adult word usage (e.g. the word *catch* in Table 4, which was used to refer to the action of throwing rather than catching).

The Acquisition of the Meanings of Referential Words: The Prototype Theory

In order to account for the occurrence of underextension, overextension and mismatch, it has been argued by Barrett (1982a; 1983b; 1986) and by Bowerman (1978) that the infant acquires the meaning of a referential word through the operation of the following two processes. Firstly, it is proposed that the infant constructs a mental representation of a prototypical referential exemplar for the word. This prototype is derived either from the infant's observations of the type of object or action in connection with which other people typically use that word (in the case of words which are used in a referential manner right from the outset), or from the infant identifying and partitioning a core element from an event representation which has previously been guiding the context-bound use of the word (in the case of words which are initially context-bound and are subsequently decontextualised). This prototypical referent then functions for the infant as a specification of the type of object or action which can be labelled with the word; at this point, the infant only uses the word to refer to objects or actions which closely resemble this prototype. Consequently, underextension may occur at this point: the word *duck*, for example, was used only to refer to toy ducks immediately after decontextualisation because a representation of a prototypical toy duck (rather than that of a real duck) had been partitioned from the event representation during decontextualisation. Notice also that, if the infant errs at this stage, a mismatch between infant and adult word usage may result. For example, the infant who produced the word *catch* (see Table 4) appeared to identify and partition the wrong action from the event representation which governed the initial context-bound use of the word (i.e. the action of throwing, rather than catching) with a mismatch therefore resulting after decontextualisation had occurred.

The second process which is proposed as underlying the acquisition of referential word meaning is the subsequent analysis of the prototypical referential exemplar into its principal features, with the word then being extended to label any object or action which shares one or more of these features with the prototypical referent. Consequently, the word is now extended to label novel referents, possibly becoming overextended in the process. Thus, to continue with the example of the word *duck*, it is suggested that the infant's representation of the prototypical referent for this word (a toy duck) was analysed by the infant into its constituent features, with the word then being extended to label real ducks, swans, geese, etc. on the basis that these objects shared one or more of these features with the prototypical referent.

This theory therefore accounts for the occurrence of underextension, overextension, and mismatch in early lexical development. In addition, the prototype theory accounts for two further major findings which have been obtained in studies of early lexical development. The first of these findings has been obtained from the analysis of patterns of overextension. These analyses have shown that the various objects or actions which an infant eventually labels with a given word do not necessarily have any features in common with one another; however, each one of these referents does usually have at least one feature in common with the object or action which originally functioned as the initial referent of the word (Barrett, 1982a; Bowerman, 1978; Nelson, 1982). For example, one infant used the word *ball* to refer to (amongst other objects) balls, an observatory dome, and crumpled pieces of paper which she used in the game of catch (Leopold, 1939). Whereas the observatory dome and the crumpled paper do not have any features in common with each other, both objects have at least one feature in common with a ball, which was the initial referent for this word. Such examples of the referents of words being linked by a family resemblance (rather than by an invariant set of common features) offer strong support for the prototype theory, according to which novel referents are identified on the basis of the features which those referents share with a central prototypical exemplar (rather than on the basis of an invariant set of necessary and sufficient features).

The prototype theory is also able to explain the patterns of results which have been obtained in studies of word comprehension. These studies have shown that when infants' abilities to comprehend words are tested by saying to them "Show me the X" or "Where is the X?" (where X is a referential word which the infants spontaneously overextend in production), those infants usually begin by choosing a referent which shares many features with the prototype of the word (i.e. they begin by choosing a central typical referent rather than an atypical overextended referent). Consequently, if comprehension testing is terminated at this point, the infants do not appear to be overextending these words in comprehension (Fremgen & Fay, 1980; Thomson & Chapman, 1977). However, if the infants are allowed to continue selecting further referents for the word, then with each successive choice they select progressively less typical referents; eventually they begin to select overextended referents which have comparatively few features in common with the prototypical referent of the word (Kuczaj, 1982). This pattern of choosing referents is precisely what would be expected on the basis of prototype theory, with the most typical referents (i.e. those which have the most features in common with the prototype) being selected first, and the more atypical overextended referents being selected last.

Thus, patterns of word overextension both in production and in comprehension provide further support for the prototype theory of referential word meaning. However, referential words do not remain overextended: infants eventually rescind these overextensions. The rescission of overextensions often occurs in conjunction with the acquisition of new words which take over the labelling of the overextended referents (Barrett, 1978, 1982a; Rescorla, 1981). For example, the infant who overextended the word *duck* to refer to swans, geese, and a picture of a quail eventually acquired the word *swan* (see Barrett, 1986). At this point in time, he stopped using *duck* to refer to swans, using *swan* instead for this purpose. He later acquired the word *geese* which he used to refer to either a single goose or a group of geese. He subsequently never used the word *duck* to refer to geese again. As far as the picture of the quail was concerned, he did not acquire the word *quail* during the period in which he was under observation, and he continued to use *duck* for labelling this picture.

In order to account for this type of phenomenon, it has been suggested that the rescission of overextensions occurs in the following way (see Barrett, 1982a, 1986). The infant first assigns the overextended word to a particular semantic field; that is, the infant groups this word with certain other words as they are acquired, possibly on the basis that the prototypical referents of these words have various salient features in common with one another (e.g. *duck* and *swan* are assigned to the same semantic field, on the basis that the prototypical referents for these words share various features). The infant then identifies those features which differentiate the prototypical referents of these words from one another, and uses these features to delimit the referential scopes of the words (e.g. the features which distinguish the prototype of *duck* from the prototype of *swan* are identified, with these features then being used to differentiate between the objects which can be called *duck* and *swan*, respectively). As a result, the overextension is totally or partially rescinded at the same time as the new and more appropriate name is acquired. Thus, most of the infant's overextensions are eventually rescinded as the growth of the vocabulary proceeds.

Non-nominal Words

The final aspect of lexical development which occurs during the single-word period is the acquisition of a variety of other non-nominal words. That is, in addition to acquiring the names of objects and actions, infants also acquire, during this period, various other words which express concepts involving, for example, the disappearance of objects (e.g. *gone*), the recurrence of objects (e.g. *more*), opposition to the actions of agents (e.g. *no*), and spatial relations (e.g. *in, up, down*) (see Barrett, 1979, 1983a, 1983b; Bloom, 1973; Gopnik, 1982; Gopnik & Meltzoff, 1986; McCune-Nicolich, 1981). The evidence which is available indicates that many of these words are first acquired in the single-word period as context-bound items. For example Barrett (1979, 1983a) and Gopnik (1982) report words as varied as *gone, no, in, on*, and *there* being produced initially in specific behavioural contexts, with these words only subsequently being decontextualised and used in a contextually flexible manner. However, the available evidence also suggests that some non-nominal words can be acquired very early on in the single-word period and used immediately in a variety of different behavioural contexts by some infants (see, for example, the word *more* in Table 3).

Theoretical accounts of how infants acquire the meanings of non-nominal words have tended to assume that these words are mapped straight on to the infant's sensory–motor concepts, with these words therefore being used to encode and express such concepts directly (see, for example, Gopnik & Meltzoff, 1986; McCune-Nicolich, 1981). As a consequence, the lexical development of the infant in this domain has usually been assumed to proceed via the same mechanisms as those which are responsible for the infant's cognitive development. The alternative position would be that there is an intermediate level of lexical representation which is only constrained, rather than constituted, by sensory–motor intelligence. This alternative position has yet to be systematically explored and tested. In addition, research into the acquisition of non-nominal words has yet to provide a detailed account of precisely how the meanings of such words are mentally represented by infants, and how these lexical entries are structured and accessed.

PRAGMATIC DEVELOPMENT IN THE SINGLE-WORD PERIOD

The linguistic developments which occur during the single-word period do not just involve the development and growth of the vocabulary; the manner in which the infant uses words to communicate with other people also changes during this period. Some of the these pragmatic changes occur as a direct consequence of the infant's lexical development. For example, as decontextualisation occurs, words which are used initially only in one behavioural context begin to be used in different behavioural contexts for different communicative functions (e.g. an object name which is used initially only while the infant performs a particular action on an object might be used later in a decontextualised manner for several different directive functions such as requesting that object, directing the attention of others to that object, etc.). Similarly, the referential and non-nominal words which are produced in a contextually flexible manner from the outset may also be used by the infant for a variety of different functions. Consequently, as the lexical development of the infant proceeds, words come to be used much more flexibly than they are at the beginning of the single-word period, with many individual words eventually being used for a variety of different communicative functions, rather than for just a single function.

The growth of the vocabulary also results in the infant acquiring a much greater specificity in the words that are used for particular communicative functions. Infants often begin by using just a single non-specific word for each individual function (e.g. *me* for requesting objects, *there* for directing attention, etc.). However, as new and more specific words (such as object names) are acquired, these begin to be used as alternatives to these earlier non-specific terms (Barrett, 1981; Griffiths, 1985; Halliday, 1975).

The Emergence of New Communicative Functions

In addition to these pragmatic changes which result from the lexical development of the infant, there are also changes during the single-word period in the range of communicative functions for which the infant uses words. As we have already seen, the earliest words are used by the infant for just two types of communicative function: for expressing internal states (e.g. for expressing affect states, reactions to objects, etc.), and for directing the behaviour of other people (e.g. for issuing orders, requesting objects, demanding attention, directing attention to objects, etc.). However, as the single-word period progresses, infants also start to answer questions, to ask questions, and to provide comments on the people and objects in their immediate environment.

Answering Questions

The most common questions that infants begin to answer, usually quite early in the single-word period, are questions which ask for the names of objects such as "What's that?", "Who's that?", etc. (Barrett, 1981, 1986; Dore, 1975; McShane, 1980). Some infants also begin, during this period, to answer questions of the form "How does the X go?" (where X is either an animal or a vehicle name) by producing an onomatopoeic word representing the sound made by X (Barrett, 1986; Bates et al., 1979), and to answer *yes/no*-questions (Barrett, 1981, 1982b; Dale, 1980; Dore, 1985; McShane, 1980). The behavioural contexts in which questions are answered by infants are usually highly ritualised, particularly in the early part of the single-word period. For example, the question "What's that?" is often produced by the mother and answered by the infant in the context of picture-book reading, a context which has been found to have a standardised and highly ritualised format (Bruner, 1983; Ninio & Bruner, 1978).

Asking Questions

The earliest questions which infants begin to ask, and which do not normally appear until comparatively late in the single-word period (Barrett, 1981; Griffiths, 1985; Halliday, 1975), are requests for the names of objects; the term *what's that?* is often used as a single-word utterance for this function (Barrett, 1981, 1982b; Goodwin, 1985; Halliday, 1975). These questions provide infants with an extremely important means of eliciting the names of objects from other people, and hence of extending their vocabularies. Some infants also acquire the word *where* during the single-word period, which they use for asking about the locations of objects (McShane, 1980). These early *wh*-questions are often produced with a rising intonation contour; some infants subsequently generalise the use of rising intonation to other words (e.g. *more, there*, and object names), in order to signal that these words are also being produced as questions that require answers (Barrett, 1981, 1982b; Dore, 1975).

Commenting

In addition to answering and asking questions, infants also begin to produce comments during the course of the single-word period. These comments are usually made about an object or a person in the infant's immediate environment. For instance, an infant might comment upon an attribute of an object, the action of a person, name the person to whom an object belongs, or comment upon the non-existence or recurrence of an object (Bloom, 1973;

Greenfield & Smith, 1976; McShane, 1980). The following example of a comment upon the non-existence of an object is taken from Barrett (1979):

> (The infant picks up her empty cup, looks inside it, then looks at her mother.)
> Infant: *Gone.*

On some occasions, the infant may produce two successive single-word utterances, where one word is used to name a person or object, and the other word is used to make a comment about either an action, an attribute, or some other feature, of the person or object (see Bloom, 1973; Greenfield & Smith, 1976; Scollon, 1976, 1979). The following example comes from Scollon (1976):

> The infant reaches out with her index finger and delicately touches a microphone.)
> Infant: *Finger. Touch.*

In some instances, the infant may await confirmation that the addressee has successfully identified the relevant person or object before producing the comment. This can result in the infant's successive utterances being produced as alternating turns in a conversational exchange with the addressee, as in the following example (also taken from Scollon, 1976):

> (The infant is looking straight into an electric fan with her hair blowing back.)
> Infant: *Fan. Fan.*
> Mother: *Hmm?*
> Infant: *Fan.*
> Mother: *Bathroom?*
> Infant: *Fan. Fan.*
> Mother: *Fan! Yeah.*
> Infant: *Cool.*
> Mother: *Cool, yeah. Fan makes you cool.*

However, in successive single-word utterances, the infant does not always identify the object or person first; sometimes the comment is produced first instead. And sometimes it may be difficult to determine unequivocally which of the two words is functioning as the comment (see Bloom, 1973, from which the following example is taken):

> (The infant is examining a Band-aid on Daddy's finger.)
> Infant: *Cut. Daddy.*

And sometimes the infant might only produce the comment (or identify the appropriate object) in response to a prompt from the addressee, as in the following example (from Scollon, 1979):

Infant: *Hiding*.
Adult: *Hiding? What's hiding?*
Infant: *Balloon*.

Single-word utterances which function as comments about objects and people have often been called "predications" in the literature on single-word speech (see, for example, Dore, 1985; Goodwin, 1985; Griffiths, 1985; McNeill, 1970; Werner & Kaplan, 1963). However, it is important to note that this informal use of the term "predication" (to denote a single-word comment about an object or person) is quite distinct from the formal linguistic use of this term (to denote the relationship between the noun phrase and the verb phrase which form the two principal grammatical constituents of a multi-word sentence). This distinction has not always been observed, with the consequence that some authors (e.g. McNeill, 1970) have argued that, because infants are able to produce predications (in the informal sense of the term), those infants must therefore possess a knowledge of the principal grammatical constituents of sentences. However, this argument conflates two quite distinct notions (i.e. single-word comments and grammatical predications). Furthermore, there is no independent evidence to support the view that infants possess any knowledge of the grammatical constituents of sentences during the period of single-word speech (see Barrett, 1982b).

Conversational Exchanges

It should be apparent from the preceding discussion of infants' abilities to use single-word utterances to answer questions, to ask questions, and to make comments about people and objects, that these abilities enable infants to participate in rudimentary conversations with other people. Prior to the emergence of these functions, the infant tends to produce isolated single-word utterances (which merely serve either to express the infant's internal states, or to direct the addressee's behaviour). However, once these new functions have emerged, the infant is able to initiate conversations by using directive words (such as personal names, *hello*, etc.), select topics for conversation and direct the addressee's attention to those topics, again by using directive words (such as object names, *look, there*, etc.), provide comments on those topics (using, for example, non-nominals, personal names, etc.), ask questions about those topics (using a term such as *what's that?*), answer questions about those topics (using nominals and sometimes non-nominals), and terminate conversations by using directive words (such as *bye*). Thus, by the end of the single-word period, the infant is able to engage in quite lengthy conversational exchanges with other people.

THE TRANSITION TO TWO-WORD SPEECH

By 19 months of age, infants have usually acquired a vocabulary of approximately 50 words, and the vocabulary explosion has normally begun (Nelson, 1973). Within another month or two, infants usually begin to combine words together to produce their first two-word utterances. Initially, these two-word utterances are produced comparatively infrequently, and infants still rely primarily upon single-word utterances in order to talk to other people; multi-word utterances begin to predominate over single-word utterances only towards the end of the second year of life (see Garman, 1979; Nelson, 1973).

Semantic Relations

Some examples of the types of two-word utterances which infants commonly produce when they first begin to combine words together are shown in Table 5. It is now quite clear from the many different studies which have been conducted into two-word speech that these utterances are not random combinations of words, but are systematic expressions of specific semantic relations (see, for example, Bloom, 1970; Bowerman, 1973; Brown, 1970, 1973; and Schlesinger, 1971). Eleven different semantic relations are illustrated by the utterances shown in Table 5.

These semantic relations are divisible into two main types (Brown, 1970). The first four relations in Table 5 are all expressed by combining a single constant term (e.g. *more, allgone*, etc.) with another word that refers to an object, action, or attribute. In the utterances expressing these relations, the meaning expressed by the constant term (e.g. recurrence, non-existence, etc.) applies specifically to the object, action, or attribute which is referred to by means of the other word. The second type of semantic relation does not involve the use of constant terms; instead, in the utterances expressing these relations, both the first word and the second word are variable. Nevertheless, in these utterances, a particular relational meaning is still being expressed by the conjunction of the two words. For example, in the utterance *big train*, the first word specifies an attribute of the object identified by the second word; in the utterance *walk street*, the second word specifies the location in which the action identified by the first word takes place; etc.

Combinatorial Rules

The appearance of two-word utterances in the speech of the infant can therefore be attributed to the infant's acquisition of two different types of combinatorial rule. The first type, the pivotal rules, specify how particular

TABLE 5
Examples of the Two-Word Utterances Produced by Infants, and of the Semantic Relations which These Utterances Express (adapted from Brown, 1970).

Two-word utterance	Semantic Relation Expressed by Utterance
that book	nomination (of object, action or attribute)
hi belt	notice (of object, action or attribute)
more milk	recurrence (of object, action or attribute)
allgone juice	non-existence (of object, action or attribute)
big train	attribute–object
mommy lunch	possessor–possessed
book table	object–location
walk street	action–location
Adam put	agent–action
mommy sock	agent–object
hit ball	action–object

pivot words (e.g. *more, allgone*, etc.) may be combined with the names of objects, actions or attributes. The other type, the categorical rules, specify how words drawn from one category (e.g. the names of attributes, agents, actions, etc.) may be combined with words drawn from another category (e.g. the names of objects, locations, etc.).

It should be noted, however, that the combinatorial rules which actually govern the two-word utterances of infants are sometimes much more limited in their semantic scope than Table 5 might imply (see Bowerman, 1976 and Braine, 1976). For example, instead of combining any action name with any object name in action–object utterances, an infant might only combine vehicle movement words with the names of vehicles (to produce utterances of the form "*drive/pull/tow + car/train/tractor*"), or might only combine oral consumption words with the names of foodstuffs (to produce utterances of the form "*eat/bite/drink + cookie/egg/milk*"). Thus, the combinatorial rules which infants actually acquire sometimes have an extremely limited semantic scope.

It should also be noted that the four pivotal rules which are illustrated by the first four utterances in Table 5 are not the only rules of this type which infants can acquire. For example, Braine (1976) found pivotal rules governing the combination of the words *want, other* and *where*, respectively, with the names of objects. The studies by Bowerman (1976) and by Braine (1976) have also revealed that infants often adopt different strategies for learning how to combine words together, with some infants relying to a large extent upon pivotal rules, and others relying primarily upon categorical rules instead. Thus, there is considerable individual variation in the type of two-word utterances which different infants produce (see also Bloom, Lightbown & Hood 1975).

Finally, Braine (1976) has shown that the two-word utterances which can be subsumed under a particular combinatorial rule do not always exhibit a fixed word order. For example, one of his infants appeared to acquire a pivotal attributive rule that specified that the word *wet* could be combined with object names; however, the two-word utterances containing *wet* which this infant produced displayed a variable word order (*shirt wet, wet nose, shoe wet, wet diaper*). These "groping patterns", as they are termed, are usually exhibited by word combinations which are only just becoming established; they are normally succeeded by further combinations displaying a fixed word order.

The Acquisition of Combinatorial Rules: The Synthetic Route

If the acquisition of two-word speech is to be explained in terms of the acquisition of pivotal and/or categorical combinatorial rules, then an explanation is required of how these rules themselves are acquired. One clue here has been provided by Branigan (1979), who compared the acoustic characteristics of isolated single-word utterances, successive single-word utterances, and two-word utterances. He found that the first word in a pair of successive single-word utterances has the same terminal intonation contour as the first word of a two-word utterance, and that this differs from the terminal intonation contour of an isolated single-word utterance. Consequently, the main acoustic difference between a pair of successive single-word utterances and a two-word utterance is the pause which occurs between the two words in the former, which is not present in the latter. This suggests that successive single-word utterances may be the ontogenetic precursors to two-word utterances.

This interpretation receives additional support from the analysis of how successive single-word utterances are used. As we saw in the previous section, these utterances are used to comment upon the actions or attributes of objects and people, the people to whom objects belong, the recurrence or non-existence of objects, etc. (see also Bloom, 1973; Scollon, 1976, 1979). That is, very similar concepts are expressed in successive single-word utterances and in two-word utterances. In addition, Braine (1976) has pointed out that the variable word orders that are exhibited by groping patterns seem to derive from the variable word orders which infants use when producing successive single-word utterances.

Thus, successive single-word utterances appear to represent an intermediate form of linguistic expression between single-word and two-word utterances, with combinatorial rules being acquired in three steps. The first step occurs when the infant begins to use successive single-word utterances for expressing a particular type of comment (for example, when pairs of successive single-word utterances such as *more* and *milk, more* and *brick*, etc. are used to comment upon recurrence; when pairs such as *daddy* and *climb, mummy* and *walk*, etc. are used to comment upon the actions which people perform; etc.). Notice that, at this point, there is no need to attribute the infant with a knowledge of any semantic or syntactic relations; instead, all that needs to be assumed is that the infant is able to produce the name of an object or person, and is able to comment upon that object or person in some way (cf. Barrett, 1982b).

The transition to the second step occurs when the infant identifies and abstracts the common elements that recur across a particular set of successive single-word utterances, and synthesises these elements together to derive a combinatorial rule (thus, the infant may derive the pivotal rule "*more* + object name" and the categorical rule "Agent + Action" from the preceding sets of successive single-word utterances). Once this combinatorial rule has been constructed, the infant may begin to combine words together in novel two-word utterances which express that particular semantic relation. However, it is possible that these word combinations take the form of a groping pattern at first. If this is the case, then the third step in the acquisition of the combinatorial rule occurs when the infant finally acquires a fixed word order preference for the realisation of that rule.

This developmental sequence therefore accounts for why two-word utterances have the same intonation as the earlier successive single-word utterances, why the semantic relations which are expressed by two-word utterances are very similar to the comments which have previously been expressed by successive single-word utterances, and why groping patterns sometimes characterise the infant's first attempts to express a particular semantic relation. Although this account presupposes that the infant's own successive single-word utterances are the major database from which the infant abstracts and synthesises combinatorial rules, such an account does not rule out the possibility that the infant is also guided by other sources of information when constructing these rules. For example, Bloom (1973) has pointed out that the infant is probably also guided here by some of the simpler multi-word utterances which the infant hears being produced by other people (thus, utterances such as *more cookies, more books*, etc. produced by other people when objects recur, could also contribute to the database from which an infant abstracts and synthesises a *"more + object name"* rule).

The Acquisition of Combinatorial Rules: The Analytic Route

The route into two-word speech which has just been described essentially involves the abstraction and synthesis of combinatorial rules from successive single-word utterances. However, this is not the only way in which infants can make the transition into two-word speech: they sometimes follow an analytic route instead. This may occur when the infant acquires a formulaic phrase which is used initially in an unanalysed form as an individual single-word utterance. For example, one infant I observed acquired the phrases *on-here, here-you-are,* and *you-do-it* (amongst many others), which were all used initially as single-word utterances for specific communicative functions (see Barrett, 1979, 1981, 1983a). These formulaic phrases, or "amalgams" as they are sometimes called, may be subsequently analysed by the infant into their constituent units, with one or more of these units then functioning as pivotal words around which multi-word utterances are constructed.

For example, the amalgam *on-here,* which was initially used to request other people to place objects in locations, was eventually analysed by the infant into two separate words, *on* and *here* (see Barrett, 1983a). The word *on* was then combined not only with *here* but also with a variety of other words; these words always referred to the location of an object (i.e. the infant produced utterances such as *on floor, on chair, on road,* etc.). These two-word utterances were thus governed by the pivotal rule *"on + location name"*; in these utterances, the word *on* was always in the first word position, mirroring its position in the original amalgam. The same infant also analysed the amalgam *you-do-it* (which she initially used to request actions on objects) into its constituents (see Table 6). She first isolated the constituent *do-it,* and began to use it in two-word combinations which were governed by the pivotal rule "Agent + *do-it*"; this rule was subsequently generalised into an "Agent + Action" categorical rule. She then isolated the constituent *it,* and derived the combinatorial rule "Agent + Action + *it*" in which *it* appeared to encode the object affected by the action (see Barrett, 1979 for the full documentation of this sequence).

In these two examples, the infant analysed a single amalgam into its constituents. In addition, Braine (1976) has suggested that infants may sometimes use a slightly different analytic route into multi-word speech. This involves the infant learning not just one but several amalgams in which one constituent repeatedly occurs; for example, the infant may learn phrases such as *all-clean, all-gone* and *all-wet* independently of one another as individual

TABLE 6
An Example of an Analytic Route into Multi-word Speech (reported in Barrett 1979). The
Age of the Infant at Each Step is given in Years, Months and Days

Age of Infant	Types of Utterances Produced	Combinatorial Rule Governing Utterances
1;9.4	you-do-it	(amalgam)
1;10.2	do-it	(amalgam)
	you do-it mummy do-it Nettie do-it	Agent + *do-it*
1;11.28	do-it	(amalgam)
	I do-it I jump you do-it you dance mummy do-it Nettie blow	Agent + Action
2;0.10	I blow you get-up Nettie pull	Agent + Action
	I blow it you bang it mummy wash it	Agent + Action + *it*[a]

[a] Three-word utterances containing the word *it* always referred to actions which were performed upon objects.

amalgams. The infant may subsequently register the fact that these various amalgams share a common constituent. This can have two consequences. Firstly, the infant may be sensitised to this type of amalgam, and may therefore preferentially acquire further amalgams with a similar form (such as *all-done, all-messy*, etc.). Secondly, the infant may go on to abstract the common constituent from this set of amalgams, and use it as a pivot around which genuinely novel two-word utterances can then be constructed (e.g. the pivotal rule "*all* + attribute/state name" might be derived from the preceding set of amalgams and used to generate new word combinations containing the word *all* in the first word position).

The Production of Dummy Forms

It has now been reported by several observers that, towards the end of the single-word period, some infants begin to combine words with semantically empty dummy forms (i.e. with words which have no apparent meaning). One very striking example, in which the infant combined the semantically empty form [*widə*] with the words *more, no, Mama, Dada, pig* and *uh-oh* in a variety of different behavioural contexts, has been reported by Bloom (1973); a slightly different type of example, in which the infant combined the word *bottle* with each of the dummy forms [*dæ*], [*mʌ*], [*te*] and (*wə*) on different occasions, has been reported by Dore, Franklin, Miller & Ramer (1976).

Dore et al. (1976) and Greenfield, Reilly, Leaper, & Baker (1985) propose that these dummy forms serve a bridging function in the development of the two-word speech of these infants. Thus, initially these infants produce single-word utterances alone (e.g. *more, bottle*, etc.). They then progress to the production of two-word utterances containing dummy forms (e.g. *more* [*widə*], [*dæ*] *bottle*, etc.) which, because the dummy forms are semantically empty, are syntactically, but not semantically, more complex than the earlier single-word utterances. Finally, it is suggested that these infants begin to substitute other meaningful words for the dummy forms in these two-element combinations, to create genuine two-word utterances (e.g. *more juice, my bottle*, etc.) that are both semantically and syntactically more complex than the earlier single-word utterances. Thus, according to this interpretation, dummy forms ease the transition from single-word to two-word speech (by allowing the infant to master the syntactic and semantic aspects of this transition separately rather than simultaneously), and hence represent a third type of route which some infants follow into two-word speech.

However, the evidence which is available concerning dummy forms is also consistent with an alternative interpretation, namely that two-word utterances containing dummy forms result when an infant acquires and tries to deploy the general syntactic principle that linguistic forms can be combined with one another, at a time when that infant has not yet acquired (via synthetic and/or analytic routes) a knowledge of any specific combinatorial rules to govern the production of appropriate and meaningful two-word combinations (cf. Bloom, 1973). According to this alternative interpretation, then, two-word utterances containing dummy forms do not actually contribute to the linguistic development of the infant (and therefore do not represent a third type of route which can be taken into two-word speech). Instead they are merely the byproducts of an incomplete knowledge system, which are eventually superseded when appropriate combinatorial rules are acquired. Given the ambiguity of the available data with respect to these two alternative interpretations, further research is clearly required in order to resolve this issue.

"Referential" and "Expressive" Infants

We have seen that there are at least two major routes that infants can follow into two-word speech, one involving the synthesis of successive single-word utterances and the other involving the analysis of amalgams. Synthetic and analytic routes depend upon different types of strategies being adopted by the infant for the construction of combinatorial rules; it has been found that infants vary from one another in the extent to which they rely upon these different strategies (Barrett, 1979; Bowerman, 1976; Braine, 1976). These individual variations form a continuum rather than a dichotomy, however, and are associated with certain other individual variations which first become apparent earlier on in the single-word period.

At one end of this continuum, there are "referential" infants who acquire a large number of object names during the course of the single-word period (Nelson, 1973). These infants tend to use their language for an extensive range of object-orientated pragmatic functions, such as drawing the attention of other people to objects, requesting objects, and commenting upon objects (Barrett, 1979, 1981; Dore, 1973; Nelson, 1973). Extreme referential infants tend to use synthetic (rather than analytic) routes into two-word speech, and their two-word utterances, which rely heavily upon object names for the encoding of semantic relations, may be based upon either categorical or pivotal combinatorial rules (Barrett, 1979; Bloom, et al., 1975; Bretherton, McNew, Snyder, & Bates 1983).

At the other end of the continuum, there are "expressive" infants who acquire comparatively few object names during the course of the single-word period (Nelson, 1973). These infants instead acquire a large number of personal names, action names, social–interactional words (e.g. *hello, ta, please, yes*, etc.), and formulaic phrases which are useful for directing the behaviour of other people (e.g. *you-do-it, here-you-are, go-away*, etc.). These linguistic expressions tend to be used by these infants for an extensive range of socially-orientated pragmatic functions, such as commenting upon people, playing games with people, and manipulating the behaviour of other people (Barrett, 1979, 1981; Dore, 1973; Nelson, 1973). Extreme expressive infants are more likely to use analytic routes into two-word speech than extreme referential infants, and their two-word utterances (which rely heavily upon pro-words such as *I, you, it*, and *here* for the encoding of semantic relations) are often based upon pivotal rather than categorical rules (Barrett, 1979; Bloom, et al., 1975).

However, the majority of infants are neither extreme referential nor extreme expressive types, but instead fall between these two end points of the continuum. Thus, most infants display a mixture of both referential and expressive characteristics (Nelson, 1973); they use both synthetic and analytic strategies for breaking into two-word speech, and their two-word utterances rely upon both nominal and pronominal words for the encoding of semantic relations (Bretherton et al., 1983).

Thus, the transition to two-word speech is achieved in different ways by different infants, and these individual differences are related to other differences which are already present earlier on in the single-word period. In addition, the two-word utterances which are produced by infants display considerable individual variation; these variations seem to result from the different strategies which are used to achieve the transition into two-word speech.

CONCLUSIONS

The development of two-word speech is usually well under way by 24 months of age. The utterances which 2-year-olds produce may seem primitive when compared with the utterances which adults produce. But as we have seen in this chapter, 2-year-olds have acquired a considerable range of linguistic skills and abilities. They have built up substantial vocabularies (which usually contain a few context-bound words, and many object names, action names, and non-nominal words); they are able to use these words for a variety of different communicative functions (such as expressing their own internal states, directing the behaviour of other people, answering questions, asking questions, and commenting upon objects and people); they can participate in rudimentary conversational exchanges; and they are able to combine words together in two-word utterances to express simple semantic relations. They are clearly no longer infants who are unable to speak: they are children with the ability to converse linguistically with other people.

REFERENCES

Anglin, J. M. (1977). *Word, object and conceptual development.* New York: Norton.

Anglin, J. M. (1986). Semantic and conceptual knowledge underlying the child's words. In S. A. Kuczaj & M. D. Barrett (eds), *The development of word meaning.* New York: Springer–Verlag.

Barrett, M. D. (1978). Lexical development and overextension in child language. *Journal of Child Language, 5,* 205–219.

Barrett, M. D. (1979). *Semantic development during the single-word stage of language acquisition.* Unpublished doctoral thesis, University of Sussex.

Barrett, M. D. (1981). The communicative functions of early child language. *Linguistics, 19,* 273–305.

Barrett, M. D. (1982a). Distinguishing between prototypes: The early acquisition of the meanings of object names. In S. A. Kuczaj (ed.), *Language Development*: Vol. 1 *Syntax and semantics.* Hillsdale, N. J.: Lawrence Erlbaum Associates Inc.

Barrett, M. D. (1982b). The holophrastic hypothesis: Conceptual and empirical issues. *Cognition, 11,* 47–76.

Barrett, M. D. (1983a). The early acquisition and development of the meanings of action-related words. In T. B. Seiler & W. Wannenmacher (eds), *Concept development and the development of word meaning*. Berlin: Springer–Verlag.

Barrett, M. D. (1983b). The course of early lexical development: A review and an interpretation. *Early Child Development and Care*, *11*, 19–32.

Barrett, M. D. (1985). Issues in the study of children's single-word speech. In M. D. Barrett (ed.), *Children's single-word speech*. Chichester: Wiley.

Barrett, M. D. (1986). Early semantic representations and early word usage. In S. A. Kuczaj & M. D. Barrett (eds), *The development of word meaning*. New York: Springer–Verlag.

Barrett, M. D., Harris, M., Jones, D., & Brookes, S. (1986a). Linguistic input and early context-bound word use. In *Proceedings of the Child Language Seminar, 1986*. Department of Psychology, University of Durham.

Barrett, M. D., Harris, M., Jones, D., & Brookes, S. (1986b, September). *The first words of the infant: Their characteristics and their relationship to maternal speech*. Paper presented at the British Psychological Society Developmental Section Annual Conference, Exeter.

Bates, E., Benigni, L., Bretherton, I., Camaioni, L., & Volterra, V. (1979). *The emergence of symbols: Cognition and communication in infancy*. New York: Academic Press.

Benedict, H. (1979). Early lexical development: Comprehension and production. *Journal of Child Language*, *6*, 183–200.

Bloom, L. (1970). *Language development: Form and function in emerging grammars*. Cambridge, Mass.: The MIT Press.

Bloom, L. (1973). *One word at a time*. The Hague: Mouton.

Bloom, L., Lightbown, P., & Hood, L. (1975). Structure and variation in child language. *Monographs of the Society for Research in Child Development*, *40*, (2, Serial No. 160).

Bowerman, M. (1973). *Early syntactic development*. Cambridge: Cambridge University Press.

Bowerman, M. (1976). Semantic factors in the acquisition of rules for word use and sentence construction. In D. M. Morehead & A. E. Morehead (eds), *Normal and deficient child language*. Baltimore, Md: University Park Press.

Bowerman, M. (1978). The acquisition of word meaning: An investigation into some current conflicts. In N. Waterson & C. Snow (eds), *The development of communication*. Chichester: Wiley.

Braine, M. D. S. (1976). Children's first word combinations. *Monographs of the Society for Research in Child Development*, *41*, (1, Serial No. 164).

Branigan, G. (1979). Some reasons why successive single word utterances are not. *Journal of Child Language*, *6*, 411–421.

Bretherton, I., McNew, S., Snyder, L., & Bates, E. (1983). Individual differences at 20 months: Analytic and holistic strategies in language acquisition. *Journal of Child Language*, *10*, 293–320.

Brown, R. (1970). The first sentences of child and chimpanzee. In R. Brown (ed.), *Psycholinguistics*. New York: The Free Press.

Brown, R. (1973). *A first language: The early stages*. London: Allen & Unwin.

Bruner, J. (1983). *Child's talk: Learning to use language*. Oxford: Oxford University Press.

Clark, E. V. (1973). What's in a word? On the child's acquisition of semantics in his first language. In T. E. Moore (ed.), *Cognitive development and the acquisition of language*. New York: Academic Press.

Clark, E. V. (1983). Meanings and concepts. In J. H. Flavell & E. M. Markman (eds), *Cognitive development*: Vol. 3 of P. Mussen (ed.), *Handbook of child psychology* (4th ed.). Chichester: Wiley.

Dale, P. S. (1980). Is early pragmatic development measurable? *Journal of Child Language*, *7*, 1–12.

Dore, J. (1973). A developmental theory of speech act production. *Transactions of the New York Academy of Sciences*, *35*, 623–630.

Dore, J. (1974). A pragmatic description of early language development. *Journal of Psycholinguistic Research*, *3*, 343–350.

Dore, J. (1975). Holophrases, speech acts and language universals. *Journal of Child Language*, *2*, 21–40.

Dore, J. (1978). Conditions for the acquisition of speech acts. In I. Markova (ed.), *The social context of language*. Chichester: Wiley.

Dore, J. (1985). Holophrases revisited: Their "logical" development from dialog. In M. D. Barrett (ed.), *Children's single-word speech*. Chichester: Wiley.

Dore, J., Franklin, M. B., Miller, R. T., & Ramer, A. L. H. (1976). Transitional phenomena in early language acquisition. *Journal of Child Language*, *3*, 13–28.

Fremgen, A. & Fay, D. (1980). Overextensions in production and comprehension: A methodological clarification. *Journal of Child Language*, *7*, 205–212.

Garman, M. (1979). Early grammatical development. In P. Fletcher & M. Garman (eds), *Language acquisition*. Cambridge: Cambridge University Press.

Goodwin, R. (1985). A word in edgeways? The development of conversation in the single-word period. In M. D. Barrett (ed.), *Children's single-word speech*. Chichester: Wiley.

Gopnik, A. (1982). Words and plans: Early language and the development of intelligent action. *Journal of Child Language*, *9*, 303–318.

Gopnik, A. & Meltzoff, A. N. (1986). Words, plans, things and locations: Interactions between semantic and cognitive development in the one-word stage. In S. A. Kuczaj & M. D. Barrett (eds), *The development of word meaning*. New York: Springer–Verlag.

Greenfield, P. M., Reilly, J., Leaper, C., & Baker, N. (1985). The structural and functional status of single-word utterances and their relationship to early multi-word speech. In M. D. Barrett (ed.), *Children's single-word speech*. Chichester: Wiley.

Greenfield, P. M. & Smith, J. H (1976). *The structure of communication in early language development*. New York: Academic Press.

Griffiths, P. (1985). The communicative functions of children's single-word speech. In M. D. Barrett (ed.), *Children's single-word speech*. Chicheser: Wiley.

Gruendel, J. M. (1977). Referential extension in early language development. *Child Development*, *48*, 1567–1576.

Halliday, M. A. K. (1973). *Explorations in the functions of language*. London: Edward Arnold.

Halliday, M. A. K. (1975). *Learning how to mean*. London: Edward Arnold.

Kamhi, A. G. (1986). The elusive first word: The importance of the naming insight for the development of referential speech. *Journal of Child Language*, *13*, 155–161.

Kuczaj, S. A. (1982). Young children's overextension of object words in comprehension and/or production: Support for a prototype theory of early object word meaning. *First Language*, *3*, 93–105.

Leopold, W. F. (1939). *Speech development of a bilingual child: A linguist's record:* Vol 1. *Vocabulary growth in the first two years*. Evanston, Ill.: Northwestern University Press.

Lock, A. (ed.) (1978). *Action, gesture and symbol: The emergence of language*. London: Academic Press.

Lock, A. (1980). *The guided reinvention of language*. London: Academic Press.

McCune–Nicolich, L. (1981). The cognitive bases of relational words in the single word period. *Journal of Child Language*, *8*, 15–34.

McNeill, D. (1970). *The acquisition of language: The study of developmental psycholinguistics*. New York: Harper & Row.

McShane, J. (1979). The development of naming. *Linguistics*, *17*, 879–905.

McShane, J. (1980). *Learning to talk*. Cambridge: Cambridge University Press.

Nelson, K. (1973). Structure and strategy in learning to talk. *Monographs of the Society for Research in Child Development*, *38*, (1–2, Serial No. 149).

Nelson, K. (1983). The conceptual basis for language. In T. B. Seiler & W. Wannenmacher (eds), *Concept development and the development of language*. Berlin: Springer–Verlag.

Nelson, K. (1985). *Making sense: The acquisition of shared meaning*. New York: Academic Press.

Nelson, K. & Lucariello, J. (1985). The development of meaning in first words. In M. D. Barrett (ed.), *Children's single-word speech*. Chichester: Wiley.

Nelson, K. E. (1982). Experimental gambits in the service of language acquisition theory. In S. A. Kuczaj (ed.), *Language development:* Vol. 1 *Syntax and semantics*. Hillsdale, N.J.: Lawrence Erlbaum Associates Inc.

Ninio, A. & Bruner, J. (1978). The achievement and antecedents of labelling. *Journal of Child Language*, 5, 1–15.

Rescorla, L. A. (1980). Overextension in early language development. *Journal of Child Language*, 7, 321–335.

Rescorla, L. A. (1981). Category development in early language. *Journal of Child Language*, 8, 225–238.

Schaffer, H. R. (ed.) (1977). *Studies in mother–infant interaction*. London: Academic Press.

Schlesinger, I. M. (1971). Production of utterances and language acquisition. In D. I. Slobin (ed.), *The ontogenesis of grammar*. New York: Academic Press.

Scollon, R. (1976). *Conversations with a one year old*. Honolulu: University Press of Hawaii.

Scollon, R. (1979). A real early stage: An unzipped condensation of a dissertation on child language. In E. Ochs & B. B. Schieffelin (eds), *Developmental pragmatics*. New York: Academic Press.

Thomson, J. & Chapman, R. (1977). Who is 'daddy' revisited: The status of two-year-olds' overextended words in use and comprehension. *Journal of Child Language*, 4, 359–375.

Werner, H. & Kaplan, B. (1963). *Symbol formation*. New York: Wiley.

Zinober, B. & Martlew, M. (1985a). Developmental changes in four types of gesture in relation to acts and vocalizations from 10 to 21 months. *British Journal of Developmental Psychology*, 3, 293–306.

Zinober, B. & Martlew, M. (1985b). The development of communicative gestures. In M. D. Barrett (ed.), *Children's single-word speech*. Chichester: Wiley.

10

The Social Structuring of Infant Cognition

Andrew Lock

Department of Psychology,
University of Lancaster, Lancaster LA1 4YF

Valerie Service

School of Psychology,
Lancashire Polytechnic, Preston PR1 2TQ

Alfredo Brito

Departmento de Psicologia Evolutiva y de la Educacion,
Universidad de Murcia,
Espinardo (Murcia), Spain

Penelope Chandler

Department of Education,
University of Bristol,
Bristol BS8 1HH

INTRODUCTION

Our focus in this chapter is two-fold. We are going to look again at the topic of individual differences in early language development that Martyn Barrett (Chapter 9) has outlined. But our purpose is not to dispute his review. Rather, on the one hand we want to expand it, and on the other, we want to take this phenomenon as a way of resuscitating a social approach to development in infancy that began to emerge in Britain in the 1970s, but which has been rather lost sight of subsequently.

Let us first be clear on what we do *not* mean by a social approach to infancy. We do not mean it as an attempt to fill in a gap in Piagetian theorising. Piaget is often said to have ignored the social environment of the infant, and the role it might play in development. He portrays infants as immature individuals who, through interaction with the physical world, construct knowledge. It would be possible to import a social dimension into this line of thought quite easily, claiming that the infant's interactions with the world are mediated by his social environment, of which some are more conducive to the construction of knowledge than others. Following this path would "fill in" some gaps in the general Piagetian framework. But this is not what we mean. Rather than seeing the infant as possessing individual knowledge and constructive abilities, we want to view these processes as *inherently* social.

An analogy drawn from attribution theory in social psychology may help clarify our intended approach. Attribution theory has grown from what has been called the *actor–observer* difference. Actors who screw up a task tend to blame situational factors for their failure; observers who watch them fail tend to blame the actor. Depending on perspective, then, the locus of responsibility for what happens can be attributed to something inherent in the individual (lack of skill, perhaps) or something inherent in the situation (it's too difficult). We can apply this to the conception of infancy inherent in the dominant paradigms. Developmental psychologists tend to act as objective observers who attribute what they see to something inherent *in* the infant, seeing the infant as responsible for what happens in the (social) situation. Instead, we want to consider the other attribution, that the responsibility for much of what infants do should be attributed, not to them, but to the situational context and the participating adult. The process of development in infancy thus becomes one of the transfer of responsibility from one "locus"—the adult—to another—the infant.

A SOCIAL CONSTRUCTIVIST APPROACH TO DEVELOPMENT

What we call here a social constructivist approach has its roots in the insights of three theorists: Macmurray, Mead, and Vygotsky. These writers do not produce an interwoven, ready-made view of the world, for their work was developed independently of each other. They use quite different terms within their theories. But they do seem to share a common view of what has to be accounted for in human development, and thus the differences in terminology do not really reflect an underlying difference in their conceptual schemes.

A preoccupation of their thinking is to elucidate what it is to be a human being. All three of them approach this through reflecting on animals and humans, and the issue of whether we, as humans, are merely very complic-ated animals, and thus of the same ilk as them, or whether there is something distinctive about us that sets us apart. They all come to the conclusion that humans are quite different from animals, but there is a remarkable similarity in the differences they posit (see later). From this, it follows that a psychology of human being and development needs to be different from one that deals with animals, because one that is adequate for animals cannot encompass beings that are not animals.

At this point, there are two obvious things we ought to do. Firstly, we should outline their arguments, the positions they lead to, and the common-alities between them. Secondly, we should outline the form of psychological theorising and practice they point to. But we are faced with a number of difficulties. The first requires a volume of its own to be done adequately. So here we try and convey only the barest gist of their work as it relates to our topic of early language. To do the second would be dishonest. It would imply that the work we are discussing in this chapter stemmed from the application of a clear theoretical position to a particular developmental problem, when in fact we are trying to make progress on two fronts simultaneously. Macmurray and Mead were philosophers; they didn't attempt to develop a clear psychology and methodology. While Vygotsky was a psychologist, his premature death meant, again, that he left us no coherent psychological programme to follow. Thus, we are as much concerned here with developing a way of looking at early language as we are with how early language develops: We are into theory development as much as theory application, then. We will say something about the sort of developmental psychology that is coming out of this at the end of the chapter.

Macmurray

[The human infant] cannot, even theoretically, live an isolated existence; . . . he is not an independent individual. He lives a common life as one term in a personal relation. Only in the process of development does he learn to achieve a relative independence, and that only by appropriating the techniques of a rational social tradition. (Macmurray, 1961, p. 50).

Macmurray's view of development is set out in two volumes stemming from his Gifford Lectures on *The Form of the Personal* given at the University of Glasgow in 1953 and 1954: *The Self as Agent* (1957); and *Persons in Relation* (1961). His argument runs something like this. A human infant can neither sustain its existence nor structure its eventual way of life on its own. Unlike other animals, he is biologically "inadequate", in that he cannot sustain his life by biological "givens", but must rely on culturally given thoughts and intentions (1961, p. 48):

ID—I

> He is . . . "adapted", to speak paradoxically, to being unadapted, "adapted" to
> a complete dependence upon an adult human being . . . He is born into a love-
> relationship which is inherently personal. Not merely his personal develop-
> ment, but his very survival depends upon the maintaining of this relation; he
> depends for his existence . . . upon intelligent understanding, upon rational
> foresight. He cannot think for himself, yet he cannot do without thinking; so
> someone else must think for him . . . He cannot do himself what is necessary to
> his own survival and development. It must be done for him by another who
> can, or he will die.

This mode of life is to be distinguished from an organic one. Organisms have
motivations, or drives, and are provided with at least the rudiments of
consummatory actions. By contrast, the human infant's motivations are
structured through intentions, where (1961, p. 51):

> the intention is the mother's, necessarily; the motives, just as necessarily, are the
> baby's own.

Put crudely, young organisms know how to be rabbits, foxes, bears, and
what have you, whereas young humans do not know how to be young
humans, or English, French, Spanish, and the like. They do not know a
"form of life".

From such considerations, Macmurray concludes, essentially, that human
babies do not exist as individuals in their own rght. Their psychological
functioning is divided between themselves and informed adults. Consequently, the unit of developmental analysis cannot be the individual—the
"I"—but the relationship in which the infant is constituted as viable—the
"You and I". Drawing from this analysis, Shotter (1974, p. 226) anticipates a
form of developmental psychology thus:

> Until he has constructed his own thought mechanisms, I shall propose that he
> *uses* his mother as a "mechanism" to do the thinking required in the realisation
> of his intentions.

How, then, are we to conceive of the processes by which this construction of
the resources for individual thought occurs? Macmurray's answer, as noted
above, is to view the constructive process as one of *appropriation*: Psychological functions exercised by the mother are gradually taken over by the infant.
But how? We need a bit more theoretical background to begin to answer this
question. It is profitable to juxtapose Macmurray with Vygotsky and Mead.
Here we will focus on their views of communication and language. In
Macmurray's (1961, p. 60) view:

> Long before the child learns to speak he is able to communicate, meaningfully
> and intentionally, with his mother. In learning language, he is acquiring a more
> effective and more elaborate means of doing something which he already can
> do in a crude and primitive fashion.

Vygotsky

For Vygotsky, the notion of "doing something one can already do" has a more precise meaning, and he gives it a central role in his account of human development. For him, on the one hand, *human* development is the gaining of control of what one can already do; and on the other, another apparent paradox, much of what one can already do one cannot be said to do at all, because other people, not you, are responsible for your being able to do it. Much of what one can do already exists as an *intermental* ability, not an *intramental* one.

Vygotsky introduces two formulations of one of his fundamental conceptualisations of development:

> In order to subject a function to intellectual and volitional control, we must first possess it. (1962, p. 90).

> Every function in the child's cultural development appears twice: first, on the social level, and later on the individual level; first, *between* people (*interpsychological*), and then *inside* the child (*intrapsychological*). This applies equally to voluntary attention, to logical memory, and to the formation of concepts. All the higher functions originate as actual relations between human individuals. (1978, p. 57).

Vygotsky's dialectical psychology of development posits a link between an individual's abilities and social relations. It is not the case that interaction *facilitates* the development of such abilities, as though they would develop anyway: rather, interaction must somehow *constitute* them—they would not develop without it. And that process of developing an ability is not one of acquiring it, or putting it together from scratch, but of gaining control of an ability that somehow already exists within social relations.

One claim we get from this juxtaposition of Vygotsky and Macmurray is that communication exists between the infant and his or her mother. Infants communicate without any knowledge or ability; maybe, then, the development of communicative abilities is really just the development of the ability to control communication? And this ability can obviously only arise in the social practice of being perceived to communicate, because it is only in conducting that social practice that an infant can find out how the practice works and how it can be used. If we now turn to Mead's writings, we find him making very similar points, but with specific reference to the development of language.

Mead

> Meaning can be described, accounted for, or stated in terms of symbols or language at its highest and most complex stage of development (the stage it reaches in human experience), but language simply lifts out of the social process

a situation which is logically or implicitly there already. The language symbol is
simply a significant or conscious gesture. (Mead, (1934, p. 79).

In Mead's symbolic interactionism, meaning is regarded as objectively
present in social interaction, having as its locus the triadic relationship
between a gesture, the response of another to it, and the result of the social
act so initiated. And being objectively present, it is there irrespective of
whether the participants whose interaction brings it about are aware of it. In
addition, social interaction is constitutive not only of objective meaning, but
also of the vehicles of that meaning. For example, gestures are constituted by
another acting on the basis of some activity, thereby elevating that activity to
gestural, communicative status. Gestures are not pre-given signals linked to
pre-given meanings, as ethologists might describe them in animals; they are
distilled in the course of ongoing interaction itself. We often assume that
crying is some such pre-given signal used by the infant to indicate hunger,
and so regulate the pattern of feeding. But even if it appears to be used in this
way in Western cultures, it is by no means a pre-given signal (Konner, 1972;
Richards, 1974, p. 88):

> among the !Kung bushmen where infants are carried on the mother's body, the
> infant's movements seem to be the usual indication to the mother that the
> infant requires access to the breast. Crying is used to signal emergencies.

Actions are constituted as gestures in the course of the interactions that
constitute their meanings, and culture, through specifying the form of the
interactions, determines the meanings they constitute.

A LITTLE HISTORY

These ideas were very much in vogue in certain areas of British developmental psychology in the 1970s (their influence can be detected in many of the
contributions to Richards, 1974, and Lock, 1978), but since then they have
somewhat disappeared, to an extent that it is perhaps difficult to believe
nowadays there ever existed a nascent school of developmental psychology
imbued by them. We think the reasons behind this disappearance were quite
subtle ones implicit in the sociology of conducting psychological research,
and the effects that dominant paradigms have on the thinking of investigators.

Before 1970, the very idea that there were such topics as pre-verbal
communication, mother–child interaction, communicative gestures, etc. was
not one which developmental psychologists had entertained. Discovering
and investigating these "things" required the creation and identification of
events that had previously not been thought about as "things". The problem

of making sense of mother–infant interaction at that time was akin to that facing a European trying to find his way around America before Columbus had discovered it: A task that is not easy, not just because he does not have a map, but because he didn't even have the idea that America existed to be mapped or explored. In the case of developmental psychology, once a set of concepts to guide our perception of early communication between people had emerged, phenomena were established as "things" which can be categorised, measured, and attributed. Psychologists are trained in how to study "things", and so there have now been a number of studies of the "thing" called gestural communication (see, for example, Zinober & Martlew, 1985). From them a possible classificatory scheme can be given (see Table 1).

Looked at this way, it is very sensible to ask how these abilities are *acquired by the infant*, how the functional systems are constructed, how in these gestures the roots of the infant's abilities as they progress into language are established, so that "the growth of the vocabulary . . . results in the infant acquiring a much greater specificity in the words that are used for particular communicative functions" (Barrett, Chapter 9, this volume). The focus comes naturally to rest on the obviously necessary, individual cognitive abilities of the individual infant who is acquiring these "things".

But why is this focus obviously necessary? Is there something in nature that makes it that way? Or is it that it just follows from the way of thinking,

TABLE 1

A possible Classificatory Scheme for pre-verbal communicative gestures.

	Function	*Origin*	*Variation*	*Vocalisation*
Expressive E.g. arm-waving, smiling, clapping, banging feet	To convey emotional states, ±	Stylisation of early rhythmic movements	Depend on infant's 'temperament'?	Accompanies from 10 months
Instrumental E.g. pick-up, headshake/nod, open palm	To control the behaviour of another person	From the act of doing the thing itself	Cultural variation in form, perhaps, but universal?	Accompanies from 10 months— convey same meaning
Enactive E.g. symbolic play— pantomime	To represent actions & attributes of people & objects	From the technical act itself	Variable at level of dyad	13–21 months
Deictic E.g. pointing, reaching	To isolate an object from its general context	?	Probably universal	Not at 9 months, 14–24 months or at 9 months?

the system of concepts that developmental psychology had in its theoretical commerce at that time? We tend now, following the analyses of such commentators as Shotter (1984), to this latter view. That one of the reasons the acquisition of abilities by individuals is a focus of much research is that it is easier to think about development that way, because the way we have of thinking about "things" naturally poses such questions, and provides a framework within which they make sense.

The individuality of the infant is assumed as a focus for explanation because of the way we have of talking about infants. To talk about them in another way is incredibly difficult, because one has to take on the tasks captured by Giddens (1984, p. 227), who, in the context of the nature of theories, argues:

> for a *deconstruction* of a whole range of theories of social change, particularly those of an evolutionary type, and for a *reconstruction* of the nature of power as inherent in the constitution of social life. To deconstruct theories of social change means to deny that some of the most cherished ambitions of social theory . . . can be realized. This does not imply making the relatively weak claim that such theories cannot be supported by the available evidence. It involves a much stronger and more controversial contention: that they are mistaken about the types of account of social change that are possible.

In the above, for "social" read "developmental"; for "evolutionary" read "cognitive". Getting to grips with questions of human development as it occurs in real life requires going through a process of deconstructing and then reconstructing one's conceptual system. Historically, perhaps as a result of the professional pressures on them, developmental psychologists have balked at this task (that is, "acceptable" empirical work can be carried out on communicative development without too much deep thought).

As we have already noted, we do not think this is the place to get embroiled in full-scale conceptual deconstruction or reconstruction in any systematic way. But it should be clear that the type of approach we have just caricatured is greatly at odds with what we have called a "social constructivist" one, and that if one accepts that a social constructivist perspective on the nature of development in infancy (and beyond) has face validity, then the position we have caricatured is in error. If we are to understand development in infancy, we must conceive and account for it in a different way: the way of social constructivism. In what follows we will look at the phenomenon of individual differences in the infant's early attempts at language as *social constructivists*, to illustrate this approach by example. We hope to show, *inter alia*, how it is possible to progress in the vein of Macmurray, Mead and Vygotsky. But to begin with, we will start within the implicit dominant paradigm, only slowly shifting to the other.

DEVELOPING A SOCIAL PERSPECTIVE ON LANGUAGE DEVELOPMENT

Styles of Early Language Development

Nelson (1973) did one of the first large-scale studies of the early period of language development: She used 30 "subjects". Prior to this everyone picked one or two children only. As a result, she found individual differences actually occurred in development; everyone else had been hung up on issues of universality. As a first-guess distinction she proposed two styles of early language development (see later). Since then there have been a number of further studies of this period (and some of them go a bit further into the two-word stage). Whereas these studies have adopted a different terminology, they have all put forward a dichotomy of ways into language that strike us as comparable. This dichotomy probably represents, in fact, the two poles of a continuum. Eschewing anyone else's terminology, children get into speaking in one of the following ways:

1. Predominant use of object labels; little imitation of what they hear; rather, the creative use of what vocabulary is possessed in ways that can be captured by rules. Such children can be thought of as creating productive grammars as a first strategy. They figure out a basic crude plan of how to put words together; categorise the words they have in their vocabulary as belonging to one grammatical class or another; and slot them into the sentence frameworks that produce the beautifully economical rule systems so typical of early papers in the grammatical paradigm of child language studies. These children really look like they have a grammar that guides them in saying new things.

2. No interest in labelling objects; the predominant use of language is for the regulation of social activities; very quickly into multi-word utterances, but in a formulaic rather than productive way; good at reproducing the intonational contours of adult speech without worrying about the words (Lancaster mothers say such children are talking "scribble"—there aren't any discernible words, but the rubbish has pretty good intonational contours). Rather than abstracting specific symbols and figuring out the general patterns (grammar) to recombine them, such children seem to be going for "one-off" holistic reproductions of what they hear. Their speech is technically called "non-productive": They will have complex utterances that come out as rituals, even though there are many other words in their vocabularies they could substitute productively for the ones they actually say.

This distinction is captured in the following crude analogy. Suppose the child is unfortunate enough to have parents who also have a parrot whom they are trying to teach to say "Joey's a pretty boy". A child following path (2) will quickly learn to say this. It will be the most complex thing he can say. By contrast, a child who is going into speech via path (1) will very quickly categorise different items in its vocabulary, figure out the basic pattern of such a statement, and say things like "Mary's a dirty girl".

This dichotomy of paths into language is quite well established. The interesting question is why children should go one way or the other. To answer that we need to look elsewhere, for it is not clear in the literature why infants might follow these different paths (see Barrett, Chapter 9, this volume). A possible answer comes from the work of Bates and her colleagues on the emergence of the symbolic ability around the end of the infant's first year.

Cognitive Bases for Different Styles of Early Language

Bates et al. (1979) offer an account of the early abilities that feed into the construction of the infant's first symbols. They develop their views from a body of data, but there is at the same time a logical nature to them that perhaps makes their empirical substantiation inevitable, i.e. it would be difficult to see how development could proceed without the exercise of these abilities. What they present is a model of symbol emergence that relies on three prerequisite skills being separately developed to a particular "threshold" level. Once each of these thresholds is reached the three skills in concert permit symbolic functioning. These can be outlined by considering how an infant comes to use words for communication.

Firstly, infants have to reproduce a vocalisation that bears some resemblance to the adult target. Thus we need credit the infants with the ability to imitate vocally what they hear. Further, imitation is a viable way of trying to reproduce events if you don't really understand what is going on, but want to try and make something you have previously seen recur. A clear example is given by behaviours Piaget has called "secondary circular reactions".

Secondly, infants have at some level to isolate what they are trying to say as a distinct event out of the flux of everyday life, and see that event as similar to a completely different class of phenomena. For example, infants who are able to request more drink by offering a beaker to another have to isolate the word "drink"out of adult speech as it crops up in dealing with this request as a target to aim at, and come to see the similarity between holding out a beaker and using the "word" "drink". Again, infants confronted with rituals around a picture-book—"that's a cow ... what does the cow say ... that's a dog ... what does the doggie say"—have to separate out from the adult speech the right target replies—"moo", "bow-wow"—and actually ignore their differences to make connection with their underlying similarities as "labels".

An analogy that Bates et al. (1979) give—cooking—shows how fundamental these abilities are to cultural skills in general. A novice cook will reproduce (imitate) the instructions in a recipe book exactly, thereby relying on the authority of another in realising an intention (dish). A novice will not have had sufficient experience to have abstracted out the similarities, and hence interchangeability, of ingredients such as cayenne pepper and chilli powder, and will likely go out for the one in any weather, even if the other is on the shelf, when the book states it is needed. Even with more experience, only if the cook exercises an analytic comparative survey of previous recipes will something like a generative grammar of cooking, an understanding of its principles, emerge. Only then will the cook be able to make the substitution.

The third ability feeding into the creation of symbols is being able to already communicate by means of conventional gestures that implicate objects (or referents) that are independent of the infant's body. Thus, within their body of data, Bates et al. (1979) find that the pointing gesture (a conventional form indicating something "out there in the world") relates to subsequent symbol use, whereas ritualised "showing off" (a conventional form involving the infant's own body as "referent") does not. Hence, even if infants have the requisite levels of imitative and analytic skills, they are unlikely to use cultural symbols in dialogue if they have not figured out the basics of communication.

While we will be going on to argue that it is wrong to conceive these phenomena as abilities to be attributed to infants as their skills, and that they should be seen as social constructions, this way of thinking is useful, for from it Bates et al. (1979, p. 361) put forward an answer to the question why infants follow the different paths into language that were outlined in the previous section [the answer she offers requires us to view the process a little differently from the way Barratt does (Chapter 9, this volume)]:

> the "expressive" child tends to employ acquisition through perception of contiguity, imitating and using unanalyzed phrases as means to ends prior to analysis of vehicle-referent relations. The "referential" child is faster at analysis, so that the use of imitated whole forms is short-lived and infrequent. When he does imitate . . . he may do so in parallel with and/or following a rapid breakdown into its components and the relationships into which that form can enter. . . . Both arbitrary and analysed learning are necessary for rapid and efficient acquisition of language. Nevertheless, individuals may vary in the "relative" use of one process over the other, and in the timing of analysis with imitation.

The obvious question at this point is why do infants show this differential reliance? We are going to claim that these differences stem from social interaction. But, as we have intimated, we think this obvious question is being cast in the wrong way, because of its focus on *individual* abilities. However, as a first strategy, we will pursue our claim in the usual paradigm, hoping to substantiate it. Only after that will we turn to a revised interpretation. But remember, this is only an expositional device to save us from doing two things at once.

THE INTERACTIVE FOUNDATIONS OF IMITATION AND ANALYSIS

In the following sections we look at two mother–infant dyads engaged in similar tasks, playing with toys and "reading" books. They interact quite differently, and it is from these differences that we believe differences in what Bates et al. (1979) identified as "the 'relative' use" of the processes of imitation and analysis are created.

Dyad 1: Creating "Parts" through Interaction

The way this happens can be illustrated by the following interchanges between a mother and her 18-month infant. They are looking at a book together. We have no rigorous data on the infant's language skills, but over the whole 25-minute session it does seem that the infant has a workable comprehension of a number of nouns and directives. He can, for example, point to aspects of the world that his mother only talks about: If she says "Where's the/Show me the/Can you see the bird", he can point at it. This is a fair skill for his age. He can direct his attention by the means of another's speech. He can also figure out another's intentions from a combination of their actions and speech: "Do you want the cup?", holding it out to him: "No", he replies, pushing it away. Because of this level of skill, we just give the mother's speech. At the same time, she is non-verbally accompanying what she says with gestures, checking she has the child's attention, what he is "saying" back to her, and so on. We are not going to be concerned with how these two "systems" interact here, though this is clearly an important factor in the social constitution of the infant's abilities.

(1) It's a hen.
There's a beak.
And two feet.
And there's a hen with lots of little chicks.
There's a tree.
And how many leaves have you got on the tree?
One, two, three . . . sixteen leaves and sixteen little birds sitting on the branch.
And look at these little birds here.

There are two big ones, and there are two more big ones, and there are two very
big ones and there's some little ones and they've got . . ., do you see where their
eyes are? Do you? Where's the birdy's eye?
Get her eye.
That's right.
And where's her nose?
Yes.
And where's her mouth?
Turn over?
Oh look, what's that?
It's a bird.
What's this one?
It's an apple.
Apple.
That's right.
It's got a leaf . . . see
That's the stalk
What's that?
That's a pretty flower
What's that one there?
It's a butterfly . . . a butterfly.
Turn over?
Yes, it's a bee . . . zzzzzzzzzzz.
There's a . . . now what are these?
They're rabbits.

There are a number of interesting things going on here, but we will focus
on one in particular. That is, the way that the mother directs the infant's
attention to objects, their parts, and the relationships between them. Look at
the hen, look it has separable parts; trees have leaves, and each one can be
counted in relation to the others; apples have leaves and stalks. Things go
together: hens and chicks; flowers and butterflies. Things vary in relation to
abstract standards: They can be big, very big, little, or pretty. In other parts
of the interaction we can pick up on the mother going further along these
lines. Parts can be in particular relations to each other.

(2) Look what the tractor's got on top of it.
(3) He's got some sand in his truck.
(4) What's he got on his foot there?

And in expanding this last relation (4), she goes on to another important
scenario: That immediate objects can be abstracted out of the overall picture
and related to objects and events that are not present.

(5) He's got boots on, hasn't he? They look like Daddy's shoes.

If we turn to the pair playing with objects, these same maternal strategies
appear again. In playing with a spinning top which has a revolving train

inside it that goes round and round, raising and lowering signals and level-crossings as it goes, she draws the child's attention to it: "Goes up ... goes down. And that one goes up. And that one goes ... up ... and then down." She uses pointing to direct the infant's attention, and paces her speech so that it co-occurs with the event: "goes ... up ... and then down". She relates present objects to absent ones, decontextualising them as parts that can be slotted in to other scenarios:

(6) It's like the clock at home.
(7) It's a snake. Remember the one you had at the fairground once?

And a lot of her play is concerned with the relationships that can exist between objects, that is, how objects can be regarded as parts of larger wholes:

(8) Show it to Teddy.
(9) Put it on the saucer.
(10) Put that bug into the bucket.
(11) Are you going to get the snake to catch this bubble?

Further, she juggles objects and contexts in a more sophisticated way than in dealing with pictures in a book, with the result that symbolic play is engineered:

(12) Would you like a cup of tea?
Yes, go on, it's a nice little cup.
You have some. (Child pretends to drink)
Give it to Teddy.
Go on, give Teddy a drink. (Child holds cup to Teddy's lips).

Here she gets the infant not just to put two objects in conjunction within the present perceptual world, but in a way which only makes sense through their relation to something that is not immediately present: The "tea" is imaginary, and must be brought in from absent contexts to inform present action. It is quite a complicated activity: One object (the cup) is to be related to another (tea) which has to be lifted out of absent contexts (and lifted out of absent objects to be put in this one), and then both the cup and its imaginary contents have to be regarded as a whole and placed in relation to a third, and not just Teddy, but the right part of Teddy—his mouth. And then, look, Mummy can be substituted for Teddy, and the cup can be related to yet another object to become another newly constituted whole:

(13) Shall I have a drink?
OK, put the cup on the saucer.
Yes, that's very proper now, isn't it?

Our claim is that this mother is transacting the world to her infant in a way that emphasises parts and their relations to wholes and each other, such that the infant's attention strategies will focus on these relations, and he will practise, and thus develop, a facility for using his analytic skills. We noted earlier how children could be conceived as placing differential reliance on part–whole (analytic) versus imitative abilities. Here we are suggesting that which path children follow results from the way the world is interactively structured for them. This child is being given excellent tuition in approaching the world analytically. Rather than finding mothers amongst our tapes who emphasise imitative reproduction, thus biasing their children towards that strategy, we presently believe that children who follow that path do so by default. That is, the world is not presented to them in a way that makes it easy for them to isolate its culturally given parts: If they are going to identify its parts and find similarities amongst them, then they are going to have to call more on their own resources. Analysis, not being socially constituted, will be less important in structuring their actions.

Dyad 2: Not Emphasising Parts

A different mother and her 18-month infant, same situations, book reading and playing with toys. The following relates to the same pages in the book as example 1:

(14) What's that one?
Yeah, chickens.
Oh look, ducks.
And a birdie, a birdie in a tree.
There's another birdie.
See the other bird there Kate.
Hey look, butterfly and flowers.
See the flowers.
And a bee.
Look at the bee.
And a rabbit.
Hmmm, bunny rabbit.

The episode is much shorter in time than episode 1. There is little sustained joint attention focused on any particular object. Whereas there is some conjunction of objects going on ("a birdie in a tree; butterfly and flowers"), the focus on isolating parts from wholes is missing. This lack is more apparent when interacting with toys, as is the greater speed at which the interaction occurs. Both mothers and infants played with the toys for close to 10 minutes. Some of the differences between them appear in the following figures. Firstly, the number of objects which the mother tried to interest the infant in: 26 in the first case versus 74 in this. Secondly, while the number of successful episodes of sharing actions around objects were similar, 9 vs. 11, their durations (in seconds) were quite different: mean 51.4; S.D. 28.7; range 16–104 vs. mean 28.4; S.D. 21.5; range 9–83. This "speeding-up" is also apparent in bookreading, where the mother changes topics for attention rapidly:

(15) What's that?
A ball.
Say ball.
And three motor cars.
Ooh look, he's clearing up.
There's a horsie.
Now, what else?
There's a train.
See?
Look.
He's got his shoes on.

It will not be in interaction that this infant develops part–whole relational skills. If he is to do so, he is going to have to draw on his own resources.

INTERACTION AND THE DEVELOPMENT OF LANGUAGE AND COGNITION

From this discussion there is an obvious hypothesis. If we are correct in supposing that the language styles reported by Nelson (1973) can be explained by children placing a differential reliance on the component skills feeding into language identified by Bates et al. (1979), and if we are correct in our argument that this differential reliance is created in mother–infant interaction, then if we can classify mother–infant dyads in terms of the extent to which analytic skills are facilitated, we can predict the path of the infant's early language development. Thus the hypothesis is that maternal styles that facilitate analysis will lead to their children's early vocabulary containing a high proportion of words which are used for naming, and vice versa. There are a number of "ifs" in this chain of reasoning, and their presence dictates quite closely the design of the study that is needed to test what we are hypothesising.

This is where we come back to one aspect of an observation we made earlier: Our concern in our work is as much with developing a theory of language development as with testing one. We are going to bring some data to bear on the hypothesis we have just put forward, but they come from a study we designed with another set of questions in mind: We hadn't figured out the present questions when we began looking at infants in the way we are about to discuss. Since the logistics of studying infants are so time consuming, we have to presently use what we do have data on.

Measures of Infants' Cognitive Development

The data come from an investigation of the relative timing of when infants attain object-permanence and person-permanence, and the role that social interaction plays in this. In pursuit of this, Brito (1986), working in our observation rooms at Lancaster, carried out a longitudinal study of 20 mothers and infants from 12 to 16 months, seeing each dyad every fourth week. On each visit: (1.) the infant was administered the tests required by the object-permanence subscales of the Casati–Lezine scale of infant development (this is essentially a French version of the more widely known, Piagetian-based Uzgiris–Hunt scale); (2.) the mothers were videoed playing with a selection of toys with their infants; and (3.) a version of the object permanence scales was developed, but instead of variously hiding and invisibly displacing objects, the infant's mother was hidden, and via an arrangement of screens enabled to invisibly displace herself. Otherwise, procedures were the same as those for determining substages in the development of the object concept, bar the fact that this form of testing is only suitable for infants who can crawl, because finding their mother involved crawling to where she might be. In addition, the mothers were asked to keep a diary of words as they appeared in the infant's vocabulary, and of the uses their children put these words to. When we asked them to do this it was with no clear question in mind, merely out of interest.

The Casati–Lezine scales, like the Uzgiris–Hunt ones, have separate subscales for tool-use (means–end analysis), imitation, object-permanence, gross motor development, and so on. Clearly, what we need to do is look for relationships between the measures of infant development on means–end analysis, imitation and language development—or at least between means–end analysis and language, for as we noted above, we suspect it is the differential development of analytic skills which is important, and are placing less reliance on imitative ones, seeing these as important only by default—and the classifications of mothers' styles of interactions (discussed later). But, to put the infants through the play session, the person permanence tests, and the object permanence ones took over an hour; And so we didn't have the time to give them all the subscales of Casati–Lezine test (an hour is a long time for an infant). Additionally we didn't think at the time that this was necessary anyway.

This means that the direct measures we need to test our present hypothesis are missing. But what we can do is regard both the object- and person-permanence measures as indices of behaviours that draw on the infant's problem-solving (analytic) abilities. Our line of reasoning here is that, especially for people as moving objects, attaining the concepts of object- and person-permanence requires a deal of abstractive cognition on the infant's part. That is, developing both the object and person concepts requires abstracting a core notion of an abstract nature; not something which is dominated by immediate perception. Developing a concept of a "person" to the extent that one may try and find one when they are hidden requires, in our view, quite a sophisticated prior analysis of what people are like. For example, people are agents: They do things. If you imagine yourself as a young infant, it becomes clear that you cannot perceive a person without perceiving their actions, because the two *conceptual* categories go together *perceptually*. To develop the concept of a person, you need to abstract out what is constant across the different perceptual arrays that people do things in: You have to ignore all the different actions they perform to discover what is constant (this is a comparable task to one we noted earlier: separating words out of rituals). The empirical literature on the relation between object-permanence and means–end analysis skills is rather confusing, so it is necessary to be cautious in going along with this line of thought: Our argument is plausible, but not yet well substantiated with solid data.

Working within this line led us to devise a scoring system from the infants' performance on (1) and (3) above (the Casati–Lezine object-permanence tests and our own person-permanence ones) that gives a picture of the infants' rate of development which we take to index their analytic abilities. This measure takes into account the highest score the infant achieved during the period of visits for both person and object permanence; the age at which these scores were attained; and the relative difference in age between these attainments.

Measures of Mothers' Styles of Interaction

It proved to be extremely difficult to classify the mothers as exhibiting particular styles of interaction on the basis of scoring different categories of their language and activity from the video of the toy-playing sessions (we will be returning to these difficulties later). Intuitively, however, there appear to be three broad interactive styles that mothers adopt, and a fourth group of mothers (in this case six) who are largely united by the fact that they do not clearly fit into the other groups.

The clearest of these styles we term *passive*, and this, at least, is clearly demonstrable by any scoring system one can devise for how mothers interact with their infants, for basically they don't. Consistently over the observation sessions, these mothers placed the box of toys in front of their infants and sat back, leaving the infant to play on its own.

Mothers in the remaining groups were much more active, and it is, we believe, the shortness of the observation session (15 minutes) that leads to the difficulty of distinguishing them one from the other. In addition, as we noted above, episodes that we used as exemplars of one style are not absent from other styles. However, in the same way as the two dyads we discussed earlier strike viewers immediately as very different, so too do many of these mothers. Two clear styles emerge that a mother consistently was classed as showing over the observation sessions. We call these *marking* mothers and *non-marking* mothers.

Marking mothers act like the one in the first dyad we discussed: *non-marking* mothers like the second. Thus the tempo of the interaction appears to differ (but is obscured in our present scoring of it because someone who operates in fast but short bursts and then takes a rest will do as much over a session as someone who more slowly paces herself). *Markers* can be described as more "in tune" with their infant, allowing the infant to determine the course of their interventions, seemingly anticipating where the infant is going with a toy, and integrating their communication more closely into, and elaborating on, the current situation. They are more "imaginative" in their play, and generally follow the pattern of pointing out and relating parts to wholes.

The final group of mothers are much more heterogeneous. A common factor amongst them was that the emotional pitch of their interactions was much higher than in the other groups: There was more laughing, squealing, exaggerated intonation, and body contact. Objects would be "loomed" at infants; they were often props in the pursuit of exaggerated surprise games, substitutes for the mother's fingers in tickling the infant, ways of eliciting laughter. In terms of emphasising parts vs wholes these mothers were less consistent over time, sometimes acting one way and then another. Yet even when parts were pointed out an emotional undertone was apparent:

(16) Ooh, look at his eyes ... Oooh what big eyes ... and ... they're ... comingtogetyou!

We have omitted these six mothers in the following discussion (although even with their inclusion the results are still clear-cut, see Table 3). As will be clear from the results, the problem of reliably indexing maternal activities is the most important issue we must face and clarify, for if the responsibility for such differences in overall development is to be attributed to interactive styles, we need to be clearer on what, in particular, distinguishes these styles.

Measures of Infants' Language Development

Again, we face some problems in measuring the language development of the infants in this study. To test our hypothesis we need to be able to classify the children by their style of development (referential vs. expressive), and this means we have to identify those styles. In her original study, Nelson (1973) classified the children when they had a 50-word vocabulary, around the age of 19 months. We only have data up to 16 months, and the largest vocabulary of any of the children was 26 words. Now, since the two styles appear to lie on a continuum, we are faced with a problem. Nelson (1985, pp. 99–100) notes that:

> For most of the children (called referential), early vocabularies consisted of a large proportion of object names, that is, nouns, with some verbs, proper names, and adjectives. For a large minority (called expressive), however, vocabularies were more diverse, with a large number of social routines or formulas (such as "stop it," "I want it," and "don't do it") included among the nouns, verbs, and adjectives.

From this, our problem should be quite clear. That is, in the very early stages of emerging language, it could prove very difficult to sort out what style children were following. For the first 10 words of children who turned out to be referential or expressive at a later date when a classification can be made more reliably could all be nouns in either case. And for the children in this study, in each case the majority of their early words were "nouns", words that referred to objects.

Thus we are forced to concentrate on object words in the attempt to see if we can somehow differentiate the children. The mothers' diaries give us information on the contexts in which words were used, and this allows us to rank the children in relation to each other in a relevant way. We can distinguish two classes of "nouns" in these eary vocabularies: specific ones and general ones. Specific nouns are words a child uses in relation to one particular object; for example "dog" in relation to only the family dog. General nouns are those which a child uses for a number of different objects; for example, "dog" in relation to the family dog, toy dogs, dogs in the park, on the television, in picture books, etc.

By making this distinction, our claim is that we have a measure relevant to the child's emerging language style, more precisely that we have an index of the cognitive skills the child is employing in developing language. That is, a general noun is only a general noun because the child has used an analytic strategy to abstract similarities out across different situations. Thus, the relative proportion of general nouns to specific ones indexes the degree to which the child is approaching language with analytic strategies. Now this is an important measure in this context, because it gets us round a number of problems with other measures we could have used. For example, if we said we will rank the children on the number of nouns in their vocabulary, on the grounds that referential children are characterised by their high use of nouns, we get a lovely relationship between high noun-users and marked maternal style, and low noun-users and non-marked maternal style. But this is not very helpful, because nouns formed the largest proportion of *all* the children's vocabularies, and what we would in fact be showing was that children with large vocabularies at 16 months had experienced marked forms of social interaction, and vice versa. This is an interesting result in its own right (that fast and slow language developers are associated with different maternal styles of interaction), but it is not the point presently at issue. Thus, ranking infants by the proportions of the two noun categories in their early vocabularies gets directly at the questions we want.

Unfortunately, though, another problem raises its head here. From the arguments we advanced earlier about the role of analytic skills in the development of language, we know such skills *must* be involved, whichever style of speech the child eventually shows, for those styles were hypothesised to result from a *differential* reliance on analytic skills, and not on their complete absence in the one case. It would seem likely that a child's first words would be context-bound in their use. That is, having abstracted a "label" out of the speech they hear, infants will initially only use that "label" in the context in which they abstracted it. They will begin with "specific" words, and only later generalise them to other contexts and referents. Thus, as their vocabulary increases, the proportion of general words to specific words may be expected to rise, irrespective of the child's style of language, and this obviously confounds the reasoning we used to justify the measure we have proposed. In fact, we find a very strong correlation ($r_s = 0.85$, $P < 0.01$) between the ratio of general to specific words and vocabulary size.

Consequently, we have had to adopt the same strategy as we did with the measures of cognitive development, and take into account the times at which new vocabulary items and usages are reported in the diaries, to give us an index of the rate at which the children are progressing from specific to general words. How accurate each mother's diary is, both absolutely and in relation to each other, is hard to say. But, if we do find anything by employing such measures, then the relationships between the factors we are considering are likely to be strong ones, for weak ones would not be detected by such coarse methods.

Summary of the Measures and Their Hypothesised Interrelations

First, we have a measure of the infants development relative to each other which we are claiming gives us an index of their use of the analytic skills which Bates et al. (1979) has hypothesised as underlying the referential style of language development. Children who are ranked high on this measure should show a tendency towards this language style.

Second, we have a measure of the infants early phase of language, which ranks them relative to their employment of strategies that are associated with this referential style of language. We hypothesise a relationship exists between this measure and the first one: Thus children ranked high on the "cognitive" measure should be ranked high on the language measure.

Third, we have categorised mothers in terms of their interaction styles into one of four groups: marked, non-marked, passive, and emotional. There are a number of hypotheses concerning how these maternal measures relate to the infant measures:

1. Marked mothers will be associated with children who score highly on the cognitive and language measures, because our general claim is that the basic building blocks that feed into the elaboration of those two skills are created in the social interactions that occur between the mothers and the infants.

2. Non-marked mothers will be associated with children who are ranked lower than the children of marked mothers, because their interactive style provides less of a resource for the constitution of the analytic skills which the child measures index.

3. Passive mothers should be associated with children who are ranked lowest on both the child measures, for if the skills which they index are being created socially, these children will have the least opportunity of all to develop them.

4. Emotional mothers could be associated with children who occur anywhere in the rankings, because this category does not distinguish mothers on the same continuum as the first three do. Emotional mothers vary along the marked–non-marked continuum, but we cannot (yet) reliably assign them to a specific position on it.

Results

The groups that we need to focus on are the marked, non-marked and passive mothers, because we are a little unclear as to what to expect for the fourth group of emotional mothers in terms of their hypothesised effects on their infants' development. Table 2 shows the mothers' styles against their infant's rank on what we are taking as both an indicator of the infant's rate of general cognitive development, and as an index of the degree of elaboration of analytic skills. The relation between the assigned maternal style and the infant measure is (embarrassingly) clear, and requires no comment. Turning to the relation between the analytic index and the infant's emerging language index, we find a significant correlation between their rankings. These results offer support for hypotheses (1)–(3) above.

Table 3 ranks the infants by their rate of development for all the infants in the study (i.e. including those with emotional mothers). As expected from hypotheses (4), the emotional mothers have children who are spread out in

TABLE 2
Relations between Mother's Style and Infant's Rankings on Analytic Skill and Language
Style Indexes

Mother's style	Analytic Skill Index	Language Style Index
M	1.0	3.0
M	2.0	5.0
M	3.0	1.0
M	4.0	2.0
M	5.0	10.0
M	6.0	8.5
NM	7.0	11.0
NM	8.5	8.5
NM	8.5	4.0
NM	10.0	6.0
P	11.0	14.0
P	12.0	7.0
P	13.0	12.0
P	14.0	13.0

NOTES:
r_s for analytic skill index by language style index $= 0.648$: $P < 0.01$
M = marked; NM = non-marked; P = passive.

the rankings, suggesting that these mothers do indeed vary along the marked–non-marked continuum. However, we need to look at them more closely before we could substantiate this, for there may well be other factors operating in their case. For example, it may be that these mothers vary more in the appropriateness of the timing, rather than the nature, of their interventions and interactions with the child, such that they marked events when the child was not looking, or in a way that disrupted joint action (and we should not forget the importance of such things for the other maternal styles just because our results happened to turn out in such a clear-cut manner). We have omitted the infants rankings on the language index in this table for no sinister reason, but because we have not calculated them at the time of writing.

DISCUSSION

There is more to developmental psychology than gathering data on the processes of development: We need to offer an interpretation. Interpretation requires a viewpoint; a "paradigmatic position" within which a "story" can be put forward. There are a number of paradigms within developmental

TABLE 3
Relations between Mother's Style and Infant's Developmental Score and Ranking

Mother's Style	Total Developmental Score	Developmental Rank
M	9.0	1.0
M	11.5	2.0
M	12.0	3.0
E	12.5	4.0
E	20.0	5.0
M	24.0	6.0
E	31.0	7.0
M	31.5	8.0
M	32.5	9.0
NM	36.5	10.0
E	38.0	11.0
E	41.0	12.0
NM	45.0	13.5
NM	45.0	13.5
NM	51.0	15.0
P	53.0	16.0
P	55.5	17.0
E	57.0	18.0
P	59.0	19.0
P	61.5	20.0

NOTE:
M = marked; NM = non-marked; E = emotional; P = passive.

psychology, and they differ in the "image" they offer of what it is to be a child; what children are like (cf. Shotter, 1984). For example, the Piagetian image of children pictures them as active individuals, constructing knowledge out of their actions *upon* the world. On the other hand, the Vygotskyan image pictures children again as active individuals, but this time acting *within* the world, with a special emphasis on the social nature of that world. The picture one gets from Macmurray is more difficult to visualise, for he takes the "You and I" as his unit of analysis, such that the psychological "entity" we are dealing with is not the possession of any one individual, and this entity performs "joint actions" that create our conception of the world and its contents, including the individuals we think we are. In addition there are other dimensions on which images of development themselves differ. We can contrast, for example, the Piagetian paradigm with the Gibsonian; one views the process at the construction of internal knowledge, the other as the picking-up of information that is already structured and available in the environment.

Given all these different images, how should we interpret our results: What sort of picture of infancy and the process of development should we put forward? We feel that there are elements of "truth" in all these paradigms, and that it would be counter-productive to plump for one at the expense of the others. In fact, we consider that the dimensions on which these paradigms differ—individual vs. social action; individual vs. social entity; internal vs. external—require us to assay a developmental theory akin to those held by quantum physicists when interpreting light, sometimes picturing it as a wave is useful, on other occasions as a collection of individual particles. Physicists do not argue whether light is "really" one or the other, for it is both at the same time.

Thus, we see little to be gained, beyond it being an interesting academic exercise, to argue for one interpretation versus another. For example, we could offer many different accounts of our findings. We could proceed as Piagetians, and claim that an individual child develops knowledge as a result of action upon the world, actions which accommodate the world. Different worlds will require different accommodations, and quite obviously, the infants of marking mothers must accommodate to very different worlds from those of passive mothers. We could argue over whether the child had a given capacity for means–end analysis which became more developed under some circumstances than others, or whether the capacity is itself constructed in the course of interactive development. We could try lots of things, actually.

Instead we want to begin a kind of "quantum" developmental paradigm, which we are calling a "social constructivist" one. To do this properly requires, as we noted earlier, a deconstruction of our present conceptual oppositions, and a reconstruction of theory on a different base, something which we cannot do here. Thus we will give here a fairly simplistic interpretation of development as we have followed it and tried to measure it in our investigation of early language. Thinking through this account further, in the light of the theoretical points we introduced earlier, will point in the direction we intend.

Compare Fig. 1 with Fig. 2. Now imagine the markers on Fig. 2 are being performed by another's finger pointing at them. Immediately one sees how the actions of another act to aid one's own abilities, and how, in the case of our investigation, a marking mother will channel and elaborate her infant's cognitive skills differently from a passive or non-marking mother. At this level, we can say the social actions of another act to construct our own *cognitive abilities*. At another level, we can also say that it is in social interactions that our *projects* are also constructed. As adults, we can read, and even if we couldn't, we could still make a shrewd guess at what we were supposed to do if confronted by figures such as these. Infants cannot read, and there is little reason to suppose that they would consider the project of looking for similarities and differences when so confronted on their own. Mother's fingers do not just point out *where* to look, but also *why* to look in the first place.

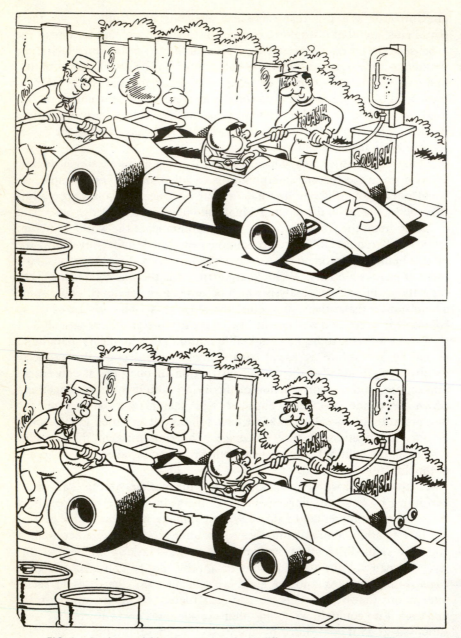

FIG. 1.   See how quickly you can spot the 10 differences between the 2 pictures.

FIG. 2.   See how quickly you can spot the 10 differences between the 2 pictures.

There are two further aspects of this social construction of abilities and projects. First of all, we suggest the way the child actually perceives the world is being changed in a phenomenological way, akin to the difference a poor reader experiences with a word as compared to a skilled reader. That is, a poor reader has to try and decipher what is written, whereas a skilled reader sees a word as meaningful. A similar difference appears to exist between novice and grand master chess players in their experiential perception of chess pieces on the board. Thus, we are suggesting that the different ways mothers interact with infants affects the way the world actually appears to their infants. In the same way that her finger can make apparent particular parts of *spatially disparate* pictures, so too with her speech and actions does she accomplish this for *temporally disparate* objects and events: this is not just *a* shoe, but it's like Daddy's shoe. What you are looking at now is imbued with a perceptual salience that has been given it through social juxtaposition of different times (*cf.* Edwards and Middleton, 1988). In a crude analogy, some mothers make aspects of the child's perceptual world more "luminous" than others.

Secondly, we suggest that developing a symbolic system such as language is a concomitant of this differential "luminosity". Symbols can be used to refer to things which are absent, but infants begin with reference to the present. But, in our view, an infant's present comes to be imbued by what is absent. Thus, it is not so much that different mothers have differentially elaborated different skills inherent in their infants that lead to their different ways of getting into language, but that they have constructed with them a whole different *Umwelt* (cf. von Uexkull, 1982[1940]) for the child. The child's perceptual world contains the same underlying structure as symbolic abilities: Both structures are constructed in the course of joint social action.

Infants develop ways of attending to the world by having their attention directed by someone else. It is not so much their knowledge of events which is being structured, but the perception of events itself. It is not easier to spot the differences in Fig. 2 because one has better knowledge, more facility in comparing representations with immediate perception; it is more that the differences have been made obvious. If "knowledge" informs this task, then it is someone else's, embedded in the way the pictures are presented. It is outside of the infant, in the structure of the interaction. The "knowledge" that guides perception is someone else's, and they employ it to make the differences more or less easy to spot.

This is especially true of the basic cultural concepts that the infant is claimed to be acquiring around this time. The concepts we attribute to the infant, like a concept of agency from around 9–10 months, are not seen in the world like cups, tables, etc., that is, as physically distinct. In a strange way they are visibly invisible: We cannot see agents as isolated phenomena, distinct from the actions they perform. Coming to see them in this way means constructing them as visible, making them perceptible. This process has to be a socially guided one: Perception is constructed intermentally. In the same way our argument is that if one wishes to attribute differential facilities with imitation vs. analysis to infants, then one should conceive of those skills as *socially constituted* and not *individually* given; not as "cognitive operations", but as embedded in the perceptual world of interaction itself. Thus, we do not conceive of infants as having differential "amounts" of analytic skills which they employ "on the world". They have different socially-constituted perceptual/conceptual worlds, some of which contain more perceptible "parts" than others. In sum, it is not that infants develop *differently* by the exercise and practice of their indivdual skills; those skills, and the infants themselves, are *constructed* differently via socially-constitutive interaction.

REFERENCES

Bates, E., Benigni, L., Bretherton, I., Camaioni, L., & Volterra, V. (1979). *The emergence of symbols: Cognition and communication in infancy*. New York: Academic Press.

Brito, A. (1986). Unpublished Ph.D. thesis, University of Murcia, Spain.

Edwards, D. & Middleton, D. (1988). Conversational remembering by mothers and children: A study of scaffolded learning. *Journal of Social and Personal Relationships*, *5*, 3–25.

Giddens, A. (1984). *The constitution of society*. Cambridge: Polity Press.

Konner, M. J. (1972). Aspects of the developmental ethology of a foraging people. In N. G. Blurton-Jones (ed.), *Ethological studies of child behaviour*. Cambridge: Cambridge University Press.

Lock, A. J. (ed.) (1978). *Action, gesture and symbol: The emergence of language*. London: Academic Press.

Macmurray, J. (1957). *The self as agent*. London: Faber & Faber.

Macmurray, J. (1961). *Persons in relation*. London: Faber & Faber.

Mead, G. H. (1934). *Mind, self and society*. Chicago: Chicago University Press.

Nelson, K. (1973). Structure and strategy in learning to talk. *Monographs of the Society for Research in Child Development*, *48*, (serial No. 149).

Nelson, K. (1985). *Making sense: The acquisition of shared meaning*. New York: Academic Press.

Richards, M. P. M. (ed.) (1974). *The integration of a child into a social world*. Cambridge: Cambridge University Press.

Shotter, J. (1974). The development of personal powers. In. M. P. M. Richards (ed.), *The integration of a child into a social world*. Cambridge: Cambridge University Press.

Shotter, J. (1984). *Social accountability and selfhood*. Oxford: Basil Blackwell.

von Uexkull, J. (1982) [1940] The theory of meaning. *Semiotica*, *42*, 25–82.

Vygotsky, L. S. (1962). *Thought and language*. Cambridge, Mass.: MIT Press.

Vygotsky, L. S. (1978). *Mind in society*. Cambridge, Mass.: Harvard University Press.

Zinober, B. and Martlew, M. (1985). The development of communicative gestures. In M. Barrett (ed.), *Children's single-word speech*. Chichester: Wiley.

11

Linking Emotion and Thinking in Infant Development: A Psychoanalytic Perspective

Cathy Urwin

Child Care and Development Group,
Free School Lane,
Cambridge,
Cambs. CB2 3RF

INTRODUCTION

The last two decades of infant research have challenged so many traditional assumptions that it is hard to believe that we might ever need to look backwards. This is particularly obvious in perception and cognitive research, which now faces the problem of squaring the complexity attributed to very young infants with the considerable development yet to be achieved. Before approaching this problem through the usual assumptions it is worth reflecting on how the new evidence has been acquired. Most has come from experimental work which has depended on sophisticated technological developments. This methodology does not make the research any the less exciting. But it is a moot point how far we can ever know infant minds directly. It is important to recognise that, like all accounts, the contemporary views are productions. As such they introduce possibilities, and also limitations. Here I want to focus on the ways in which experimentation has contributed to a general tendency for emotion to be bypassed in accounts of infant cognition and perception. That is, whereas elaborate experimentation enables investigators to make more refined claims about what the baby knows or perceives, what the baby feels in these situations is marginalised. This marginalisation is somewhat remarkable given how often emotional responses, like cries and other measures of distress or surprise, are used as evidence that a young baby has perceived a difference of some sort, has expected an object or different object from behind a screen, or has shown "puzzlement" at its disappearance (see Butterworth and Harris, Chapters 3 and 5, this volume). But the contribution of these kinds of emotional resonses to the organisation of perception and cognition is not incorporated within the experimental paradigm. Similarly, on closer inspection, the supposedly objective experimenters are less detached than at first appears. Inevitably they make judgements about the meaning of observed behaviour in terms of pleasures and interests, and soon discover the importance of taking account of the infant's state, as not too tired, distressed, hungry, or anxious. Indeed the design of a successful experiment depends on harnessing infants' motivations and emotional preoccupations.

The marginalisation of emotion and emphasis on observer detachment are examples of what I have described elsewhere as a pervasive split in psychology between emotion and thinking. This is rooted in a longer tradition of separating emotion and reason and was inscribed in the way developmental psychology first began at the end of the last century within a movement committed to recording and studying child behaviour according to the methods of biological science (Urwin, 1986). One heritage is that it remains difficult for investigators to put together the study of emotional experience and the development of thought and perception, even where this is intended. For instance, in fact there has been a flowering of research into infants' emotions over the last few years (e.g. Lewis & Rosenblum, 1978; Stern, 1985; Trevarthen, 1985). This has followed a longer tradition aiming to examine effects of social interaction on cognitive development in infancy, or even to locate the emergence of cognition and symbolic functioning within a social matrix (e.g. Butterworth & Light, 1980; Lock, 1978). Nevertheless, when emotions are put together with cognitive processes, explanatory accounts generally reduce to one of two alternatives. Either emotional phenomena, such as what emotional states the infant perceives, expresses, or recognises, are rendered as things the infant knows about, and then reduced to underlying cognitive schemes which are taken as determining or primary. Alternatively, emotion tends to be viewed as a kind of energy, positively or negatively charged, that speeds up or slows down cognitive processes without entering into the formation of these processes themselves (see Urwin, 1984, 1986 for a more extended discussion).

To cut across dualistic approaches to relations between emotion and cognition it may be necessary to look outside the theories and methods offered by traditional psychology. In this chapter my aim is to illustrate the relevance of clinical work and psychoanalytic accounts of infancy, beginning with Freud but concentrating on the work of Melanie Klein and her followers. The latter psychoanalytic tradition makes assumptions about the relative sophistication of young infants' mental equipment which are in many ways comparable to the views of contemporary developmental psychologists. It also has a distinctive view of relations between emotion and thought, in which what is crucial is the infant's discovery of mind itself as a mental space.

But my aim here is not to suggest that this or any other psychoanalytic theory is simply applied to the study of infancy or immediately translated into empirical predictions. In this kind of uptake some of the most distinctive or challenging aspects of psychoanalysis can get lost (Urwin, 1986). Rather I hope to demonstrate the possibilities for productive dialogue beween developmental psychology and psychoanalysis. This involves illustrating relations between psychoanalytic theory and its own methods for producing evidence. In particular in clinical contexts the psychoanalytic method both generates theoretical concepts and is a tool for evaluating their explanatory power and therapeutic relevance. Following an account of theoretical assumptions, I will give examples from the psychotherapy of two school-aged children. Both children have particular problems in thinking which have clear emotional concomitants and several factors indicate that these problems originated very early in infancy. After outlining developments shown in these children's psychotherapy I will conclude by examining their relevance to relations between emotion and thinking in infancy under more ordinary circumstances, and to findings produced by contemporary psychological studies.

PSYCHOANALYSIS AND THINKING: FREUD

Though psychoanalysis is often regarded as a theory of emotional relationships which applies to people with problems or the mentally ill, in actuality it is also a theory of mental representations, meanings, and symbols which applies to all of us. Arguably all of Freud's work addresses the lifelong relations between emotion and mental processes. But for present purposes one of the most influential accounts is the speculative paper "Formulations on the two principles of mental functioning" which pursues the problem of how we come to think at all (Freud, 1911). Here Freud asserts the importance of the unconscious mental processes discovered by psychoanalysis and argues that they represent the ontogenetically and phylogenetically oldest form of thought. He proposes that these "primary processes" are governed by a "pleasure principle" which aims to obtain or prolong pleasure and avoid unpleasure by adapting or denying reality. In contrast, the "reality principle" is concerned with detecting what is useful to the individual rather than what is necessarily pleasurable. This is governed through the ego or the monitor of the conscious part of the mind and lays the foundations for rational thought and other achievements associated with consciousness, or what Freud calls the "secondary process". Speculating on how or why the reality principle should emerge, Freud takes further an hypothetical reconstruction first put forward in *The Interpretation of Dreams*, proposing that the realities of life first confront the infant in the form of major somatic needs, for food, for example (Freud, 1900). The experience of the satisfaction of these needs, when the crying baby gets fed, would be accompanied by particular perceptions remaining as mnemic images associated with the memory trace of the excitation produced by the need. When this need arises next time, a psychical impulse would recreate the pleasurable affect associated with the original satisfaction by reinvoking an image resembling the perception itself, giving rise to what we call a wish. Thus, Freud argued, in its primitive state the psychical apparatus might be able to deal with the unpleasure associated with hunger with a wish fulfilment phantasy, ending in hallucinating. Wish fulfilment is, of course, the stuff of dreams, when sleep provides a cover for rejecting external reality. In waking life, hallucinations occur under conditions of extreme deprivation, and in some kinds of psychosis. But though we all deny, split off, or confuse reality with phantasy in some degree, we can also tell the difference. What accounts for this? In the "Two principles" Freud suggests that a capacity for judging reality might come about with the discovery that actually, hallucinating failed to remove the physical discomfort or displeasure. The disjunction would oblige the psychical apparatus to form a conception of the real circumstances, however disagreeable, in order to make a change in them by acting on the world. This would provide a developmental basis for giving rise to a new principle of mental functioning and secondary system thought. But this system would not entirely replace the primary process, since reality testing safeguards the pleasure principle by postponing gratification through work or sublimating instinctual processes into cultural achievement. Moreover, the ego which monitors external reality ultimately derives its energy from the individual's instinctual life, though this is outside conscious awareness.

Thus Freud is proposing an affective basis for the emergence of conscious cognitive activity, in which the emergence of the secondary system depends on an already functioning mode of thought, the primary process and its capacity for wish fulfilment through primitive mental representations. The "Two principles" was written relatively early in Freud's career and there are a number of problems with the account, some of which I have discussed elsewhere (Urwin, 1986). Nevertheless, this paper set out important parameters for future theorising, some of them pursued by Freud himself. Though hypothetical, the argument brought to the forefront the particular dependence of the human infant, and the importance of the relationship to the breast. This heralded a shift away from a model based on the management of instinctual energy *per se* towards one in which the psychic apparatus achieves its aims through its relationships with "objects", that is, people or parts of people, in phantasy and reality. It also paved the way for a number of theoretical accounts which emphasise the first object relation established in infancy. One of the most influential of these is Melanie Klein's.

MELANIE KLEIN AND INFANT DEVELOPMENT

Where Freud's developmental theories were largely derived from reconstructions from adult patients and a knowledge of contemporary child study literature (Urwin, 1986), Klein was one of the first analysts to work with children. Following suggestions which Freud had actually made himself, Klein began using children's play as a means of gaining access to their desires, conflicts, or sources of inhibition. Like Freud she came to the conclusion that the differentiation unconscious/conscious was less clearly marked in children than in adults and that play was a medium through which children sought to represent their preoccupations, master their anxieties, or bring about wish fulfilment in phantasy. "It was by approaching the play of the child in a way similar to Freud's interpretations of dreams that I found I could get access to the child's unconscious" (Klein, 1955, p. 19). But from the outset, Klein's ways of confronting children's phantasies provoked controversy. Much of this centred round the "transference", the phenomenon discovered in adult work where particular past events, anxieties, desires or phantasies are re-experienced in relation to the person of the analyst (Freud, 1909). In very general terms, how the patient responds to interpretations of these phenomena is a test of the therapeutic adequacy of the theory of early development which informs the therapists' interpretations. With her child patients, Klein found both a highly positive or affectionate transference and also considerable anxiety. This was often associated with terrifying phantasies. Interpretations relating these to the children's own aggressive impulses provided considerable relief. Klein also found that a transference extended beyond the person of the analyst to the toys, objects, and even the play-room itself, which were experienced as part of the mother/therapist. These observations contributed to a broadened notion of transference that includes the totality of desires and phantasies invoked in relation to the therapist. Though experienced as vividly present, these phenomena are assumed to have roots in infancy and to reveal fundamental aspects of the individual patient's psychic organisation. Eventually Klein took her discoveries into work with adults, including schizophrenic and psychotic patients. This is in contrast to Freud, who had argued that such thought-disordered individuals could not be helped through analysis, though he accepted that their difficulties originated early in infancy.

Unsurprisingly, these developments led to distinctive theoretical accounts of the earliest phases of development (see Klein, 1935; 1940; 1946). Unlike many psychoanalytic theorists who forefront infancy, such as Winnicott and representatives of the British Object Relations School, Klein accepted a distinction which Freud (1920, 1923) introduced in his later work between life preservative instincts and the "death instinct", a tendency within the organism to bring about its own destruction or to return to some prior state of being. Klein emphasised that throughout life the life drive, manifested in love and creativity, is constantly threatened by destructive impulses, emanating from within, and saw the infant as coming into the world with conflicting impulses of love and hate. She proposed that the new-born infant has already established a primitive ego capable of some form of reality testing and object relating, or that there was an active search for a primal relation to the mother/other object as provider of food, comfort, and love. This view is in contrast to most psychoanalytic accounts which assume an initial adualism or lack of differentiation between self, other and environment. It is also seen in Piaget's work (Piaget and Inhelder, 1969) but it is consistent with the claims of those contemporary developmental psychologists who stress the relative sophistication of the new-born's perceptual and cognitive apparatus, and who argue for a particular adaptation towards properties of other people (e.g. Stern, 1985; Trevarthen, 1985). Unlike psychologists, however, Klein proposes that a major function of the primitive ego is to deal with a high level of anxiety which might otherwise overwhelm the tiny baby. Though this anxiety is partly reality-based, since the very young infant is extremely vulnerable, it is also fuelled by the death instinct, as feelings of hatred or resentment stirred up in the baby bring about a tendency to destroy the self. Fortunately for the infant, the primitive ego quickly organises "mechanisms of defence" to deal with this anxiety. These mechanisms operate throughout life and are well attested within all psychoanalytic traditions. They include the "denial" of feelings or reality, "splitting", whereby parts of the personality or of the ego or objects are kept apart so as not to be available to consciousness simultaneously, "idealisation" and "projection". In the latter feelings or phantasies are effectively disowned by the individual through being projected into someone or something else (e.g. *He* is just so infantile!). How did Klein see such processes as applying to the infant? Imagine a tiny baby who is very hungry. According to Klein, anxiety emanating from the death instinct is partly dealt with by turning the self-destructive tendencies outwards in the form of aggression, so that the baby becomes enraged, and partly by projection. The infant projects the aggression into a part of an object, prototypically into the breast, which is felt to be the source of discomfort and anxiety. This gives rise to the phantasy of the "bad breast" which is now felt to be dangerous and persecuting and hence should be avoided at all costs, along with the mother associated with it, who becomes a "bad object". This kind of process can be observed in a very hungry baby who nonetheless rejects the breast initially, as if the present, external object is experienced as bad or dangerous. For Klein the baby does not experience hunger as absence of food but as having the "bad breast" inside. It is the attempt to expel or push this out that leads to projection. Thus, the defence mechanism contributes to the formation of primitive phantasies, the first mental representatives of instinctual and bodily processes. Over the same developmental period the infant establishes the phantasy of the "good breast", as an infant deflects the life instinct outwards into an object in the external world. Initially this relation is "idealised" as the infant believes the object is partly a result of his or her own creation. But gradually the ideal is merged with gratifying experiences from the real external mother, which are taken in or "introjected", giving rise to the phantasy of the "good object". For Klein, the young infant's aim is to try to acquire and keep inside the good object, seen as life giving and protective, and to identify with it, and to keep out the bad object and those parts of the self felt to be dangerous and potentially annihilating. The infant thus "splits" the ego and the object into parts felt to be "good" or "bad", aiming to keep them apart. Splitting is generally accepted as a defence mechanism of very early origin. But Klein also identified another early mechanism through her work with children and psychotic adults, "projective identification". This is a difficult concept to understand outside the psychoanalytic context and will be illustrated more fully later. In brief, in projective identification parts of the self are split off and projected into an object, which then becomes possessed by or controlled by the projected parts. This may serve the function of disowning these parts if they are felt as bad or dangerous, as when a young baby defecating phantasises attacking the mother. Alternatively, parts of the self felt to be good can be projected in order to preserve them, or to avoid the pain of separation.

These defences are used excessively over the first 3 or 4 months after birth and Klein uses the term "paranoid–schizoid position" to characterise the ego's relations with its objects over this period. But it is important to recognise that they remain with all of us, serving sometimes valuable functions. In the first months they both protect the infant's psyche and pave the way for subsequent developments. Projective identification, for example, eventually contributes to the capacity to "put yourself in someone else's shoes", and provides the basis for the earliest form of symbol-formation, as parts of the self are projected into the object using some basis of perceived similarity. Similarly, splitting into good and bad is a primitive form of discrimination which is a vital precondition for later integration and provides the basis for what becomes an ability to suspend one line of thought in order to engage with potentially competing information (Segal, 1986).

Nonetheless an alternative form of object-relating is implied. For Klein this can be seen from 4 to 5 months as the infant moves into what she calls the "depressive position". This is not a distinct developmental stage, but refers to a reorientation in the ego's relations to objects which must be worked through over several months or even years. Crucial to this phase is the infant's recognition of the mother or significant other as a whole object. This development has been embodied in psychological studies, including Bower's (1971) "multiple mothers" experiment in which very young infants confronted with multiple images of their mothers through an arrangement of mirrors were apparently unperturbed. But from about 5 months, which for Klein marks the onset of the depressive position, this situation provoked acute distress. Bower argued that the baby now knows that the same object, the mother, cannot be in two places at once, and assumed an underlying and determining cognitive achievement, a coordination between place and movement (Bower, 1982). Though Klein implies the contribution of cognition, assuming, for example, neurological developments over the first few months, which facilitate memory and perceptual motor control, what is crucial about the depressive position is that it is premised not on a determining cognitive structure but on an emotional shift as the "good" and "bad" mother is recognised as one and the same, and the infant experiences ambivalence for the first time. This has revolutionary implications, but also ushers in a whole new range of anxieties. Firstly, the leading anxiety of the paranoid–schizoid position was that the ego would be attacked by the bad object or objects. But in the depressive position the main anxiety of infants is that their *own* impulses will destroy the good objects, both internal and external. Second, since the infant attempts to defend against this anxiety by intensifying the use of introjections, aiming to incorporate the external mother in order to protect the inner objects, this promotes the phantasy that the infant has brought the good, loved object under attack, giving rise to feelings of guilt, often of crippling intensity. Thirdly, recognising the mother as a whole person means increasingly recognising her as separate, with independent relationships with other people. As a corollary, the baby discovers helplessness, dependency, and jealousy. It is for this reason that Klein (1945) asserts, in contrast to Freud, that the Oedipus complex begins with the depressive position and competition for the mother's attention in the middle of the first year.

Observation of infants suggests many ways in which they attempt to deal with these new anxieties. They may become clinging, no longer allowing their mothers out of sight, showing the stranger and separation anxieties much studied by psychologists. They may become ill or may suddenly start having sleep disturbances. They may revert to defences of the earlier period, rejecting their mothers temporarily in favour of their fathers or other caretakers. Alternatively they may become "manic", keeping themselves going as a way of denying dependence and the pain associated with the threatened loss of their mothers. But partly because of these anxieties, the depressive position promotes radical developmental changes, in social–emotional relationships, in thinking, and in symbolic functioning. Crucial is the fact that, in addition to ambivalence and guilt, the infant in the depressive position may now mourn or pine for a good object, remembered but felt to be lost or destroyed. At the same time, because of the acceleration of introjection and identification, the infant may now suffer on behalf of the mother. This immobilises the infant to try to restore the mother and other objects, and to "make reparation".

Ultimately it is the infant's wish to restore the mother, internally and externally, that leads to a resolution of depressive anxieties. Initially, and arguably necessarily, the infant's attempts to make reparation are omnipotent. Since, in omnipotence, infants believe that their own destructive attacks are responsible for the damage, they also believe that their own love and care can undo the effects of the aggression, independent of what is actually the case. To resolve this there must be radical alterations in the infants' capacity for testing reality. For Klein, this is not a simple discovery of the existence of an external world. Rather, what is crucial is the perception of a disjunction between what is happening in psychic reality, the destruction of the mother and her omnipotent restoration, for example, and a reality actually existing outside the self. That is, as infants begin to discover the ambivalence of their own feelings and their dependence on external objects, they become aware that their own psychic impulses can be differentiated from external reality, and it is the perception of this disjunction which has radical implications for what in psychology we would think of as cognitive development. Although, for Klein, reality testing exists from birth, to begin with it is based on primitive classification of good or bad. The differentiation between inside or outside is weak, and made more so through projective identification, as parts of the self are projected into an external object in phantasy. But in the depressive position, infants' increasing awareness of their own impulses and concern for their objects makes them follow closely the actual impact of their actions, leading them to test out their own power and their objects' resilience. This increases their acknowledgement of and capacity to bear separation, and motivates them to discover more and more ways of actuality affecting external reality, contributing to the ability to keep track of objects, or hold them in mind, despite alterations in their locations. This itself is linked to the development of symbol formation. In psychoanalysis symbol formation is a means whereby instinctual aims are displaced onto objects or other substitutes. For Klein the creative use of symbols always involves a renunciation or a loss as the original instinctual aim, or object, is given up. Only then can the symbol be differentiated from that which it replaces, such that the infant feels the symbol has been created by the self, to be used freely by the self (Segal, 1952). This is in contrast to the "symbolic equation" in which the symbol is equated with the original object, giving rise to the concrete thinking characteristic of some schizophrenics and autistic children, such as the borderline autistic child I will describe later.

Thus although the depressive position involves considerable pain, it is the seat of change, laying the foundations for thinking and symbolic activity. However, in no individual is the process of working through the depressive position fully completed. In all of us situations invoking guilt, ambivalence, and loss re-awaken depressive anxieties which have to be worked through all over again. In some individuals such stresses reinvoke the dread or actual threat or a breakdown. In a fortunately very small number of children, the movement into the depressive position is never achieved. What accounts for these kinds of differences?

Crucial to the satisfactory working through of the depressive position is the developing ability of infants to retain a belief in the goodness of their objects and the capacity to regain them internally and externally when they are experienced as lost or destroyed. It is the attempt to restore or maintain good objects in the internal world that provides the anchor point for active curiosity. Although Klein is often presented as being entirely concerned with internal processes, she describes various ways in which environmental support can contribute to the infant's passage through this period. For example, a mother's reappearance after absences and her care and attention can help to modify infants' belief in the omnipotence of their destructive impulses, and her firmness can diminish the baby's belief in magical re-paration. Similarly, in the paranoid schizoid position predictabilities in parental handling provide the baby with opportunities for introjecting good objects and for learning that bad experiences and good experiences can both be located in the same source. But care-taking practices do not simply determined development. On the one hand, the mother's own internal life may be important. On the other hand, the mental processes of the baby remain fundamental. That is, for a baby to make use of a predominance of good over bad experiences, the processes for ordering and differentiating, the splitting, projective, and introjective mechanisms of the paranoid schizoid phase, also need to have been established satisfactorily. What contributes to this early organisations and, once on the threshold of the depressive position, what enables the infant to sustain depressive anxiety rather than reverting to previous modes of defence?

Here it is useful to turn to the work of Bion, an analyst who also worked extensively with psychotic patients who, by definition, have had difficulties moving into the depressive position. Working intensely in the transference, like Klein, Bion identified splitting, defensive disintegration of the ego, and the mammoth use of projective identification. However Bion took Klein's discoveries further. Where Klein emphasised the patient's attempts to get rid of unwanted parts to control the object and/or defend against intolerable anxiety, for Bion what was also at issue was a primitive form of communica-tion. He came to recognise this through making use of the "counter-transference", the feelings invoked in the therapist during the analytic encounter. Doing this depends on the therapist's understanding the part he or she is playing in some ongoing phantasy of the patient, and may involve experiencing feelings which the patient is as yet unable to bear.

The communicative aspect of projective identification is well illustrated by O'Shaugnessy (1981) who describes herself experiencing an incredible feeling of isolation during a therapy session with a 9-year-old girl, who moved swiftly and systematically from one activity to another, one imagines like an oh-so-busy grown up. Following Bion, O'Shaugnessy understood the counter-transference experience as the child's way of making known the feelings of isolation and impotence which terrified her. Her interpretation to the little girl included the recognition that she wanted the therapist to know how she felt. By this time Bion had taken forward his insights theoretically (Bion, 1962, 1967). Linking analytic experience with observations of young infants and their mothers, Bion came to argue that, in addition to being a mechanism of defence, projective identification was also one of the first forms of communication between baby and mother. Furthermore, he proposed that thinking originates in this process through which the baby projects feelings, fears and so on into the mother for her to receive and know them. Following Freud's emphasis on the aim of the pleasure principles as the avoidance and discharge of unpleasurable stimulation, Bion speculated that the infant discharges unpleasure by splitting off and projecting anxiety, arousing perception, sensitivity, feelings, and so on into the mother for her to contain them or bring them into manageable proportions in what he called the mother's "reverie". This form of thought is no more or no less evidenced than in the processes underlying comments like "Where *has* that wind gone to, hey?" or "I know, I know, you've had such a long wait". None the less, it is indicative of the availability of a psychic space in which anxieties can be understood, made bearable, and meaningful.

Though consistent with Klein's general perspective, Bion's account adds a further dimension. This is the idea that as fundamental to the introjection of the good breast for psychic development is the availability and introjection of a containing mental space through which thought can be differentiated and organised. This has contributed to understanding the phenomenology of the precipitating factors in psychosis. At its simplest, if there is no notion of a mental capacity for understanding and making tolerable the terrifying, the individual will retreat from the demands and pain of the depressive position, the getting to know external reality and psychic qualities in others. Bion's work has also had important technical implications. One, pointed out by Mary Boston (1987), is an emphasis on the therapist's function in holding or "containing" the patient's projections, while pondering over them, tolerating the uncertainly until the patient is able to take them back. Another is a recognition of the value of working with the counter-transference. In the next section I will illustrate these implications in the psychotherapy of two children who show difficulties in object relations and in thinking outside of a two-dimensional world.

TWO CASE STUDIES

Nicholas

Nicholas is a 9-year-old child who I have been seeing 4 times a week for 2 years. Nicholas could be described diagnostically as "borderline autistic". At first referral he showed many of the limitations in symbolic functioning characteristic of autistic children. His language had been delayed initially and at 7 years he relied heavily on ritual phrases and parroting. His use of "I" and "You" was not firmly established. His drawings were obsessionally neat but stereotyped. He was preoccupied with drawing flat cars, with no people inside and a two dimensional "Dobbin" (see Fig. 1), a hobby horse showing one leg, one eye, and a smiling mouth. Later we understood that this drawing encapsulated parts of himself that he was prepared to reveal. He also showed more obviously psychotic features, or confusions between phantasy and reality, and marked paranoid anxieties. Objects which were slightly broken or out of place would terrify him, as if he believed that the objects themselves were out to get him. The cause of Nicholas' autism and other difficulties is not known. It is known that he had a very difficult birth and that his mother was very depressed through much of his infancy. Now, at 9 years Nicholas could be extremely affectionate but was still strongly tied to his mother and there were marked separation problems.

Communicating with a child in whom concrete thinking is so marked is not easy. For example, in his early sessions Nicholas would start on some activity, become blocked, and attempt to deal with his anxiety by calling out "Put that away now", "When's my Mummy coming?" and/or by sliding into an autistic ritual. From the outset it was clear that splitting was a dominant defence. But it was utilised rigidly, so that it was ineffective in organising his experience. He soon discovered, for example, that there was a "good boy" Nicholas, kept apart from parts of his internal world which terrified him, and which was unable to project effectively. Projective identification from the outset was a way in which he attempted to avoid the anxiety of separation. In his case it took the form of a massive intrusion. For instance, his early sessions were occupied in building an enormous chimney out of building bricks, designed to take up the whole space. Hearing a noise outside, he would in phantasy project himself into the corridor, imagining that he was making the noise. This would lead to terror of intruders, and a general difficulty in distinguishing whether noises came from inside or outside the playroom, or from inside his own head. As many people find with children like Nicholas, initially it was necessary to be much more actively involved than with children whose difficulties are less severe. I might, for example, act a part for him which he was not yet ready to acknowledge as part of himself. I also had to accept and take on board the full weight of his projection and acknowledge and make explicit the totality of his experience. As a little

FIG. 1.   Nicholas' "Dobbin".

exuberance led to a rapid clampdown, for example, I might comment, "To you, Nicholas, the room is *full* of policeman", or "A tiny little tear, and you feel the *whole* thing is spoiled". Through acknowledging the anxiety, drawing a contrast with his phantasy and the actual reality, it also gradually became possible to make explicit his own feelings as he experienced them in relation to me.

One of the consequences of this kind of interpretation was that gradually Nicholas came into closer contact with his own impulses such that he could own them. This facilitated his interest in communication and his use of "I" and "You" became much more consistent. Splitting became more flexible and it was a big step forward when he was able to announce, "There are *two* Dr Urwins!", one good, one bad. On the other hand, the intensification of our relationship and the appreciation of my wholeness which this implied presented him with further difficulties, revealing levels of anxiety of incredible intensity. Firstly, allowing me greater freedom of movement in his phantasy brought to the forefront the existence, real and imagined, of competitors for my interest and affection. But expressions of intense jealousy which this provoked were complicated by the fact that in his mind he had not yet established an object sufficiently robust to withstand his attacks, limiting his capacity for symbol formation and movement into the depressive position. This is vividly demonstrated in a phobic reaction which began after he smashed the toy cars belonging to his therapy box, a box containing his toys and materials available for him at each session. This occurred after the Christmas holiday. For several months afterwards Nicholas would not go near the box containing the broken toys. The damage was equated with damage to me his therapist/mother and my phantasy babies and was felt to be irreparable and total. But the guilt could not be thought about. The reaction became somatised and he developed eczema all over his hands. Secondly, beginning to acknowledge my separateness also increased his anxiety about the consequences of separation, which for Nicholas revealed an anxiety which can only be described as a fear of his own annihilation. Something of the flavour of this anxiety is suggested in the following example, which also illustrates the value of and necessity for working with the counter transference.

Child psychotherapy, like adult psychotherapy, is usually organised on a regular basis, such that the setting is predictable with respect to time and place, as well as the therapist. On this occasion Nicholas arrived unusually early from school and had to wait in the waiting room, which was particularly crowded with other families with small children. As I picked him up he was hunched behind the door. "Phew!", he said, getting up. He hurried downstairs into the playroom nipping ahead, and slamming the door. When I got inside he was nowhere to be seen. On the far side of the room were two barrels, about 3 feet high, one containing soft balls, the other empty. I knew Nicholas must be hiding behind one of them and I approached them as if playing a game.

'Where's Nicholas' I said. 'I can't see Nicholas. Nicholas wants *me* to find *him*. He's making me wait now. How can I find Nicholas?' I saw him reach out from behind the barrel for a silver helmet with slit eyes and a visor from the dressing up box, sticking it out above the barrel. It looked macabre. 'I can see a helmet. But no face. Where's *Nicholas's* face?' He stuck an arm out to one side. 'I can see one hand. And *another* hand', as he stuck out the other one, withdrawing the first. He was behind the empty barrel. 'I'm not in here' he said, 'Look in there', pointing in the direction of the other barrel. 'Is Nicholas in here?' I said, going up and peering into the barrel full of soft balls. By this time he could see me. 'Is Nicholas there? I'm not looking for all *those* children. I'm looking for Nicholas. *There* he is', as I turned and looked at him, looking at me and grinning broadly. 'You found me', he said, getting up. 'I thought I was losted. For a minute I thought I was losted. I thought I'd drunk something nasty and got losted."

At the time my experience was that Nicholas had felt not only swamped by the other children, rendered faceless, but that he had totally disappeared. But the example illustrates an important developmental shift. On this occasion I was put in the position of the one who was shut out, unable to find what I was looking for. In finding Nicholas I was required to "push out" the intruding children, to establish a boundary constituting the session as a safe place in which anxieties could be contained, understood and made tolerable. But it was Nicholas who took the initiative. In signalling his need to be reclaimed, Nicholas was checking that I had been able to hold in my mind his face, the alive Nicholas, parts of himself which he had projected into me for safe keeping. In doing so he was using my mind, my mental space, as a basis for distinguishing between psychic and external realities. "I thought . . ." but "You found me".

The relative frequency of sessions has been particularly important to Nicholas, enabling him to establish some notion of my continuity and to feel safe enough to express extremes of emotion. But some children, like Jacqueline, can use the predictability of psychotherapeutic sessions at less frequent intervals. Here I will describe an early phase in her therapy.

Jacqueline

Jacqueline is 8 years old and has one brother, 2 years younger. Though Jacqueline was born at term, her labour was protracted and the birth was difficult. Jacqueline spent a short period in special care.

From the parent's account, Jacqueline was an impossible baby for the first 6 months. She cried or grizzled virtually continually and gave her mother the feeling that there was nothing she could to to satisfy her. The fractiousness or irritability settled down from 7 months, when Jacqueline was able to sit upright and her mother weaned her onto a cup. Although she was somewhat stiff in her movements, there was no gross delay in milestones with the exception of some initial delay in expressive language. She took a long time to settle at school, the teaching staff finding her alternatively clinging and babyish, or in a world of her own, often backing out of tasks which her teacher felt were within her capacity. Eventually she was placed in a special class for children with learning difficulties, but was referred for psychotherapy because of a general suspicion that emotional difficulties were contributing to her learning problems.

One of the most striking of Jacqueline's early sessions was an unwillingness or inability to talk about any of the thoughts going on in her head. At our first session she was excited about coming to see this "lady" but could not volunteer any suggestions as to why she was here. "I don't know" was a favourite reply, second only to a repetitive, whining "No?". She spent much of this session and many of the subsequent ones pulling at the arm of her chair, sucking her fingers, rubbing her hands on the top of the table, wriggling. Alternatively, she would run her nails on the edge of the table more destructively, and lapse backward looking round the room. Unsurprisingly with this inhibition, Jacqueline needed coaxing to investigate her particular therapy box and I had to open the box and take things out. At the first session, Jacqueline showed interest in the little dolls, and particularly the baby doll. "It's the smallest one", she said timidly, showing me that, although it had a long dress stretching below its feet, it was really very small. "Is it a boy baby or girl baby?" I asked. "A girl baby", she said firmly, picking up the boy doll and putting it to one side. I said that here was a baby part of Jacqueline that she felt needed looking after. Perhaps she felt, too, that she wished she was the smallest one. She smiled, now starting to play more enthusiastically with the animals, particularly with two little lambs, who nuzzled each other, mouth to mouth. But despite this enthusiasm, for several months she was unable to initiate opening her box herself. Anxieties about the contents or the inside of the box overwhelmed her. A main line of defence was to "empty" her mind, leaving the initiative to me. I resorted to a kind of half-way strategy. I would open the box and watch what she looked at, and what made her freeze. I might then take out the ruler, for example, and put it on the table, saying "It seems, Jacqueline, that for you this ruler stands for something nasty. Perhaps if we put it here, it's easier to get started". She would look at what I was doing with interest, and then start to take out the animals and dolls herself. The preoccupation with the two lambs continued. She also enjoyed drawing in these early sessions, some of the drawings showing a stereotyped quality similar to Nicholas's. She was interested in drawing her own house, invariably giving it a very small roof. The front door had the number of her house on it. In the example in Fig. 2, the room on the right, given pink curtains, was Jacqueline's room. Her brother's room, with yellow curtains, was on the far side. The parents' room was forgotten, then added later, and given patterned curtains. I assumed while she was drawing these that she was trying to represent flowers. "Those are spiders", she said, matter-of-factly, putting down her felt-tip with satisfaction. Jacqueline insisted that this was a picture of her own house. I suggested that maybe part of her was concerned about what was going on in her parents room in the middle. Perhaps she felt shut out, and that made her angry with her parents. Then whatever goes on inside turns nasty for her, like a room full of spiders. "They *do* let me in", she said, plaintively, but with feeling. She slammed the drawing book shut and pressed it flat. I commented on how painful she found it that she could not be with Mummy and Daddy when *she* wanted. But at this time Jacqueline could not tolerate this kind of comment. Her reaction was to shut out the nasty frightening thoughts, or attempt to empty her mind completely. One consequence of this was a marked inhibition in thinking and curiosity. The possibility of opening her mind as a space for thinking has again involved working through and making use of countertransference.

It is hard to put across how excruciating I found working with Jacqueline in the initial sessions: The wriggling, the negativism which at times felt wilful, and the lack of any clear signs of initiative. I also experienced feelings of frustration, impotence, anger, and a kind of limp despair, whereas Jacqueline arranged herself in queenly fashion, before staring or looking blank.

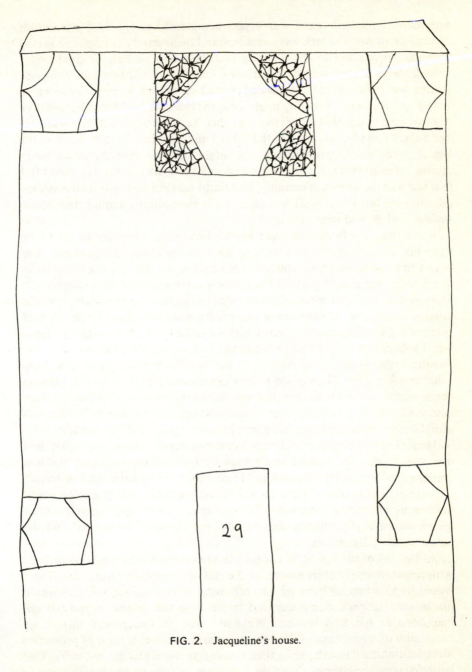

FIG. 2.   Jacqueline's house.

Gradually I realised that I was experiencing feelings of which she herself seemed unaware. The task was to understand these parts of herself, projected into me, in relation to the ongoing phantasy and underlying anxieties. I talked about the baby part of her who found it *so* hard to find a way of getting what she wanted and needed. It was such hard work to try to make herself understood. This baby might imagine that she could feed herself, like the two little lambs that talked to each other. Jacqueline smiled, and removed her fingers from her mouth. On the other hand, as I had to open her box for her to facilitate the proceedings, she might imagine that *she* could be in control of everything. If she got me to do all the work, maybe she could feel that she was the grownup mummy, and that I was the little girl who was shut out, and did not know what was going on in the mummy's mind. Jacqueline smiled, and peeped over into the box.

From this time Jacqueline went for her box more determinedly. "I know what I'm going to do today", making me guess, but more adventurous. She began to provide more information about what she did outside her session times. "I'm excited. My friend Catherine's coming to tea this afternoon". The relative elaborateness of these communications was striking. While acknowledging the importance of these relationships in the outside world, I pointed out that she was very curious about what I did when I was not seeing her. Perhaps she was telling me that *she* had a friend Catherine, who was coming to *her* house to tea because it was hard to have to think about the other children I see. How could I see other children and *still* have a place in my mind for her? Perhaps, too, she was telling me that she could feed herself because the baby part of her wanted good things to eat *so* much, but she was afraid someone, some other baby would come along and replace her.

Jacqueline responded to these transference interpretations with relief, and used the insight. She became more openly curious about the other children she glimpsed in the waiting room. "The naughty boys have made a mess", she said with glee, over a bit of sand spilt on the floor. Interpretation could now focus on rivalries, on her wish to displace or project messy parts of herself into analytic siblings, and on the split between the big girl and the infant parts of Jacqueline.

At the end of the first term Jacqueline approached the Christmas holiday with trepidation, producing some of the classic separation phantasies. There would be a Christmas baby who would move in and replace her, or I would not be coming back. She attempted to push the two lambs together as she had done in her first session. We had come to understand this as an expression of a phantasy of the breast as part of herself, a form of projective identification used in defence against separation. Now this did not work. One lamb fell over the edge of the table and clung on with its fingernails, tearing the edge as if in pain. To give some concrete representation of the length of the holiday and the fact that I would be returning again, we made a calendar in which Jacqueline's sessions were marked with circles. She appeared to have been helped by this preparation, returning after the 3-week break with enthusiasm. She spent much of her first session back drawing her house. Although initially it appeared to be the usual house, three small clouds were placed in the sky, the sun peeping below one of them. "These are raindrops", she said, drawing in pear shaped drops. But she also added a rainbow, a glorious expanse of colour going across from one side of the page to the other.

Jacqueline was beginning to be in touch with depressive feelings aroused by the separation. But it was also a picture that expressed hope partly consequent on the fact that her mind had begun to open. This shift was indicated in a series of drawings produced a few weeks later. The series began with a house which differed from the previous drawings in that the number of the door and the door bell were given boundaries. In addition she put in a path leading up to the front door. This was Jacqueline, thinking ahead, I suggested, to her time with me. It was also a house with an inside and an outside. Jacqueline cut round the edge of the door so that it would open, "Opening to go inside". She then turned out to the next page and drew a female figure with arms outstretched. She turned back the first page and then opened the door to reveal the figure waiting inside (see Fig. 3). This was Jacqueline claiming her time, her number, my thinking, I commented. She smiled, and opened up the page with the figure on it. 'There's an awful lot of space in here', she mused. But Jacqueline, of course, faced a related problem on leaving. How could there still be a space for her in my mind when she left, and indeed, what was she to carry away herself? Towards the end of that session she noted "I've got an idea". She turned to a new sheet of paper and drew a teddy bear. I guessed that this was inspired by the teddy bear permanently on the window sill in the playroom. She agreed, and admitted that part of her wished that she could be like the teddy bear, who never had to leave and could watch all the comings and goings. However she denied that she was afraid that I would forget her. Perhaps, I suggested, it was the thoughts that she was looking for? What were her thoughts about leaving? Jacqueline smiled and said that she had another idea. She wrote "Mummy" near the top of the same page, then "Daddy", "Jacqueline", and her brother's name, her outside world family. She put rings around all these words so that they looked like thought balloons, drawing a vertical balloon to link them all together. Then she transformed the thought balloons into the air filled variety, tracing long threads to the teddy's hand, so that the teddy held them all together (see Fig. 4).

In this drawing, Jacqueline seemed to be grappling with the problem of how to represent her own thoughts, linking different members of her family together in her mind and preserving the thread of continuity to her place in the therapy room, represented by the teddy bear. Of course, her omnipotence

FIG. 3.   Jacqueline's house with open door.

was still evident. Her name was the biggest, and the teddy held the threads, cushioned by the balloons against the threat of separation. Nevertheless, it indicates movement in the thinking, room for imagination, and the beginnings of a space for thinking about thinking.

FIG. 4.   Jacqueline's teddy plus thought balloons.

DISCUSSION

In this chapter I have outlined three psychoanalytic accounts of relations between emotion and thinking in infancy and have illustrated phenomena described by Klein and Bion with examples from two children's psycho-therapy. Though their difficulties differ, I have indicated how interpreting the

ID—K*

children's anxieties and phantasies experienced in the transference contributed to a more adaptive use of defences and a greater awareness of a distinction between psychic and external reality. In both cases this was accompanied by developments in symbol formation, increasing curiosity and, however fleeting, movement from two-dimensional to a multidimensional mental space.

What, if anything, do the psychoanalytic accounts and these developmental shifts tell us about relations between emotion and cognitive development under ordinary circumstances? Despite differences in methods for obtaining evidence there are significant points of correspondence between the psychoanalytic accounts and many contemporary studies. Firstly, though there are differences between the psychoanalytic accounts, they concur in stressing an early-established form of mental activity which is consistent with recent claims for some form of primitive mental representation in very strong infants. Secondly the recent experiments in infant perception and cognition give strong support to claims which Klein made for an early functioning ego. Though Freud himself was somewhat equivocal about this (Segal, 1986, p. 24) evidence presented in various chapters of this book suggests that very young infants are equipped with mechanisms which fulfil what he outlined as the basic requirements for a system for testing reality (Freud, 1911). These are mechanisms for differentiating between stimuli emanating from outside and inside the body, for selecting, noting, and rapidly recognising information, and there is some primitive control over attention. But the psychoanalytic work now raises the question, at a time when actual control over external reality through action is minimal, how do these systems relate to the regulation of pleasure and anxiety and the construction of primitive phantasy? Here I am struck by the plausibility of Klein's claims for early mechanisms of defence when seen in relation to descriptions of early organised systems for matching movements of body parts and communicating affects between self and others. For example many chapters in this book have discussed the evidence for imitation and cross-modal matching put forward by Meltzoff and his colleagues (Meltzoff & Moore, 1977; Meltzoff, 1981). Like all forms of identification, the defence mechanism of projective identification through which parts of the self are split off and projected into another could not be employed if there were not a basis for using the correspondence between self and other. Evidence for projective identification as communication is found in many of the studies of play exchanges between mothers and babies described by Stern (1974; 1985), Trevarthen (1974, 1985) and others. Though the mother's attentions and following responses clearly play an important part, there seems to be some capacity in very young infants to induce particular mood states or affective responses in an interacting partner, a process which Trevarthen has described as "primary intersubjectivity", or more recently as a system permitting the practice of a structured, mutual emotional experience (Trevarthen, 1985; see also Stern, 1985). Though much of the social interaction work has concentrated on pleasurable affectivity, infants also show negative emotions and avoidance reactions in communicative episodes (Sylvester-Bradley, 1981). This may be less of an indication of a failure in interaction than a demonstration of the baby's attempts to use projective processes in order to get rid of unwanted anxiety, as described by Bion.

Thus psychoanalysis implies that attention regulating systems are not simply indices of what the infant does or does not know. They also function in relation to emotional states, operating both externally and internally, influencing the form of primitive representations. This emphasis may be relevant to paradoxes in current literature on infant cognition which imply, like psychoanalysis, both continuity and discontinuity in development. One of the most intriguing paradoxes surrounds evidence for integration in very young infants which is apparently temporary. For example several experiments suggest early coordinations between different perceptual and motor systems, like vision and audition, and vision and prehension, which apparently disintegrate in the first weeks or months, to be re-established later in development (see Butterworth and Bower, Chapters 3 and 4, this volume). Here further evidence from Nicholas is particularly interesting. This is on a form of splitting which involved separating and keeping apart parts of his own body, and using his senses in isolation. Earlier I referred to his "Dobbin" drawings in which only one side is revealed. As indicated in Fig. 5, he also produced a stereotyped "Chad" or "Mr Wot", representing "Look, but don't bite or speak", and finally, a drawing which allows "Touch, but do not look", each of these drawings depicting concretely ways in which he attempted to deny parts of himself. A complete dismantling of perceptual systems is characteristic of autistic children in acute anxiety states (Meltzer et al., 1975) and the tendency to use one sense in isolation rather than in synchrony or in a way which allows one sense to disambiguate information from another sense is frequently found in children with paranoid anxieties. It is also seen in a milder form in children like Jacqueline who cut out or go blank. In Nicholas's case, as I described, a defensive use of listening in isolation contributed to his difficulties in distinguishing between whether sounds were coming from inside or outside the playroom. But in more usual circumstances, the combination of auditory and visual information allows developing infants to assess the relative distance of noise making objects (Bower, 1982). So why should perceptual dismantling arise? Following the infant cognition experiments on early coordination and subsequent reintegration, a psychological argument might suggest than an initial coordination was not established, and/or that something has impeded the subsequent recoordination. This would produce a cognitive deficiency contributing to subsequent impediments in thinking and curiosity. On the other hand one

'Dobbin' show/use one side
at a time

'Chad' Look, smell but
don't speak or bite

Touch but don't look

FIG. 5.   Nicholas splitting the senses.

could ask instead, firstly, what role could the early coordinations play in the management of anxiety in the new-born infant, and speculate on the psychic significance of their absence. Secondly, one could ask, for these children, what emotional shift has not taken place that would allow or demand subsequent coordination and multiple use of senses, so that earlier patterns of use could be given up as outmoded?

From available case history information, we can assume, I think, that circumstances surrounding birth may have rendered both these children especially vulnerable. These vulnerabilities have been compounded with difficulties in early relationships, leaving the children not "unattached" to their mothers but bound up with them, stuck on, as it were, such that separation threatens annihilation. In Nicholas's case, this was illustrated in the fear that he had totally disappeared; in Jacqueline's case, that something was being ripped or torn away. This form of object relation, in which the separateness of the object cannot be allowed or recognised, has aptly been called "adhesive identification" by Bick, who has put forward an account that may shed light on general functions of neonatal coordinations. Using evidence from infant observation and analysis, Bick (1968) argues for a primal phase in neonatal development which necessarily precedes and sets the stage for the elaboration of the defences in the paranoid–schizoid phase as proposed by Klein. Bick argues that once the infant's body lacks the support previously provided within the womb, parts of the personality are not immediately differentiated from parts of the body, and that they lack a binding force between them. She proposes that establishing an internal function drawing together the parts of the self initially depends on the introjection of an external object, experienced as capable of fulfilling this function through its capacity for holding the body and personality together (1968, p. 484):

> The need for a containing object would seem, in the infantile integrated state, to produce a frantic search for an object—a light, a voice, a smell, or other sensual object—which can hold the attention and thereby be experienced, momentarily at least, as holding the parts of the personality together. The optimal object is the nipple in the mouth, together with the holding and talking and familiar smelling mother.

Such a holding function is of course enhanced by mechanisms in the newborn through which parts of the body and perceptual systems are coordinated around the infant's body axis, thus mapping out an immediate spatial frame of reference (Trevarthen et al., 1975). Bick goes on to argue that identification with this holding function of the object gives rise to the first sense of a boundary, and a primitive phantasy of internal and external spaces. The introjection of this function is a necessary precondition for the concept of a space within a space, setting the stage for the elaboration of internal objects through the mechanisms of splitting and idealisation of self and objects described by Klein. Under ordinary circumstances, one might speculate that the slow elaboration of mechanisms for distributing attention and the disengagement of previously coordinated schemes are cognitive counterparts to the splittings and differentiations of the paranoid–schizoid phase (see Mounoud, 1977 for a similar argument). Under less optimal circumstances, where there has been a failure in introjection "the function of projective identification will necessarily continue unabated, and all the confusions of identity attending it will be manifested" (Bick, 1968, p. 484).

In these children, the implications of such difficulties are clear; in the particular terror associated with separation, the persistent and excessive use of projective identification, the maladaptive splitting, the inhibited curiosity, and the restrictions in world view to two dimensions. But in themselves the existence of initial coordinations may be neither necessary nor sufficient to ensure the subsequent development of mental phantasy. In both these children, the intensity of their early anxiety and other difficulties imposed considerable impediments on early social relationships. On the other hand, some development has been observed in the psychotherapeutic context. Does this development shed any light on the functions of early social relations in promoting the development of phantasy and thinking?

Here I have tried to illustrate how, in order to reach these children, I relied heavily on counter-transference information, receiving the full weight of the children's projections and acknowledging the anxieties in a form that the children could comprehend before they could begin to take them on board as parts of themselves. This is consistent with Bion's concept of "containment" through which the availability of a psychic space is communicated to the infant or young child. To Bick's emphasis we might also add that a precondition for the later awareness of psychic reality is the infant's understanding that parts of the self are held together in another's mind, providing the idea of a mental space which is subsequently introjected.

Through the inclusion of spaces within spaces, Jacqueline's later drawings illustrate the identification with this holding function. But would one see these kinds of developments in infants and young children under more usual circumstances? One place to look is in the motivational basis for the infant's passage through the object permanence task, where, again, despite evidence for some form of representation of permanence in infants under 6 months, there is much about the developmental problem which has to be unravelled (see Harris, Chapter 5, this volume). Bower (1982) points out that the classic object permanence problem, when the baby eventually looks under clothes and in alternative locations, is not simply a problem of knowledge of existence of objects. It is also one involving container/contained relationships. These, I think, may be fundamental. From the present perspective, prerequisites leading the baby to first pull off the cloth and to persevere with subsequent conflicts are not to be found in a unitary, determining cognitive structure. Following Klein the achievement may mark a change in reality testing inaugurated through the depressive position as the infant discovers the distinction between psychic and external reality, the disjunction contributing to a spatial differentiation between "inside" and "outside". After Bion we might add that the capacity to sustain the associated anxiety may be enhanced by a history of containment which enables the infant to discover that he or she is held in another's mind, and the existence of mind as a mental space. It is at this point, one might speculate, that the child in therapy obliges by opening her therapy box, and the baby in the object permanence task pulls away the screen.

REFERENCES

Bick, E. (1968). The experience of the skin in early object relations. *International Journal of Psychoanalysis*, *49*, 484–486.
Bion W. (1962). *Learning from experience*. London: Heinemann.
Bion, W. R. (1967). *Second thoughts*. London: Heinemann.

Boston, M. (1987, January). Splitting image? The child observed and the children within. Paper presented to BPS Medical and Psychotherapy Section.

Bower, T. G. R. (1971). The object in the world of the infant. *Scientific American, 225*, 30–38.

Bower, T. G. R. (1974, 1982). *Development in Infancy* (2nd ed.), San Francisco: Freeman.

Butterworth, G. and Light, P. (eds) (1982). *Social cognition: Studies in the development of understanding*. Brighton: Harvester Press.

Freud, S. (1900). *The interpretation of dreams*. London and New York: Hogarth. Standard edition, 4–5. London: Penguin Books. Freud Library, 4.

Freud, S. (1909). *Notes upon a case of obsessional neurosis*. London and New York: Hogarth. Standard edition, 10. London: Penguin Books. Freud Library, 9.

Freud, S. (1911). *Formulations on the two principles of mental functioning*. London and New York: Hogarth. Standard edition, 12. London: Penguin Books. Freud Library, 11.

Freud, S. (1920). *Beyond the pleasure principle*. London and New York: Hogarth. Standard edition, 18. London: Penguin Books. Freud Library, 11.

Freud, S. (1923). *The ego and the id*. London and New York: Hogarth. Standard edition, 19. London: Penguin Books. Freud Library, 11.

Klein, M. (1935). A contribution to the psychogenesis of manic depressive stages. In *Love, guilt and reparation and other works 1921–1945*. London: Hogarth.

Klein, M. (1940). Mourning and its relation to manic–depressive states. In *Love, guilt and reparation and other works 1921–1945*. London: Hogarth.

Klein, M. (1945). The Oedipus complex in the light of early anxieties. In *Love, guilt and reparation and other works 1921–1945*. London: Hogarth.

Klein, M. (1946). Notes on some schizoid mechanisms of defence. In *Envy and gratitude and other works, 1946–1963*. London: Hogarth.

Klein, M. (1955). The psychoanalytic play technique: Its history and significance. In M. Klein, P. Heimann and R. E. Money–Kyrle (eds), *New directions in psychoanalysis*. London: Tavistock.

Lewis, M. and Rosenblum, K. (eds) (1978). *The development of affect*. New York: Plenum Press.

Lock, A. (ed.) (1978). *Action, gesture and symbol: The emergence of language*. London: Academic Press.

Meltzer, D., Bremner, J., Hoxter, S., Weddell, D., & Wittengerg, I. (1975). *Explorations in autism*. Aberdeen: Clunie Press.

Meltzoff, A. (1981). Imitation, intermodal coordination and representation in early infancy. In G. E. Butterworth (ed.), *Infancy and epistemology: An evaluation of Piaget's theory*. Brighton: Harvester Press.

Meltzoff, A. N. & Moore, M. K. (1977). Imitation of facial and manual gestures by human neonates. *Science, 198*, 75–78.

Mounoud, P. (1977). La relation mere–enfant du point de vue des theories psychologiques et psychoanalytiques. *Science Psychomotrice, 4*, 147–155.

O'Shaugnessy, E. (1981). A commemorative essay on W. R. Bion's theory of thinking. *Journal of Child Psychotherapy, 7*, 181–192.

Piaget, J. and Inhelder, B. (1969). *The psychology of the child*. London: Routledge & Kegan Paul.

Segal, H. (1952). Notes on symbol formation. *International Journal of Phychoanalysis, 38*, 391–397.

Segal, H. (1986). *Introduction to the work of Melanie Klein*. London: Hogarth.

Stern, D. (1974). The goal and structure of mother–infant play. *Journal of American Academy of Child Psychiatry, 13*, 402–421.

Stern, D. (1985). *The interpersonal world of the infant*. New York: Basic Books.

Sylvester-Bradley, B. (1981). Negativity in early infant–adult exchanges and its developmental significance. In P. Robinson (ed.), *Communication in development*. London: Academic Press.

Trevarthen, C. (1974). Conversations with a two month old. *New Scientist, 2*, 230–235.

Trevarthen, C. (1985). Facial expressions of emotion in mother–infant interaction. *Human Neurobiology, 4*, 21–32.

Urwin, C. (1984). Power relations and the emergence of language. In J. Henriques, W. Hollway, C. Urwin, C. Venn and V. Walkerdine (eds), *Changing the subject: Psychology, social regulation and subjectivity*. London: Methuen.

Urwin, C. (1986). Developmental psychology and psychoanalysis: Splitting the difference. In M. P. M. Richards and P. Light (eds), *Children of social worlds: Development in a social context*. Cambridge: Polity Press.

AUTHOR INDEX

Acredolo, L. P., 116, 117, 119, 129–131, 135, 136, 140
Adams, A., 135
Adams, J. L., 198
Adams, N., 165
Adamson, L. R., 206
Ainsworth, M. D. S., 203, 204, 207, 208
Aitken, S., 86, 88, 89, 91, 93, 95
Albano, J. E., 22
Alexander, K. R., 11
Allik, J., 68, 69
Anglin, J. M., 221, 238
Antell, S. A., 68, 69
Arden, G. B., 50
Arend, R. A., 173
Ariel, M., 28
Aron, M. 171
Aronson, E., 80
Aslin, R. N., 20–23, 27, 36, 43–45, 69
Atkinson, J., 8, 9, 12–16, 18–23, 28, 29, 31, 36, 37, 50, 52, 58

Badcock, D. R., 15, 37
Baillargeon, R., 109–111, 120, 168, 177

Baisel, E., 133
Bakeman, R., 206, 208
Baker, N., 236
Banks, M. S., 8, 9, 12, 15, 16, 27, 29, 37, 46, 64, 69
Barlow, H. B., 7, 37
Barnes, I., 22
Barrera, M., 65
Barrett, M. D., 212–229, 233–235, 237–239, 243, 249, 252, 253
Bartsch, K., 119
Bates, E., 161, 164, 177, 212–216, 218, 220, 227, 237, 239, 252–254, 258, 263, 271
Bauer, J., 20, 27
Bausano, M., 135
Benasich, A. A., 61
Benedict, H., 211, 239
Benson, J. B., 135, 140
Berman, N., 28
Bernstein, P., 156, 157
Bertenthal, B. I., 77, 82, 134, 136, 140, 173, 177
Bhana, K., 48
Bick, E., 296–298
Bigelow, E., 151, 164, 175

Bion, W. R., 282, 283, 293, 294, 298
Birch, E. E., 20, 21, 37
Bjork, E. L., 117, 120
Blakemore, C. B., 10, 24, 27, 37
Blehar, M. C., 203
Bloom, L., 211, 212, 217, 218, 225, 227, 228, 230, 232, 233, 236, 237, 239
Born, W. S., 79
Bornstein, M. H., 10, 11, 37, 61, 69, 153
Borton, R. W., 64, 154
Boston, M., 283, 299
Bouma, H., 17, 37
Bower, T. G. R., 60, 61, 63, 66, 69, 74, 77, 78, 80–82, 85–90, 95, 96, 106, 120, 128, 154, 155, 161, 177, 279, 280, 295, 299
Bowerman, M., 218, 220–223, 230–232, 237, 239
Bowlby, J., 193, 201, 202, 204, 205, 209
Braddick, O., 8, 9, 12–14, 16–18, 20–23, 26, 28, 29, 31, 37, 38, 50, 52, 58, 69
Braine, M. D. S., 231, 232, 234, 237, 239
Branigan, G., 232, 239
Bremner, J. G., 125–127, 137, 140, 163, 177
Bresson, F., 22, 161, 177
Bretherton, I., 161, 205, 209, 237–239
Brill, S., 11, 13
Brito, A., 173, 211, 243, 259, 271
Brody, L. R., 153
Bronson, G. W., 18, 38, 50, 51, 69, 195, 209
Brookes, S., 212
Brooks, J., 91
Broughton, J. M., 80, 89, 154, 155
Brown, A. L., 168, 169, 172, 175
Brown, R., 230, 231, 239
Bruce, V., 7, 38
Bruner, J. S., 144, 145, 148, 151, 164, 170–173, 175–177, 194, 199, 205, 207, 209, 214, 227, 239

Bryant, P. E., 125, 126
Burnham, D. K., 59, 60, 63, 64, 69
Bushnell, E. W., 173, 177
Bushnell, I. W. R., 17, 38, 51, 52, 64–66, 69
Butterworth, G. E., 5, 57, 66, 79, 80, 82, 113, 114, 120, 125, 140, 156, 157, 164, 176, 177, 198, 209, 273, 274, 295, 299

Campbell, F. W., 12, 14, 17, 26
Campos, J., 133, 134, 139, 141
Campos, R. G., 134
Carlson, V. R., 61
Carlson-Luden, V., 161
Caron, A. J., 61, 69
Caron, R. F., 61
Carstens, A. A., 154
Carulli-Rabinowitz, V., 154
Cavanagh, P., 149, 177
Chaika, H., 153
Chandler, P., 173, 211, 243
Chapman, R., 224
Chu, F., 79
Ciccheti, D., 80
Clark, E. V., 221, 239
Cleaves, W., 59
Cobb, H. V., 171
Cochran, E., 198
Cohen, D., 66, 154
Cohen, L. B., 13, 38, 54, 55, 69, 85, 96
Collis, G. M., 197, 198, 207, 209
Conel, J. L., 19, 38
Copoper, G. F., 27
Cornell, E. H., 130, 131, 141, 164, 177
Corrigan, R., 163, 174, 178
Crisafi, M. A., 175, 178
Cross, D., 119
Cross, T., 108, 209
Cummings, E. M., 117
Cupolillo, M., 164
Cutting, J. E., 77, 82
Cynader, M., 28, 38

Dale, P. S., 227, 239
Dannemiller, J. L., 16, 38, 64, 69

Darby, B., 64
Davidson, M. L., 149
Davis, J. M., 149, 178
Davis, R. T., 171, 178
Daw, N., 28, 38
Day, J., 20, 28
Day, R. H., 22, 45, 59–61, 70, 130, 131
De Courten, C., 10, 19
De Schonen, S., 22, 38, 89, 96, 161
De Valois, R. L., 14, 38
De Vries, L., 50
DeCasper, A. J., 65, 70, 154, 178
DeLoache, J. S., 168, 169, 172, 178
Diamond, A., 115–118, 120, 151, 170, 178
Dobson, V., 8, 10, 38
Domminney, C., 172, 173, 175
Dore, J., 212, 214–216, 220, 221, 227, 229, 236, 237, 239, 240
Dubowitz, L. M. S., 50, 70
Dumais, S. T., 20
Dunkeld, J., 87, 96
Dutton, S., 164
Dziurawiec, S., 65, 70

Edwards, D., 270, 271
Eichorn, D. H., 190
Eimas, P. D., 193, 209
Ellis, H. D., 65
Emde, R. N., 139, 190, 209
Emerson, P. E., 201, 202, 204
Engeland, B., 203
Evans, C., 22
Evans, D., 130
Ewy, R., 66

Fabricius, W. V., 147
Fagan, J. F., 14
Fagen, J. W., 149, 157, 178
Fantz, R. L., 14, 38, 47, 70
Fay, D., 224
Feinman, S., 199, 209
Fenson, L., 199, 209
Field, D. J., 15, 38
Field, J., 136, 153, 161, 178

Field, T., 154, 178
Field, T. M., 66, 70, 153, 178
Fifer, W. P., 65
Finger, I., 164
Fischer, K., 163, 173, 174, 178, 190, 209
Flavell, E. R., 174
Flavell, J., 174
Fogel, A., 195, 197, 209
Fox, R., 20, 38, 77, 82
Franklin, M. B., 236
Freeman, R. D., 27
Fremgen, A., 224, 240
French, J., 9
Freud, S., 274–277, 280, 283, 294, 299
Frisby, J. P., 7, 38
Frye, D., 161, 163, 178

Gaensbauer, T. J., 190
Garey, L., 10, 19, 38
Garman, M., 211, 217, 230, 240
Gayl, I. E., 12, 38
Gekoski, M. J., 149, 154, 178
Gelber, E. R., 85
Genova, P., 164
Gewirtz, J. L., 203, 209
Gibson, E. J., 74, 77–79, 82, 104–106, 109, 111, 132, 133, 141, 154, 178
Gibson, J. J., 73, 74, 82, 86, 96, 104–106, 109, 111, 132, 141, 266
Giddens, A., 250, 271
Ginsburg, A. P., 12
Goldfield, E. C., 174, 178
Goldstein, E. B., 7, 38
Goldstein, S., 154
Golinkoff, R. M., 169
Goodwin, R., 227, 229, 240
Goodwyn, S. W., 135
Gopnik, A., 218, 225, 240
Goren, C. C., 65, 70
Granrud, C. E., 58, 59, 75, 83
Gratch, G., 117, 120
Green, P., 7
Greenberg, R., 66, 153
Greenfield, P. M., 215, 228, 236, 240
Greenhalgh, T., 26

Griffiths, P., 215–227, 229, 240
Gruendel, J. M., 221, 240
Gwiazda, J., 13, 20, 27, 39

Haake, R., 165, 178
Haegerstrom, G., 27
Hainline, L., 21, 39
Haith, M. M., 12, 39, 45, 47, 48, 67, 70
Halliday, M. A. K., 215, 217, 226, 227, 240
Hamer, R. D., 11, 39
Harding, C. G., 144, 169, 178, 179
Harmon, R. J., 190
Harnick, F. S., 175, 179
Harris, M., 212
Harris, P. L., 22, 39, 45, 68, 70, 113, 114, 117, 119, 120, 123, 151, 153, 170, 179, 273
Hartmann, E. E., 15
Hauert, C. A., 151
Hein, A., 28, 132–134
Held, R., 13, 20, 21, 27, 39, 132–134, 141
Hendrickson, A., 9
Hess, R. F., 17, 26, 39
Heth, C. D., 130, 131, 164
Hickey, T. L., 27, 39
Hicks, L., 125
Hieman, M. L., 165
Hilton, A. F., 17, 39
Hoffman, K. P., 23, 39
Hogarty, P. S., 190
Hollis, J. H., 171, 179
Hood, B., 111, 120, 155, 156, 168, 179
Hood, L., 232, 237
Hopkins, N., 156
Horobin, K., 116, 117, 119, 120
Horowitz, F. D., 48, 70
Howland, H. C., 9, 13, 39
Hubley, P., 200
Humphrey, N. K., 19, 39
Hunt, J. McV., 144, 151, 259
Hutt, S. J., 193, 209

Ihsen, E., 60, 70, 130
Illingworth, R. S., 136, 141
Inhelder, B., 278

Jacobson, S. G., 27, 39
Jager, B., 78
James, W., 63, 70
Jansson, G., 73
Jarrett, N. L. M., 125, 151, 164, 175, 179
Jennings, K. D., 172, 173, 179
Johansson, G., 73, 76, 81, 83, 91, 93, 96
Jones, D., 212
Judge, S. J., 29
Julesz, B., 17, 39

Kagan, J., 199, 205, 209
Kalnins, I. V., 171, 179
Kamhi, A. G., 220, 221, 240
Kaplan, B., 198, 229
Kaplan, M. G., 149
Karmel, B. Z., 12, 39
Karmiloff-Smith, A., 160, 179
Kauffman, F., 76
Kaufman-Hayoz, R., 76, 78, 83
Kaye, K., 154, 159, 160, 176, 179, 194, 197, 207, 209
Kearsley, R. B., 199
Keating, D. P., 68
Keating, M. B., 131, 136, 141
Kellman, P. J., 75, 76, 83, 106–108, 110, 120
Kessen, W., 48, 70
Klahr, D., 160, 164, 176, 179
Klein, M., 274, 276–282, 293, 294, 297, 299
Klein, S. A., 15
Kleiner, K. A., 16, 39, 64, 70
Klinnert, M., 139
Kohler, W., 147, 179
Konner, M., 205, 209, 248, 271
Kopp, C. B., 164, 179
Koslowski, B., 164, 170–172, 175, 179
Krinsky, S. J., 61
Kuczaj, S. A., 224, 240
Kuhl, P. K., 79, 83
Kujawski, J., 91, 96
Kupersmidt, J., 171

Lamb, M. E., 153–155, 179, 204, 209

Langlois, J. H., 67, 70
Latz, E., 47
Lawden, M. C., 17, 39
Leaper, C., 236
Lee, D., 80, 83, 86, 96
Lempers, J., 174, 180
Leopold, W. F., 223, 240
Leslie, A. M., 168, 180
Letson, R. D., 27
Lettvin, J. Y., 17, 39
Lewis, M., 91, 96, 274, 299
Lewis, T. L., 19, 50
Light, P., 274
Lightbown, P., 232, 237
Lipsitt, L. P., 65, 70
Lishman, R., 86
Lock, A., 173, 211, 216, 218, 240, 243, 248, 271, 274, 299
Lockman, J. J., 164, 180
Lucariello, J., 212, 214, 220

MacFarlane, A., 22, 39, 45
Macmurray, J., 244–247, 250, 266, 271
Maisel, E. B., 12
Malkin, C. M., 154, 155
Mandler, J. M., 168, 180
Marcus, J., 160, 176
Marr, D. C., 17, 39
Martello, M., 13
Martin, P. P., 173
Martlew, M., 211, 216, 249
Massar, B., 116
Mast, V. K., 157, 180
Matas, L., 173, 180
Maurer, D., 13, 19, 39, 50, 65, 70
Maury, L., 161
McCall, R. B., 190, 209
McComas, J., 136, 141
McCrickard, D., 152, 180
McCune-Nicolich, L., 218, 225, 240
McCutcheon, E., 51
McDaniel, C., 77
McKechnie, J., 170, 171, 180
McKenzie, B. E., 22, 40, 45, 60, 61, 66, 70, 130, 131, 136, 137, 141, 151, 164, 175, 180

McNeill, D., 229, 240
McNew, S., 237
McShane, J., 220, 227, 228, 240
Mead, G. H., 244–248, 250, 271
Melhuish, E. C., 64, 71
Meltzer, D., 295, 299
Meltzoff, A. N., 66, 71, 79, 83, 90, 96, 154, 168, 180, 218, 225, 294, 299
Messer, D. J., 198, 209
Meuwissen, I., 131, 141
Michotte, A., 91, 96
Middleton, D., 270
Miles, F. A., 29, 40
Milewski, A. E., 17, 40, 154, 180
Miller, R. T., 236
Millodot, M., 27
Miranda, S. B., 14, 46
Mitchell, D. E., 24, 27, 40
Moar, K., 22
Moerk, E., 208, 210
Mohindra, I., 13, 27, 40
Mohn, G., 22
Molfese, D. L., 193, 210
Molfese, M., 206
Molfese, V. J., 193
Mollon, J. D., 7, 11, 40
Moore, M. K., 63, 66, 71, 79, 80, 89, 90, 154, 155, 168, 294
Morison, V., 46–49, 51, 54–56, 58, 59, 61, 62, 71, 76, 108
Morrison, D. C., 154
Morrongiello, B. A., 149, 171
Mounoud, P., 151, 180, 297, 299
Movshon, J. A., 24, 40
Muir, D., 153, 180
Murphy, C. M., 198, 210
Mushin, J., 50

Nachmias, J., 15
Nadolny, I., 116
Nelson, K., 208, 210–212, 214, 217, 220, 230, 237, 240, 241, 251, 258, 261, 262, 271
Nelson, K. E., 223, 241
Newell, A., 144, 176, 180
Nilsson, N. J., 145, 146, 180
Ninio, A., 227, 241

Norcia, A. M., 8, 40

O'Connell, K. M., 20
O'Connor, M. J., 164
O'Shaugnessy, E., 283, 299
Over, R., 66

Paden, L., 48
Painter, M., 206
Papousek, H., 156, 157, 180
Peeples, D., 10, 11, 40
Petrig, B., 20, 40
Petterson, L., 59
Pettigrew, J. D., 19, 40
Piaget, J., 63, 66, 103–106, 109, 111–
    120, 123–125, 128, 132, 138, 139,
    141, 144, 147–155, 157, 159–161,
    163, 164, 167, 168, 175, 180, 190,
    204, 205, 244, 252, 259, 266, 278,
    299
Pick, H. L., 21, 164
Pieraut, G., 161
Pimm-Smith, E., 22
Pipp, S., 12, 40
Pisoni, D. B., 43, 44
Pope, M. J., 80, 83
Proffitt, D. R., 77
Pulos, E., 11, 40

Rader, N., 135, 141
Rakic, P., 19, 40
Ramer, A. L. H., 236
Rauschecker, J. P., 27, 40
Raviola, E., 29, 40
Regal, D., 8, 40
Reilly, J., 236
Rentschler, I., 17, 40
Rescorla, L. A., 222, 224, 241
Rheingold, H. L., 198, 210
Richards, J. E., 135, 141
Richards, M. P. M., 248, 271
Richardson, H. M., 161, 180
Rieser, J., 130, 141, 165, 181
Roberts, J. O., 12
Robinson, M., 164, 176
Rose, D. H., 46, 48, 49, 51, 54, 58, 59,
    76

Rosenblum, K., 274
Rosie, K., 166
Rovee-Collier, C. K., 149, 154, 157,
    171, 181
Roy, C., 206
Ruff, H. A., 60, 71
Rutkowska, J. C., 144, 181

Sage, S., 165, 170
Sai, F., 51, 65
Salapatek, P., 8, 12, 21, 22, 29, 40, 45,
    46, 48
Samuels, C. A., 66, 71
Sarty, M., 65
Scafidi, F., 154
Schaffer, H. R., 190, 191, 196, 197,
    199, 200–202, 204, 205, 207, 210,
    211
Schiller, P. H., 19, 40
Schlesinger, I. M., 230, 241
Schmid, D., 134
Schwartz, A., 133, 134, 141
Scollon, R., 228, 232, 241
Segal, H., 279, 281, 294, 299
Sekel, M., 11
Self, P., 48
Service, V., 173, 211, 243
Shaw, R. E., 74
Shea, S. L., 20
Sherod, L. R., 192, 202, 210
Sherwood, V., 205
Shimojo, S., 20, 21, 40
Short, K. R., 108
Shotter, J., 246, 250, 266, 271
Simon, H. A., 144, 176
Sinclair, J., 51
Singer, W., 27
Slater, A. M., 13, 41, 46–49, 51, 54–
    56, 58–62, 71, 76, 83, 108, 121
Smith, J. H., 215, 228
Smith, P. K., 164, 181
Snow, C. E., 198, 210
Snyder, J., 237
Somers, M., 108
Somerville, S., 165
Sophian, C., 147, 165, 170, 181
Sorce, J., 139, 141

Spelke, E. S., 75, 76, 79, 83, 105–111, 120, 168
Spetner, N. B., 77
Sroufe, L. A., 173, 203
Stanley, J. C., 17
Stechler, G., 47, 71
Stephens, B. R., 15, 16, 64
Stephenson, C. M., 17, 41
Stern, D. N., 195, 210, 274, 278, 294, 295, 299
Streri, A., 154, 181
Stromeyer, C. F. III, 15, 41
Sugarman, S., 168
Sugarman-Bell, S., 199, 210
Sullivan, M. W., 149, 157
Svejda, M., 134, 141
Sykes, M., 13
Sylva, K., 164, 181, 206, 210
Sylvester-Bradley, B., 154, 181, 295, 299

Teller, D. Y., 8, 10, 11, 41
Thomas, M. A., 77
Thomson, J., 224, 241
Thorn, F., 27
Tootell, H. E., 61
Town, C., 46, 59, 76
Treutwein, B., 17
Trevarthen, C. B., 154, 181, 200, 210, 274, 278, 294, 295, 297, 300
Triesman, A., 29, 41
Tronick, E., 22, 41, 154, 181
Tweedlie, M. E., 51
Tyler, C. W., 8

Urwin, C., 274–277, 285, 300
Uzgiris, I. C., 135, 136, 151, 160, 181, 259

Valsiner, J., 68
Van Hof-van Duin, J., 22, 41
Van Sluyters, R. C., 24
Varner, D., 11, 41
Vaughn, B., 203, 210
Vega-Lahr, N., 154
Vinter, A., 79, 83
Vital-Durand, F., 10

Volbrecht, V. J., 11, 41
Von Hofsten, C., 57, 70, 73, 74, 80, 83, 154, 179
Von Uexkull, J., 270, 271
Vygotsky, L. S., 206, 210, 244–247, 250, 266, 271

Walk, R. D., 132, 133
Walker, A., 77, 78, 83, 154
Walker-Andrews, A., 78, 83
Wall, S., 203
Wallace, J. G., 160
Warren, W. H., 74, 83
Wasserman, S., 109, 110, 168
Waters, E., 203, 205, 210
Wattam-Bell, J., 13, 16, 18, 20, 28, 41, 52
Webb, R. A., 116, 121
Weiskrantz, L., 19, 41
Wellman, H. M., 118, 119, 121, 144, 147, 164, 165, 172, 173, 181
Werner, H., 85, 96, 198, 210, 229, 241
Werner, J. S., 10, 11, 41
Wertheimer, M., 78, 83
Whitecraft, R. A., 171, 181
Wiesel, T. N., 29
Willatts, P., 111, 151, 155–159, 161, 162, 164–166, 168, 171–173, 175, 176, 182
Winston, P. H., 145, 182
Wishart, J. G., 128, 141, 161, 182
Wolff, P. H., 194, 210
Woodson, R., 66, 153
Woodward, W. M., 150, 182
Wooten, B. R., 10
Wu, P. Y. K., 65
Wurtz, R., 22, 41

Yarrow, L. J., 173, 182
Yonas, A., 21, 41, 58, 59, 71
Youdelis, C., 9, 41
Younger, B. A., 13, 54

Zelazo, P. R., 153, 182, 199
Zinober, B., 211, 216, 241, 249, 271
Zusne, L., 53, 71

SUBJECT INDEX

Abnormal visual development, 24–29
Accommodation of sensori-motor schemes, 160
Acoustic characteristics of early utterances, 232
Active movement and spatial orientation, 132–139
Active vs. passive perception, 47, 49
Actor-observer difference, 244
Adualism, 278
Affect expressions, 214–215
Affordances, 79–81
Amalgams in early utterances, 234–235
Amblyopia, 24–28, 32
  anisometropic, 24, 32
  deprivational, 24, 33
  meridional, 27, 34
A not B search error, 112–119, 151
  and/number-separation of containers, 119
  memory accounts, 113–114, 116–119
  under different delays, 115
  with a visible object, 113–114
Answering questions, 227

Apprenticeship, 207
Asking questions, 227
Astigmatism, 9, 32
Attachment, 189, 200–205
  and parental sensitivity, 207–208
  and security, 202
Attentional control, 21–24, 295
Attribution theory, 244
Audiovisual coordination, 78–79
Autism, 281, 284–287

Barrier problems, 150–151
Binocular disparity, 12, 20, 32, 58–59
Binocular vision, 3
  development of, 20–21, 28–29

Capture by visual stimuli, 47
Categorical rules in language, 231
Coaction, 196
Colour vision, 3, 10–11
Combinatorial rules in language, 230–232
Commenting, 227–228
Comprehension of words, 223–224
Constructionism,
  Piagetian, 99–100
  social, 140, 192

Context-bound word use, 212–214, 218

Contrast sensitivity, 3, 8–9, 33, 46–47

Conversational exchanges, 229

Coordination of schemes, 165
  in the psychoanalytic perspective, 297

Cortical control over midbrain, 19

Counter-transference, 282–283, 288

Critical periods in visual development, 26–28

Cultural concepts, 270

Death instinct, 277–278

Decontextualization,
  of objects, 256
  of word use, 218–220, 222

Defence mechanisms, 278

Deletion at an edge, 75–76

Depressive position, 279–281, 285

Depth cues, 58–59
  pictorial, 59
  sequence of development, 58

Depth perception, 58–59
  stereoscopic, 20

Detection of impossible movements, 109–110

Detour tasks, 159–160, 164–167, 173

Dichromacy, 11, 33

Directive word use, 215–216

Direct perception, 99

Dummy forms in early language, 235–236

Dynamic approach to perception, 74

Ecological psychology, 73–74

Ecological validity, 57

Ego, 275–276

Egocentrism, 112, 124

Emmetropization, 29, 33

Emotional development, 185
  and cognition, 186, 273–298

Empathetic perception, 91

Encounters in perception, 79–81

Environment of evolutionary adaptedness, 201

Error detection and inhibition, 168–172

Event perception, 73–74
  events vs. encounters, 73–82

Event representations and language, 214
  core elements of, 219–220
  partitioning of, 220

Eye movements, 3
  control of, 9
  cortical and subcortical mechanisms, 23–24
  smooth pursuit, 23, 35
  vergence, 28, 36

Existence constancy, 63 (see also Object permanence)

Expressive word use, 215–216

Externality effect, 17

Face perception, 45, 64–67, 193

Fear of strangers, 201

Feature constancy, 62–63

Field of view, 45

First words, 212–216
  as performatives, 215
  their communicative functions, 215–217

Fixation reflex, 22

Flicker detection, 8

Focal attention, 31

Formal properties of stimulation, 88

Form perception, 53–56

Fovea, 9, 33

Gestures, 211, 215–216, 248–249

Goal corrected behaviour, 202

Goal directed behaviour, 101, 144–177, 149, 157, 161

Goal terminated behaviour, 144–177

Groping patterns in language acquisition, 232

Habituation techniques, 3, 33, 48
  and colour vision, 11
  and object permanence, 106–107
  and perception of occlusion, 75

infant controlled procedure, 49
   in newborns, 48
Heuristics in problem solving, 145
Hyperopia, 28–29, 33

Idealization, 278
Imitation,
   by neonates, 66, 90–91, 153
   in the psychoanalytic framework,
   294
   the interactive foundation of, 254–
   258
Individual differences,
   in language development, 216, 221,
   243, 251–271 (see also Styles of
   early language)
Inferences, 165
Information processing constraints,
   and problem solving, 173–174
Intentionality, 101, 144–45, 157–159,
   191
Interception skills, 80–81
Intermental abilities, 247, 270
Intersensory perception, 78–79, 154
   in the psychoanalytic framework,
   294
Intonation contour, 217
Intramental abilities, 247

Landmarks and spatial orientation,
   129–131
Language acquisition, 186, 208, 211–
   238
   and cognitive development, 225
Language styles,
   referential vs. expressive, 186
Lateral geniculate nucleus, 10, 33
Lateral inhibition, 9, 34
Lexical development, 218–225
   discontinuity in, 221–222
Linear systems analysis, 12, 34, 46–47
Locomotor development,
   and spatial orientation, 101, 135–
   139
   and visual cliff avoidance, 133–135
Locus of habituation, 50–51

Looming (see Visual expansion)

Maternal styles, 260–263
Means-ends separation/analysis, 146,
   149, 153, 161
Measures of cognitive development,
   Casati-Lezine scale, 259
   Uzgiris-Hunt scale, 259
Models of perceptual development, 44
Modular model of early skill, 194
Monotropism, 202
Motion parallax, 58, 68
Motivation, 274
Movement perception, 59–60
   coherent vs. incoherent movement,
   77
   human movement, 60, 76–78, 91–93
Moving room technique, 80
Multiple attachments, 202
Mutual gaze, 195–196
Myelinization, 10, 34

Nativism vs. empiricism, 43, 85
Neural development, 4, 9–10
Neural mechanisms of early visual
   perception, 50–51
Nominal word use, 218
Non-nominal word use, 218, 225

Object identity, 63–64
Objective perception, 124
Object-occluder relationships, 123–124
Object permanence, 63–64, 100, 103–
   120, 259–260
   and psychoanalytic theory, 298
   and social development, 205
   Piagetian stages of, 106
Object search, 104, 106, 112–119, 123–
   124
   and spatial orientation, 124–128
   as problem solving, 150–151
Object unity, detection of, 105
Oculomotor control, 21–24
Oedipus complex, 280
Olfactory discrimination, 65
Optical development, 9–10

Optic nerve, 9
Optokinetic nystagmus, 21, 23, 34
   binocular vs. monocular, 23–24
Overextension, 222–224

Paranoid-schizoid position, 279–280
Parental style, 187
Parent-infant interaction, 248–271
   and development of language and
   cognition, 258–271
Part-whole analysis, 255–258
Peer interaction, 206–207
Perception of emotion, 78
Perception of gender, 91–93
Perception of higher order variables,
86–93 (*see also* Superordinate
qualities)
Perception of superordinate qualities,
78
Perception vs. cognition, 99–100
Period of undiscriminating social
responsiveness, 200–201
Person-object integration, 199–200
Person permanence, 259
Phantasy, 277, 290
Phobic reaction, 285–286
Phonemic discrimination, 193
Photoreceptors, 9, 10, 34
Pivotal rules in language, 230–232,
234
Planning, 143
   planned vs. planful solutions, 147
   planning a series of actions, 166–
   167
Plasticity in visual development, 24–
29
Pleasure principle, 275–276
Pointing, 253
Position coding, 116–117, 124–131
   self-referent vs. external-referent,
   125–131
Position updating during movement,
128, 130
Postural development and spatial
orientation, 101, 136–139
Pragmatic development in single word
use, 226–229

Predication, 229
Preparedness and perceptual
development, 45–47
Pre-verbal communication, 247–248
Primary intersubjectivity, 294
Proactive interference and search
errors, 113
Problem reduction, 147, 153
Problem solving, 101, 143–177
   directed groping, 151–152
   flexibility in, 151–152
   persistence, 172–173
   Piaget's theory, 148–153
   strategies in, 145–147
   trial-and-error, 143
Projection, 278, 282, 294
Prototype theory of acquisition of
word meanings, 222–225
Prototypical referent, 222
Pseudo-dialogue, 196
Psychoanalytic theory, 187, 273–298
Psychotherapy, 284–292
Purposive behaviour, 202

Reaching in newborns, 89–90, 154
Reaching in the dark, 111, 155–156
Reality testing, 187, 278, 294, 298
Recall memory,
   and problem solving, 170
Receptive field, 9–10, 34
Recognition memory, 51
Referential vs. expressive infants, 237–
238
Referential word use, 212, 216, 220–
222, 237–238
Refractive error, 9, 28–29, 35
Relative movement, 76
Representation, 99
   and problem solving, 147, 174–175
   and social development, 205
   in psychoanalytic theory, 275–276
   of higher level properties, 31–32
Rescission of overextensions, 224–225
Retinal adaptation, 50–51
Retinal ganglion cells, 9, 35
Rhythmic patterns in behaviour, 194

Saccades, 35
  control of, 21–22
Scaffolding, 207
Secondary circular reactions, 148–149, 252
Semantic field, 224
Semantic relations, 230
Sensory-motor intelligence, 225
Shape constancy, 61–62
Single-word utterances, 212–229
  successive single-word utterances, 228, 233
Size constancy, 60–61
Skill acquisition, 145
  and problem solving, 163–164
  levels of skill, 174
Social construction of cognition, 243–271
Social context, 191, 205
Social development, 185, 189–208
  interrelationship with cognitive development, 204–205
  stages of, 191, 194–200
Social interaction, 185, 191, 195–196, 248
  and cognitive development, 186, 247–271
Social perception, 77–78
Social pre-adaptation, 192–194
Social referencing, 199
Sonic guide, 81, 86–89
Spatial awareness, 101, 123–140
Spatial frequencies, 35, 45
Spatial orientation, 124–131
Spatial primitives, 17–18
Spatial reference systems, 136–137
  and the psychoanalytic perspective, 297
Spectral sensitivity, 10, 35
Speech perception, 79, 193
Splitting, 278, 282, 284
Stereoacuity, 21, 35
Stereopsis, 20–21, 35
Strabismus, 24–29, 35
Strange situation procedure, 203–204
Striate cortex (*see* Visual cortex)

Styles of early language, 251–252
  their cognitive bases, 252–254
Superior colliculus, 19, 35, 50
Support tasks, 158, 161
Symbolic interactionism, 248

Terminal intonation contour, 232
Textons, 17–18
Top-down processing, 32
Topic sharing, 197–199
Transference, 277, 290
Transfer of problem solution, 175
Trichromacy, 11, 36
Turn taking, 194
Two-word utterances, 211
  the analytical route to, 234–235
  the synthetic route to, 232–234
  transition to, 230–238

Unconscious mental processes, 275
Underextension, 222–224

Violation of expectancy studies,
  in reaching for a virtual object, 155
  in social interaction, 154
Visual accommodation, 9, 32
Visual acuity, 3, 8–9, 32, 44–45
Visual anticipation and spatial orientation, 128–131
Visual cliff technique, 133
Visual coorientation, 197
Visual cortex, 10, 12, 36, 50
  functional development, 18–21
Visual discrimination
  of angular relationships, 54–55
  of orientation, 13–14, 52, 55
  of spatial frequencies, 8, 10, 14–15
  of spatial relations, 15–18
Visual evoked potentials, 8, 13, 33, 36, 52
Visual expansion, 79–80, 86
Visual memory, 4
  in newborns, 50
  persistence of, 51
Visual perception, 3–96
  of lower vs. higher order variables, 55, 68

Visual perception—*cont.*
  of movement, 59–60
  of occlusion, 74–76, 104
  of static vs. dynamic stimuli, 57–58
  segmentation in, 29
  selective sensitivity in, 12–18
Visual preferences, 3, 8, 34, 46, 192
  eye movements in, 22
  for attractiveness, 67
  for curved stimuli, 46
  for faces, 16–17, 64
  for high contrast stimuli, 46

  for moving stimuli, 46
  for three-dimensional stimuli, 46
Vocabulary explosion, 217
Vocal interchange, 196
Voice discrimination, 65

Wish fulfilment, 276–277

Zero-crossings, 15, 36
Zone of proximal development, 206–207